THE ROUTLEDGE CO............ ...
CHRISTIAN HISTORY

The Routledge Companion to Christian History is an indispensable aid for anyone seeking wide-ranging coverage of the key facts in clear, concise language. It covers:

- the chronology of events in Christian history from the persecution of the Roman Empire to the fall of Communism and the rise of fundamentalism;
- the impact of Islam, the Crusades, monasticism and the spread of popular religious movements throughout the world;
- Western Christendom, the Orthodox churches of the East and the 'new' churches of Asia and Africa.

Fully cross-referenced throughout with a combination of timelines, glossaries and statistics, this packed volume contains a wealth of information for the first-time student or for anyone revisiting the subject.

Chris Cook is former Head of the Modern Archives Unit at the London School of Economics.

THE ROUTLEDGE COMPANION
TO CHRISTIAN HISTORY

Chris Cook

LONDON AND NEW YORK

First published 2008
by Routledge
2 Park Square, Milton Park, Oxon OX14 4RN

Simultaneously published in the USA and Canada
by Routledge
270 Madison Ave, New York, NY 10016

*Routledge is an imprint of the Taylor & Francis Group,
an informa business*

Typeset in Times New Roman by
Keyword Group Ltd
Printed and bound in Great Britain by
MPG Books Ltd, Bodmin

British Library Cataloguing in Publication Data
A catalogue record for this book is available
from the British Library

Library of Congress Cataloging in Publication Data
A catalog record for this book has been requested

ISBN 10: 0-415-38362-5 (hbk)
ISBN 10: 0-415-38363-3 (pbk)
ISBN 10: 0-203-09963-X (ebk)

ISBN 13: 978-0-415-38362-2 (hbk)
ISBN 13: 978-0-415-38363-9 (pbk)
ISBN 13: 978-0-203-09963-6 (ebk)

CONTENTS

CONTENTS

PREFACE AND ACKNOWLEDGEMENTS

This new Routledge Companion has attempted to provide, within the constraints of a single, medium-sized volume, an introductory overview of the history of Christianity from its early beginnings to the present day. No volume of this length can begin to attempt to be comprehensive. Rather, it has concentrated on the key historical themes, events and terms in the history of a movement that now spans two millennia and every continent.

This is essentially a book of historical reference for teachers, lecturers, students and the general public (of whatever religious persuasion, or indeed none). It has been designed as a desk-top companion for quick reference, a digest and compendium of information assembled from a large array of sources and not easily found assembled elsewhere in one volume. It is not primarily a book for theologians (although it is hoped that they will find here key facts and dates on such themes as the background to the divisions that have afflicted Christianity over the centuries and the relationship of Christianity to the other faiths). Rather, the primary aim of the book has been to provide, within a wide-ranging but concise chronological framework, the historical and particularly the political background in which Christianity first flourished and later declined (and, in various parts of the world, is now witnessing a renaissance).

The book is intended particularly to provide some of the background dates, data and other key information concerning the role and place of Christianity in the world of the twenty-first century. Hence the chronologies and other material in this volume grow larger and more voluminous from the sixteenth century Reformation onwards, filling out even more after the French Revolution. Recent years have seen a growing need for a book of this kind. In the twentieth century, the study of the history of religion became unfashionable, almost to the point of extinction. Religion itself (and particularly Christianity) seemed very much consigned to the past, at least in the Western world. This was the age of science and technology, of communism and consumerism, of the Internet and the infallibility of human progress. The events of 1989 (with the collapse of Communism) and the devastating terrorist attack on America in 2001 have altered that perspective.

Religion, and religious fundamentalism, is once again at the forefront of world affairs. The rise of militant Islam, the revival of Christianity in the former Soviet Union, the embracing influence of the 'religious right' in the USA – all these are key themes for the student of contemporary history. Some of the current problems affecting the Christian churches in the modern era are also treated in this volume: the troubled relationship of Church and State; the relations of Christianity with other faiths, particularly Judaism and Islam, over the centuries; the shifting 'balance of power' within the Roman Catholic and Protestant churches away from Europe and America, towards Africa and Asia; the revival of Orthodoxy after its troubled history under Communism in Russia and Eastern Europe. Even within these relatively limited objectives, selectivity is important. Until recently, geographical coverage of the history of Christianity concentrated heavily on Europe (and particularly Western Europe). The emphasis was on European Catholicism and Protestantism, and missionary work overseas.

Now, attention has shifted to once-forgotten areas: the Orthodox churches of Eastern Europe, Russia and the Balkans; the 'ancient churches' of the East (Armenian, Syrian, the Nestorian missions and so forth; and (yet more recently) to the newly independent churches of the African continent, the radical liberation theology movement of South America and the growing fundamentalist right in North America. This volume has attempted to give some background coverage to some of these new themes. At the same time, no doubt the primary readership of this book, whether students and lecturers, laymen or clergy, will be in Britain and America. Hence particular attention has still to be given to such traditional areas of study as the Crusades, the medieval papacy and the Protestant Reformation, without excluding these new areas of study.

The compilation of any book of this kind owes much to the innumerable standard histories and reference works on particular aspects of the history of Christianity. Some of these are included in the Bibliography, but particular mention should be made of such invaluable works as the *Oxford Dictionary of the Christian Church* (2nd edn, 1983) and the more recent encyclopaedia *Christianity: The Complete Guide* (2005). I am also indebted to such friends and colleagues as Philip Broadhead, John Paxton, Ken Powell and John Stevenson, who have generously given me permission to use material in their copyright. Much of the research work for this volume was done in the libraries of the London School of Economics and the Institute of Historical Research. I am deeply grateful to the staff there. For the preparation of the manuscript, I am indebted to the long labours of Linda Hollingworth and Elizabeth Teague, copy-editor. At Routledge I must thank Rosie Waters and her staff for their practical help and encouragement. This list would not be complete without thanks to James Robinson.

I
OUTLINE TOPIC CHRONOLOGIES

THE EARLY CHURCH (FROM THE APOSTOLIC AGE TO THE COUNCIL OF NICAEA)

c. 30/33

Possible dates for crucifixion of Jesus Christ outside Jerusalem.

c. 35

Possible date for martyrdom of Stephen (by stoning).

Possible date for conversion of St Paul.

c. 43–44

Herod Agrippa I inaugurates persecution of Christians.

c. 45–64

Start of missionary journeys of Paul to Cyprus, Asia Minor, northern Greece, Athens and Corinth.

c. 48–49

Council of Jerusalem accepts that Gentile Christians do not need to observe Jewish laws and customs.

c. 49–62

Paul's Letters to the Churches.

c. 60–100

Parameters within which majority consensus of scholars agrees the Gospels were written.

c. 62

Possible date for death of James, the brother of Jesus, and leader of the Jerusalem Church.

64

Blame for fire of Rome laid on Christians. Subsequent persecution by Nero.

Possible deaths of Peter and Paul in Rome (or perhaps AD 67 for Paul). Supposed inauguration of Linus as Bishop of Rome.

66

Revolt of Jews against Rome. First Jewish revolt leads to Roman War.

70

Destruction of Jerusalem by Roman forces under Titus deals major blow to Christians.

81–96

Traditional period of persecution during reign of Emperor Domitian (though many scholars now doubt this). Domitian had demanded he be worshipped as a god.

84

Excommunication from Jewish synagogue of Christians.

96

Accession of Emperor Nerva (following murder of Domitian) sees relaxation of any anti-Christian and anti-Jewish measures.

c. **100–115**

Christianity reaches Edessa (beyond the eastern frontier of the Roman Empire).

107

The 'Seven Letters' of Ignatius, Bishop of Antioch. Written on his way to Rome (where he was martyred), the letters call for government of the Church by bishops. Scholars believe he was the first to use the phrase 'Catholic Church'.

108

Polycarp's Letter to the Philippians.

110

Martyrdom of Ignatius.

111–113

Emperor Trajan's letters to Pliny the Younger, the governor of Bithynia, on the treatment of Christians. Trajan forbids a witch hunt, but 'obstinate' Christians to be punished.

115

Jewish revolt (extends to Mesopotamia, Cyrenaica, Egypt and Cyprus).

120

Gnostic Christian centres flourish (e.g. Basilides in Alexandria and Valentinus elsewhere in Egypt).

124

Minucius Fundanus (governor of Asia) receives rescript of Emperor Hadrian concerning the Christians.

130

Conversion of Justin Martyr (*c.* 100–165), early Christian apologist.

132–135

The Second Jewish Revolt led by Bar Kochva.

140

Emergence of Christian writings known as 'Apologies'. These aim to clarify Christian beliefs among non-believers, removing any untruths and false accusations. Over the next 50 years, gradual emergence of an agreed canon of those books which will eventually constitute the New Testament.

144

Excommunication of Marcion (who had advocated rejection of Jewish scriptures). Subsequent church founded by Marcion extends from southern Gaul to Syria.

150

Growing disputes over the dates Easter to be celebrated. The Acts of the Martyrs, collected accounts of the events surrounding early martyrs.

c. **151**

First Apology of Justin Martyr.

c. **155–156**

Polycarp, Bishop of Smyrna, martyred. Beginning of a 'cult of the martyrs'.

161–180

Marcus Aurelius is Emperor. Persecution of Christians.

c. 165

Justin Martyr executed in Rome.

c. 170

Montanists (who await an early establishment of the New Jerusalem on Earth) active in Asia Minor.

178

Irenaeus begins work in Gaul as Bishop of Lyons.

c. 197

Apology of Tertullian (the first to be written in Latin, not Greek). Tertullian later a Montanist.

200

Establishment of Christian School of Alexandria (under Clement, then Origen). Beginning of use of Latin by some churches.

202

Persecution of Septimus Severus. Imperial edict bans conversion to Christianity or Judaism.

235

Exile of theologian Hippolytus to Sardinia.

249

Persecution of Emperor Decius. Victims include Origen and Fabian, the Bishop of Rome. Novatian (the first theologian to write in Latin) establishes separate church for those who refuse to accept apostates back in the Church.

257–258

Renewed persecution of the Christians.

Cyprian, Bishop of Carthage, is martyred.

Flourishing joint cult of Peter and Paul at Rome (and Petrine supremacy invoked against Cyprian).

c. 260

First edict of toleration in the Empire by Gallienus. Christian worship now permissible.

268

Bishop of Antioch, Paul of Samosata, deposed.

c. 271

St Anthony becomes first hermit in Egypt. By c. 280, other hermit communities emerge in Egyptian and Syrian deserts (see p. 26).

280

Armenia becomes first Christian 'state' after conversion of its ruler.

298

Expulsion of Christians from the armies of the Empire.

303

Beginning of the Great Persecution (21 Feb.), which results in many martyrdoms and apostasies. Churches closed, all Christians forced to sacrifice to the Emperor; scriptures destroyed.

305

Cessation of persecution in the West (but in the East at its worst until 311 under Galerius, whom Diocletian had chosen). Rule for hermits drawn up by St Anthony of Egypt.

306

Resumption of persecution.

310

Further tranche of martyrdoms.

311

Galerius renounced persecution, being forced into an edict of toleration by threat from Constantine in the West.

Donatist schism in North Africa when new Bishop of Carthage rejected (he had been made Bishop by a bishop who had sacrificed during the persecution).

312

Battle of the Milvian Bridge (28 Oct.), where famously Constantine had a vision before the battle of a flaming cross.

313

The 'Edict of Milan' in favour of Christianity follows death of Maximin, Galerius's successor (proclaimed after Conference of Milan) (Feb.). Edict issued by Constantine and Licinius, the Eastern Emperor. The Emperors agreed to tolerate all religions equally.

Council of Rome (2 Oct.) opens.

314

Council of Arles (30 Aug.) (summoned by Constantine to deal with the Donatists).

316

Condemnation of the Donatists (see p. 242) by Constantine (Nov.).

321

Beginning of persecution of Donatists.

325

Council of Nicaea opens (20 May).

CHURCH AND EMPIRE, 313–476

313

Toleration granted to Christians in the Empire by the Edict of Milan.

314

Beginning of reign of Pope Silvester I (to 335). The Council of Arles.

316

Condemnation of Donatists by Constantine.

320

Construction began of first Church of St Peter's in Rome (completed *c.* 349).

321

Beginning of persecution of Donatists.

323

Intervention of Constantine in Arian dispute.

324

Control of all Roman Empire in hands of Constantine. *Ecclesiastical History* of Eusebius.

325

Council of Nicaea (one of the most important gatherings so far in the history of the Church) (20 May).

First draft of Nicene Creed agreed.

Continuation of the Arian controversy over the definition of the Trinity (named after Arius, a priest of Alexandria). Controversy racks Eastern churches until 381. Monasticism proper under Pachomius (see p. 17).

326

Pilgrimage of Helena, mother of Emperor Constantine, to Holy Land. Building begins of the Church of the Holy Sepulchre (traditionally considered to be the site of Christ's crucifixion).

327

Second session of Council of Nicaea opened (Autumn).

328

Byzantium (under the new name of Constantinople) created capital of the Empire by Constantine.

330

Athanasius becomes Bishop of Alexandria (May). Deposition of Eustatius of Antioch.

334

Council of Caesarea (Spring).

335

Councils of Tyre and Jerusalem. Dedication of the Church of the Holy Sepulchre in Jerusalem (13 Sept.).

336

Exile of Athanasius. Death of Arius. Marcellus of Ancyra deposed.

337

Bishop Eusebius of Nicomedia baptizes Emperor Constantine. Death of Constantine (22 May). Constantius (Constantine's son) eventually becomes sole emperor.

339

Death of first great church historian, Eusebius of Caesarea. Second exile of Athanasius.

341

Conversion of many Germans by Ulfilas, Bishop of the Goths. Bible translated into Gothic.

c. **353**

Hilary becomes Bishop of Poitiers.

354

Birth of Augustine of Hippo (at Thagaste, 13 Nov.).

356

Third exile of Athanasius.

361–363

Reign of the last non-Christian Emperor, Julian, the cousin of Constantius, sees the pagan reaction.

362

Fourth exile of Athanasius.

365

Persecution of the Orthodox under Valens, fifth exile of Athanasius.

370

Basil became Bishop of Caesarea in Cappadocia.

372

Gregory elected Bishop of Nyssa. Gregory Naz Bishop of Sasima. Martin became Bishop of Tours.

373

Death of Athanasius.

374–397

Ambrose begins influential period as Bishop of Milan (the Western imperial capital).

c. **375**

Appearance of *Apostolic Constitutions*.

378

Rome suffers disastrous defeat at hands of the Goths at Battle of Adrianople.

379

Theodosius I becomes Emperor (until 395).

380

Baptism of Theodosius. The *Five Orations* of Gregory Naz.

381

Council of Constantinople (the second Ecumenical Council) settles disputes over the Nicene Creed and the Arian controversy, and elevates Constantinople itself to a patriarchate (see p. 300). Antioch witnesses preaching of St John Chrysostom.

Gregory Naz becomes Bishop of Constantinople.

382

Establishment of canon of Old Testament and New Testament. Jerome at Rome.

386–387

Conversion of Augustine of Hippo (in North Africa) to Christianity. Beginning of work of Jerome on translation of Bible into Latin (the Vulgate version). Jerome did this work living as a hermit at Bethlehem (where he had gone *c.* 385).

391

Augustine ordained priest at Hippo.

392

Banning of heathen worship in the Empire by Imperial decree (not fully enforced). Heresy of Theodore, Bishop of Mopsuetia.

395

Beginnings of Western monasticism (see p. 17).

396

Augustine becomes Bishop of Hippo (in North Africa), one of the key theologians of the Western church.

398

St John Chrysostom becomes Patriarch of Constantinople (until 404).

c. **400**

Pelagius and Celestius at Rome. The *Confessions* of Augustine.

402

Innocent I becomes Bishop of Rome.

404

Capital of the Western Empire moved to Ravenna.

406

The Imperial frontier on the Rhine breached by invading Germans.

410

Capture of Rome by Alaric, the Visigoth chief.

412

Augustine begins work on *City of God*. Cyril becomes Bishop of Alexandria.

414

Ending of the Antiochene Schism (divergence between Antioch and Alexandria became most bitter with the fifth-century disputes over the nature of Christ).

415

Pelagius in Palestine.

416–425

Spain taken by the Vandals.

422

Celestine Bishop of Rome.

426

City of God completed by Augustine.

428

Beginning of Nestorian controversy.

429–430

Vandals take North Africa.

430

Death of St Augustine at Hippo (28 Aug.).

431

The Council of Ephesus (the third Ecumenical Council). Significant for deposing Nestorius, Patriarch of Constantinople. See p. 300 for details. See p. 28 for later Nestorian churches. Missions to Ireland begin (see p. 41).

438

First Christian code of laws (the Theodosian Code) drawn up in reign of Theodosius II.

440

Election of Leo I as Pope. An important papacy for the exercise of wide papal authority in the West outside of Italy. Beginning of Eutychian Controversy (Eutychianism was a form of Monophysitism).

448

Publication of *Tome* of Leo I.

451

Council of Chalcedon (the fourth Ecumenical Council) failed to end Monophysite controversy over nature of Christ (i.e. one person in one nature). See p. 300. Major groups of churches in the East reject Chalcedon. Jerusalem created a patriarchate.

452

Invasion of Italy by Vandals.

455

Sack of Rome by Gaiseric.

476

Traditional date for the final collapse of the Roman Empire in the West (when Romulus Augustus is deposed).

EARLY HERESIES AND COUNCILS

c. 95

Ebionite heresy (denying Christ was Son of God).

c. 100

Appearance of Gnostics (although their origins were pre-Christian). Principal first century exponent was Simon Magus.

c. 120

Saturninus at Antioch.

Second century

Continuation of Gnostic heresy (with such figures as Marcion, Basilides (*c.* 125) and Valentinus (*c.* 135)).

c. 156/157

Montanist heresy, when Montanus proclaims himself 'prophet of the Spirit'. Condemned by synods in Asia, 175.

c. 190–200

Theodotus of Byzantium founds Dynamists (sometimes called Adoptionists). Monarchianism in evidence at Rome.

Third century

Gnostic heresy continues (e.g. Mani). Dynamist/Adoptionist heresy dies out.

202/205

Tertullian joins Montanists.

215

Emergence of Sabellians (also known as Medallists or Patripassians) with arrival of Sabelius in Rome.

217

Schism of Hippolytus at Rome.

251

The Novatianist schism (a form of rigorism named after Novatian).

255

Baptismal controversy of Carthage and Rome.

260

Monarchianism rift of Paul of Samosata, Bishop of Antioch.

311

Donatist heresy when followers of Donatus (see p. 242), Bishop of Carthage, oppose Majorinus. Meletian schism in Egypt.

313

Opposition of Pope Melchiades to Donatists. Beginning of Arian heresy at Alexandria when Arius (*c.* 250–336) in conflict with Bishop Peter.

314

Council of Arles opposes Donatists.

318

The Arian Controversy grows.

321

Synod at Alexandria condemns Arius.

325

The Council of Nicaea (see p. 300) condemns such heresies as Monarchians, the Arians, etc.

341–359

Succession of synods attempts to deal with Arianism (Antioch, 341; Sardica, 343; Antioch, 344; Arles, 353) (where the Western bishops were forced to condemn Athanasius); Milan, 355 (which confirmed Arles); Sirmium, 357 (which adopted the 'Blasphemy' creed); Ancyra, 358 (where the semi-Arians condemned the Blasphemy creed); and Ariminum (West) and Seleucia (East) (both eventually accepted the modified 'Dated Creed').

360

The Council of Constantinople ratifies the Nicene Creed as the official creed of the whole Church. A drawing together of the Orthodox and semi-Arian.

362

Council of Alexandria again reaffirms the Nicene Creed, with a definition of terms which leads to increased understanding between Eastern and Western supporters of Nicaea. Macedonianism condemned.

381

Arianism loses its hold (except among the Goths) after Second Council of Constantinople. Macedonianism condemned and reaffirmation of Nicene Creed.

c. **400**

Final disappearance of Montanist heresy in the East and in Africa.

403

The Synod of the Oak (a district of Constantinople) debates Chrysostom.

c. **405**

Start of preaching of Pelagius at Rome. Pelagianism condemned at Councils of Carthage (418) and Semi-Pelagians at Orange (529).

411

Donatists finally condemned by Council of Carthage. Donatists eventually disappear from North Africa after Muslim invasions.

412

Council of Carthage debates Pelagianism.

416–418

Condemnations of heresy of Pelagius in Africa and Rome.

430

Councils of Rome and Alexandria debate Nestorianism.

431

The Council of Ephesus, the third Ecumenical Council of the Church (see p. 300).

448

Council of Constantinople debates Eutychianism.

451

The Council of Chalcedon, the fourth Ecumenical Council of the Church. Monophysites ousted, but still hope that their fortunes might recover with a sympathetic emperor.

Postscript

482–484

Formula of union (the Henoticon) devised by the Emperor Zeno, on his sole authority and without a council of bishops, to accommodate the pro-Monophysites. Signed by the (pro-Monophysite) Patriarchs of Alexandria and Antioch even though it failed to condemn Chalcedon outright. The Henoticon (and the fact that Acacius of Constantinople had entered into communion with the Monophysites unilaterally) infuriated Rome. In 484 both Acacius and the Byzantine Emperor excommunicated by the Pope. Schism not ended until 518.

CHRISTIANITY IN NORTH AFRICA (TO 698)

In the early centuries, Christianity flourished in Roman North Africa, in great centres such as Alexandria and Carthage. Africa played a vital and vibrant role in the evolution of the early Church from Clement of Alexandria to the death of Augustine of Hippo in 430. The archaeological remains of churches across Mediterranean North Africa are testimony to this vibrant (though often divided) Church before it fell before the advance of Islam. Christianity was marked by a large number of 'bishops' and a bitter dispute over Donatism.

130

Disturbances among Christians reported in Alexandria. Gnostic influence was strongly established there.

180

Cathecal School established (the Didascalia) in Alexandria by Pantaenus to counter Greek philosophers and advocate Christianity.

c. 180

First mention of the Church in Carthage (by Tertullian). The *Acts of the Scillitan Martyrs*.

c. 200

Persecution of Christians in Alexandria.

202/203

The *Passion of Perpetua and Felicitas*.

215

Death of Clement of Alexandria (Patriarch).

225

Seventy bishoprics in Carthage alone reported on death of Tertullian.

248

Attack on Christians in Alexandria in major pogrom. Influence of Origen at its height.

250

Severe persecution of Decius. Bishops Cyprian of Carthage and Dionysius of Alexandria escape only by going into hiding. Around 150 bishops in Carthage area.

258

Death of Cyprian of Carthage.

284

Coptic Calendar begins (in commemoration of the persecution of Egyptian Christians).

302–311

Severe persecution by Diocletian disrupts life of the Church in Egypt.

312

Beginning of Donatist split over the election of Caecilian (in 311) as Bishop of Carthage. Donatists oppose state intervention in the

Church, favour a programme of social revolution and stress penance and martyrdom. The immediate cause was Caecilian's consecration by a *traditor* (see p. 267). Caecilian replaced by Majorinus (himself replaced by Donatus). However, Donatism takes on a partly nationalist Numidian strain against Carthage.

313

Around 250 bishops in Carthage when Edict of Milan published. Pope Miltiades decides in favour of Caecilian (decision rejected).

314

Council of Arles summoned by Constantine to attempt to settle dispute with the Donatists.

317–321

Persecution of Donatists.

c. 320

Establishment of early monasticism by Pachomius (see also p. 17).

321

Following the failure of persecution, Constantine granted toleration to the Donatists.

325

Cyrenaica under the jurisdiction of the see of Alexandria.

348

Despatch of legates Paul and Macarius by Constans in fruitless attempt to enforce church unity.

c. 355

Death of Donatus in exile in Gaul.

361

Return of exiled Donatists under Emperor Julian the Apostate.

362–392

Parmenion Bishop of Carthage (partly in exile).

c. 370

Birth of Synesius of Carthage (*c.* 370–413), one of the Fathers of the Eastern Church.

373

Death of Athanasius, Patriarch of Alexandria.

381

Constantinople takes over from Alexandria as second Christian centre.

388

Return of Augustine of Hippo to Africa (where Donatism now strongly entrenched).

391

Pagan cult centre of Serapeum in Egypt destroyed by Christians.

391/2

Death of Donatist leader, Parmenion, Bishop of Carthage.

394

Unity restored in Donatist ranks at Council of Bagai.

395–398

Uprising in Numidia against the authorities supported by powerful Donatist bishops (e.g. Optatus of Timgad, bishop from 388 to 398).

396–430

Augustine's period as Bishop of Hippo (when he wrote *Confessions* and the seminal *City of God*).

405

Promulgation of edicts banning the Donatists under Emperor Honorius.

411

Council of Carthage condemns Donatism. Donatists banned by Edict (412) and property confiscated, etc.

415

Greek philosopher Hypatia murdered by Christian monks.

419

Ruling of Council of Carthage on appeals to the see of Rome.

429

Coming of the Vandals to North Africa. They occupy the region until 534.

430

Death of Augustine of Hippo (354–430).

444

Death of Cyril, Patriarch of Alexandria.

451

Deposition of Dioscorus, Patriarch of Alexandria. Breakaway of Egyptian Coptic Church following Council of Chalcedon.

534

Belisarius, the general despatched by Emperor Justinian, restores Byzantine rule with his attack on the Arian Vandals in Africa.

619

Persians take Alexandria.

629

Restoration of Byzantine rule in Egypt by Heraclius.

640/641

Patriarch Cyrus negotiates as Islam advances into Egypt (Alexandria formally under Muslim control in 642).

698

Fall of Carthage to Muslim Arabs followed by mass exodus of Greek and Roman population.

EARLY MONASTICISM (TO 910)

Note: The earliest hermits and the origins of monasticism in the Egyptian and Syrian deserts may well have been spurred on by persecution. St Anthony is usually regarded as a key early figure.

c. 270

Early beginnings of monasticism when St Anthony enters the desert.

302

Armenian monastery of Echmiadzin founded near Erivan.

c. 327

Birth of Macrina (older sister of Basil the Great), who headed monastic community at Annesi in Cappadocia.

330

Birth of St Basil the Great (d. 379). The main influence (especially after 370) and organizer of Greek monasticism from his monastic complex of Caesarea (in Cappadocia).

c. 335

Birth of Martin, Bishop of Tours, a major figure in development of Western monasticism.

346

First Christian monastery in Egypt founded by St Pachomius.

350

Athanasius builds Chapel of the Great Meteoron at Meteora in Greece (site of early anchorite communities).

358–364

Monastic rule of St Basil propounded (the basis of subsequent Orthodox monasticism).

c. 360

John Cassian (d. 435). Author of books on basic rules of community life and founder of monastic centres near Marseilles.

361

Legugé, first monastery in Gaul, founded by Martin of Tours.

386

Jerome settles at a Bethlehem commune (a symbol of the appeal of sheltered monasticism).

395–430

Growth of monasticism in the West – at Nola (near Naples), the island of Lérins near Marseilles, etc. Arrival of John Cassian from Egypt.

410

Foundation of monastery of Lérins by Honoratus.

423–529

Life of Theodosius 'the Cenobriach' who heads the cenobites in Palestine.

432

Convent founded on Mount of Olives by Melania the Younger (*c.* 373–439).

486

Monastery of Mar Saba in Kidron Valley in Judaea founded by Sabas of Cappadocia.

c. **500**

The golden age of Irish monastic scholarship (see p. 41).

c. **515**

Appearance of the Benedictines (Black Monks).

529

Monte Cassino, north of Naples, founded by St Benedict.

540

Benedict of Nursia composes his monastic rule (later the generally accepted guideline in Western Christianity for monastic observance after *c.* 800).

543

Death of Benedict.

c. **557**

Foundation of the monastery of St Catherine's in Sinai (on the supposed site where Moses witnessed the burning bush).

590

Luxeuil in Burgundy first great monastery founded by St Columban.

591–615

Missions undertaken and monasteries founded in Europe by Irish monk Columbanus.

612

Foundation of Bobbio Monastery (between Milan and Genoa) by Irish monk Columbanus.

649

Death of hermit John Climacus at Mt Sinai.

744

Benedictine Abbey founded at Fulda by St Boniface.

780

Aniane Monastery founded by St Benedict.

880

Foundation of Montserrat Monastery.

909–910

Cluny Abbey (founded by William, Duke of Aquitaine). Located in Burgundy, south of Dijon (see p. 57).

CHRISTIANITY IN THE EASTERN EMPIRE: FROM JUSTINIAN TO THE GREAT SCHISM

519

Peace with papacy re-established.

525

Pope John I visits Constantinople.

527–565

Reign of Emperor Justinian, who attempts to re-establish old imperial frontiers by constant war and to revive the universal Christian Roman Empire (with himself as master of the Church). But cleavage of Latin and Greek Christianity intensifies.

529

The 'Code of Justinian'. Justinian's suppression of heresy and paganism reflected in closure of Neoplatonic Academy at Athens.

532–538

Beginning of rebuilding of Cathedral of St Sophia in Constantinople.

533

Byzantine reconquest of North Africa.

535–554

Reconquest of Italy. Ostrogoths decisively beaten at Battle of Tagina (552). All Italy under Byzantine rule.

540–562

The Persian War against Chosroes (Khusru I).

568–571

Most Byzantine possessions in Italy lost following Lombard invasions (Ravenna, Rome and Naples retained).

586

Patriarch John IV the Faster assumes title Oecumenical Patriarch.

610–641

Eastern Empire becomes distinctly Greek and Byzantine under Heraclius I, who founds new dynasty. Strong support from Patriarch Sergius.

614

Fall of Jerusalem to Persians.

622–630

The 'Byzantine Crusade', the outburst of religious enthusiasm which helped Heraclius I win a major victory over the Persians at Nineveh (Dec. 627). Persia returned all conquered land. The 'Holy Cross' returned to Jerusalem after Heraclius recovers Jerusalem in 629.

634

The advance of Islam and the Arab conquests. Rapid series of Muslim gains follows (see p. 30).

637–638

Fall of Jerusalem to Muslims.

638

The *Echthesis* issued by Heraclius, a formula prepared by Patriarch Sergius to try to reconcile Monophysites. It recognized one will in the two natures of Christ (Monothelitism). Not accepted by Egypt and Syria.

643

Fall of Alexandria, last Greek outpost in Egypt, to advancing Muslims.

647–648

North Africa invaded by Muslims.

648

Fall of Cyprus to Arabs.

649

Monotheletism condemned at Lateran Synod by Pope Martin I.

653

Emperor takes captive Pope Martin I (having been arrested by the Exarch of Ravenna). Conquest of Armenia by Arabs.

654

Rhodes plundered as Arabs advance. Death of Pope Martin I.

673–678

Constantinople finally beats off repeated Muslim land and sea blockades. Arab threat never so severe again.

680–681

Sixth Ecumenical Council meets at Constantinople (see p. 300). Condemnation of monothelitism and return to Orthodoxy. Following loss of other patriarchates after Muslim conquests, Constantinople becomes ever more important and Roman claims very nominal.

692

The 'Quinisext' Council at Constantinople (strongly anti-Roman).

698

Carthage falls to advancing Muslims.

717

Accession of Leo III (the Isaurian). Growing influence of elements in the Empire hostile to icons – in particular the Monophysite heresy, the Manichean strands within the Paulicians and the advance of Islam. Excessive use of icons seen as barrier to their conversion.

718

End of second great siege of Constantinople by the Arabs.

726

Edict of Leo III published. All images declared idolatrous and all to be destroyed. Start of iconoclast controversy. Rapid growth of serious opposition to Leo's Edict (led by Patriarch Germanus).

727

Revolt in Greece against iconoclasts. Pope Gregory II joins condemnation.

730

Patriarch Germanus (*c*. 640–*c*. 733) deposed. Forced into retirement at Platonium. Systematic persecution, especially of the monks.

731

Synods at Rome called by Pope Gregory III denounce the iconoclasts.

733

Leo III detaches Calabria, Sicily and Illyricum from jurisdiction of Rome.

741

Death of Leo. Succession of his son, Constantine V. Two-year revolt by Artabasdus (Constantine's brother-in-law). Iconoclasm policy then pursued.

751

Fall of Exarchate of Ravenna to the Lombards.

753

Constantine calls Synod of Hieria, which leads to increased persecution and martyrdom. Some secular clergy accept new doctrine. Synod seen as unrepresentative (neither the Patriarchs of Antioch, Jerusalem or Alexandria, nor the Pope, attended). Major attacks on monks and numerous monasteries suppressed.

755–764

Empire involved in successive campaigns against Bulgars.

775

Death of Constantine V. Accession of his son, Leo IV. Easing of the persecution.

778–779

Expulsion of Arabs from Anatolia after Byzantine victory at Germanikeia.

780

Death of Leo IV. Under his widow, the Empress Irene, regent for her young son Constantine I, iconoclasm policy reversed.

782

Arabs again advance to Bosporus.

784

Tarasius becomes Patriarch of Constantinople. Opening of conciliatory negotiations with Pope Hadrian I.

787

Seventh General Council meets at Nicaea. Total reversal of the iconoclastic Synod of Hieria. Icons restored throughout the Empire and agreement reached on the degree to which they can be venerated. Support for iconoclasm remains strong in imperial army and will later resurface.

790

Army (opposed to the monks) revolt puts Constantine VI in power.

809

Monks of Studion (led by Theodorus of Studion) banished and subsequently appeal to the Pope.

814

The 'Second Iconoclastic Controversy' begins under Leo V the Armenian (who was himself a general and had been elected Emperor by the army in 813). Removal of icons from churches etc. begins afresh.

815

Deposition at Council of St Sophia of Patriarch Nicephorus. The leading defender of icons among the monks, Theodorus of Studion, forced into exile. Further imprisonments and martyrdoms.

820

Assassination of Leo V. His successor, Michael II, continues a less harsh form of iconoclasm.

829

Death of Michael II. Accession of his son, Theophilus, followed by return to rigid iconoclasm.

832

Iconoclast Patriarch John the Grammarian enthroned. Increased persecution and violence by iconoclasts.

842

Death of Theophilus brings ending of persecution under Theodora (widow of Theophilus).

843

Election of monk Methodus as Patriarch. Defeat for iconoclasts. Triumphant rejoicing at great feast in celebration of the icons (later celebrated as the Feast of Orthodoxy). The dispute was widely regarded as another episode on the road eventually leading to schism with the Latin churches of the West in 1054.

858

Photius replaces Ignatius as Patriarch.

863

Missionary work of Cyril and Methodius among the Slavs of Bohemia and Moravia (see p. 40).

865

Baptism of Tsar Boris of Bulgaria (see p. 40) under pressure from Constantinople. Revolt by noble leaders after forced baptism of population.

867

Growing schism with Rome (following appeal by Ignatius for an inquiry into events of 858). Photius, with much support on his side, dominates Council of Constantinople. The Council anathematises the Pope, declares that the papacy is pursuing doctrinal aberrations and rejects any papal primacy.

867–874

Serbs converted to the Orthodox Church. Banishment of Photius, recall of Ignatius.

869

The Council of Constantinople (eighth Ecumenical Council). Not recognized in the East. Death of St Cyril in Rome.

870

After flirtation with Rome, Bulgaria looks to Constantinople.

871–879

Chronic warfare with Arabs in East but also campaign against the Christian Paulician sect.

877

Restoration of Photius as Patriarch (until 886) and renewed break with Rome.

879–880

Synod under Photius rejects the decisions of the 869 Council of Constantinople.

885

Slavonic liturgy introduced to Slavs of Bulgaria.

886

Accession of Leo VI. Photius deposed again and the Ignatians restored to power.

889–893

Brief heathen reaction to Christianity in Bulgaria until Boris returns from retirement (893) and reorganizes the Church.

900

Renewal (at least superficially) of union with Rome.

913–917

Growing threat to Constantinople from Tsar Symeon of Bulgaria.

926

In Bulgaria, Tsar Symeon establishes Leontius of Preslav as Patriarch.

c. **950**

Beginnings of Bogomil heresy in Balkans (see p. 235).

955

Constantinople visited by Princess Olga of Russia. Subsequent baptism of Olga.

961

Reconquest of Crete by Byzantines. Expulsion or conversion of Muslims. Foundation of the great lavra (monastic complex) on Mt Athos by Athanasius the Athonite (d. 1003).

964–968

Greeks reconquer Cyprus and briefly take Aleppo and Antioch.

969

Patriarchate of Preslav abolished.

972–976

Byzantines take Damascus (976) and Beirut (976). Halted at Jerusalem by Muslim forces from Egypt.

976–1014

Under Samuel as ruler of Bulgaria, the patriarchate ultimately based at Ochrid.

987–988

Conversion of Prince Vladimir of Russia at Cherson.

1014

Defeat of the Bulgars by Emperor Basil II (the 'Bulgar Slayer') at battle of Balathista.

1016–18

Bulgaria incorporated into Byzantine Empire. Abolition of the Bulgar Patriarchate (but effective independence of Archbishop of Ochrid).

1028

Emperor Romanus III allows Patriarchate to persecute Monophysites in Syria. This persecution facilitates subsequent Seljuk Muslim successes against Byzantium.

1040

Following revolt of the Bulgars, Bulgaria incorporated into the Empire and the autocephalous Church of Ochrid subservient to the Patriarch of Constantinople.

1054

The 'Great Schism' with Rome (see p. 61).

CHRISTIANITY IN THE EAST: THE ORIENTAL ORTHODOX CHURCHES

THE ARMENIAN CHURCH

Third century

Reliable independent historical evidence of established bishoprics in western Armenia.

313–314

Following Edict of Toleration (313), Gregory the Illuminator baptizes Tiridates III (298–330), the King of Armenia, in 314. Armenia first nation with Christianity as its religion. Gregory consecrated chief bishop (*catholicos*) of Church in Armenia. Catholicate established at Echmiadzin (formerly Vagarshapat). The catholicate an eastern province linked to the see of Caesarea (Cappadocia).

325

Gregory succeeded as *catholicos* by his son. The catholicate hereditary in his family.

c. 354

Catholicos Nerses I calls first Armenian Church Council in Ashtisat. Rules for moral conduct, monastic institutions, etc. laid down.

387

Greater Armenia divided between Rome and Persia. Weakening of links to see of Caesarea.

389

Sahak I becomes *catholicos* with no involvement of Caesarea.

Fifth century

The catholicate becomes elective. A 'golden age' of Armenian Christianity.

c. 404

Mesrop begins work creating a Bible in Armenian.

444

Hovsep I succeeds Sahak I as *catholicos* at Council of Shahapivan. Effective autonomy of Armenian Church.

451

Armenian Church rejects Council of Chalcedon (and again in 491).

481

Second Armenian revolt against Persian attempts to force Armenians to renounce their faith leads to full religious freedom for Armenians.

484

Catholicate moved to Duin (until 901).

653

Conquest of Armenia by Muslims.

Postscript

1113

Long-running schism begins with rival *catholicos*, David, on island of Al'thamar, Van.

1116

Establishment of the catholicate in Cilicia.

1441

Further schism when see of Cilicia transferred back to Echmiadzin.

1831

An Armenian Rite Catholic Church legally recognized by Rome (now based in Beirut).

Postscript

For the Armenian massacres, see p. 283.

THE COPTIC CHURCHES

Egypt

40s

Tradition that founder of ancient church of Egypt (and its patriarch) was Mark the Evangelist, preaching in Alexandria.

Second century

Important centre of Christian scholarship at Alexandria including Clement, Origen, the Cappadocian Fathers and Jerome.

230

Heraclas, a pupil of Origen, becomes Patriarch of Alexandria (until 246). Heraclas deemed the first with the title of Pope in the Coptic Church.

247

Dionysius Bishop of Alexandria.

284

Severe persecution of Egyptian Christians following accession of Diocletian as Emperor. The Coptic 'Calendar of the Martyrs' begins.

c. **300**

Withdrawal of Egyptian Christians to the desert symbolized by St Anthony (*c.* 250–356). Rise of the Desert Fathers and such monastic centres as Nitria, Cellia, etc.

313

Rapid rise in prominence of Alexandria as a major theological centre after Christians granted freedom of worship.

326–373

Athanasius Patriarch of Alexandria. A champion of orthodoxy in the *homoousios* ('of one being') Christological debate on the relationship of the Son with the Father.

346

First monastery founded by St Pachomius in Egypt.

412–444

Cyril Patriarch of Alexandria. A champion of Mary as *Theotokos* (Mother of God) in theological debates.

444

Dioscorus (nephew of Cyril) becomes Patriarch of Alexandria.

449

Authority of Alexandrian theology seemingly reaffirmed at Second Council of Ephesus (the Council that was bitterly denounced by Rome).

451

Council of Chalcedon (called by pro-Western Emperor Marcion) attacks Dioscorus. Deposition and exile of Dioscorus. Beginning of split in Coptic Christianity between the pro-Byzantine element (Melkites, 'the king's men') and the pro-Cyril faction. Byzantines subsequently give military support to pro-Chalcedon patriarchs of Alexandria.

457

Accession of Coptic Patriarch Timothy Aelurus, who is forced to live mainly in exile.

477

Accession of Coptic Patriarch Peter Mongus. Remains in hiding until 482, with the compromise of the Henoticon of Zeno (see p. 13).

537–566

Exile of anti-Chalcedonian Patriarch Theodosius in Constantinople.

616–629

Persian occupation of Egypt disrupts life of the Church.

629–642

Byzantine recovery of Egypt (629) and imposition of a Chalcedonian patriarch (631)

in the person of Cyrus. Benjamin, the anti-Chalcedon patriarch, 622–662, a fugitive in Egypt.

640s

The Muslim conquest of Egypt. Subsequent good relations of Patriarch Benjamin and the Muslim governor.

Seventh century

Growth in importance of monasteries as Christianity in Alexandria and the Delta declines.

725–831

Series of Coptic revolts accelerates the Islamization of the region.

969–1171

Generally a period of stabilization and recovery for Coptic Church under the Fatimid dynasty, but persecution under Caliph el-Hakim in the years 996–1021.

Postscript: Christianity survived the difficult period of the Mamluk era (1250–1517). There were occasional outbursts of anti-Christian mob violence (as in 1321 and 1354). Under the Ottomans after 1517, Egypt became relegated to the position of a backwater.

Ethiopia

Fourth century

Conversion of the Ethiopian kingdom of Axum to Christianity begins the long association with the see of Alexandria. Frumentius appointed first Bishop for Ethiopia by Patriarch of Alexandria.

c. 500–550

Kingdom of Axum in northern Ethiopia an important Christian power under King Kaleb.

Translation of Bible and key patristic writings into Ge'ez (Ethiopic).

Seventh century

The coming of Islam and increased isolation of Ethiopia. Major gap in historical knowledge of the Church until the Zagwe dynasty.

Twelfth century

The Zagwe dynasty. Construction of the famous churches at Lalibela from the rock.

1270 onwards

Revitalisation of the Church by reforms of Tekla Heylamot. Foundation of monastery of Debra Libanos.

Fourteenth–fifteenth century

Further period of translation of theological texts into Ge'ez.

THE ASSYRIAN CHURCH OF THE EAST

Note: This church (called incorrectly Nestorian from the fifth century and Assyrian from the nineteenth) was an Antiochene breakaway from Eastern Orthodoxy. Its doctrines developed from St Theodore of Mopsuestia. Centred on Edessa (the present-day Urfa in Turkey), it was influential in territories east of the former Byzantine Empire (SE Turkey, Iraq and Persia).

Second century

Christianity had spread from Najran (SW Arabia) through southern Turkey and Iraq to SW Persia.

Third century

Christianity reportedly spread to Fars (in far south of Persia), to Socotra (in Indian Ocean)

and to Sasanid capital of Seleucia-Ctesiphon. The Bishop of Seleucia-Ctesiphon was under the jurisdiction of the Antioch Patriarchate.

309–379

Persecution by the Sasanid King Shāpūr II (who sees Christians as allies of the Byzantines).

379–383

Continued persecution under Ardashīr II.

410

Synod of Seleucia convened by Marutha (representing the Emperor and Patriarch) made the metropolitan of Seleucia-Ctesiphon a *catholicos*. The new *catholicos* exercises all authority in the east except over see of Riyordashir. The Synod of Seleucia accepted Canons of first Council of Nicaea (the Church of the East had taken no part in this Council).

428

Nestorius (*c*. 381–*c*. 451) becomes Patriarch of Constantinople. Beginnings of the Nestorian Schism (Nestorius taught that Christ had two natures, human and divine).

431

Nestorius condemned at Council of Ephesus. Assyrian Church rejects Council of Ephesus, especially its adoption of the title *Theotokos* (Mother of God) for the Virgin Mary.

457

Barsumas metropolitan of Nisibis (Persia). Founds Nestorian school.

484

Effective separation from mainstream Orthodox churches of Persian Nestorian

Church. Intermittent persecutions and martyrdoms of Assyrian Church.

489

Closure of the 'Persian School' at Edessa, which had considerable impact on the doctrinal Antiochene theology (via the School of Nisibis) and on Nestorians.

c. **523**

Persecution of Christians in Najran.

527–565

Orthodox and Monophysite missions sent to Nubia during reign of Justinian.

542–577

Episcopate of Jacob Baradaeus (organizer of the Jacobites). Many monastic foundations and important monastic writers (e.g. Isaac of Nineveh).

628

Death of Babai the Great, author of the *Book of the Union* and most important theologian of Nestorian Church.

635

Nestorianism brought to Ch'ang-an, China, by A-lo-pên.

641

Edessa falls to the Arabs.

650

Conversion of many Turks by Nestorian Metropolitan of Merv.

651

End of Sassanid rule in Iran. Christians treated fairly in the 'dhimma' under Muslim rule.

698

Buddhist reaction in China against Christian mission.

750–780

Apogee of Nestorian missions in China.

845

Christians and Buddhists persecuted in China by Wu Tsung.

944

Byzantines briefly take Edessa.

c. **1009**

Conversion to Christianity of some of the Keraits.

1144

Zengi captures Edessa.

1295

Conversion of Mongol dynasty to Islam results in serious reversal for the Church.

Sixteenth century

Church of the East divided when separate Uniat line emerged (Chaldean Christians).

CHRISTIANITY AND THE RISE OF ISLAM

c. 570

Birth of the prophet Mohammed (Muhammad).

610

First revelation to Mohammed.

622

The Hegira (Hijra), the migration to Medina from Mecca (since 619, with the death of his wife Khadija and his uncle Abu Talib, Mohammed had no protector in the city). First year of Islamic calendar dates from 622.

624

Although outnumbered, Muslims win battle of Badr with what is seen as divine help.

625

Muslims defeated at battle of Uhud by Meccans.

627

Muslims win battle of the Trench over Meccans and other Bedouins. Leadership of Muslims consolidated in Mecca.

628

Muslims permitted to undertake pilgrimage to Mecca by Treaty of Hudaybiyah.

630

Mecca occupied by Mohammed.

632

Death of Mohammed. Succeeded by Abu Bakr, the first Caliph. Expansion into Syria and Iraq follows.

634

Umar (Omar) Ibn al-Khattab becomes second Caliph on death of Abu Bakr.

636

Major defeat for Byzantine army at Battle of Yarmuk (south of Lake Tiberias).

637

Major Muslim victory over Persians at Qadisiya. Muslims subsequently capture Ctesiphon (Al-Madain).

638

Fall of Jerusalem (one of Christianity's ancient Eastern patriarchates) to Muslims follows rapid Muslim subjugation of northern Syria, Aleppo and Antioch (another of the ancient patriarchates).

642

Surrender of ancient Christian Patriarchate of Alexandria to advancing Muslims.

644

Fatal stabbing of Caliph Umar. Uthman Ibn Affan becomes third Caliph. His reign sees final assembly of the Quran (Koran).

646

Conquest of Mesopotamia (roughly modern Iraq) completed by Muslims.

649/650

Muslims overrun Fars.

656

Death of third Caliph Uthman. Civil war among Muslims over succession leads to Sunni–Shia split. Fourth Caliph Ali Ibn Abi Talib victorious at Battle of the Camel over Aisha.

661

Assassination of Caliph Ali Ibn Abi Talib. The Ummayad dynasty founded by Muawiya Ibn Abi Sufyan.

670

Most of NW Africa conquered by Muslims.

680–692

Husayn, son of Caliph Ali, is martyred after leading rebellion against Umayyad Caliph Yazid (the second Muslim civil war). The first creation of the saga of the suffering Shi'ites.

697

North African city of Carthage (with strong Christian tradition) overrun. Marks end of Byzantine rule in North Africa.

711

Straits of Gibraltar crossed by Berber converts to Islam. Beginning of Moorish conquest of Spain (see p. 46).

31

THE WESTERN CHURCH, 402–910

402–417

Papacy of Innocent I, regarded by some as the first true pope with his claim to be custodian of apostolic tradition.

406

The 'great invasions' of tribes across the Rhine.

410

The sack of Rome by Alaric the Goth.

429–439

Catholic Christianity in North Africa destroyed by the Vandals.

440–461

The papacy of Leo I ('Leo the Great').

445

Leo I obtains edict from Emperor Valentinian II declaring papal decisions have force of law.

449

The 'Robber Council' of Ephesus, later denounced by Leo I.

455

Rome captured by Vandals.

476

Romulus Augustus, last Roman Emperor in the West, deposed.

484–519

The first schism between Rome and Constantinople (the Acacian Schism over the Henoticon dispute) (see p. 13).

492–496

Papacy of Gelasius II, who developed the idea of a world divided into two powers – State and Church – with the Church supreme. Founding of Ostrogothic kingdom in Italy by Theodoric (to 553).

496

Baptism of Clovis, King of the Franks, on Christmas Day at Rheims. Key date in the conversion of the German tribes to Christianity.

507

Battle of Vouillé. Victory of Clovis forces Visigoths to withdraw over the Pyrenees and establish new capital at Toledo.

519

Ending of first schism with Constantinople.

527

Justinian reconquers North Africa from Vandals and Italy from Goths.

529

Monte Cassino founded by Benedict.

561

The Arianism of Sueves condemned at Council of Braga under St Martin.

565–578

Holy Cross founded at Poitiers by Radegund.

568

Beginning of Lombard rule in Italy.

580

Sack of Monte Cassino by Lombards.

587–589

Conversion of King Recared from Arianism to Roman orthodoxy in Spain. Third Council of Toledo. Visigoths in Spain finally accept Catholicism as their official faith. Insert of *filioque* (see p. 244) into Nicene Creed at Toledo Council (589).

590

Beginning of papacy of Gregory the Great (Gregory I), who (like Leo I and Gelasius II) invoked the Petrine supremacy theory. Gregory was the first pope who had been a monk.

596

Despatch of Augustine to England by Pope Gregory (see p. 42).

597

Death of Columba on Iona (see p. 42).

c. **600**

Jews forced to accept baptism in Spain.

604

Death of Gregory the Great.

614

Columbanus at Bobbio.

615

Death of St Columbanus.

620–629

Expulsion from Spain of Byzantine forces.

625–638

Papacy of Honorius I.

633

Council of Toledo IV under Isidore assumed the right to confirm elections to the crown.

636

Death of Isidore of Seville.

640–642

Papacy of John IV.

641

Christianization of Croatia begun by Pope John IV (a native of Dalmatia). Mission of Abbot Martin to the Croat lands. Eligius becomes Bishop of Noyon.

649

Condemnation of Monotheletism at Lateran Synod.

653

Pope Martin I arrested by the exarch. Died in exile.

657–662

Papacy of Pope Vitalian.

662

Death of St Maximus the Confessor.

663

Roman Church prevails over Celtic Church in England at Synod of Whitby (see p. 42).

669

St Theodore becomes Archbishop of Canterbury (until 690).

674

Eastern Christianity threatened by Arab siege of Constantinople. Siege ended in 678.

679

The Council of 125 Bishops of Pope Agathos.

680/681

Birth of St Boniface. The Council of Constantinople (Sixth Ecumenical Council) (see p. 300), important for condemnation of Monotheletism.

690

St Willibrord Archbishop of Utrecht. Death of St Benet Biscop.

692–695

Consecration of Willibrord in Rome as Clement.

***c*. 700**

Conversion of Germany (see p. 37) begun by Wilfred of York, Willibrord and Boniface.

711

Conquest of Spain by the Moors (see p. 46). Pope Constantine I invited to Constantinople by Justinian II. Beginning of the Papal States in Italy.

715–731

Papacy of Gregory II.

723

Consecration of St Boniface as bishop by Gregory II.

726

Iconoclasm in the East opposed in Italy.

731

Pontificate of Pope Gregory III. Condemnation of iconoclasm.

732

Defeat of Muslims near Poitiers by Charles Martel halts advance into France.

732–733

Transfer of East Illyricum to jurisdiction of Constantinople.

735

Death of St Bede the Venerable at Jarrow. The ablest church historian of his time.

751

Fall of Exarchate of Ravenna to Lombards.

756

Expansion of the Papal States by the Donation of Pepin laid foundation of papal temporal power.

767

Synod of Chantilly.

768–814

Charlemagne King of the Franks.

769

The Lateran Synod.

772–795

Papacy of Hadrian I.

787

The Council of Nicaea (Seventh Ecumenical Council) condemns iconoclasm. First Vikings land in England (see p. 43).

794

Synod of Frankfurt.

798

Flight of Pope Leo III to Paderborn.

800

Coronation of Charlemagne by Pope Leo III on Christmas Day. 'Restoration' of the empire in the West.

804

Death of Alcuin.

809

Council of Aachen.

814

Death of Charlemagne.

816–817

Rule of St Benedict to be followed by all monasteries throughout the Empire.

817–824

Papacy of Paschal I.

824–825

Synod of Paris.

826

First missionary journey of St Anskar to convert Scandinavia. No permanent achievement (see pp. 37–8).

843

Iconoclasm ended in east by Council at Constantinople (see p. 300). The Treaty of Verdun.

845

Hincmar Archbishop of Rheims (until 882).

846

Muslim raiders sack St Peter's Rome (in 847 Pope Leo IV walls the 'Leonine City' to increase defences).

c. **850**

Possible date for the forged decretals.

858

Nicholas I (the last pope to be styled 'The Great') becomes Pope, the only one of any effective power in this period. Photius became Patriarch of Constantinople (see p. 336).

863

Missionary work in Moravia by Orthodox missionaries Cyril and Methodius (see p. 40).

871

Reign of Alfred in England. Beginning of the Christianisation of Danes in England by time of his death in 901.

879–892

Croat national church organized by Pope John VIII.

910

Foundation in Burgundy of Abbey of Cluny (see p. 57).

THE CONVERSION OF EUROPE (TO 1198)

WESTERN AND CENTRAL EUROPE, 491–1198

491

Theodosius closes last pagan temple in Rome.

496

Clovis, King of the Franks, and his subjects baptized.

589

Conversion of the Visigoths.

***c*. 590–591**

Mission of Irish monk Columban of Leinster (Columbanus) to Europe. His work results in major foundations (Gall, Würzburg, Salzburg, Bobbio, etc.).

597

Despatch by Pope Gregory the Great of Augustine to England (see p. 42).

678

Landing of St Wilfrid in Friesland.

690

Mission of Willibrord to the Frisians.

716

First mission of Winfrith (St Boniface) to the Frisians.

718–719

Boniface makes first visit to Rome and first mission to the Rhineland.

723

The sacred oak of Geismar, a major pagan symbol, cut down by Boniface.

739

Death of Willibrord.

754

Death of Boniface.

772

Launching of first campaign by Charlemagne against the Saxons.

784

Pagan Frisians stage last major revolt.

787

Consecration of Willehad as first Bishop of the Saxons.

801

Birth of Anskar.

826

Harald baptized at Mainz.

37

845

Baptism of 14 Czech princes.

865

Death of Anskar.

910

Foundation of Cluny (see p. 57).

911

Baptism and recognition of rule in Normandy of Rollo.

929

Death of King Wenceslas (Vaclav) at hands of Boris the Cruel.

948

Foundation of sees of Brandenburg and Havelberg by Otto I.

955

Magyar advance halted by Otto I.

965

Conversion of Danish King Harold Bluetooth to Christianity.

c. **966–967**

Duke Mieszka of Poland (reigned to 992) baptized. Polish Court accepts Christianity as a result.

968

Foundation of Archiepiscopal see of Magdeburg.

c. **960–990s**

Establishment of first Christian churches among the West Slavs, Danes, Poles and Russians.

973

Founding of the diocese of Prague.

983

Revolt among the Wends.

988

Orthodox see of Kiev founded (see p. 40).

997

St Adalbert (Vojtêch) of Prague martyred by Prussians.

1000

Iceland accepts Christianity. Foundation of Gniezno as a Polish archbishopric. Beginning of reign of Stephen of Hungary.

1002

Anti-Christian rising in Transylvania defeated by Stephen.

1021

Death of first Christian King of Sweden (Olof Skötonung).

1037

Popular anti-feudal and anti-Christian rising in Poland.

1066

Christianity suffers reverse when missions are expelled from the West Slavs (the 'revolt of the Wends').

1086

King Canute IV of Denmark martyred.

1088

Second Czech diocese founded (at Olomouc).

1103–04

Lund established as metropolitan see of the North.

1118

Foundation in Jerusalem of Hospital of St Mary for Germans.

1124–25

Start of missions of Otto of Bamberg in Pomerania (new mission in 1127–8). Beginning of conversion of south Baltic coast.

1126–54

Missionary labours of Vicelin among the Wends.

1139–43

Wagria and Polabia conquered by Saxons.

1143

Foundation of Lübeck, which becomes major commercial centre.

1143–44

Cistercians begin work in Denmark and Sweden.

1147

First northern crusade against Baltic Slavs launched.

1152

Foundation of see of Trondheim as major centre.

1164

Saxons and Danes put down revolt of the Abotrites. Foundation of archiepiscopate of Uppsala.

c. **1168–69**

Paganism among the Wends of Rügen destroyed by the Danes under Valdemar I.

1171

Crusade against east Baltic heathens authorized by Alexander III. Submission of Pomeranian Slavs to Canute VI of Denmark.

1180

Concessions in favour of the clergy by Grand Duke Casimir II of Poland.

1184

Construction of church near mouth of the Dvina by Meinhard.

1188

First missionary work begins among the Livs.

1190–91

Origins of the Teutonic Knights when hospital founded at Acre by merchants of Bremen and Lübeck. This became connected to the Church of Mary the Virgin in Jerusalem.

1198

Brethren of the hospital at Acre raised to a military order (the Teutonic Knights).

For subsequent history, see pp. 75–7.

EASTERN EUROPE, 587–1054

587

Patriarch of Constantinople assumes title 'Ecumenical' and seeks coordinated Christian missions to barbarians on frontiers of Byzantium.

c. 800

Rule of Christian Slavic Prince Viseslav at Nin.

858

Patriarch Photius the Great sends missions to Moravia, Bulgaria and Russia.

860

Mission to the Khazars of Constantine-Cyril.

c. 861

Death of first Christian Slav prince in Slovakia (Pribina).

862

Mission to Greater Moravia (Constantine-Cyril and his brother Methodius) at the request of Ratislav.

c. 864/865

Conversion of Khan (King) Boris of Bulgaria.

866

Basil I becomes Emperor. Beginning of forced baptism of Serbs of the Narenta Valley.

869

Death of Constantine-Cyril.

c. 884/885

Death of Methodius.

891

Death of Mutimir (during whose reign the conversion of the Serbs had been achieved). The main organization of the Serb Church came with Sava after 1174.

927

Death of Simeon (during whose reign conversion of the Bulgars was achieved).

c. 954/955

Baptism of Olga of Kiev in Constantinople.

c. 987/988

Vladimir, Grand Prince of Kiev, baptized.

1015

Death of Vladimir of Kiev.

c. 1050

Foundation of Monastery of the Caves in Kiev (see p. 136).

1054

Beginning of the Eastern Schism (see p. 61).

For developments after 1054, see p. 136 for Kiev and Russia, see p. 61 for main developments in the Byzantine Empire and the Balkans.

CHRISTIANITY IN THE BRITISH ISLES

BACKGROUND NOTE

c. 200

Tertullian reports existence of Christianity in parts of Britain.

c. 304

Traditional date for martyrdom of St Alban, the legendary first English martyr.

306

Proclamation of Constantine as Emperor at York.

314

Evidence that Council of Arles attended by British 'bishops'.

410

Withdrawal of Roman troops from Britain.

429

Controversy between St Germanus on visit to Britain and the Pelagians.

CELTIC CHRISTIANITY, *c.* 430–664

c. 431

Date traditionally given for mission of Palladius to Ireland.

c. 432–450

Churches founded by Patrick on his mission to Ireland in Meath, Ulster, Connaught, etc.

Still much paganism survives, and early churches established by Patrick subsequently partly collapse.

c. 450

Mission of St Ninian to the Picts.

c. 500

Start of the Golden Age of Irish monasticism (to *c.* 800).

c. 500

Foundation of Celtic monastery at Tintagel (Cornwall).

c. 520

Establishment of monastery at Clonard, major centre for important later missions.

c. 521

Birth of Irish monk Columba.

c. 550

Mission to Wales of St David.

563

Columba settles on Iona, the mother church of Scotland and seen as a model of true monasticism.

591

Monasteries founded and missions undertaken by Irish monk Columbanus in Europe (see p. 37).

(see p. 37)

596/597

Death of St Columba on island of Iona.

664

The Synod of Whitby (see below).

FROM AUGUSTINE TO THE VIKINGS

597

Mission of St Augustine in Kent. Aethelbert, King of Kent, accepts Christianity. Death of St Columba (596/7).

604

Death of Pope Gregory the Great.

615

Death of Columban (Columbanus).

616

Following death of Aethelbert of Kent, his successor Eadbald eventually returns Kent to Christianity.

617

Return of paganism to London (until 654).

627

Baptism of King Edwin at York by St Paulinus.

c. 630–635

Start of East Anglian mission of St Felix; missionary work of St Aidan in Northumbria from Lindisfarne (where he had been summoned from Iona by Oswald of Northumbria).

c. 635

Christianity introduced into Mercia by St Aidan.

c. 650

Missionary work among Mercians and West Saxons by St Finan.

c. 651

Death of Aidan.

c. 654

Abbey of Peterborough founded (destroyed by Danes in 870).

656

First missionary bishop of Mercia appointed.

657

Foundation of Whitby Abbey by St Hilda (its first abbess until her death in 680).

662

Thorney Abbey founded.

664

Celtic Christianity brought back into conformity with Roman Church at the Synod of Whitby (e.g. over date of Easter, etc.).

669

Theodore of Tarsus becomes Archbishop of Canterbury. Introduction of strictly Roman parochial system and centralized episcopal system. His period as Archbishop (until 690) an important era in development of early English Church.

c. 673–675

Work of St Etheldreda at Ely.

674

Monastery of Wearmouth (Northumberland) founded by Bishop Biscop.

680

Cuthwin appointed first Bishop of Leicester (a see of the early Church until 870).

681

First Bishop of Selsey appointed. Jarrow monastery founded by Bishop Biscop.

681–686

St Wilfrid converts the South Saxons.

685

Church at Winchester founded.

686/687

Last pagan region of England (Isle of Wight) accepts Christianity.

687

Death of St Cuthbert.

c. 695

Production of *Lindisfarne Gospels*.

699

Arrival of St Guthlac at Crowland.

710

Death of St Wilfrid.

716/718

Beginning of mission to the Rhineland by St Boniface, the Anglo-Saxon monk (see p. 37).

731

Ecclesiastical History of the English People completed by Bede.

735

Death of Bede. Archbishopric of York founded.

775

St Boniface martyred.

782

Alcuin undertakes work at Charlemagne's court.

789

First recorded attack by Vikings in England (along Dorset coast).

793

Lindisfarne raided and sacked by Norsemen.

794

Jarrow sacked.

795

Vikings attack isle of Skye and Iona.

798

Isle of Man attacked.

800

Attack on St Andrew's tomb shrine.

802

Further attacks on Iona (finally abandoned in 807 as a result of attacks).

807

Irish settlement of Sligo attacked.

823

Norwegian conquest of Ireland begins.

832

Sack of Armagh.

833

Danish attacks on England begin.

840

Dublin founded as centre of Norse trade with Europe (along with Limerick and Waterford).

856–875

Main Viking assault on England.

866

The Great Library at York destroyed.

870

Danes destroy monastery at Ely.

FROM ALFRED TO THE NORMAN CONQUEST

871–900

The period of Alfred the Great in sustaining Christianity in Wessex (although almost destroyed by the 878 winter invasion). Eventually Guthrun the Dane becomes a Christian following the Peace of Wedmore.

Tenth century

Under the influence of the revival at Cluny (see p. 57), some improvement to the corruption and decadence into which the Church had fallen during the period of the invasions.

943

Glastonbury Abbey founded by St Dunstan. Revival of monasticism in England (especially under Oswald, Archbishop of York).

959

Edgar becomes King, with Archbishop Dunstan as chief counsellor who undertook ecclesiastical reform.

972

Oswald becomes Archbishop of York (until 992).

973

Coronation of Edgar as King of England by St Dunstan.

c. 993

Aelfric's *Lives of the Saints*.

1012

Martyrdom of St Alphege.

1014

Wulfstan's *Sermo Lupi ad Anglos* at York.

1016

Knut succeeded to English Crown.

1035

Death of Knut.

1062

St Wulfstan Bishop of Worcester (until 1095).

1065

Death of St Edward the Confessor.

1066

The Norman Conquest (see p. 87).

MOORISH AND CHRISTIAN SPAIN, 711–1492

711

Visigothic King Roderick defeated by mixed force of Arabs and Berbers who had crossed Straits of Gibraltar from Africa under the Berber Tariq at the battle on the Guadelete. Cordoba and Toledo swiftly fall.

712

Musa, Tariq's master, rapidly conquers Medina Sidonia, Seville, Merida and Saragossa.

714

Muslims begin the conquest of Visigothic Lusitania (Portugal).

718

Muslim advance temporarily halted by Christian victory at Covadonga.

719

Muslim forces reach the Pyrenees. Christian remnants forced into the mountains of north and west Spain. Kingdom of the Asturias created by Pelayo (until 737).

732

Charles Martel and the Franks inflict decisive defeat on Moors who had pushed into France at the battle of Tours.

739–757

Church receives generous portion of lands reconquered from Moors by Alfonso I.

756–788

Emir Abd ar-Rahman I. In return for payment of a poll tax, Christians tolerated. Jews well treated.

759

Expulsion of Moors from present-day France completed.

816

Introduction of Malikite rite to al-Andalus.

***c.* 830**

Supposed discovery of relics of St James. Subsequent rise of Santiago de Compostela.

837

Revolt of Christians and Jews in Toledo suppressed.

852–886

Rule of Muhammad I. Christian rising in Cordoba suppressed. Intermittent military operations against Christian states of Leon, Galicia and Navarre.

899

Miraculous discovery of the bones of St James the Greater at Santiago de Compostela.

912–961

Gifted and able rule of Abd ar-Rahman III. General pacification of the country. Continued toleration for Christians and Jews. Continued wars with Leon and Navarre.

955

Muslim peace treaty with Ordono III of Leon recognizes independence of Leon. Muslim frontier now on the Ebro. Peace ineffective, continued wars against Leon.

976–1009

Beginning of decline of Umayyad dynasty. Muslim Spain gradually reduced to civil war and petty kingships. Path for Christian reconquest opens.

1031

End of the Andalusian Caliphate.

1033

Extension of influence of the Cluniacs and French elements.

1034

Christians establish their Portuguese frontier with the Moors at the Mondego River. End of Caliphate at Cordoba.

1055

Reconquest of much of Portugal continues with victories of Ferdinand the Great.

1056–1147

The Almoravids, a Berber dynasty, invited to Spain by the Abbasids to aid them against the Christians.

1064

Coimbra (Portugal) conquered by Christian forces. Beginnings of the Aragonese reconquest.

1070

Building of cathedral at Santiago de Compostela.

1074

Alfonso VI of Castile and Leon asked to establish Roman rite by Pope Gregory VII.

1085

Toledo captured from the Moors by Alfonso VI of Castile. Christian advance to Tagus frontier. Strengthening of Cluniac influence in Spain.

1086

Defeat of Alfonso of Castile at Zallaka in counter-offensive by Moors.

1093

Henry of Burgundy, son-in-law of Alfonso VI of Castile, created Count of Portugal.

1097

El Cid returns to Castilian service, then returns to Muslims, eventually becoming ruler of Valencia.

1099

Death of El Cid. Valencia returns to Almoravids (in 1102).

1112

Accession of 3-year-old Afonso Henriques in Portugal.

1114

Catalan crusade to the Balearic Islands.

1118

Spanish crusade of Pope Gelasius II. The fall of Saragossa to the crusaders (Dec.).

1128

Afonso assumes authority in Portugal. Victories over Moors culminate in battle of Ourique (1139).

1140

First Cistercian foundations in Spain.

1143

Burgundian Count Afonso proclaimed King of Portugal. Under the Treaty of Zamora Castile recognizes Portuguese independence and Portugal accepts suzerainty of the Pope.

1146–1150

Invasion and conquest of Moorish Spain by the Almohades. Moorish divisions pave way for resumption of the *reconquista* (e.g. into Andalusia).

1147

Lisbon conquered from Muslims (with assistance from English crusaders). Establish their frontier on the River Tagus.

1158

Establishment of Spanish Order of Alcántara (most clerical of the three Spanish Orders).

1164

Spanish Order of Calatrava confirmed by the Pope.

1171

Spanish Order of Santiago founded, subsequently the largest and richest of the three Spanish military orders (with *c.* 700,000 members in 1492).

1172

Muslim unity in Spain restored.

1179

Independence of Portugal formally recognized by Pope Alexander III.

1185

Accession of Sancho I in Portugal. Subsequent establishment of military orders of knighthood.

1189

Fall of Silves (in Portugal) to the crusaders (3 Sept.).

1193

Crusade in Spain.

1197

Further crusade in Spain.

1200

The Order of San Jorge de Alfama founded.

1211–1223

Conflict between Crown and Church in Portugal under Afonso II. Subsequent papal interference.

1212

Expulsion of Almohades from Spain following Christian victory at the Battle of

Las Navas de Tolosa (16 July). A major Christian victory which leaves only local Muslim dynasties in Spain.

1229

Intense period of crusade in Spain (to 1253). Crusade of James I of Aragon to Majorca.

1231

Crusade of Ferdinand III of Castile in Spain.

1232

The conquest of Valencia by James I of Aragon begins. Major advance in 1238.

1236

Cordoba taken by Ferdinand III of Castile (June) after attacks on Moors in Guadalquivir Valley. Muslim resistance begins to crumble and *reconquista* accelerates.

1243

Fall of Murcia to Christians.

1245

Deposition of Sancho II in Portugal by the Pope.

1248

Fall of Seville to forces of Ferdinand III. Granada remains as main Moorish bastion in Spain.

1250

Silves, the last Muslim city in Portugal, finally falls to the Christians.

Postscript
1340

Alfonso IX of Castile defeats the Muslims at the Battle of Salado.

1473

Massacre of *conversos* in Andalusian towns.

1492

Conquest of Granada. Expulsion of the Jews. Columbus discovers America.

1502

Moriscos forced to choose between baptism and expulsion.

THE MEDIEVAL PAPACY, 1049–1198

1046

Synod of Sutri deposes Benedict IX, Sylvester III and Gregory VI after period of rival popes and antipopes. Svitgar, Bishop of Bamberg, made Pope by Emperor Henry III. First of a series of German popes strongly reflecting Cluniac influences.

1047

Decrees against simony and clerical marriage by Synod of Rome.

1049

Bruno, Bishop of Toul, elected Pope as Leo IX. Beginning of a period of revival of spiritual primacy of the papacy and recovery of lost influence following Council of Rheims.

1052

Duchy of Benevento granted to the papacy by Henry III.

1054

Breach with Constantinople, with mutual excommunication of the other (see p. 61). Acrimony had developed over rival claims in southern Italy. Successive attempts to heal the breach never succeeded and it eventually became permanent.

1055–57

Papacy of Victor II, dominated by Hildebrand.

1057–58

Papacy of Stephen IX also continues reforms. Period of the Pataria in Milan, a popular movement calling for the end of such abuses as simony, a return to the simpler apostolic life and the introduction of clerical celibacy.

1058–61

Papacy of Nicholas II.

1059

The Synod of the Lateran sets procedures for future election with rules for the College of Cardinals.

1061–73

Papacy of Alexander II (although the Synod of Basel elected a rival pope). Alexander II gave his blessing to the Norman invasion of England in 1066.

1072

Start of Norman conquest of Sicily (Bari having been conquered in 1071 by Robert Guiscard). Ending of Greek power in southern Italy.

1073–85

The important papacy of Gregory VII (often called by his own name of Hildebrand). Major effort to wrest the Church from lay control and reform it. The investiture of bishops and abbots by lay princes forbidden (at 1075 Synod of Rome), leading to the Investiture

Struggle (see below). The papal claims were summarized in his *Dictatus*. During his papacy, Gregory asserted suzerainty over Hungary, Spain, Sardinia and Corsica.

1076

The conflict of Gregory VII and the Emperor Henry IV (the Investiture Struggle) leading to the excommunication of Henry. The Synod of Worms, called by Henry IV at the urging of the German bishops, deposed Gregory.

1077

The famous penance of Henry IV at the castle of Canossa (north Italy).

1080

Clement III crowned (Antipope) (Antipope until 1100).

1084

Founding of the Carthusians (see p. 57) at the Grande Chartreuse.

1088

Beginning of papacy of Urban II.

1095

Pope Urban II called for the First Crusade at the Synod of Clermont to free the Holy Land from the Muslims (see p. 65). Jerusalem falls to crusaders in 1099.

1098

Founding of the Cistercians (see p. 57). The Synod of Bari, in which papacy fights to keep leadership of the crusade.

1099–1118

Papacy of Paschal II. Excommunication of Henry IV renewed.

1103–7

Investiture battle fought in England by Anselm, Archbishop of Canterbury (see p. 87).

1111

Pope Paschal II permits lay investiture to Emperor Henry V. Humiliating retreat by papacy over papal fiefs and secular revenues has major impact on Europe.

1112

Paschal repudiated his concessions.

1115–53

Period when St Bernard was Abbot of Clairvaux.

1115

The lands of Matilda (subject of donations to papacy in 1086 and 1102) left in her will to Emperor Henry V, provoking new conflict of empire and papacy.

1118–19

Papacy of Gelasius II. Forced to flee Rome and finished up in France. An antipope in Rome.

1119–24

Papacy of Calixtus II. The Synod of Rheims continues attack on simony, clerical marriage and lay investiture. Confirmation of *Carta caritatis* by the Pope.

1120

Foundation of Premonstratensians and military knights (see p. 57).

1121

The condemnation of Abelard at Soissons.

1122

The Concordat of Worms which produced the compromise.

1123

The First Lateran Council (The ninth Ecumenical Council of the West; see p. 304).

1130

Election of corrupt Anacletus II as Pope provoked schism. His rival, Innocent II (1130–43) supported by most princes and by Bernard of Clairvaux. Major supporter of Anacletus II was Roger II of Sicily.

1139

Schism ended by the Second Lateran Council (tenth General Council of the West). For details, see p. 304.

1140

Condemnation of Abelard at Sens. Publication of the *Decretum* of Gratian, the basis for the study of canon law.

1142

The death of Abelard.

1143

Advent of the Commune of Rome. Subsequently defied the weak papacies of Celestine II, Lucius II and Eugene III. The campaign of Arnold of Brescia (see p. 233) against clerical wealth and call for return to apostolic simplicity.

1147–49

The Second Crusade (see p. 67).

1151

Death of Abbot Suger of St Denis.

1153

Death of Bernard of Clairvaux.

1154–59

Papacy of Hadrian IV (Nicholas Breakspear), the only Englishman ever elected Pope.

1156

Foundation of the Carmelites (see p. 58). Death of Peter the Venerable.

1159–81

Papacy of Alexander III (defied by the Imperial-sponsored antipopes Victor IV, Paschal III and Calixtus III). The Synod of Pavia, called by Frederick and ignored by Alexander III, recognized Victor.

c. **1159**

The four-volume *Sentences* of Peter Lombard, Bishop of Paris, became major medieval theological textbook. Peter Lombard dies *c.* 1161–64.

1167–68

Frederick's fourth expedition to Rome. Flight of Alexander III to the Normans. Rome captured by Emperor Frederick.

1170

The murder of Thomas à Becket (see p. 58). Birth of St Dominic, 1170–1221.

***c.* 1170s**

Preaching of the life of simplicity and poverty by Peter Waldo. The birth of the Waldenses.

1179

The Third Lateran Council (eleventh General Council of the West; see p. 305 for details).

1181–88

Papacy intermittently forced out of Rome by anarchy in the city.

1189

Launch of the Third Crusade (see p. 68).

1198

Election of Pope Innocent III (see p. 54).

THE MEDIEVAL PAPACY, 1198–1305

1198

Election of Lothar dei Conti as Pope Innocent III following the death of Celestine III (Jan.). In 1189 he had been created Cardinal Deacon of SS. Sergio and Bacco by his uncle, Pope Clement III. His election was swiftly followed by a dispute for the Crown of Germany. (Archbishop of Cologne crowns Otto in Cologne, Philip crowned in Mainz.) Sale of relics prohibited by new Pope.

1199

Accession of King John in England.

1200

The 'Proposita' of the Humiliati. Pope and cardinals meet in secret consistory to seek end to Imperial schism (Dec.).

1201

Innocent III comes down in favour of Otto (March). Philip Augustus of France takes back Ingeborg of Denmark as his lawful wife (May). In August Philip's children by Agnes of Meran legitimized. Papal bull concerning the Humiliati (June).

1202

Beginning of the Fourth Crusade (see p. 69). In the wake of the crusade, Innocent III organized new Latin Church of Constantinople after fall of Constantinople in 1204.

1205

Archbishop Adolf of Cologne threatened with excommunication and deposition (he had changed sides in the imperial dispute).

1208

Papal legate in Toulouse (Pierre de Castenau) murdered (Jan.). Followed by launch of the Albigensian Crusade against heretics (see p. 72). Papal Interdict issued on England (March).

1209

Excommunication of King John of England (Jan.). Papal claims to Sicily recognized by Otto in Declaration of Speyer (March).

1210

Verbal approval by Innocent for Francis of Assisi's Rule for the Friars Minor. Otto excommunicated by Pope after invading Sicily.

1212

The semi-legendary Children's Crusade.

1213

Calling of a General Council of the Church for November 1215 (April). England now held as a papal fief by King John (May). The Golden Bull of Eger (July).

1215

The Fourth Lateran Council began, the climax of Innocent's pontificate (see p. 305). A hugely important event in church history. Beginning of reign of Frederick II as Holy Roman Emperor and a dangerous foe of the medieval papacy.

1216

Death of Innocent III at Perugia (16 July). Election of Honorius III as Pope (until 1227).

1221

Death of Spaniard Dominic.

1226

Death of Francis of Assisi. Beginning of reign of (St) Louis IX of France.

1227

Election of Gregory IX as Pope.

1228

Canonization of Francis of Assisi.

1232

Systemization of the Inquisition (partly a result of the Albigensian heresy).

1234

Canonization of Dominic.

1243–54

Papacy of Innocent IV whose pontificate saw final downfall of the Hohenstaufen.

1255

Position of friars at Paris University confirmed in papal bull *Quasi lignum vitae* of Alexander IV.

1257–72

Period of St Bonaventure as minister-general of Franciscans.

1260s

Bonaventure produces the Franciscan Narbonne Constitutions.

1271

Election of Gregory X (a Visconti).

1274

Deaths of St Thomas Aquinas and St Bonaventure. Second Council of Lyons (fourteenth Ecumenical Council) proclaimed reunion with Greek Church and changed arrangements for papal conclaves (see p. 305).

1277

Election of Nicholas III (Orsini). Nicholas III and subsequent popes preoccupied with affairs in Italy, the anarchy in Rome and promotion of their own family interests.

1279

The Franciscan *usus pauper* approved by Pope Nicholas III in bull *Exiit qui seminat*.

1294

Eventual election (after two years of rivalry and infighting in Rome) of the unwilling hermit Celestine V as Pope. He never saw Rome, was induced by dubious means to resign, and subsequently kept prisoner by Boniface, his successor. Election of Benedict Gaetani as Boniface VIII (24 Dec.). Widely seen by historians as the last of the medieval popes, asserting universal authority in the tradition of Gregory VII and Innocent III, and also promoting the interests of his family (the Gaetani) and regaining Sicily for the papacy.

1296

Papal bull *Clericos laicos* (publication ordered in France and England, 18 Aug.) intended to force the kings of France and England to accept papal intervention. Clergy forbidden to pay taxes to lay rulers without papal agreement. Strong popular support of the rulers of France and England. Papal claims ended in humiliation (1302–3).

1297

Canonization of St Louis (Aug.). Vendetta by Boniface VIII against the Colonna family.

1298

The Decretals (Sext) of Boniface VIII (March).

1300

The 'Great Jubilee' promulgated (22 Feb.). This marked the zenith of Boniface VIII's pontificate. Relations of bishops and friars settled in bull *Super cathedram* (18 Feb.).

1302

Peace of 1302 ended War of the Sicilian Vespers. The bull *Unam sanctam* (18 Nov.), marking climax of papal claims. Papacy defeated in its conflict with the nation-states.

1303

Seizure of Boniface in papal apartment at Anagni by Nogaret and Sciarra Colonna.

1303

Death of Boniface (12 Oct.). Succeeded by Benedict XI, who sought to escape Roman anarchy in Perugia. Sudden death of Benedict XI (1303–4). Ten-month conclave of divided cardinals followed.

1305

Election of French Archbishop of Bordeaux, Bertrand de Got, as Clement V (see p. 78 for the subsequent 'Babylonian Captivity' at Avignon).

THE RELIGIOUS ORDERS

THE REVIVAL OF MONASTICISM

909/910

Foundation of Cluny by William, Duke of Aquitaine.

927–942

Odo's time as Abbot of Cluny.

943

Maieul becomes Abbot of Cluny.

994–1048

Peak period of Cluniac influence under Abbot Odilo (994–1049).

1001

Reorganization of Fécamp Abbey in Normandy.

1027

Death of Romuald of Ravenna (b. 950).

1030

Birth of St Bruno (d. 1101), founder of the Carthusian Order.

***c.* 1050**

Appearance of the Augustinian Canons (Austin Canons or Black Canons).

1059

Papal approval for the Augustinian Canons (confirmed again in 1063).

1084

Carthusian Order founded by St Bruno at La Grand Chartreuse in Dauphiny. Another aspect of the great monastic expansion.

1098

Monastery at Cîteaux (France) founded (hence the term Cistercian for this Order of White Monks). The Cistercians aimed to keep the rule of St Benedict in a simpler form. Cîteaux founded by Abbot Robert and 12 monks from Molesmes.

***c.* 1100**

Robert of Arbrissel founded Order of Fontévrault.

1113

Victorines (community of Augustinian Canons) founded by William of Champeaux (Abelard's teacher).

1120

Founding in Jerusalem of the Knights Templar and also the Knights Hospitaller (the Order of St John of Jerusalem). Premonstratensians (White Canons) founded by St Norbert of Xanten (*c.* 1080–1134) at Prémontré (near Laon) in France. Sometimes called Norbertines. First Cistercian foundation outside France (in Italy).

1122–57

Peter the Venerable the Abbot of Cluny.

1131–32

Foundation of major Cistercian houses in England (Tintern, Rievaulx, Fountains).

1131

Foundation of the Gilbertines (only medieval religious order originating in England) by Gilbert of Sempringham (the order comprised both nuns and regular canons on the same site).

1134

Death of Norbert of Xanten, founder of the Premonstratensian Order of White Canons (in 1120).

1151

333 Cistercian men's abbeys in existence.

1155–56

Foundation of Order of Our Lady of Mount Carmel (the Carmelites).

1198

Order of the Most Holy Trinity founded in France by St John of Matha.

1201

Spanish Order of the Trinity, a religious order of women, founded.

THE COMING OF THE FRIARS

1209

Francis of Assisi called to a life of poverty and preaching of penance.

1210

Oral permission granted by Innocent III for the Franciscan brethren (the Friars Minor or Grey Friars).

1215

Fourth Lateran Council forbade the creation of any further religious orders. However, four Mendicant Orders were subsequently approved at the Council of Lyons in 1274 (see p. 305). Emergence of the Poor Clares (St Clare had taken the veil on 18 March 1212).

1216

The Dominicans (Friars Preachers, Black Friars) founded by St Dominic (provisional approval granted by papacy in 1215; formal bull of approval by Innocent III on 22 Dec. 1216). Conceived as a band of preachers to convert the Albigensians.

1219

Franciscans appoint 'ministers' for various regions; certain regulations imposed by papacy.

1220 (and 1221)

First two general chapters of the Dominicans held at Bologna. In 1221, Blessed Jordan of Saxony became Master General (1221–37). Emergence of the Carmelite Friars. Francis of Assisi composed 'Second Rule' for his Order (but never applied).

1223

Papal confirmation by Honorius III of the Franciscans (29 Nov.) and adoption of the 'Third Rule'.

1226

The 'Testament' of St Francis, reaffirmed his commitment to poverty, etc. Death of St Francis.

1247

'Second Rule' formulated for the Poor Clares.

c. **1250**

Number of Cistercian abbeys reached 647.

1238–63

Rapid spread of Dominicans under their Masters General (St Raymond of Peñafort (1238–40), John of Germany (1240–52) and Humbert of Romans (1254–63).

1256

Organization by Pope Alexander IV of various houses of hermits in central and northern Italy into one rule by the 'Great Union' (the Order of Hermit Friars of St Augustine – the Augustinian Hermits). Their hermit life was transposed into work in the cities. Rapid spread into England, France, etc.

1257–74

The generalate of St Bonaventure in the Franciscan Order.

1260s

The Narbonne Constitutions for governance of Franciscans promulgated by Bonaventure.

1274

Approval at Council of Lyons of four Mendicant Orders: the Franciscan, Dominican, Carmelite and Augustinian Friars.

Fourteenth century

Growing split in Franciscan ranks between the Friars Conventual (advocating a less austere community life) and the Friars Spiritual.

1322–23

Pope John XXII settled Franciscan dispute in favour of the Conventuals. Breakaway from Franciscans of the Fraticelli.

1415

Order of Friars Conventual broke away from Franciscans (these became known as the Observants).

1435

Foundation of the Minimus by St Francis of Paola.

1475

Dominicans granted permission by papacy for the corporate ownership of property.

Note on the religious orders since 1500

1517

Observants become a separate religious order.

1525

Capuchins (Order of Friars Minor Capuchin) formed by Matteo da Bascio from Franciscans to pursue a more austere life.

1535

Capuchins receive papal confirmation and separate government under a vicar-general.

1542

Defection of the Capuchin second general (Bernardo Ochino) to Protestantism.

1530

Barnabites founded.

1535

Order of St Ursula founded in Italy, the first community of women dedicated to the education of girls.

1625

Foundation of the Congregation of the Mission in France by St Vincent de Paul.

1721

Foundation in Italy of Congregation of the Passion by St John of the Cross. Strong missionary emphasis.

1732

Order of the Congregation of the Most Holy Redeemer (Redemptionists) founded in Italy by St Alphonsus Liguori.

1814

Foundation of Congregation of the Most Precious Blood in Italy.

1837

Establishment of Congregation of the Holy Cross in France, dedicated to missionary work and education.

1858

Society of Missionary Priests of St Paul formed by American Isaac Hecker. A men's religious order.

Note: For further details of mission orders, see pp. 293–94.

THE BYZANTINE CHURCH, 1054–1453

1054

Simmering dispute with papacy results in schism. Partly precipitated by Norman conquests of parts of southern Italy. The Patriarch of Constantinople, Michael Kerularios, disputes Pope Leo IX's claim to jurisdiction in southern Italy. Friction exacerbated by conduct of the papal legates. Assumes the dimensions of a schism (even if not recognized as such at the time).

1071

Following the Byzantine loss of Otranto, Bari, the last Byzantine outpost in southern Italy, falls to the Normans. End of Byzantine rule anywhere in Italy.

Seljuks victorious at Battle of Manzikert. Decisive Byzantine defeat. Subsequent plight of Eastern Christendom was a factor in the launch of the Crusades (see p. 65).

1084–87

The heretic Bogomils (p. 235) revolt in Thrace and Bulgaria. Byzantines temporarily defeated at Battle of Drystra (1087).

1096–97

The First Crusade. Byzantines recover much of Anatolia.

1098–1108

Antioch, captured by crusaders, given to Bohemund. War of Bohemund and Emperor Alexius over refusal of Bohemund to recognize suzerainty. Bohemund eventually gave in (1108).

1100

Trial and imprisonment of Bogomils in Constantinople. Bogomil beliefs take hold in twelfth century in Serbia and Bosnia.

1117

Reprieve for Byzantines after victory over Seljuks at Philomelion (1116) results in recovery of coastal Anatolia at Peace of Akroinon.

1143–80

Reign of Manuel I Comnenus, the pinnacle of Comneni dynasty, but who neglected the East and was preoccupied with the Normans (e.g. war with Roger of Sicily), and with war against Hungary and Venice.

1147–49

Clash with crusaders of the Second Crusade narrowly averted at Constantinople. Greeks signally failed to aid the crusaders in Anatolia.

1174

Birth of Sava, who was to organize the Serbian Orthodox Church during his lifetime.

1183–85

Amid the endless court changes, Andronicus I Comnenus becomes ruler and ends Latin influence of the earlier regency of Maria of Antioch for Alexius II Comnenus.

1185–95

Rule of Isaac Angelus marks signs of disintegration of the Empire.

1185–88

Major insurrection in Bulgaria against the Greeks.

1187

Alliance of Isaac Angelus (fearful of another crusade) with Saladin. Fall of Jerusalem to Muslims.

1189

The Third Crusade (see p. 68).

1193

Death of Saladin relieves pressure from the East on Byzantium.

1198

Proclamation of the Fourth Crusade by newly elected Pope Innocent III (Aug.).

1202

Venetians led by Doge Enrico Dandalo begin crusade (Sept.). Zara taken by Crusaders (24 Nov.). Zara looted by crusaders and given to Venice.

1203

Durazzo taken by crusaders. Beginning of siege of Constantinople (July) by French and Venetians after sailing via Corfu, Euboea and Chalcedon. Major assault on city fails (17 July) but results in flight of Alexius III Angelus. Alexius IV Angelus and the blinded

Isaac II crowned as co-emperors (1 Aug.), wholly under crusader control (effectively puppets).

1204

Alexius V Ducas deposes Isaac II and Alexius IV is strangled (Feb.) following a revolt. Crusaders agree plan to attack the city and divide the spoils. Storming of the city (12 April). Alexius V escapes, but the city is sacked amid terrible carnage and wholesale looting. Ending of the Fourth Crusade. Baldwin of Flanders elected Latin Emperor by the crusaders (May) and Byzantine empire partitioned (Oct.). Boniface of Montserrat becomes King of Thessalonika. The Venetian Pier Morosini made Patriarch of Constantinople. Catholic primate Basil crowns Ioannitsa King of Bulgaria.

1205

Conquest of Morea completed. Lordship of Athens created and the Principality of Achaea. Emperor Baldwin captured and killed by Ioannitsa. Baldwin's brother Henry is regent. Crusaders fail to establish themselves in most of Anatolia (present-day Turkey). Major territorial gains by Venice include parts of Constantinople itself, Crete, Gallipoli, Euboea, Durazzo and numerous Ionian and Aegean islands. Michael Angelus Comnenus (Greek) becomes despot of Epirus. Empire of Trebizond founded on north coast of Anatolia. Henry I, brother of Baldwin, becomes Latin Emperor (until his death in 1216). The ablest of the Latin Emperors.

1208

Theodore I Lascaris crowned Greek Emperor at Nicaea.

1216

Death of Latin Emperor Henry. Succeeded by Peter of Courtenay (until 1219).

1219

St Sava consecrated as autocephalous Archbishop of Serbia. Rule of Latin Emperor Robert of Courtenay, whose power was effectively reduced to Constantinople.

1222–54

Expansion of power and prosperity of Nicaean Empire under John III.

1228

Accession of Baldwin II (the 11-year-old son of Peter of Courtenay) as Latin Emperor, with regency of John of Brienne.

1230

Battle of Klokotnitsa. Defeat and capture of Theodore of Epirus by Bulgarian John Asen, who seizes much territory.

1261

Constantinople reconquered by Greek army under Alexius Stragopoulos. Flight of Baldwin II. End of the Latin Empire.

1274

'Union of Lyons'. Acceptance by Byzantine Emperor Michael VIII of the *filioque* clause, the use of unleavened bread and the supreme authority of the Pope at the Council of Lyons.

1278

The Arsenite council held (Thessaly or Epirus).

1281

Pope Martin IV ended the Union of Lyons.

1282

Revocation by Andronicus II of the 1274 union of Eastern and Western churches.

1296

Birth of Gregory Palamas (d. 1359). One of the foremost Orthodox theologians with great influence on the councils of 1341, 1347 and 1351.

1321

Threat to Byzantium grows as Ottomans reach Sea of Marmara.

1326

Byzantine Bursa taken by Ottomans.

1329

Nicaea captured by Ottomans.

1331–55

Serbian medieval empire at its height under Stephen Dusan (1331–55).

1337

Nicomedia also captured by Ottomans.

1340

Start of oppression of the Cathars in Bosnia (see p. 72 for the Albigensian crusade against the Cathars in France).

1345

Entry of Ottoman Turks into Europe, initially as mercenaries in the pay of Byzantium.

1346

Head of Serbian Church assumed title of Patriarch with his seat at Peć.

1350

Salonika captured by Ottomans.

1352

Serb forces defeated by Ottomans at Battle of Maritza River.

1354

Adrianople falls to Ottomans.

1360

Crusade against Cathars in Bosnia.

1362

Thrace added to Ottoman conquests.

1363

Byzantine Emperor recognizes Ottoman Sultan's rule of conquered territories in Europe.

1371

Important Ottoman victory at Second Battle of Maritza River. Nis captured and Bulgaria attacked. Ottomans reach the Adriatic.

1375

Serbian Patriarchate recognized by Constantinople.

1378–85

Important Ottoman advances in Anatolia.

1389

Historic defeat of Serb Prince Lazar and his allies at battle of Kosovo (15 June) by Ottomans under Murad I. Overthrow of Serb Empire.

1393

Bulgaria overrun by Ottomans.

1396

First siege of Constantinople by Ottomans abandoned in order to defeat crusaders of Nicopolis.

1402

Second Ottoman siege of Constantinople. Mongol invasion of Asia Minor forces its abandonment.

1444

Hungarian-led anti-Ottoman crusade defeated at battle of Varna. Last real crusading attempt to halt Ottomans.

1448

Ottoman rule in the Balkans consolidated at Second Battle of Kosovo.

1453

Fall of Constantinople to Ottoman forces (see p. 140).

1459

Conquest of Serbia completed by Ottomans.

THE CRUSADES

THE BACKGROUND

1054

Growing schism between Rome and Byzantium precipitated by Cardinal Humbert (the Pope's legate) and Patriarch Michael Cerularius (July).

1071

Norman conquests reach Bari (April). Battle of Manzikert (26 Aug.): major defeat of Byzantine army.

1085

Toledo conquered by Alfonso VI of Castile and Leon (May).

1088

Odo of Lagery elected Pope Urban II (March).

1089

Acre, Tyre and other ports in Holy Land captured by Fatimids.

1091

Conquest of Sicily completed by Normans.

1095

Opening of Council of Piacenza (March).

THE FIRST CRUSADE

1095

Urban II calls for crusade at Council of Clermont (27 Nov.). Severe persecution begins of European Jews in Germany, etc. (Dec.).

1096

'People's Crusade' of Peter the Hermit, Walter Sans-Avoir etc. arrives at Constantinople (July–Aug.). Annihilation of 'People's Crusade' at Nicaea by the Turks.

1097

Battle of Dorylaeum (1 July). Siege of Antioch begun (21 Oct.).

1098

Edessa taken by Baldwin of Boulogne (March). Crusaders take Antioch (3 June). Bohemond of Taranto becomes Prince of Antioch. Battle of Antioch (28 June). Crusaders victorious over Kerbogha of Mosul. Jerusalem taken for the Fatimids from the Artukids (Aug.).

1099

Capture of Jerusalem by the crusaders (15 July). Godfrey of Bouillon elected Advocate of the Holy Sepulchre and first Latin ruler of Jerusalem (22 July). The Fatimid army defeated near Ascalon by the crusaders (12 Aug.).

1100

Death of Godfrey of Bouillon (18 July). Bohemond captured by Turcomans (Aug.).

Coronation of Baldwin I as King at Bethlehem (25 Dec.).

1101

Tancred becomes regent of Antioch for Bohemond. Arrival of final wave of crusader armies at Constantinople (March). Subsequent series of defeats for crusaders near Mersivan and near Heraclea (Aug.) and again near Heraclea (Sept.).

1103

Bohemond resumes rule of Antioch after he is freed (May).

1104

Further crusader setbacks when Baldwin of Edessa and Joscelin of Courtenay captured at Harran (May). Cilicia regained by Byzantine forces. Bohemond leaves for Europe, Tancred left as regent.

1105–7

'Crusade' of Bohemond of Taranto against Byzantines with papal blessing.

1108

Surrender of Bohemond to the Greeks (Sept.). Baldwin recovers Edessa from Tancred (Sept.).

1109

Tripoli falls to crusaders under Bertram, son of Raymond of St Gilles (12 July).

1112

Roger of Salerno succeeds Tancred.

1113

Hospital of St John at Jerusalem receives first papal privilege.

1118

Death of Baldwin I (April). Succeeded by Baldwin II.

1119

Roger of Antioch defeated and killed (June). Baldwin II regent of Antioch for Bohemond II. Joscelin of Courtenay installed as Count of Edessa.

1119/20

Formation of the Templars (see p. 57).

1122

Joscelin captured (Sept.).

1123

Baldwin II captured (April). (Released Aug. 1124).

1124

Capture of Tyre by crusaders aided by Venetian fleet (July).

1127

Zengi appointed Governor of Mosul.

1129

Templars recognized by Council of Troyes. Damascus attacked by crusaders (Nov.).

1130

Bohemond II of Antioch killed in Cilicia.

1131

Death of Baldwin II (Aug.). Succeeded by son-in-law Fulk of Anjou (Sept.). Joscelin II succeeds his father as Count of Edessa.

1137

Invasion of Cilicia and siege of Antioch by Emperor John Comnenus. Enters Antioch, then withdraws (April–May 1138).

1142

Construction of Crusader fortress of Krak (Kerak). Reappearance of John Comnenus before Antioch.

1143

Succession of Manuel Comnenus as Emperor. Death of Fulk. Joint crowning of Melisend and son Baldwin III (25 Dec.).

1144

Edessa falls to Muslims under Zengi (Dec.) for first time.

1145

Proclamation of Second Crusade by Pope Eugenius III (see below).

THE SECOND CRUSADE
1145

Bull *Quantum praedecessores* issued by Pope Eugenius III proclaiming new crusade.

1146

Preaching of a Second Crusade by St Bernard of Clairvaux at Vézelay (31 March). Renewed anti-Semitism in the Rhineland. Edessa finally captured and sacked by Nūr-ad-Din (Nov.).

1147

Conrad III and the German crusaders arrive at Constantinople (Sept.). Followed by Louis VII and French crusaders (Oct.). Defeat of Conrad III near Dorylaeum (Oct.).

1148

French crusaders under Louis VII defeated near Cadmus (Jan.). Crusaders withdraw from siege of Damascus (July).

1149

New Church of the Holy Sepulchre consecrated (July). Gaza granted to the Templars. Defeat of Army of Antioch near Inab. Death of Raymond.

1150

Capture of Joscelin II (May). (He dies in captivity in 1159.)

1151

Last remaining part of Edessa captured from Byzantines.

1153

Surrender of Ascalon to Baldwin III.

1157–84

Repeated calls by papacy for crusade in the East meet with only limited response.

1158

Baldwin III marries Theodora, niece of Emperor Manuel.

1163–69

Expeditions to Egypt made by King Amalric of Jerusalem.

1164

Capture of Bohemond III and Raymond III by Nūr-ad-Din.

1169

Succession of Saladin following death of Shirkuh. Saladin soon in control of Egypt.

1171

Proclamation of Abbasid Caliphate in Egypt by Saladin (Sept.).

1174

Death of Nūr-ad-Din (May).

Damascus occupied by Saladin (Oct.). Unsuccessful attempt on life of Saladin by Assassins.

1175

Saladin formally invested with government of Egypt and Syria by Caliph (May).

1176

Second unsuccessful attempt on life of Saladin (May).

1177

Defeat of Saladin's forces at Mont Gisard by Baldwin IV.

1179

Fortress at Jacob's Ford destroyed by Saladin (Aug.).

1180

Saladin and Baldwin IV conclude truce (May). Broken by Reginald of Kerak (1181).

1183

Submission of Aleppo to Saladin (June).

1186

Submission of Mosul to Saladin (March).

1187

Military defeats for crusaders in the Holy Land. Battle of Hattin (4 July). Capture of Guy, execution of Reginald. Fall of Jerusalem to Saladin (20 Oct.) followed by wave of conquests by Saladin. Third Crusade proclaimed by Pope Gregory VIII (29 Oct.). Failed siege of Tyre by Saladin (Nov.–Dec.).

THE THIRD CRUSADE
1187

Following Battle of Hattin (4 July), when crusaders badly defeated, Jerusalem falls to the Muslims under Saladin (Oct.). Third Crusade proclaimed by Pope Gregory VIII in his bull *Audita tremendi* (29 Oct.). Saladin continues to take more Christian territory, but unsuccessfully besieges Tyre (Nov.–Dec.).

1188

'Saladin Tithe' imposed on England (Jan.). Emperor Frederick I Barbarossa takes the cross at Mainz (March).

1189

Both Henry II of England and Philip II of France take the cross. Death of Henry II (6 July), succeeded by Richard I. German crusaders under Frederick I travel overland from Regensburg (Ratisbon). Siege of Acre by Guy of Lusignan assisted by fleet from Pisa.

1190

Dardanelles crossed by the German crusaders (March). Iconium taken by crusaders

68

(18 May). Emperor Frederick I drowns in Cilicia (10 June). Richard I and Philip II set out on crusade from Vézelay (4 July). Crusaders under Henry of Champagne arrive at Acre (July).

1191

Richard I takes Cyprus from Isaac Comnenus (May). Surrender of Acre after assault by combined crusader armies (12 July). Richard left in sole command when Philip II sails from Acre. Saladin's forces defeated at battle of Arsuf by Richard I (7 Sept.).

1192

Death of Conrad of Montferrat at Tyre at hands of Assassins. Following marriage to Isabel, Henry of Champagne rules Kingdom of Jerusalem (May). Cyprus bought from Templars by Guy of Lusignan. Treaty of Jaffa concluded (2 Sept.). Third Crusade ended when Richard I set sail from Acre (9 Oct.).

1193

Death of Saladin (4 March).

THE FOURTH CRUSADE
1198

Newly elected Pope Innocent III proclaims Fourth Crusade.

Note: For the diversion of the Crusade to Constantinople, and the subsequent sack of the city and the creation of the short-lived Latin Empire, see p. 62.

THE FIFTH CRUSADE AND AFTER
1216

Honorius III becomes Pope (July) on death of Innocent III.

1217

Beginning of Fifth Crusade with Hungarian crusaders under Andrew II.

1218

Andrew II leaves Acre for Hungary with nothing accomplished. Main body of Fifth Crusade arrives off Damietta to attack Egypt. Siege of Damietta (May 1218–Nov. 1219). Damietta abandoned to crusaders.

1221

Battle of al-Mansura inflicts defeat on crusaders in Egypt (Aug.). Damietta evacuated (Sept.).

1225

Frederick II marries Isabel of Brienne and claims the throne of Jerusalem.

1227

Gregory IX succeeds Honorius III as Pope (March). Excommunication of Frederick II (Sept.).

1228–29

The last act of the Fifth Crusade marked by departure of Emperor Frederick II on crusade (June).

1229

Restoration of Jerusalem to Frederick II by treaty (Feb.) with al-Kāmil. Frederick II sails from Acre to save Apulia.

1231

Crusade of John of Brienne to give aid to Constantinople.

1236

New crusade proclaimed to support Constantinople (and again in 1239–40).

1239

Crusaders under Theobald IV of Champagne defeated near Gaza (Nov.). Jerusalem surrenders to Ayyubids. Fortifications dismantled.

1244

Fall of Jerusalem to the Khorezmians. Sacking of city.

1248

Beginning of first crusade of Louis IX of France (St Louis).

1249

Damietta captured by crusaders (June).

1250

Defeat of crusaders in Egypt at al-Mansura (Feb.).

1250–54

Louis IX in the Holy Land. Sails for France (1254) after strengthening position in Palestine.

1256–58

War of St Sabas in Acre.

1259

Battle of Pelagonia in which Greeks defeat Latins of Achaea.

1261

Constantinople reoccupied by the Greeks (July). End of the Latin empire.

1268

Mamluks under Kalavun capture Antioch (May). Sacking of the city.

1270

Landing of Louis IX and French crusaders in Tunisia (July). Death of Louis IX (Aug.).

1270–2

Crusade of Edward I of England to Tunisia and Palestine.

1271

Fall of crusader castle-stronghold, Krak des Chevaliers, to Mamluks under Baybars after siege of one month.

1274

'Union' of Latin and Greek churches at Lyons (repudiated in the East).

1277

Claim to throne of Jerusalem purchased by Charles of Anjou.

1286

Henry II of Cyprus crowned King of Jerusalem.

1291

Fall of Kingdom of Jerusalem after Acre falls to Mamluks (18 May). Surrender of remaining Frankish towns to Mamluks.

1307–14

Suppression of the Templars (see p. 266).

1309

Surrender of Rhodes to Knights Hospitaller. Subsequent establishment of their order there.

Note: Although numerous minor crusades continued to be launched, none achieved lasting success. For the struggle in Europe and the Mediterranean with the Ottoman Empire, see pp. 140–43.

MEDIEVAL HERESY: THE ALBIGENSIAN CRUSADE*

The Cathar 'heresy' had a long history in southern France before the launch of the Crusade itself in 1208 following the murder of Peter of Castelnau, the papal legate. For a note on the Cathars, see p. 236.

Tenth century

The Bugomil heresy, with its dualist emphasis and other similarities to the Cathars, active in the Balkans (whence it had spread from deported Paulician heretics in Armenia and Asia Minor).

1002

Orleans and Toulouse witness first executions of Cathars in France.

1025

Heretics from Italy brought before Synod of Arras.

1049

Council of Rheims discusses appearance of Cathar heresy in France.

1077

A Cathar burnt at the stake in Cambrai.

1126

Peter de Bruys burnt at the stake at Saint-Gilles (in Languedoc).

c. **1160**

Birth of the Waldensian movement in Lyons.

1163

Denunciation of Cathar heresy at Council of Tours.

1167

Cathar organization and beliefs developed at Albigensian Council at Saint-Felix-de-Caraman.

1177

Rapid development of Cathars reported by Raymond V, Count of Toulouse.

1179

Attack on Albigensian heretics launched at the Third Lateran Council.

1180

Papal Legate Henry, Cardinal Bishop of Albano, preaches crusade against Albigensians in French Midi.

1184

Excommunication of Waldensians by Pope Lucius III.

1198

Innocent III elected Pope (see p. 54).

1203

Appointment of Peter of Castelnau as papal legate.

1204

The theological debate between Catholics and Cathars at Carcassonne (instigated by Peter II of Aragon).

1209

Beginning of series of massacres of Cathars (e.g. at Béziers).

1210

Second excommunication of Count of Toulouse (Sept.). Foundation of Franciscans.

1211

Massacres of Cathars after fall of Lavaur (400), Cassès (94) and other places.

1212

Pamiers Assembly summoned by Simon de Montfort to settle legal and political status of the defeated Cathars. Further series of massacres.

1213

Battle of Muret (Sept.). Simon de Montfort inflicts defeat on Cathars.

1214

Battle of Bouvines.

1215

Opening of the Lateran Council. Sanctioning of the Dominican Order by Pope Innocent III.

1216

Siege of Beaucaire and first defeat of crusaders (May–Aug.). Death of Innocent III (July). Entry of Simon de Montfort into Toulouse. Dominicans confirmed by bull of Honorius III.

1218

Death of Simon de Montfort.

1221

Death of St Dominic.

1222

Death of Raymond VI.

1223

Formal ratification of the Franciscans as a corporation (also known as Minorites, Grey Friars, and Cordeliers). Death of Philip II; Louis VIII crowned at Rheims (Aug.).

1225

Pieusse Assembly of Cathars.

1226

Excommunication of Raymond VII by Council of Bourges.

1227

Election of Gregory IX as Pope.

1229

Independence of the Princes of the South effectively ended. Scourging of Raymond VII in Notre Dame in Paris.

1231

Montségur now the key stronghold of the Cathars.

1233

Inquisition given definitive powers by Gregory IX and Dominicans authorized to play a key role in it. Ratification by the Pope of foundation of Toulouse University to be a strong Catholic force.

1234

'Statutes against Heretics' published by Raymond VII.

1235

Expulsion of Dominicans from Toulouse ordered by the Count.

1239

Burning of 183 Cathars at Montwimer in Marne.

1242

Rebellion of Raymond VII.

1243

Decision to destroy Montségur taken at Council of Béziers. Siege of Montségur opened (13 May). Absolution granted to Raymond VII by Innocent IV (Dec.).

1244

Capitulation and subsequent massacre at Montségur.

1255

Quéribus, one of last Cathar refuges, falls to crusaders.

1271

Languedoc passes under French Crown.

*Principal sources: Z. Oldenbourg, *Massacre at Montségur* (1961); R. Weis, *The Yellow Cross* (2000).

THE TEUTONIC KNIGHTS: THE NORTHERN CRUSADES AND THE BALTIC

1198

Brethren of the hospital at Acre raised to a military order (the Order of the Knights of the Hospital of St Mary of the Teutons in Jerusalem). Commonly known as the Teutonic Order, with membership open only to Germans. Following the failure of the crusades, they turned their efforts to other areas. Livonian crusade authorized by Innocent III. Killing of Bishop Berthold.

1201

Foundation of Riga as major missionary centre and crusader base. Bishop Albert founds see of Riga. Establishment of the Livonian Brothers of the Sword. Cistercians lead conversion of Livonia to Christianity.

1210

Beginning of period of Herman von Salza (a friend of Emperor Frederick II) as first great Grand Master of the order.

1215

Consecration by Innocent III of a Christian bishop of the Prussians.

1217

Crusade against Prussians authorized by Honorius III.

1219

Northern Estonia the target of Danish crusade. Reval founded by Valdemar II.

1226–29

Golden Bull of Rimini of Frederick II organizes the Knights to be the main pioneer missionaries of the eastern frontier. The knights are assigned Prussia and are introduced into Poland by Conrad of Mazovia.

1230

Knights granted Kulmerland by Conrad of Mazovia.

1234

The Teutonic Knights, having transferred their holdings to the Pope, receive them back as fiefs of the Church.

1236

Destruction of the Swordbrethren by Lithuanians at Siaulas.

1237

In Livonia, the Swordbrethren absorbed by the Teutonic Order. Notable successes soon follow.

1239

Finland the target of Swedish crusade.

1240

Effective completion of conquest of western Prussia (begun 1229) by the Knights. First crusade against the Russians unsuccessful. Defeat of Swedes on the Neva.

1241

First Mongol invasion of Poland.

1242

Battle of Lake Peipus (April) follows first revolt in Prussia against Teutonic Order.

1251

Mindaugas accepts Christianity and is crowned King of Lithuania. Foundation of Memel to secure conquests in that area.

1260–83

Revolt and final subjugation of the southern Letts, Prussians and Curonians after disastrous defeat of Knights at Durben (1260).

1304

Teutonic Knights joined by crusaders from Rhineland against Lithuania.

1308–9

Gdansk and Eastern Pomerania captured by Teutonic Knights.

1309

Headquarters of the Teutonic Order moved to Marienberg from Venice. The Teutonic Order now at its height. Knights advance into Poland and also Lithuania, the last major heathen region in Europe.

1318

Finland raided and Abö cathedral burnt by Novgorodians.

1323

Peace of Vilnius between the Teutonic Order and Gediminas of Lithuania.

1324

Teutonic Knights faced by alliance of Poland and Lithuania against them.

1326

Start of first Polish War. After initial setbacks, this Polish reaction to Teutonic advances was overcome (truce concluded in 1333).

1329

King John of Bohemia's crusade.

1331

Battle of Plowce. Teutonic Knights defeated by Wladyslaw the Short.

1343

Under the Peace of Kalisch, Poles forced to recognize claim of Teutonic Order to Pomerania.

1343–45

Major uprising in Estonia. Estonian revolt suppressed and Estonia bought from Valdemar IV of Denmark in 1346 by the Order.

1348–50

Crusades of King Magnus of Sweden and invasion of Russia.

1362

Capture of Kaunas by the Knights and crusaders.

1364

Continuation of war on Lithuania urged by Pope Urban V.

1382

Vilnius taken by Teutonic Knights.

1385

Union of Poland and Lithuania, creating barrier to further eastern advance by the Order.

1386

Lithuanian Grand Duke Jagiello (Jogailo) baptized. Subsequently marries Jadwiga, Queen of Poland. Beginning of the Jagiellonian dynasty.

1387

Diocese of Vilnius established. Final conversion of Lithuanians to Catholicism.

1410

Teutonic Knights defeated in Battle of Tannenberg by Poles and Lithuanians.

1411

First Peace of Thorn. Teutonic Knights cede Samogitia but Poles effectively fail to exploit their famous victory at Tannenberg.

Postscript

1454

Major rebellion against oppressive Teutonic Order in the revolt of Prussia (with support from Casimir of Poland).

1466

Under Second Peace of Thorn, Poland acquired West Prussia. Teutonic Order retains East Prussia, with its capital at Königsberg, but East Prussia now cut off from rest of Germany. Knights surrender their headquarters at Marienburg and the Grand Master of the Teutonic Order is forced to swear fealty to Poland. Henceforth the Teutonic Knights are in decline.

1525

End of their territorial power as the order is secularized.

THE MEDIEVAL PAPACY, 1309–1449

THE BABYLONIAN CAPTIVITY:
THE PAPACY AT AVIGNON: 1309–76

1305

Election of the Frenchman Clement V as Pope. Reluctantly under French royal domination.

1307

Destruction of the Templars (see p. 266).

1309

Clement V finally moves from France to Avignon (an enclave in the Venaissin, so part of papal territory).

1310–13

Expedition of Emperor Henry VII to Italy (Pope Clement V and French King Philip IV unite to oppose him).

1311

The Council of Vienne (the fifteenth ecumenical council of the West).

1312

The bull *Exivi de Paradiso* of Clement V.

1316

Election of John XXII as Pope. Lengthy struggle with Empire over validity of Emperor Lewis IV's title (from 1323–47). Continued anarchy in Italy.

1322–23

Bulls *Ad conditorem canonum* and *Cum inter nonnullos* (declaring as heresy those who claimed the non-ownership of property by Christ).

1324

Lewis IV deprived of the Empire by John XXII.

1328

Flight of William of Ockham from Avignon to join the Emperor.

1334

Death of John XXII. Election of Benedict XII. Beginnings of the Observant Franciscans.

1335–39

Benedict XII promulgates bulls on monastic reform.

1342

Death of Benedict XII. Election of Clement VI.

1347

Popular revolution of Cola di Rienzi in Rome.

1349

Deaths of William of Ockham and Archbishop Brandwardine.

1352

Death of Clement VI. Election of Pope Innocent VI.

1353–63

Cardinal Albornoz restores the papal states in Italy.

1357

New government (the Egidian Constitution) for the papal states.

1361

Death of John Tauler.

1362

Election of Pope Urban V on death of Innocent VI. Temporary return to a poverty-stricken Rome facilitated by Emperor Charles IV. Cardinals urge Urban V to return to Avignon.

1370

Death of Urban V. Election of Gregory XI.

1377

Return of Gregory XI from Avignon to Rome (Jan.).

1378

The Great Schism in the Catholic Church (see below). An Italian pope (Urban VI) elected by a conclave under intimidation from the Roman crowd.

THE GREAT SCHISM 1378–1449

1378

Death of Gregory XI (March). Succeeded by Urban VI (Bartolomeo Prignano, Archbishop of Bari) (April). Election of rival Pope Clement VII (Cardinal Robert of Geneva) by the cardinals at Anagni. Beginning of the Great Schism.

1379

Henry of Langenstein advances arguments supporting the Conciliar Movement.

1382

Condemnation of Wycliffe's teaching by English church synod (May) (see p. 95).

1389

Death of Urban VI, followed by election of Boniface IX (Piero Tomacelli) (Oct.).

1393

University of Paris attempts to revive discussion on ending the schism. Statute of Praemunire in England (see p. 260).

1394

Death of Clement VII. Succeeded by Benedict XIII (Pedro da Luna) (Sept.).

1395–96

Continued attempts by French bishops to seek diplomatic means of ending the schism. A national synod urges resignation of both popes. Benedict XIII requested to end schism by the Way of Cession.

1398

Withdrawal of obedience from Benedict XIII by the French (July). French clergy (endorsed by the King) voted to withhold papal taxes and dues. Reaction sets in against King.

1402

Hus given charge of Bethlehem Chapel, Prague (see p. 96).

1403

Restoration of obedience to Benedict by the French (May).

1404

Death of Boniface IX (Oct.). Succeeded by Innocent VII, the Neapolitan Cosimo dei Migliorati. The Urbanist Innocent VII forced to flee Rome. Rome occupied by Ladislas of Naples.

1405

Benedict XIII at Genoa.

1406

French King proclaims second withdrawal of obedience from Benedict XIII (Sept.) (following earlier calls from University of Paris). Death of Innocent VII (Nov.) followed by election of Urbanist Venetian Gregory XII. Gregory XII offers to resign if Benedict XIII does likewise.

1407–8

Fruitless period of frustrating negotiations between Benedict XIII and Gregory XII. (Gregory XII refused to meet Benedict XIII when Benedict was in Porto Venere on the Italian riviera).

1409

Benedict XIII held the Council of Perpignan. Opening of the Council of Pisa (March) called to resolve schism. Deposition of both Gregory XII and Benedict XIII by Council of Pisa (June), which elects a third Pope, the elderly Cardinal Peter Philargi,

as Alexander V. Dissolution of Council of Pisa with continuing three-fold division of Western Christianity and pledge that church reform will be dealt with at a later council.

1410

Death of Alexander V. Election of John XXIII as Pisan Pope, continuing a three-fold division. John XXIII expelled from Rome. Forced by Emperor Sigismund to call a General Council (the 1414 Council of Constance).

1413

Renewed condemnation of Wycliffe (Feb.).

1414

Council of Constance opened by John XXIII (Nov.). Arrest of Hus (28 Nov.). For a summary of the Council of Constance, see p. 305.

1415

John XXIII persuaded to abdicate (March). The decree *Haec sancta* enacted (April). John XXIII deposed (May). Communion in both kinds forbidden (June). Hus burnt as a heretic (6 July). Abdication of Gregory XII announced (July). English victory over French at Agincourt (Oct.). Spanish withdrawal of obedience from Benedict XIII.

1416

Burning of Jerome of Prague (associate of Hus) (May).

1417

Deadlock intensifies at Constance. Benedict XIII deposed (26 July). Death in October of Gregory XII. Cardinal Otto (Oddo) Colunna elected as Martin V (Nov.). Election of Martin V ends the schism.

1418

National concordats agreed between Pope Martin V and the German, French and English nations (Feb.). Final sessions of the Council of Constance, which is dissolved in April. Agreement that next council to be held at Pavia (as outlined in *Frequens*).

1419

Death of John XXIII in Florence (22 Dec.).

1423

Opening of the General Council at Pavia (April). Council transferred to Siena (July).

1424

Dissolution of the General Council without any real achievement.

1431

Death of Martin V. Election of the obdurate Venetian Gabriel Condulmer as Eugenius IV (Feb.). Formal opening of the strongly anti-papal Council of Basel (July). Eugenius IV attempts to dissolve the Council without success (Dec.).

1432

Haec sancta reissued by the Council. Emperor Sigismund mediates between Eugenius IV and the Council.

1434

Revival of republicanism in Rome forces Eugenius IV to Florence.

1435

Annates abolished by Council of Basel (thus putting pressure on Eugenius IV to accept its claims by depriving him of revenue).

1437

Deep polarization of views at Basel over union with the Greek church (April). Transfer by Eugenius IV of Council of Basel to Ferrara for meeting with the Greeks. Conflict continues between Eugenius and remnants of Council at Basel (the Council suspending Eugenius (Jan. 1438), Eugenius dissolving the Council (Sept. 1437)).

1438

Charles VII and a French national synod accept the Pragmatic Sanction of Bourges (this endorses most of the anti-papal decrees of the Council of Basel). A key element of Gallicanism, it halted the haemorrhage of money to the papacy from France.

1439

Transfer of council of union (with the Greek delegates) to Florence from Ferrara (Jan.). Deposition of Eugenius IV by Council of Basel (June). Greek delegates at Florence forced to accept Roman terms for union (July). The union of the churches was in name only since it was repudiated by the Greeks in Constantinople and not implemented. Election of Amadeus VII, Duke of Savoy, as Pope Felix V by Council of Basel (thus renewing the schism) (Nov.). The Diet of Mainz accepts the Pragmatic Sanction of Mainz.

1441

Council of Florence transferred to Rome by Eugenius IV and eventually disperses without formal closure (1443).

1444

Defeat of crusading army at Varna, with papal legate Cardinal Cesarini killed in the battle.

1446

Concordat of Eugenius IV and Frederick III.

1447

Election of Cardinal Parentucelli as Pope Nicholas V, following death of Eugenius IV (Feb.).

Nicholas V recognized by Charles VII and the French clergy who attempt to force Felix V to abdicate.

1448

The Council forbidden to continue in Basel by Frederick III. The remnant moves to Lausanne (July).

1449

Abdication of Pope Felix V, aided by the diplomacy of Charles VII and attitude of Nicholas V. Nicholas V elected by Council of Lausanne, which subsequently dissolved itself. End of the 'conciliar epoch' with the dissolution of the Council of Basel.

1450

Jubilee celebrated papal victory over the conciliar movement.

Postscript

1458

Election of Aeneas Sylvius Piccolomini as Pope Pius II.

1460

Issue of bull *Execrabilis* (against appeals to a council).

1464

Death of Nicholas of Cusa.

1467

Institution of a separate church in Bohemia.

MEDIEVAL ANTI-SEMITISM: FROM THE CRUSADES TO THE COUNTER-REFORMATION

BACKGROUND NOTE

Persecution, discrimination and sometimes enforced baptism was an enduring theme in Christian treatment of the Jews in this period. There were examples in Western Europe of forcible conversion in Clermont (576), Arles and Marseilles (591), Spain (600) and Paris (629). Among major campaigns of forcible conversion in the Byzantine Empire were those in 640, 721, 873 and 930.

Although many fared better under Islam, there were episodes of repression (as in 888 when the Muslim Sicilian ruler Ibrahim forced Jews to wear a 'badge of shame').

Persecution tended to intensify in Western Europe in the age of crusades, although there were happier episodes, as in the invitation to England in 1066.

1010

Jews of Limoges forced to convert.

1066 onwards

Jews arrive in England after William the Conqueror's victory. Coming via Rouen, many were moneylenders to the Crown and the barons.

1096

Jews of Worms forced to convert.

1099

Massacre of Jews in Jerusalem by crusaders.

1144

First false accusations of ritual murder against Jews in Norwich.

1146

Forcible conversion of Jews in Spain (and again in 1391, 1411 and 1492). Jews of Tunis forced to convert.

1189

Beginning of systematic persecution (at a time of crusading fervour).

1190

The Jews of York killed themselves rather than surrender after violent attacks by crusaders.

1222

The Council of Oxford decrees Jews must wear the Star of David or other distinguishing badge.

1240

The Paris Disputation (the first of three great medieval disputations between Jews and Christians).

1255

Ritual murder charge against Jews in Lincoln: 18 Jews subsequently executed.

1263

The Barcelona Disputation (the second great disputation).

1266

Jewish 'ghetto' established in Breslau.

1268

Total destruction of Jewish community of Trani (near Bari) in Italy. Synagogues turned into churches.

1279

Council of Buda decrees Jews must wear the 'Star of David'.

1281

Synod of Exeter forbids Jews to hold public office.

1290

Expulsion of all 5,000 Jews from England. Property confiscated and they crossed to Flanders and France.

1307

Expulsion of the Jews from France.

1310

Conference of Italian Jews at Foligno debated how to aid the persecuted German Jews.

1312

Jewish 'ghetto' established in Palermo.

1349

Persecution of Jews widespread in Germany (following Black Death).

1391

Massacre of Jews in Sicily under House of Aragon. The 'Holy War' of Archdeacon Ferrán Martinez targets Jews of Seville. Spreads to parts of Castile and Aragon.

1412–15

Anti-Jewish laws passed in Aragon following preaching of the Dominican Vicent Ferrer.

1413–14

The Tortosa Disputation (third great medieval debate).

1434

Toleration for Jews in Florence (until 1494).

1445

Jews expelled from Lithuania (with further expulsions in 1495).

1449

Toledo Jewish community revolts.

1475

Execution of several Jews in Trent (in north Italy) after they are accused of ritual murder of a Christian boy.

1480

First Inquisitors appointed in Castile (for the growth of the Inquisition, see pp. 118–20).

1492

Jews expelled from Spain, Sicily and Malta. A landmark in history of modern Jewry.

1494

Anti-Jewish legislation in Florence inspired by Savonarola.

1497

Portuguese Jews forced to convert to Christianity following expulsion edict.

1510

Expulsion of many Jews from Naples (complete expulsion in 1541). Execution of several Jews in Brandenburg, where they had been charged with desecrating a consecrated Host.

1517

Jewish ghetto established in Venice.

1519

Jews expelled from Regensburg (Ratisbon) in Germany.

1523

Luther writes *That Jesus Christ was Born a Jew*, in which he expresses the hope that Jews will be converted to Christianity by evangelical preaching.

1526

Extension of Spanish Inquisition to Granada.

1527

Jews expelled from republican Florence.

1541

Expulsion of remaining Jews from Naples results in migrations to northern Italy, the Ottoman Empire, etc.

1543

Call on secular authorities to extirpate Judaism by force by Luther is his forthright *On the Jews and Their Lies*.

1550

Expulsion of Jews from Genoa.

1553

The *Talmud* declared to be blasphemous by Pope Julius III.

1555

Christians and Jews required to live separately by the bull *Cumnimis absurdum* of Pope Paul IV.

1575

Expulsion of Jews from the German Palatinate.

1597

Authorities in Cremona (north Italy) expel 1,000 Jews.

1614

Jewish ghetto looted during the Fettmilch riots in Frankfurt-am-Main.

Postscript

1655

Cromwell allows Jews to return to England.

1655–56

Sabbatai Zevi claims to be the Jewish messiah and achieves a large following among Jews in Central Europe.

1672

Amsterdam has a Jewish population of 7,500, drawn to the city by its relative tolerance; e.g. Jews are not obliged to reside in a ghetto.

1728

Frankfurt Jews no longer required to wear distinguishing marks on their clothing.

1745

Jews expelled from Prague.

1750

Prussian General Privilege allows Jews to have their own schools, cemeteries and synagogues but maintains restrictions upon owning property.

1762

Jews allowed to settle in Munich.

THE ENGLISH CHURCH, 1066–1485

1066

Conquest of England after Battle of Hastings by William I; the 'Norman Conquest'.

1070

Consecration of Lanfranc as Archbishop of Canterbury (Aug.).

1077

First Cluniac foundation in England.

***c*. 1082**

Chichester created a bishopric.

1088

Bath created a bishopric.

1093

Consecration of Anselm as Archbishop of Canterbury (Dec.). Rebuilding of Durham Cathedral.

1095

Death of St Wulfstan, Bishop of Worcester since 1062.

1097–1100

Anselm absent from England.

***c*. 1100**

First house of Augustinian canons in England.

1107

Ecclesiastical investiture and homage dispute ended by compromise (Aug.). Urban of Llandaff becomes first Welsh bishop to make allegiance to Canterbury.

1109

Death of Anselm. Ely created a bishopric.

1128

Building of first Cistercian house in England at Waverley.

1131

Foundation of the Gilbertine Order by Gilbert of Sempringham.

1133

Carlisle created a bishopric.

1147

St Ailred Abbot of Rievaulx (until 1167).

1154

Coronation of Henry II at Westminster (Dec.). Election of Nicholas Breakspear as Pope Adrian (Hadrian) IV (the only English Pope).

1160

Construction of new cathedral at St Andrews.

1164

Flight of Archbishop Thomas à Becket to France.

c. **1167**

Migration of English scholars at Paris to Oxford.

1170

Murder of Becket in Canterbury Cathedral (29 Dec.). Cult of martyrdom rapidly develops and Canterbury becomes major pilgrimage centre.

1174

Rebuilding of Canterbury Cathedral after fire.

1186

St Hugh of Avalon becomes Bishop of Lincoln.

1190

Violent pogrom of Jews in York. Massacre and mass suicide (March). Departure of Richard I from Vézelay on Third Crusade (July).

1191

Richard reaches Acre (8 June). Acre falls to crusaders (12 July).

1208

Proclamation of Interdict on England (24 March).

1209

Move of some Oxford scholars to Cambridge (Oxford University chartered in 1214).

1213

England a papal fief.

1214

Lifting of the Interdict (2 July).

1215

Fourth Lateran Council (see p. 305). King forced to concede to barons in Magna Carta.

1220

Beginning of construction of Salisbury Cathedral.

1221

Dominicans now active in England.

1224

England reached by the Franciscans.

1235

Robert Grosseteste becomes Bishop of Lincoln.

1250

Margaret, Queen of Scotland, canonized.

1269

Rebuilding of Westminster Abbey by Henry III.

1279

Gifts of property to religious houses regulated by First Statute of Mortmain.

1286

The writ *Circumspecte agatis* concerning the relationship between ecclesiastical and spiritual jurisdictions.

1289

Bull prohibits foreigners from being appointed heads of religious houses in Scotland.

1290

Expulsion of the Jews from England (see p. 84).

1291

The *Taxatio* of Pope Nicholas IV.

1292

Roger Bacon dies.

1296

Conflict provoked over royal taxation of the Church by papal bull *Clericos laicos* of Boniface VIII. Conflict won by the Crown.

1297

Edward I outlawed the clergy.

1301

Papal claims repudiated in Parliament of Lincoln.

1307

Grievances of the Church stated in the Parliament of Carlisle.

1312

Expulsion of the Order of the Templars from England (see p. 266).

1316

Relationship of ecclesiastical and spiritual jurisdictions defined in *Articuli cleri*.

1317

The bull *Execrabilis* of Pope John XXII.

1320

St Thomas Cantelupe canonized.

1327

Series of attacks on the great abbeys.

1343

Papal provisions curtailed by Ordinance on Provisors.

1349

Simon Islip appointed Archbishop of Canterbury (until 1366).

1351

The first Statute of Provisors.

1352

Benefit of clergy defined by statute *Pro clero*. John Thoresby appointed Archbishop of York.

1353

First Statute of Praemunire.

1357

Protest against the Friars by Archbishop Fitz-Ralph.

1363

Passing of Second Statute of Praemunire.

1366

Papal overlordship of England repudi- ated. Launching of inquiry into pluralism (see p. 259) in province of Canterbury.

1371

Growing calls for ecclesiastical disendow- ment.

1377

First clerical poll tax introduced.

1378

Wycliffe charged with heresy (see p. 95 for John Wycliffe and the Proto-Reformation).

1379

Second clerical Poll Tax.

1380

Clerical Poll Tax.

1381

Murders of Archbishop Sudbury (Chan- cellor) and Sir Robert Hales (Treasurer) during Peasants Revolt. William Courtenay appointed Archbishop of Canterbury.

1383

Flanders crusade of Bishop Despenser of Norwich.

1384

Death of Wycliffe.

1389

Second Statute of Provisors.

1391

Guilds and fraternities affected by Second Mortmain Act.

1393

Third Statute of Praemunire.

1396

Thomas Arundel becomes Archbishop of Canterbury.

1397

Political upheaval deprived Thomas Arundel of Canterbury. Restored 1399.

1401

Statute *De Haeretico Comburendo* (see p. 96). St John of Bridlington canonized.

1404

Temporary seizure of ecclesiastical temporal- ities called for by Coventry Parliament.

1405

Percy revolt and execution of Archbishop Scrope.

1409

Transfer of England's allegiance in Great Schism from Gregory XII to Alexander V (and his successor John XXII). The consti- tutions of Archbishop Arundel published to limit the spread of heresy.

1414

The Oldcastle revolt (see p. 96). Justices given powers to deal with heresy by new Act. Alien priories suppressed by legislation (effects not immediate). Opening of Council of Constance (see p. 305).

1428–31

Series of heresy trials in Norwich diocese.

1456

St Osmund of Salisbury canonized.

1457

Reginald Pecock condemned for heresy.

1482

Establishment at Greenwich of house for Observant Franciscans.

CHRISTIANITY AND WITCHCRAFT IN EUROPE*

BACKGROUND NOTE

Although the widespread persecution of witches reached its height in the early modern period, most particularly between 1580 and 1650, the widespread concern of the Church over this supposed problem dates back to the early medieval period. During the worst period of persecution, witches were prosecuted throughout Europe, but mostly in Germany, France and Switzerland. The exact numbers of those arrested and subsequently executed are not known, but recent estimates suggest that 110,000 were arrested and 60,000 were executed. Of these, probably 80 per cent were women.

1184

Pope Lucius III gives formal direction to bishops to investigate all deviations from Church's teachings.

1233

Establishment of Papal Inquisition (see p. 118).

1320–35

Church increasingly tries persons accused of heretical sorcery.

c. **1435**

Johann Nider writes *Formicarius*, a treatise on witches.

1473–83

Three bulls of Sixtus IV link heresy to sorcery.

1484

Pope Innocent VIII publishes a bull against witchcraft, *Summis desiderantes affectibus.*

1486

Publication of *Malleus Maleficarum* by Dominican Inquisitors, Heinrich Kramer (Institoris) and Jacob Sprenger. This brought together many contemporary beliefs about witchcraft and emphasized that female weaknesses and failings meant that most witches were women.

1524

Publication of *Tractatus de Haereticis et Sortilegiis* by Paulus Grillandus, which disseminated to prosecutors ideas about the witches' sabbath.

1532

Lex Carolina in the Holy Roman Empire requires witches to be punished by death for *maleficia* (black magic). White magic is also to be punished, but not as severely.

1538

Spanish Inquisition warns its officials against accepting statements on witchcraft made in the *Malleus Maleficarum.*

1541

Four witches are burnt in Wittenberg, to the approval of Luther.

1550s and 1560s

Ninety witches tried in Geneva.

1563

Johann Weyer publishes *De Praestigiis Daemonum*, claiming that witches have no powers, but are merely deranged or deluded. They should not be brought to trial or executed. He supports this idea in *De Lamiis* (1582). Witchcraft statutes are enacted in England and Scotland.

1580s

Great upsurge of witch trials in Germany, Sweden, France and England.

1580

Jean Bodin publishes *De la Démonomanie des Sorciers*.

1588

Michel de Montaigne publishes *On Lameness*, criticizing belief in diabolism.

1590–91

King James VI of Scotland (James I) takes an active role in the prosecution of witches, whom he believes are plotting his death. The North Berwick witch trial becomes the most celebrated in Scotland.

1595

Nicholas Remy publishes *Demonolatreiae*, a comprehensive account of the activities of witches and the dangers they pose to society.

1597

Publication of *Daemonologie*, written by James VI.

1602

Henri Boguet publishes *Discours des Sorciers*. The *Parlement* of Paris establishes its right to review all sentences relating to witchcraft. Many of the sentences submitted to it are overturned.

1609–14

Basque witch trials.

1612

First occasion that the evidence of a witches' sabbath is given in a witch trial in England.

1617

Diabolism made a crime in Denmark.

1623

Pope Gregory XV orders that any who confess to having made a pact with the devil be executed by the secular authorities.

1624–31

Witch-hunt in Bamberg (Germany). At least 300 people are executed, including the mayor, Johannes Junius.

1626

Sole example of the Portuguese Inquisition ordering the execution of a person for witchcraft.

1631

Friedrich von Spee (a Jesuit) publishes *Cautio criminalis seu de processibus contra sagas liber*, which criticizes the conduct of the Inquisitors and witchcraft trials.

1634

A priest, Urban Grandier, in Loudon (France) is charged with witchcraft and executed.

1641

The Paris *Parlement* orders that suspect witches should not be subject to ordeal by water.

1645–46

English witch trials are led by Matthew Hopkins. Nineteen people are executed.

1661–62

Scottish witch-hunt and trials.

1669–76

Swedish witch-hunt. About 200 people are executed as witches.

1670

Series of witch panics in Normandy.

1682

Louis XIV prohibits prosecutions for witchcraft in France.

Postscript
1692

Salem witch trials in Massachusetts.

1714

Prosecutions for witchcraft forbidden in Prussia.

1736

Prosecutions for witchcraft forbidden in England.

1755

Last execution of a witch in Germany.

1776

Witch trials forbidden in Poland.

Main source: Chris Cook and Philip Broadhead, *The Routledge Companion to Early Modern Europe, 1453–1763* (2006).

THE PROTO-REFORMATION

JOHN WYCLIFFE AND THE LOLLARDS

1324

Birth of Wycliffe at Hipswell, near Richmond (Yorkshire).

1340

Wycliffe begins studies at Oxford.

1356

Wycliffe Master of Balliol College, Oxford.

1361

Ordained priest.

1372

Increasingly radical views put forward by Wycliffe, including strong emphasis on preaching and primacy of scripture. Wycliffe also denies the doctrine of transubstantiation. Bitter attacks on the Pope's authority as Antichrist since it lacked scriptural justification. Also attacks corruption of Mendicant Friars.

1374

Parish priest of Lutterworth (Leicestershire).

1377

Accused by Bishop of London of error before Archbishop of Canterbury (rescued by intervention of John of Gaunt). Papal bulls issued against Wycliffe.

1378

Wycliffe charged with heresy at Lambeth (saved by Queen Mother) and retired from Oxford.

c. 1380

Nicholas of Hereford heads first Lollard group of Oxford scholars.

1381

Wycliffe's retreat from Oxford to Lutterworth begins prolific period of writing. The Peasants' Revolt. Some blame Lollards for its anti-clerical aspects.

1382

Council at Blackfriars condemns Wycliffe. Wycliffe, summoned to Rome, suffers stroke. Some Oxford Lollards forced to renounce their views by William Courtenay, Archbishop of Canterbury. Lollards none the less continue to flourish.

1384

Death of Wycliffe, 'the Morning Star of the Reformation', following a second stroke.

1395

The posting in London of the Lollard 'Twelve Conclusions'.

1399

Accession of King Henry IV. Wave of repression against heresy.

1401

Statute for burning of Lollards who repeat heresy (*De Haeretico Comburendo*). Burning of William Sawtrey, first Lollard martyr.

1410

Lollard Disendowment Bill.

1411

Further heresy detected in Wycliffe's writings by Oxford University.

1414

Rising of Sir John Oldcastle. Severe reprisals against Lollards drive movement underground. Oldcastle burned in 1417.

1415

Burning of Jan Hus as a heretic at the Council of Constance (see below).

1427

Remains of Wycliffe exhumed, burnt and scattered in local River Swift.

THE HUSSITE MOVEMENT

Background

973

Founding of the diocese of Prague.

1088

Founding of second Czech diocese (in Moravian town of Olomouc).

1344

Prague diocese raised to an archbishopric by Pope Clement VI (1342–52).

1348

Prague University founded by Emperor Charles IV.

1409

Jan Hus (1371–1415) elected Rector of Prague University.

1412

Hus leaves Prague (having been excommunicated and thus preventing the city coming under interdict).

1414

Appearance of Jan Hus before Council of Constance to defend his views (having been given a guarantee of safe conduct by Emperor Sigismund). Arrested on papal orders and abandoned by Sigismund.

1415

Burning of Jan Hus as a heretic at the Council of Constance (6 July). His death does not stop the movement.

1416

Burning of Jerome of Prague, one of the close associates of Hus (May) (despite having recanted in Sept. 1415).

1419

Death of King Václav IV (Aug.). Succession of his younger brother, the Holy Roman Emperor Sigismund, rejected by the Czech Estates.

1420

Promulgation by both moderate and radical Hussites of the Four Articles of Prague (July) (these were free preaching, communion in both kinds, the ending of the secular authority of the clergy and the application of civil punishment of mortal sins to priests). Continuing divisions between moderate Hussites (Utraquists–mainly aristocracy and wealthy urban dwellers) and more radical, peasant Hussites (Taborites). Outbreak of the Hussite Wars. First of five crusades against Bohemia launched and defeated (March). Hussite armies led by Jan Žižka and Prokop Holý (Prokopius the Great).

1425–26

Germany threatened after Hussites take the offensive (March).

1429–30

Punitive Hussite expeditions against Germany.

1430

Renewed divisions of moderate and radical Hussites.

1431

Flight of the crusading army (accompanied by Cardinal Cesarini) from the Bohemians at Taus.

1433

Hussite negotiators arrived at Basel (Jan.) (see p. 305). The *Compactata* agreed at Council of Basel accepts the chief demands of Czechs for communion in both kinds (Nov.). Growing divisions with radicals who refuse to compromise on the original Four Articles of Prague.

1434

Battle of Lipany (central Bohemia) (30 May). Defeat of Taborites (who had refused to accept the *Compactata*) by moderate Hussites combined with Catholics.

1436

End of the Hussite Wars. The Four Articles of Prague enshrined in the Compact of Iglau (July). This paved the way for recognition of Sigismund by the Bohemians.

THE CHURCH ON THE EVE OF THE REFORMATION

c. 1448

Johannes Gutenberg invents the process of printing using moveable type.

1454

Gutenberg prints copies of the Bible.

1469

Brethren of Common Life establish a school at Deventer, followed by several more schools, such as those at Utrecht, Groningen, Trier, and 'sHertogenbosch. Those educated by the Brethren include Erasmus and Luther.

1474

Pope Sixtus IV grants papal approval to the new order of Minims, founded by Francesco Paola. They follow strictly the rule of St Francis.

1475

Establishment of the Brotherhood of the Rosary in Cologne by the Dominican friar Jacob Sprenger. It aims to encourage the use of the rosary and rapidly spreads, attracting many members, especially women.

1476

Pope Sixtus IV rules that indulgences bought by the living can bring benefit to souls in Purgatory.

1478

So-called Cologne Bible is printed, one of the earliest illustrated printed Bibles.

1483

Appointment of Tomás de Torquemada as Inquisitor General in Spain. This is followed by an increase in the persecution of Jews and Jewish converts to Christianity (*conversos*).

1491

Girolamo Savonarola, a Dominican friar in Florence, begins preaching of the imminent purging of the Church, and the need for general repentance.

1494

Sebastian Brant publishes his *Ship of Fools* (*Narrenschiff*) in Basel. It is an indictment of the folly and worldliness of all sections of society.

1495

Cardinal Jiménez de Cisneros (Ximénez) is made Archbishop of Toledo and begins reforms within the Franciscan, Benedictine and Dominican Orders in Castile.

1497

Foundation of Oratory of Divine Love in Genoa. Composed largely of laymen, its members emphasize the importance of attendance at the sacraments, prayer and charitable work.

1498

Execution of Savonarola.

1499

Cardinal Jiménez begins forcing Muslims in Spain to convert to Christianity or face expulsion.

1502

Work begins on the Complutensian Polyglot Bible at Alcalá which, by providing parallel texts of Scripture in Hebrew, Greek and Latin, facilitates detailed biblical study. It is published in 1514.

1504

Erasmus publishes *Enchiridion Militis Christiani* (*The Manual of the Christian Soldier*).

1507

Pope Julius II grants an indulgence to raise money for the rebuilding of St Peter's Church in Rome.

1508

Erasmus publishes *In Praise of Folly*, an attack on corruption within the Church and on the role of monasticism.

1511

The Congregation of Windsheim (a group of monasteries and convents associated with the reforming aims of the *devotio moderna*) has grown to include 97 houses.

1512

Jacques Lefèvre d'Étaples publishes a commentary on the Epistles of St Paul. It was to influence subsequent evangelical thought. Fifth Lateran Council is summoned. It identifies the need for the reform of clerical education and discipline. It also criticizes the over-involvement of the papacy in temporal matters.

1515

Appointment of Guillaume Briçonnet as Bishop of Meaux. As a humanist, he encourages the introduction of reforming measures in his diocese.

1516

Ulrich von Hutten and Crotus Rubeanus publish *Epistolae obscurorum virorum* (*The Letters of Obscure Men*), a satirical attack on the opponents of humanist scholars, particularly directed against those attacking the Hebraist Johannes Reuchlin.

Death of Abbot John Trithemius of Sponheim. An innovative scholar, he had done much to encourage the reform of Benedictine monasteries in North Germany.

Erasmus publishes his edition of the New Testament in Greek (*Novum Instrumentum*).

1517

Division of the Franciscan Order into the Friars Minor and the Conventual Friars by Pope Leo X.

1518

Erasmus publishes *Julius Exclusus* (*Julius Excluded*), a satirical attack on the military exploits of Pope Julius II in Italy.

LUTHER AND THE GERMAN REFORMATION

1483

Martin Luther born in Eisleben (10 Nov.).

1501

He enrols at the University of Erfurt.

1502

He graduates with the degree of bachelor of arts.

1505

He is awarded the degree of master of arts (Jan.) and prepares to study law. In September he abandons the idea of legal study and enters the house of the reformed Augustinians in Erfurt as a novice.

1507

Luther is ordained a priest.

1510

He travels to Rome to represent the reformed Augustinians of the Saxon province in a conflict within the order.

1511

He returns to Germany and moves to the Augustinian house in Wittenberg.

1512

Luther is awarded the degree of doctor of theology.

1513

He begins his first series of lectures on the Psalms to theology students at Wittenberg.

1515

He gives a series of lectures on St Paul's Epistle to the Romans. These indicate that Luther has already begun to question the teaching of the Church on how salvation is achieved. He criticizes the belief that individuals can accumulate spiritual merit which will influence whether they are saved or damned.

1517

The Dominican Johann Tetzel begins selling indulgences in the area around Electoral Saxony.

Luther produces his *Ninety Five Theses*. These were in Latin and were intended to stimulate a debate over what he considered to be false teaching concerning salvation and bogus claims for the power of the indulgences which had been made by Tetzel. Within a month, the *Theses* have been translated into German, printed and circulated throughout Germany without Luther's consent. They stimulate widespread interest and support.

1518

Luther is summoned to Rome to defend his criticisms of the Church. Following the intervention of his ruler (Elector Frederick the Wise of Saxony), Luther is allowed to present his case to the papal legate (Cardinal Cajetan) at the meeting of the Imperial Diet in Augsburg (Oct.). At the meeting Cajetan rejects the justifications offered by Luther. He calls on Frederick the Wise to hand Luther over to the ecclesiastical authorities, but Frederick refuses.

1519

Attempt by the papal envoy Karl von Miltitz to negotiate a compromise between Luther and the papacy, but no real progress is made. In July a disputation is held at Leipzig between Luther and Johann Eck. Some views held by Luther are shown by Eck to have been previously condemned as being heretical by the Church. Luther insists that the authority of Scripture is paramount. In October, Luther begins to question the sacramental teaching of the Church in sermons on penance, baptism and the mass.

1520

Luther publishes *On the Power of Excommunication* (Jan.). In May he publishes *Treatise on Good Works*, in which he emphasizes that amends for sins can be made only by faith in God's redeeming love, and not by human acts. In June he publishes *On the Papacy at Rome*, which challenges papal authority over the Church and its doctrine. Luther is threatened with excommunication by the papal bull *Exsurge Domine* if he refuses to recant. In August Luther publishes *Address to the Christian Nobility of the German Nation*, in which he describes the failings of the Church, and urges the Emperor and the secular authorities in Germany to support the introduction of religious reform. In September he publishes *The Babylonian Captivity of the Church*,

in which he condemns the sacramental teaching of the Church for imposing a tyranny over the souls of the faithful. He also accuses the papacy of being the Antichrist. In November he publishes *The Freedom of the Christian*, in which he shows that faith and not outward acts are of benefit to the soul, but that true Christians would freely wish to perform acts of love towards their neighbours. In December Luther publicly burns the papal bull *Exsurge Domine*, signalling his break with the papacy.

1521

Luther is excommunicated by the papal bull *Decet Romanum Pontificem* (Jan.). He is summoned by Charles V to the Imperial Diet to be held at Worms (March). He is granted a promise of safe conduct. Luther appears before the Imperial Diet at Worms and refuses to recant his works (April). On his way home from the Diet, Luther is taken into protective custody by soldiers of Frederick the Wise. He is held at the fortress of the Wartburg until March 1522. Charles V declares Luther to be an outlaw by placing him under the ban of the Empire (May). In the Edict of Worms he declares his intention to root out all Lutheran teaching.

1522

While at the Wartburg, Luther translates the New Testament into German. He publishes *A Sincere Admonition by Martin Luther to All Christians to Guard Against Insurrection and Rebellion* and *Temporal Authority: To What Extent It Should Be Obeyed*, in which he expounds his view that each person is subject to two kingdoms, the kingdom of God and a secular kingdom. Secular government is to be obeyed in worldly matters, but should not attempt to constrain people in matters of religion. Rebellion is not justified by unchristian acts by rulers, but passive refusal to carry out unchristian commands is justified. In March Luther returns to Wittenberg from

101

the Wartburg. He preaches against radical religious changes which have been introduced there under the influence of Karlstadt.

1523

Luther begins work on revising the form of worship in Wittenberg. He publishes *That Jesus Christ was Born a Jew*, expressing the hope that Jews would wish to become members of a Christian church which is based on evangelical teaching.

1524

Luther publishes *To the Councillors of All Cities in Germany That They Establish and Maintain Christian Schools*, emphasizing the importance of education for boys and girls. Luther ceases to wear the habit of a friar.

1525

In April Luther publishes *An Admonition to Peace: A Reply to the Twelve Articles of the Peasants of Swabia*, in which he upbraids princes for their oppressive rule but insists that rebellion by subjects cannot be justified. In May, following the outbreak of violence and rebellion, Luther publishes *Against the Robbing and Murdering Hordes of Peasants*, in which he urges the German princes to put down the peasant rebellions by force. Luther marries Katharina von Bora, a former nun (June). In December he publishes *De servo arbitrio*, which responds to criticism, made by

Erasmus, of Luther's denigration of the role of free will.

1527

Luther publishes his views on the eucharist in *That These Words of Christ, 'This Is My Body' Still Stand Firm Against Fanatics*.

1529

Luther and Zwingli meet at the Colloquy of Marburg, but are unable to agree over eucharistic teaching (Oct.).

1534

Luther publishes his translation of the entire Bible into German.

1540

Luther supports the bigamous marriage of Philip of Hesse.

1543

He publishes *On the Jews and Their Lies*, an intemperate call for the suppression of Jewish belief and for the expulsion of Jews from Germany.

1546

Luther dies in Eisleben (18 Feb.). He is buried in Wittenberg.

ZWINGLI AND THE REFORMATION IN ZURICH

1484

Huldrych Zwingli is born in a village near Glarus in Switzerland (Jan.).

1498

He enrols at the University of Vienna.

1502

He enrols at the University of Basel.

1506

Zwingli obtains the degree of master of arts. He is made parish priest in Glarus. He continues humanist studies and is strongly influenced by the ideas of Erasmus.

1515

Zwingli accompanies Swiss mercenary troops to Italy and witnesses heavy loss of life at the battle of Marignano. As a result he becomes an opponent of mercenary service.

1516

Zwingli is made people's priest at the pilgrimage church of Einsiedeln.

1518

He is made people's priest at the Great Minster in Zurich.

1519

Zwingli begins preaching sermons critical of abuses within the Church and of the moral failings of society.

1520

Under the influence of the writings of Erasmus, and probably also of those of Luther, Zwingli begins to develop his own evangelical teaching.

1522

Zwingli is present when a group of citizens eat meat during Lent, a time when the Church demands that people abstain from eating meat (March). Zwingli publishes a defence of their defiance in *Regarding Freedom and Choice of Foods*. Zwingli secretly marries Anna Reinhart.

With some other clerics in Zurich, he petitions the diocesan bishop for the abolition of clerical celibacy (July). In September he publishes *Of the Clarity and Certainty of the Words of God*, a brief introduction to evangelical study. Zwingli resigns as people's priest and is reappointed by the city council as preacher (Oct.).

1523

First Disputation is held at the town hall in Zurich (Jan.). Zwingli prepares 67 theses for discussion of the main issues which separate evangelical teaching from that of the Roman Catholic Church. These include: the authority of the papacy; the doctrine of the mass; the existence of Purgatory. The diocesan bishop (Hugo von Hohenlandenberg, Bishop of Constance) refuses to participate, allowing Zwingli to present his views unchallenged and to consolidate his influence. In August he publishes *An Essay on the Canon of the Mass*, in which he attacks the belief that the mass was a re-enactment of the sacrifice of Christ. Second Zurich Disputation, in which Zwingli argues against the presence of religious images in churches (Oct.).

1524

The Zurich city council orders the removal of all images from churches (June). Some parents refuse to have their babies baptized (Aug.). Zwingli publishes *Who Is the Source of Sedition?*, in which he calls for reform to the system of tithing, urging that tithes be used only for their original purpose of supporting the work of the Church and the poor in the locality.

1525

Measures are established to eliminate begging in Zurich and to create a common fund for the relief of the poor. This is partly funded from the secularized revenues of the Church. Zwingli completes *On the True and the False Religion*, a statement of his views on evangelical beliefs. These include: justification by faith alone; a rejection of the mass; the need for infant baptism; the

rejection of papal authority. In April the mass is abolished in Zurich and is replaced by a service in German. In May a marriage court (*Ehegericht*) is established to regulate all matters relating to marriage. Instruction in biblical studies and languages is established for the clergy in classes known as the 'Prophecy' (*Prophezei*).

1526

Zwingli publishes *A Clear Exposition of Christ's Last Supper*, in which he rejects belief in transubstantiation and insists that the bread and wine in the eucharist are symbolic. This leads to conflict with the Lutherans, who insist that Christ is present in the elements.

1527

Zwingli publishes *Refutation of the Tricks of the Anabaptists*. He meets Luther at the Colloquy of Marburg (Oct.), but is unable to come to an agreement with him over eucharistic teaching.

1530

Zwingli compiles his *Confession of Faith*.

1531

Zurich is at war with the Catholic cantons in the Swiss Confederation. Death of Zwingli at the Battle of Kappel.

CALVIN AND GENEVA

1509

John Calvin is born at Noyon in France.

1523

He enrols in the arts faculty at the University of Paris.

1525–26

He enrols at the University of Orléans to study law.

1531

He leaves Orléans as a licentiate in law and returns to Paris to resume his studies.

c. **1532**

Calvin develops an interest in evangelical theology.

1534

During a period of persecution of French Protestants, in the wake of the Affair of the Placards, Calvin flees from France and settles initially in Basel.

1535

Calvin completes the first edition of the *Institutes of the Christian Religion.*

1536

Religious reform is introduced in Geneva (May). In August Calvin passes through Geneva and is persuaded to stay and assist in the consolidation of the Reformation there. Calvin presents his *Confession of Faith* to the Genevan city council, which appoints him as preacher (Nov.).

1537

Calvin presents his 'Articles on the Government of the Church' to the council (Jan.). This seeks to impose reform on religious and moral life, and is accepted with some alterations by the council.

1538

Opposition grows in Geneva to Calvin and his attempts to impose reform. Calvin is ordered to leave Geneva (April). He moves to Strasbourg.

1539

Publication of the second edition of the *Institutes of the Christian Religion.*

1540

Supporters of Calvin regain influence within the council and summon him back to Geneva to establish order and discipline within the Church. Some civic leaders believe that Geneva needs a strong Protestant identity in order to survive prolonged conflict with its former bishop and the neighbouring territory of Savoy.

1541

Calvin returns to Geneva. His *Ecclesiastical Ordinances for the Church of Geneva* are accepted by the city council. It is established that the church will be run by a consistory, composed of pastors and elders of the Church. The consistory has responsibility for upholding religious and moral discipline among the servants of the Church and the wider community, although the council insists that the work and the powers of the consistory should in no way impair its own authority. This becomes the model for church government in Calvinist churches throughout Europe.

1546

Pierre Ameaux, a playing-card maker whose business has suffered as a result of the reform of morality, is accused of slandering Calvin. He is forced to perform public penance, and this, along with other similar incidents, prompts riots by opponents of Calvin.

1547

Council approves Calvin's plans for visitations of rural parishes controlled by Geneva, to ensure that Catholic observance is eradicated. Opposition in Geneva to Calvin and the 'French' influence coalesces around Ami Perrin, in a faction known as the 'Libertin'. Perrin is removed from his position on the council.

1549

Increasing numbers of French Huguenots flee to Geneva from the late 1540s. This leads to anxiety among the citizens and some on the council of being overwhelmed by religious migrants.

1550

Establishment of annual household visitations by members of the consistory to examine people on matters of religion.

1551

Council receives suggestions from Calvin aimed at punishing swearing and blasphemy.

1553

Michael Servetus, a Spanish intellectual, is arrested in Geneva on account of his anti-trinitarian writings. He is sentenced by the council to be burnt at the stake, despite an attempt by Calvin to intervene and have the sentence changed to execution – the less barbaric punishment favoured by Calvin.

1555

Election of council which strongly supports Calvin's reforms.

Measures are passed allowing increased numbers of refugees to obtain citizen status. These changes prompt riots led by Perrin and the 'Libertin' faction. The riots are put down and the 'Libertin' leaders are punished by exile or execution. This marks the triumph of Calvin and his supporters over their opponents in the city.

1559

Establishment of the Genevan Academy to train pastors. Publication of the fifth edition of the *Institutes of the Christian Religion*, the definitive version of Calvin's teaching.

1564

Death of Calvin (May).

THE REFORMATION AND THE CIVIL WAR IN FRANCE

1520

Lutheran teaching is condemned as heretical by the theology faculty of the University of Paris.

1520s–30s

Occasional persecution of evangelical supporters in France by Francis I and the *Parlement* of Paris.

1534

The Affair of the Placards (Oct.). Evangelical supporters in Paris and in other towns secretly put up posters denouncing the clergy and the mass. This angers and alarms Francis I, who instigates a campaign against heresy, including the execution of heretics and measures for censorship. Many evangelicals (including Calvin) flee abroad.

1540s–50s

Secret Huguenot conventicles are established in many parts of France. In many cases they are in touch with Calvin and his supporters in Geneva. Huguenots gain significant support from among the French nobility.

1551

Edict of Châteaubriant aimed at eliminating heresy in France.

1559

Death of Henry II (July). His successor, Francis II, is a minor, and his government is dominated by the strongly Catholic Duke of Guise.

1560

Tumult of Amboise (March), an attempted coup by Huguenots led by Prince de Condé. It aimed at wresting control over government from the Guise faction, but ended in failure. Death of Francis II (Dec.), who is succeeded by his brother Charles IX. His mother (Catherine de Medici) becomes regent, and in seeking to bolster the authority of the monarchy, attempts to achieve a settlement between the Huguenots and Catholics.

1561

Colloquy of Poissy is organized by Catherine de Medici and attended by leading theologians, including Théodore de Bèze, representing the Calvinists, and James Laynez, the head of the Jesuits. Despite long discussions, a compromise proved unobtainable. The failure of the Colloquy was followed by a growth of support for Huguenots and an increase in their militancy.

1562

Outbreak of the French Wars of Religion.

This great series of conflicts convulsed France from 1562 until it was settled in

1598 by the Edict of Nantes. The conflict is usually divided into the following eight phases.

1. First civil war (April 1562–March 1563), ended by the Edict of Amboise.
2. Second civil war (Sept. 1567–March 1568), ended by the Peace of Longjumeau.
3. Third civil war (Oct. 1568–Aug. 1570), ended by the Peace of Saint-Germain.
4. Fourth civil war (Sept. 1572–July 1573), ended by the Edict of Boulogne.
5. Fifth civil war (Sept. 1574–May 1576), ended by the Edict of Beaulieu or the Peace of Monsieur.
6. Sixth civil war (April 1577–Sept. 1577), ended by the Peace of Bergerac.
7. Seventh civil war (April 1580–Nov. 1580), ended by the Peace of Fleix.
8. Wars of the League (Aug. 1585–March 1598), ended by the Edict of Nantes.

1598

Edict of Nantes (see p. 243) ended this phase of religious conflict.

1610

Henry IV assassinated by Ravaillac.

1614

Civil war headed by Prince de Condé.

1615

Civil war. Condé and the princes unite with the Huguenots.

1616

Louis XIII and Condé conclude the Peace of Loudon (May).

1618

Exile of Richelieu to Avignon (April). Publication of his *Instruction du Chrétien*. Beginning of Thirty Years War in Europe.

1621

Assembly of La Rochelle under Rohan and Soubise. Louis XIII fights the Huguenots.

1622

Royalist successes against the Huguenots are followed by the Treaty of Montpellier in October.

1625

Outbreak of the Huguenot Rebellion, provoked by the repressive measures of Cardinal Richelieu. With their strength centred on La Rochelle, the Huguenots were led by Duke Henry of Rohan and his brother Soubise. The Huguenot fleet (under Soubise) was defeated by Duke Henry of Montmorency, the High Admiral of France, and La Rochelle was progressively blockaded. English forces, under the Duke of Buckingham, twice attempted to relieve La Rochelle without success.

1628

La Rochelle finally surrendered on 29 October 1628 (with a mere 5,400 people still alive from a pre-war population of 28,000).

1629

Huguenots under Rohan in Languedoc were defeated by Montmorency.

1630

Final crushing of Huguenot revolt freed France to enter the Thirty Years War.

1648

Peace of Westphalia ended Thirty Years War.

1660s

Period of increasing legal pressure against Huguenots.

1679

Intensification of attacks on Huguenots in France.

1680

Edicts issued against Huguenots (and continuation of persecution of Jansenists).

1681

The Dragonnades (attacks on Huguenots) begin. Large numbers emigrate from the north and west. Influx of refugees to England.

1682

Louis XIV's Declaration of Four Articles is endorsed by an assembly of the French clergy.

1685

Revocation of the Edict of Nantes.

1687

Hostility with Pope Innocent XI results in the occupation of Avignon (in Oct. 1688).

1689

Revolt in the Cévennes (*Enfants de Dieu*).

1693

Reconciliation of the Gallican Church with the papacy.

1702

Rebellion of the Camisards (Protestant peasants in the Cévennes region).

1704

Revolt in the Cévennes largely put down by Villars.

1705

Jansenism condemned in the papal bull *Vineam domini*.

1710

Infamous destruction of the Jansenist convent at Port-Royal by soldiers.

1711

Camisard rising is finally quelled.

For the Church in France after 1714, see p. 144.

THE ENGLISH CHURCH, 1485–1603

1485–1547

1485

Tudors come to the throne following Battle of Bosworth.

1487

Attack on rights of sanctuary amid growing unease about legal privileges of the clergy. Benefit of clergy limited in 1489 and 1491 by statute.

1511

First teaching by Erasmus at Cambridge University.

1514

Death of Richard Hunne (a London Lollard) while in the custody of the Bishop of London arouses anti-clerical feeling.

1515

Cardinal Wolsey appointed Chancellor of England.

1521

Henry VIII publishes his *Assertio Septem Sacramentorum* (a confutation of Luther) and in October a copy is presented to Pope Leo X. The latter granted Henry the title of *Fidei Defensor* (Defender of the faith).

1525–26

William Tyndale's translation of the New Testament into English published (see p. 310).

1527

Henry VIII's disillusionment with his marriage to Catherine of Aragon and his sincere doubts about its legality (Catherine being the widow of his brother Arthur). Beginning of proceedings for annulment of the marriage.

1529

Dismissal of Wolsey as Chancellor and the meeting of the Reformation Parliament. Legislation passed limiting some rights of sanctuary, mortuaries, non-residence, pluralism, and clerical involvement in leasing. No papal dispensation against terms of the act allowed.

1530

Death of Wolsey at Leicester.

1533

Thomas Cranmer is appointed Archbishop of Canterbury. He annuls the marriage of Henry VIII and Catherine of Aragon. The Act in Restraint of Appeals forbids any appeals being heard at Rome.

1534

Act of Supremacy is passed by Parliament, establishing Henry as supreme head of the Church in England. Act in Restraint of Annates forbids the payment of annates to Rome. Act for the Submission of the Clergy.

1535

Thomas More and John Fisher executed for refusing to swear the oath to the Act of Succession. *Valor Ecclesiasticus* is compiled, providing an assessment of clerical income.

1536

Anne Boleyn is executed. The Pilgrimage of Grace, a rebellion in the north of England, is prompted by religious reform and action against the monasteries. The Ten Articles, a statement of doctrine allowing for a Protestant understanding of the sacraments, are published. Smaller monasteries are dissolved.

1539

Second Dissolution Act followed by dissolution of the larger monasteries. All religious houses dissolved. Six Articles, asserting Catholic teaching on major points of doctrine, are published. The Great Bible is published.

1541

Creation of new bishoprics (for list see p. 278).

1543

The King's Book promulgated.

1545

Dissolution of the chantries proposed in first Chantry Act.

1547

Death of Henry VIII and accession of Edward VI.

REFORM AND REACTION: RELIGIOUS CHANGE UNDER EDWARD AND MARY, 1547–58

1547

Accession of Edward VI. Edward Seymour, Earl of Hertford (and later Duke of Somerset) chosen as Protector. Protestant feelings now erupted in England and there was widespread iconoclasm, especially in London. Arrival of a number of foreign reformers, most notably Peter Martyr and Martin Bucer. Radical programme of religious reform (Oct.–Dec.). Chantries, etc. dissolved, Act of Six Articles and repeal of previous heresy acts.

1548

Cranmer issued the *Order of the Communion* in English (Jan.). Abolition of many ceremonies (including those of holy water and holy bread) and destruction of remaining images. Many stone altars were demolished (Jan.–March).

1549

Publication of the Book of Common Prayer. All Latin services abolished, but the Book was conservative in tone, providing for an English mass, vestments, prayers for the dead, private confession, extreme unction and commemorations of the saints. First Act of Uniformity passed to enforce the Prayer Book. Fall of Duke of Somerset. His replacement, John Dudley (Earl of Warwick and later Duke of Northumberland) supported radical Protestants. Clerical marriage now permitted.

1550

Support for extreme Protestants by Warwick (created Duke of Northumberland in 1551). Rise of Zwingli's follower John Hooper. Appointment of radical John Ponet as Bishop of Rochester. Many parish churches ordered to remove altars and screens. Some Anabaptists (e.g. Joan Bocher) burned in London.

1551

Ponet promoted Bishop of Winchester when Stephen Gardiner deprived of the see. Heath deprived of bishopric of Worcester.

1552

Second Act of Uniformity passed through Parliament. This repeated the terms of the 1549 Act (adding penalties for persons attending illegal services) and ordered the use of the revised Book of Common Prayer from November. The new second Prayer Book reflected the influence of English radicals (notably Hooper) and of continental reformers, especially Bucer. The mass was totally abolished, plain bread, surplices and communion tables replacing hoses, chasubles and altars. Prayers for the dead also abolished.

1553

The 42 Articles published (June). Directed against Anabaptists. Death of Edward VI (July). Unsuccessful attempt to place Lady Jane Grey on the throne. Accession of (Catholic) Mary I (Mary Tudor). Rapid exodus of leading English Protestants into exile (e.g. to Zurich, Geneva and Strasbourg). Leading Protestant bishops deprived or gaoled (Cranmer, Latimer, Hooper, Ridley). Release of Gardiner and Bonner from detention. Parliament passes Act of Repeal, revoking nearly all the legislation after 1547 and unmaking the Edwardian reformation.

1554

Marriage of Mary to Philip of Spain announced. Anti-Spanish rebellions (e.g. of Sir Thomas Wyatt in Kent suppressed by force). Injunctions issued to the bishops (March) to continue to suppress 'heresy' and restore Catholic traditions. Reginald Pole, Mary's Archbishop of Canterbury, arrives in London. Second Act of Repeal (Nov.) removes all anti-papal measures passed since 1529, so undoing the religious revolution enacted under Henry VIII.

1555

The newly revived heresy laws used to condemn the first Protestant martyr, John Rogers, who was executed (Feb.). Other martyrdoms followed, the victims including Hooper, Ridley and Latimer. Over 300 executions of Protestants followed. Many ordinary men and women suffered death for their opposition to the revived Catholic faith. In November, Bishop Gardiner died.

1556

Religious unrest continued in many areas and many more persons were burned for heresy (including Cranmer).

1558

Death of Mary (and death of Pole a day later). Accession of Elizabeth.

THE SEARCH FOR A SETTLEMENT, 1558–1603

1558

Death of Mary and accession of Elizabeth I.

1559

Act of Uniformity and Act of Supremacy restore Protestantism to England. Elizabeth becomes 'Supreme Governor' of Church of England. Publication of the revised version of Prayer Book. All Acts repealed by the Marian regime were revived and the Acts of Repeal repealed. The heresy Acts were revoked and papal supremacy abolished. The Oath of

Supremacy was to be taken by all clergy, justices, officers and royal servants. Gradual return of the Protestants who had been in exile during Mary's reign. Matthew Parker is appointed Archbishop of Canterbury.

1560

The Geneva Bible (in an English translation by William Whittingham) published in England.

1562

John Jewel's *Apology of the Church of England* published. This powerful defence of the Elizabethan Settlement of religion was aimed chiefly at Catholic critics.

1563

Publication by John Foxe of *Acts and Monuments* (*Book of Martyrs*).

1564

Many Puritan clergy were deprived for refusal to wear the surplice.

1566

Further conflict with radicals over vestments.

1568

Mary, Queen of Scots, flees to England. As a danger to the Crown (being both a Catholic and Elizabeth's heir), she was put into custody. William Allen secured the foundation of a college to train English Catholic priests at Douay (Douai) in Flanders.

1569

Rebellion of northern earls in favour of Catholicism.

1570

The Catholic threat increased with the issue by Pope Pius V of a bull, *Regnans in Excelsis*, excommunicating the Queen and calling on all Catholics to assist in her deposition.

1571

Parliament met and Puritan Members planned a strong campaign of church reform. William Strickland introduced a bill to amend the Prayer Book and abolish many usages, including the wedding-ring, surplice and kneeling at communion. The bill was quashed by the Privy Council. The Thirty Nine Articles defined Anglican beliefs.

1572

Growing Puritan anger and frustration.

1575

Death of Archbishop Parker, who was succeeded by the Archbishop of York, Edmund Grindal.

1576

In Parliament, bitter attacks on the failings of the clergy were made by a number of Members led by Peter Wentworth. The Puritans demanded more preaching in the Church.

1577

Archbishop Grindal is suspended from office for refusing to act against prophesying (a means of instructing Puritan preachers).

1579

An English College at Rome is founded under the patronage of Pope Gregory XIII and the supervision of the Jesuit Order.

1583

A French plot to invade England is uncovered. Its chief English agent was Francis Throckmorton, a Catholic squire, and Parsons and other Jesuits were deeply implicated. In August John Whitgift becomes Archbishop of Canterbury. He was a known anti-Puritan.

1586

The authorities discovered the involvement of Anthony Babington, page to Mary, Queen of Scots, and several priests in a plot to murder Elizabeth. Mary was to have been placed on the throne.

1587

Puritans Cope, Wentworth and Lewknor jailed. Henry Barrow and John Greenwood, the leaders of the London Separatists, imprisoned (Oct.). The execution of Mary Stuart in February was popular with Parliament but did not remove the very real threat of Catholic invasion of England.

1588

The Marprelate tracts attacking bishops are published. The defeat of Philip of Spain's Armada did not lessen the government's determination to crush Catholicism. Thirty-one priests were executed.

1591

In May, Cartwright and other Puritans were finally brought before Star Chamber on charges of slandering the bishops, attacking the Prayer Book, and participating in Presbyterian organizations. The charges were not finally proved, but the men spent 18 months in gaol.

1593

Legislation against 'Popish Recusants'. Puritans Henry Barrow and John Greenwood executed.

1597

Archbishop Whitgift draws up a set of constitutions dealing with abuses in the Church, which were approved by Convocation (e.g. pluralism, fees in church courts).

1598

The Pope appoints George Blackwell archpriest of England to control the Catholic clergy. Jesuits excluded from Blackwell's jurisdiction and many Catholics saw his appointment as a Jesuit attempt to dominate their Church in England.

1603

Death of Elizabeth. Accession of James I.

THE REFORMATION IN SCOTLAND, 1472–1603

1472

Creation of first Archbishopric in Scotland (at St Andrews).

1480s

Independence from English province for Scottish Franciscans and Dominicans.

1492

See of Glasgow created an Archbishopric (9 Jan.).

1494/95

Foundation of King's College, Aberdeen by Bishop Elphinstone.

1495

Papal bull of Alexander VI (10 Feb.) institutes Aberdeen University.

1525

First Act against heretical literature.

1528

Abbot of Ferne burnt for heresy.

1534

Norman Gourlay and David Straiton burnt in Edinburgh for heresy (27 Aug.).

1535

Passing of further Acts against heretical literature.

1546

George Wishart burnt for heresy (2 March). Murder of Cardinal Beaton (29 May).

1547

John Knox moved to France.

1549

First reforming council of the Church.

1552

Second reforming council.

1555

Return of John Knox to Scotland.

1556

Knox goes to Geneva (July).

1557

Knox returns to Scotland; the First Covenant of the Lords of the Congregation is signed (3 Dec.).

1558

Walter Milne, last of the Scottish Protestant martyrs, burnt (April). Protestant riot in

Edinburgh (1 Sept.). Publication of John Knox's *The First Blast of the Trumpet against the Monstrous Regiment of Women*.

1559

Reformation movement in Scotland advances. Knox in Fife (May). Riots in Perth (May–June) against Mary of Guise and Roman Catholicism.

1560

Treaty of Edinburgh (6 July) constitutes triumph for the 'Lords of the Congregation'. Scottish Parliament ('Reformation Parliament') abolishes papal jurisdiction (Aug.). Calvinism now adopted. First *Book of Discipline* (Dec.).

1568

Catholic rising in Scotland. Escape of Mary Queen of Scots from Loch Leven (2 May). Battle of Langside (13 May). Flight of Mary to Carlisle (19 May).

1571

Archbishop of St Andrews hanged (7 April) for complicity in murder of Moray.

1572

Death of John Knox at Edinburgh (24 Nov.).

1573

Edinburgh Castle surrendered by Sir William Kirkcaldy. Virtual end of Mary's party and supporters.

1574

Return from Geneva of Andrew Melville.

1578

Publication of *Second Book of Discipline*.

1581

James VI signs second 'Confession of Faith' (28 Jan.).

1587

Execution of Mary, Queen of Scots (18 Feb.).

1592

Establishment of *Second Book of Discipline*. Fraserburgh University founded (1 July).

1593

Presbyterianism strengthened by discovery of Catholic plot.

1600

'Commissioners' appointed to the ancient sees by James VI.

1603

Accession of James VI as King James I of England.

THE NORTHERN REFORMATION

1478

Foundation of Copenhagen University, which becomes a focal point for religious ideas.

1520

Revolt in Sweden led by Gustav Vasa after massacre of leaders of the Swedish party by the Danish king.

1526

Catholic clergy and evangelicals in Denmark and Sweden in dispute. Beginnings of the Reformation. Translation of New Testament into Swedish by Olaus Petri.

1527

Sweden sees introduction of Lutheranism. Crown acquires property of the Catholic Church. Bishops become entirely dependent on the Crown. Discontinuation of payment of 'Peter's pence' to the papacy. Secularization of the monasteries in Denmark.

1529

Örebro Synod in Sweden. Feast days are abolished and the Latin mass modified.

1534

Protestant Christian III becomes King of Denmark after civil war (elected against opposition of the bishops). Continued secularization of church property, followed by establishment of a Lutheran national church (on the lines drawn up by Johann Bugenhagen). Seven new bishops consecrated. Intervention of Christian III on side of Protestant princes in Germany against the Emperor.

1536

Lutheran Reformation takes hold in Denmark.

1537

The Church Ordinances complete the Lutheran Reformation in Denmark.

1539

Örebro *Riksdag* establishes royal authority over the Church in Sweden.

1541

Publication of the 'Gustavus Vasa Bible' (in Swedish).

THE INQUISITION

1233

Institution by Pope Gregory IX of the papal Inquisition 'for the apprehension and trial of heretics'. Prompted by the earlier emergence of the Cathars and Waldenses. Its use was mostly in northern Italy and southern France, only rarely in northern Europe.

1252

Use of torture to obtain confessions and to obtain names of other suspects authorized by Pope Innocent IV.

1478

Pope Sixtus IV authorized the Spanish Inquisition (following the *reconquista* (see p. 262) and the desire of the Spanish monarchy to root out apostate former Jews and Muslims). Inquisitor appointed in Castile and Aragon (Spanish Crown has power of appointment and dismissal).

1480

Inquisitors start activities in such Andalusian towns as Seville and Cōrdoba.

1481

Six *conversos* burnt at the stake in first auto-da-fé at Seville (6 Feb.).

1482

Tomas de Torquemada among additional appointments of Inquisitors. *Conversos* face long period of punishment. New offices of Inquisition established at Cōrdoba, Saragossa, Ciudad Real and Jaen, etc. Ciudad Real transferred to Toledo in 1485.

1483

Creation of the *Suprema* (the *Consejo de la Suprema y General Inquisition*) as a branch of royal council of Castile with its president the Inquisitor-General.

1484

Inquisition established at Barcelona.

1485

Inquisition established at Llerena (for Extremadura).

1487

Sicily witnesses introduction of Inquisition at Palermo.

1488

Inquisition established at Valladolid (for Leon and Old Castile) and at Murcia and Palma (for Majorca and Balearics).

1492

Fall of Granada (last Moorish stronghold in Spain).

1498

Diego de Deza, Archbishop of Seville, becomes Inquisitor-General.

1505

Inquisition established in Las Palmas (Canary Islands).

1510

Nobility in Naples reject attempt of Ferdinand of Aragon to introduce Spanish-style Inquisition.

1512

Inquisition established in Logroño (Navarre and Basque Country).

1517

Adrian Dedel (later Pope Adrian VI) becomes Inquisitor-General for Aragon (and Castile in 1518). Inquisition introduced into Sicily.

1521

Inquisitor-General issues first ban on Lutheran books in Spain (April).

1522

Inquisition introduced into the Netherlands by Emperor Charles V.

1524

Inquisition lists 48 heresies of the *alumbrados* in Spain (Sept.).

1526

Inquisition established in Granada.

1529–32

Suspected Lutherans, *alumbrados*, etc. undergo show-case trial in Castile.

1531

Portuguese Inquisition instituted by first papal bull in December.

1536

Cum ad nil magis (second papal bull regarding the Portuguese Inquisition) (May).

1542

Papal bull *Licet ab initio* establishes central Congregation of the Inquisition at Rome (4 July). Subsequently, offices of the Inquisition established elsewhere in Italy in Naples, Milan and Florence.

1545

Roman Inquisition holds 'show trial' at Lucca, following an anti-Spanish conspiracy.

1546

Strengthening and reorganization of the Inquisition in the Netherlands. Edict on sale and publication of forbidden books.

1547

Beginnings of Inquisition in Venice with establishment of three 'Deputies on Heresy'. Failure of attempt by Emperor Charles V to introduce Inquisition into Naples. Portuguese Inquisition offices established at Lisbon and Evora.

1548

Siena Index of forbidden books published.

1549

Venetian Index of forbidden books instituted.

1551

Publication of First Spanish Index of prohibited books. Extension of Venetian Inquisition to all its possessions. Florence witnesses first Italian auto-da-fé.

1555

Election of hard-line Gian Pietro Carafa as Pope Paul IV.

1557

Further tightening of the Index in the Netherlands.

1559

Publication of Second Spanish Index of prohibited books.

1561

The *Instrucciones nuevas* modify the procedures of the Inquisition.

1564

The Roman Index published. Publication of Third Spanish Index of prohibited books.

1565

Confederation of the Nobles to resist introduction of the Inquisition into Dutch lands.

1565–70

Establishment of Inquisition in Mexico (for Central America and the Philippines).

1570

Inquisition established in Lima (for Peru, Chile and Argentina).

1571

Publication of Fourth Spanish Index of prohibited books.

1572

Three Salamanca university professors arrested for suspected heresy by the Inquisition.

1574

Inquisition established at Santiago (for Galicia).

1583

Publication of Fifth Spanish Index of prohibited books.

1609

The expulsion of the *moriscos* (see p. 255).

1610

Inquisition established at Cartagena (for Colombia, Venezuela and the Spanish Caribbean).

1612

Publication of Sixth Spanish Index of prohibited books.

THE JESUITS

1539

First draft outline of the organization of the Order.

1540

The Society of Jesus confirmed on 27 September by Pope Paul III in the bull *Regimini militantis ecclesiae*. Its founder was Ignatius of Loyola (see p. 250)

1541

First edition of the *Constitutionales* (Constitutions).

1542

Missionary work in India begun by Francisco Xavier, the 'conquistador of souls'. Peter Canisius (1521–97) approached to work in southern Germany. First Jesuit College (at Padua).

1547–48

Jesuit missions to Congo and Morocco. First Jesuit school opens (at Messina in Sicily).

1549

Arrival of Jesuits in Brazil led by Manuel de Nobréga. Jesuit College of Ingolstadt founded (centre of Jesuits in Germany).

1551

Principal Jesuit College at Rome founded.

1552

Death of Francis Xavier.

1556

Death of Ignatius of Loyola (31 July). Succeeded as 2nd General by James Laynez (1512–65). By now 12 Jesuit provinces created (9 in Europe, along with Brazil, India and Ethiopia). Total Jesuit numbers pass 1,000.

1558

Final form of the *Constitutionales* approved by the General Congregation of the Order.

1563

Work of Jesuits dominates Council of Trent.

1564

First Jesuits arrive in Poland. Subsequently achieve great success.

1565

Death of James Laynez. Succeeded by Francis Borgia as 3rd General.

1566

Beginning of unsuccessful Jesuit mission to Florida.

1568

First Jesuit missions in Peru.

1580

Three Jesuits invited to the court of Emperor Akbar.

1583

Jesuits Michele Ruggieri and Matteo Ricci (1552–1610) begin mission in China.

1588

Spanish Jesuit Luis Molina publishes controversial work on divine grace and human free will.

1595

Expulsion of most Jesuits from France by order of the *Parlements*.

1599

Ratio studiorum approved, the curriculum for instruction in Jesuit schools.

1610

Foundation of first of the Guarini missions in Paraguay.

1615

Peak of Jesuit worldwide influence; death of Father General Claudio Aquaviva.

1617

Jesuit theologian Francisco Suárez dies.

1618

Total number of Jesuit provinces reaches 32.

1621

Death of Robert Bellarmine (b. 1542).

1622

Canonization of Ignatius of Loyola (12 March).

1626

Jesuit numbers total 15,544.

1646

Conflicts between Jesuits and local bishops in Latin America (e.g. with Bishop Juan de Palafox in Mexico, with Bishop Bernardino de Cárdenas in Paraguay).

1654

Death of the 'Apostle of the Black Slaves', Pedro Claver.

1656–57

Bitter attack on Jesuits by Blaise Pascal (1623–62) in his *Lettres provinciales*.

1666

Jesuit influence in Spain as Austrian Jesuit Eberhard Nithard the *de facto* ruler.

1697

Death of António Vieira, Portuguese Jesuit missionary.

1711

Death of Eusebio Kino, Jesuit missionary among Pima Indians of Sonora and Arizona.

1743

Acclaim for Jesuit regime in the Guarani missions by Spanish king.

1749

Total Jesuit numbers estimated at 22,589.

1754

Outbreak of Guarani rebellion (subdued by Spanish and Portuguese troops by 1756).

1755

Fall of Jesuit Francisco de Rávago as confessor to the Spanish king.

1757

Attack on Jesuit influence at Portuguese Court by Pombal. Expulsion of first Jesuit missionaries from Amazonas.

1759

Expulsion or imprisonment of all Jesuits in Portugal and Portuguese territories following assassination attempt on Portuguese king.

1761

Jesuit missionary Malagrida burned at the stake in Lisbon.

1764

France suppresses Jesuit Order.

Last papal bull to praise work of the Jesuits.

1766

Expulsion of the Jesuits from Spain following 'Hat and Cloak' riots. Expulsion of Jesuits from throughout the Spanish Empire.

1768

Jesuits depart from Paraguay missions.

1773

Dissolution of Jesuits by papal bull *Dominus ac Redemptor* of Clement XIV (only re-established in 1814).

THE EXPANSION OF
CHRISTIANITY OVERSEAS

THE SPANISH IN THE AMERICAS

1493

Under papal bull *Inter Caetera Eximiae Devotionis* (recognizing Spanish claims to the newly-discovered regions) the Spanish Crown has the obligation to promote and spread Christianity in the new territories. In 1494, first mass celebrated in the New World.

1500

Arrival of first Franciscan mission in the Caribbean.

1504

The first three bishops in the Americas (Manso, Deza and Garcia Padilla).

1508

Spanish Crown given rights to found dioceses and nominate to all benefices in New World by bull *Universalis Ecclesiae*.

1509–10

Despatch of first Dominican mission to the Caribbean.

1511

Establishment of dioceses at Puerto Rico and Santo Domingo (preaching of Antonio de Montesino in Santo Domingo).

1513

First diocese established in Central America (Panama).

1514

Conversion of Bartolomé de Las Casas in Cuba. He protests at the *encomiendas*.

1518

Creation of bishopric in Cuba (Santiago de Cuba).

1519

First Bishop of Mexico (Julián Garcés). Series of missions begun to New Spain and Peru.

1522

Bartolomé de Las Casas (1474–1566) becomes a Dominican. Subsequently famous for his defence of the rights of the native Indians against cruelty and abuses.

1524

The Franciscan 'Twelve Apostles' arrive in Mexico.

1526

First Dominicans arrive in Mexico.

1530

Dioceses of Mexico City and Guatemala established.

1531

First diocese in South America (Coro) established.

1538

Appointment of Vicente de Valverde as Bishop of Cuzco (Peru).

1539

Concentration of missionary work by Dominicans in Peru; creation there of a Dominican province. Founding of University of Santo Domingo. Bishop Zumárraga establishes first printing press in colonial America (in Mexico).

1542

Proto-martyr of the USA, Fray Juan de Padilla, killed by Indians on the plains of Kansas.

1546

Bishoprics of Popayán and Quito created in South America.

1547

Creation of three archdioceses in the Americas: Santo Domingo, Mexico City and Lima.

1551

First Bishop of Bahia (Brazil) appointed. Organization of the Church consolidated (e.g. First Provincial Council of Lima under Loaisa).

1553

Opening of universities in Mexico and San Marcos University in Lima.

1555

First Provincial Council of Lima under St Toribio de Mogrovejo and First Provincial Council of Mexico under Montufar.

1561

Diocese of Yucatan established.

1564

Diocese of Santa Fé de Bogota established.

1565

Parish founded at St Augustine, Florida (the first Catholic parish in what was to become the USA).

1568

First Jesuit missions in Peru.

1577

José de Acosta writes his *De procuranda indorum salute*.

1582

Third Council of Lima under St Toribio de Mogrovejo.

1585

Third Council of Mexico under Moya and Contreras.

1609

Archbishopric of La Plata created. Founding of Santa Fé, later the headquarters of the New Mexico missions.

1617

Buenos Aires created a diocese. Carranza becomes first bishop (1620).

1622

Congregation de Propaganda Fide established (Catholics in America remain under this jurisdiction until 1908).

1638

Missionary activity of the Jesuits in Amazon area.

1680

New Mexico missions destroyed by Indian rebellion.

1687

Missions in Arizona begun.

1692

New Mexico reconquered and friars return. Ten Reductions set up among Chiquitos Indians in Bolivia.

1697

First permanent mission established in Baja, California.

1738

University of Santiago founded.

1759

Expulsion of the Jesuits from Brazil.

1763

Jesuits banished from Louisiana and Illinois country.

1767–68

Expulsion of the Jesuits from Spanish America.

1769

Founding of the first of the California missions at St Diego.

THE PORTUGUESE EMPIRE

1452

Papal bull, *Dum Diversas*, grants to the Crown of Portugal the lands, property and persons of all the unbelievers whom they encountered on their voyages.

1455

Portuguese are confirmed in their African possessions by the papal bull *Romanus Pontifex* of Nicholas V.

1456

Papal bull *Inter Caetera* grants Portugal spiritual jurisdiction over all lands and peoples 'discovered' by Portuguese explorers.

1494

Treaty of Tordesillas.

1500

Papal bull *Cum sicut maiestas* (March) gives authority over the region from Cape of Good Hope to the Indies (i.e. the Indian Ocean) to authority of an apostolic legate.

1511

Goa (capital of the Portuguese Asian Empire) becomes centre for later religious activity.

1542

Francis Xavier, the 'conquistador of souls', begins missionary work in India. He had been nominated in 1541 as legate for the Indies by Pope Paul III.

1543

Thousands converted by Xavier in southern India.

1545

Xavier undertakes missionary work in Malaya and the Spice Islands.

1549–51

Xavier in Japan.

1552

Death of Xavier on island of Shangwan while awaiting permission to enter China.

1557

Cochin (India) and Malacca (Malaya) established as bishoprics.

1563

(Japan) Baptism of first local ruler, important initial success.

1575–78

(Philippines) Arrival of Augustinian missions (1575), followed by Franciscans (1577) and Dominicans (1578).

1576

(China) Macao created a bishopric.

1580

(India) Three Jesuits invited to the court of Emperor Akbar.

(Japan) Christian numbers estimated at 150,000.

1583

(China) Jesuits Michele Ruggieri and Matteo Ricci begin mission in China.

1587

(Japan) Hideyoshi issues order for expulsion of Christian missionaries from Japan (but order not implemented).

1588

(Japan) Bishopric created at Funai.

1597

(Japan) Persecution and mass martyrdom of Christians and missionaries. Crucifixion of 26 missionaries after being taken to the Nagasaki Hills (5 Feb.).

1600

(India) Bishopric created at Angamale (from 1609 at Cranganur).

(Japan) Christian numbers in Japan estimated at 210,000.

1603

(Japan) Local Japanese rulers begin to reject Christianity.

1606

(India) Diocese of Mailapur created.

1613–14

(Japan) Banishment of Europeans and Imperial decrees against Christians.

1615

(China) Christian converts estimated at around 5,000.

1622

(India) Canonization of Francis Xavier.

THE ENGLISH CHURCH, 1603–88*

1603

Death of Elizabeth and accession of James I. The Millenary Petition, which seeks greater concessions for Puritans, is presented to James. The Bye and Main Plots. Three priests and a number of Catholic gentry were involved in a scheme to seize the King and force him to grant toleration to Roman Catholics.

1604

Hampton Court Conference is held. James refuses to accept a Presbyterian system of church government. New Prayer Book proclaimed (5 March) which embodied minor changes proposed at the Hampton Court Conference. Whitgift succeeded as Archbishop of Canterbury by Bancroft.

1605

The Gunpowder Plot, an attempt by Catholics to murder James and blow up Parliament, is discovered.

1606

Guy Fawkes and the Jesuit superior, Henry Garnet, executed. Under the Penal Laws Catholics were required to take the Oath of Allegiance renouncing the doctrine that the Pope could depose kings.

1607

Archpriest Blackwell deposed for his approval of the Oath of Allegiance. He was succeeded by Birkhead.

1610

Bill to abolish pluralities. Commons Petition on Religion (July). The Petition took up the demands of the Millenary Petition and denied the King's right to alter laws concerning religion without Parliament's consent.

1611

The Authorized Version of the Bible published. George Abbott becomes Archbishop of Canterbury.

1612

Thomas Helwys's General Baptist congregation comes to England from the Netherlands.

1618

The Book of Sports is issued by the King in response to growing Sabbatarianism. It listed games and pastimes permitted on Sundays.

1623

William Bishop appointed Bishop of Chalcedon by the Pope, with jurisdiction over the secular clergy in England and Wales but without the powers of an ordinary (i.e. of a bishop with a diocese).

1625

Death of James I and succession of Charles I. Montague published *Appello Caesarium*, which was a more definite statement of the Arminian position.

1626

Declaration against Controversy (16 June). (An attempt to end the Arminianist debate.)

1627

The Sibthorpe sermon emphasizing royal supremacy and law-making (and the requirement of all subjects to obey these laws – as in the case of forced loans).

1628

William Laud made Bishop of London. The Commons Remonstrance (11 June) called for the strict enforcement of the Penal Laws and the suppression of Arminian doctrines.

1629

King Charles dissolves Parliament–ruling without it until 1640–after it renewed its criticisms over taxation, religion, etc.

1633

Archbishop Abbot died, having been suspended in 1621 and 1627–28 and succeeded by Laud. The Book of Sports of 1618 reissued.

1637

Prynne, Burton and Bastwick have their ears clipped and are sentenced to perpetual imprisonment and heavy fines, and Prynne to branding as well, by the Star Chamber. All three had written attacking the church hierarchy and Laud's ecclesiastical policy. Charles I orders the universal adoption in Scotland of a Prayer Book based on the English Book of Common Prayer. Revolt ensued in Scotland.

1638

Formation of National Covenant in Scotland.

1639

The First Bishops' War, which was concluded in June by the Treaty of Berwick.

1640

The Second Bishops' War, concluded in October by the Treaty of Ripon. The Canons of 1640 published (June), in effect a codification of Laud's innovations. Controversy erupts again. The Root and Branch Petition (11 Dec.) supposedly subscribed by 15,000 Londoners petitioning for the complete abolition of episcopacy. Parliament declares that the 1640 Canons bound neither clergy nor laity because they had not been confirmed by Parliament (15 Dec.). The Canons declared illegal (16 Dec.). Archbishop Laud is impeached in the Commons and imprisoned in the Tower (18 Dec.).

1641

Crisis intensifies between King and his opponents. News arrives (1 Nov.) of the outbreak of rebellion in Ireland. The Grand Remonstrance (1 Dec.) demands the removal of bishops' temporal powers and of the oppressions that they were responsible for introducing.

1642

The Clerical Disabilities Act (13 Feb.) deprives bishops of their temporal jurisdiction and their seats in the House of Lords. The Nineteen Propositions (1 June) offered as the terms of a dictated peace by Parliament. They included the proposal that the King should accept the reformation of the Church by a synod. Charles refused to accept. Beginning of Civil War in England between King and Parliament.

1643

Westminster Assembly of Divines. Solemn League and Covenant with the Scots, to harmonize religious observance in Britain. In accordance with this all members of Parliament and the army and other office holders had to take the Solemn League and Covenant (Sept.).

1644

Ordinance enjoining taking the Covenant by everyone else passed (5 Feb.). The Uxbridge Peace Propositions (24 Nov.) proposes posts of all bishops and cathedral clergy to be abolished and religion reformed according to the advice of the Assembly of Divines, based on the Covenant.

1645

Ordinance (4 Jan.) for abolishing the Book of Common Prayer. Replaced with Directory of Public Worship, prescribing no set forms of service, only instructions on how 'meetings' should be conducted. Archbishop Laud executed (10 Jan.). Ordinance (26 April) for none to preach but ordained ministers. The Newcastle Propositions for peace (13 July).

1646

Ordinance (9 Oct.) for abolishing bishops and archbishops. Their lands and possessions are settled on trustees for the use of the Commonwealth, and all courts which had operated under their jurisdiction are abolished.

1647

The Heads of Proposals (see p. 246).

1648

Ordinances (29 Jan.) for settling counties into classical Presbyterian and Congregational elderships and (29 Oct.) for the form of church government to be used in England and Ireland.

1648–49

The Whitehall Debates (Dec.–Jan.) on the Agreement of the People, especially on its religious terms.

1649

Repeal (9 Feb.) of the Oaths of Obedience, Allegiance and Supremacy. The Trustees for the Maintenance of Preaching Ministers are appointed (5 April). Act for Abolishing Deans, Deans and Chapters, etc. of cathedrals, administration of their possessions and abolition of archdiaconal courts.

1650

The Blasphemy Act is passed against the Ranters (9 Aug.), because of the political threat implied by their extreme Antinomianism. Repeal (27 Sept.) of the laws imposing penalties for not attending church.

1653

The Prerogative Court of Canterbury abolished, thus removing the final remnants of the old ecclesiastical jurisdiction. The Instrument of Government (16 Dec.) proposes some sort of state church and toleration (but not for Roman Catholics).

1654

The Commissioners for the Approbation of Public Preachers, or 'Triers', appointed (20 March). Commissioners for ejecting scandalous, ignorant and insufficient ministers, or 'ejectors', appointed (22 Aug.).

1655

The Jews readmitted to England.

1657

The Humble Petition and Advice (25 May), (see p. 248).

1660

The Declaration of Breda (4 April). Charles II offered to give his assent to any legislation that offered a measure of religious toleration. Restoration of the monarchy and the Church of England. Parliament passes the Clarendon Code, enshrining Anglicanism as the state religion.

1661

Savoy Conference (April) between bishops and Presbyterians. The Corporation Act (Nov.) requires all local officials to take Anglican communion, thereby excluding all Nonconformists (Dissenters). Venner's rising (an attempt to establish the Fifth Monarchy of King Jesus) discredits Nonconformists.

1662

Revised Prayer Book is published. The Act of Uniformity requires all ministers to conform to Prayer Book services. Those ministers refusing forced to resign. The Quaker Act imposes punishments on Quakers who attend meetings of more than five people.

1664

The Conventicle Act forbids meetings of five or more people not members of the same household. In effect the Act acknowledged the existence of a separate Protestant community. It expired in 1668.

1665

The Five Mile Act. Ministers ejected by the Act of Uniformity and other unlicensed preachers were forbidden to come within five miles of the parish where they had been incumbent, or of any city or town.

1670

The Treaty of Dover (May) with Louis XIV. In its secret clause Charles II agreed to declare war on Holland and grant toleration to Roman Catholics.

1672

The Declaration of Indulgence (March). Charles declares the suspension of the Penal Laws against Nonconformists and recusants. It was a great source of relief for Protestant Nonconformists, despite actually being intended for Roman Catholics.

1673

Test Act excludes Catholics from public office.

1678

Publication of John Bunyan's *Pilgrim's Progress*. The 'Popish Plot' (see p. 259) and the Exclusion Crisis (1678–81).

1679

The First Exclusion Bill (May). Catholics attempt to discredit Presbyterians with the spurious Meal Tub Plot (Oct.).

1680

The Second Exclusion Bill (it had been intended to free dissenters from the Elizabethan statutes intended against Catholics, but which actually operated against dissenters as well).

1681

The Third Exclusion Bill.

1682

William Penn gets charter for Pennsylvania. Subsequent emigration of over 2,000 Welsh Quakers to Pennsylvania.

1683

The Rye House Plot (April). Followed by renewed persecution of Protestant Nonconformists. The intention of the plot was to assassinate Charles II and put Monmouth on the throne to save the Protestant cause.

1685

Death of Charles II. He is succeeded by his brother James, a Roman Catholic. Monmouth's rebellion (June). The Revocation of the Edict on Nantes means the end of toleration for Protestants in France.

1686

Catholics are admitted to the commissions of the peace and other positions in the county administration after being dispensed from the terms of the Test Act by James II. The Court of Ecclesiastical Commission is established illegally (Aug.) by James II.

1687

Roman Catholics admitted to government offices by dispensation from the Test Act by James. In the spring James tries to force the Fellows of Magdalen College, Oxford, to elect a Roman Catholic president, in contravention of their statutes. Major confrontation ensues. The First Declaration of Indulgence (4 April) suspends the operation of the Penal Laws and of the church courts on both Roman Catholics and dissenters. Announcement of the Queen's pregnancy.

1688

The 'Glorious Revolution' and flight of James II.

For subsequent events see pp. 149–53.

Principal source: C. Cook and J. Wroughton, *English Historical Facts, 1603–88* (1980).

RELIGION IN THE AMERICAN COLONIES AND CANADA* 1603–1776

1603

First religious activity of Europeans by French Catholics in Arcadie (Nova Scotia) and Quebec (1608).

1607

Settlement of Jamestown, Virginia with a Church of England chaplain. The first permanent English settlement in North America.

1619

Anglican Church in Virginia established by law.

1620

Pilgrim Fathers sail for America.

1629

Charter granted for Massachusetts Bay Company.

1630

Launch of Congregationalism in Massachusetts Bay Colony by John Winthrop.

1631

Massachusetts Bay restricts franchise to church members.

1633

Charles I of England decrees that worship in Newfoundland be Anglican.

1634

Puritan movement to Connecticut begins.

1636

Rhode Island founded by Roger Williams (after his banishment by General Court of Massachusetts). Church and State separate in Rhode Island.

1637

Banishment of Roger Williams by Massachusetts Bay.

1643

Catholics disfranchised and priests outlawed in Virginia.

1647

Anti-priest law enacted in Massachusetts Bay Colony.

1649

Degree of toleration introduced with the 'Act Concerning Religion in Maryland'.

1654

Repeal of the tolerant Maryland Act followed by Puritan suppression of the Catholics.

1659–61

Hanging of four Quakers on Boston Common.

1662

Massachusetts Bay adopts the Half-Way Covenant. Franchise still restricted to those formally baptized (even if not full members of established Congregational churches).

1663

Experiment of complete religious toleration in Rhode Island and Providence plantations. John Eliot publishes first complete Bible to be printed in North America.

1665

Dutch allowed toleration in New Amsterdam (New York) by Duke's Laws.

1669

Draft of Fundamental Constitutions of Carolina. Multiple establishment proposed.

1670

William Penn's *Great Case of Liberty of Conscience* published (in England).

1683

Religious toleration for all Christians enacted by New York Assembly and Governor Thomas Dongan. Mennonites began to arrive in Pennsylvania.

1684

Massachusetts becomes a royal colony (having lost its charter).

1689

The Act of Toleration passed in England.

1691

Under new Charter, liberty of conscience granted to all Christians in Massachusetts Bay except Catholics.

1692

Maryland establishes Church of England by law.

1699

Birth of Brattle Street Church in Boston.

1702

Magnalia Christi Americana published by Cotton Mather (1728).

1708

Non-Congregational Protestant worship allowed in Connecticut (but taxes still required to support Congregationalists).

1718

Catholics in Maryland disfranchised.

1719

Arrival of first German Dunkers, founded by radical Pietist Alexander Mack (1679–1735).

1734

First beginnings of the 'Great Awakening'. Introduction of the principle of voluntaryism (e.g. with Jonathan Edwards in Massachusetts).

1739

Methodist Whitefield on first American tour reinforces 'Great Awakening'. 'Great Awakening' at its peak, 1740–42.

1749

City of Halifax established, includes Protestant settlers from England and also Hanover.

1760–71

First arrival of Baptists (1760), Quakers (1762) and Moravians (1771) in Canada.

1767

Public arguments over introduction of Church of England bishops into America.

1774

Hostility to Catholicism revived by passage of Quebec Act by English Parliament (which allowed much greater level of toleration to Roman Catholics).

1775

First arrival of Methodists in Canada.

1787

Consecration of first Anglican bishop for Nova Scotia (Canada) by Archbishop Moore of Canterbury.

1791

Canada divided into two by Constitutional Act. This aided spread of Anglicanism.

Source: Everett Emerson, *Puritanism in America, 1620–1750* (1977).

CHRISTIANITY IN THE RUSSIAN LANDS

ORIGINS AND EARLY HISTORY, 954–1448

c. 954/955

Baptism of Olga, Regent of Kiev, in Constantinople.

c. 987–988

Baptism of Grand Prince Vladimir of Kiev (d. 1015) forces Christianity on Russia.

1037

Construction of Cathedral of Holy Wisdom in Kiev.

c. 1040–50

Active Christian communities in Novgorod and Pskov, but threatened by Latin Christian crusades from the West.

c. 1050

Pecherska Lava (Monastery of the Caves) founded in Kiev.

1062–74

St Theodosius abbot of the Monastery of the Caves.

1072

Death of Anthony of Kiev.

1074

Death of Theodosius.

Thirteenth–fifteenth century

Russia under Mongol rule.

1240

Destruction of Christian Kiev by the Mongol invasion. Growing importance henceforth of Moscow. Swedish invaders defeated by Russian Prince Aleksandr Nevsky (d. 1263).

1242

Teutonic Knights' encroachment repulsed and Orthodoxy prevails in Moscow.

1270

Russian Church obtains immunity from taxation.

1308–26

St Peter of Kiev served as Metropolitan.

1326

Cathedral of the Assumption built in the Kremlin.

1328

Moscow now seat of the Metropolitan in place of Kiev.

1350

Monastery of the Holy Trinity founded by St Sergius of Radonezh (now Zagorsk). Most famous religious centre in Russia.

1354–78

Period of St Alexis as Metropolitan of Moscow.

1380

Russian forces victorious at Kulikovo over Tatars and Mongols following the exhortations of St Sergius of Radonezh. Beginning of consolidation of the state of Muscovy.

1392

Death of St Sergius of Radonezh, patron saint and nation builder of Russia.

1448

Russian bishops elect their own Patriarch without recourse to Constantinople. Russian Church now autocephalous.

THE RUSSIAN ORTHODOX CHURCH AFTER 1453

1453

Fall of Constantinople (the 'second Rome') to Ottoman forces (see p. 140).

1462–1505

Russia ruled by Ivan the Great (Ivan III).

1470

Spread of Judaizer heresy throughout Novgorod.

1472

Marriage of Ivan III to Sophia Palaeologue (niece of the last Byzantine Emperor). Strengthens Russian claim to be heir to the Byzantine Orthodox tradition.

1475

Construction of new Cathedral of the Assumption (Uspensky Sobor) begins in the Kremlin, Moscow. Completed 1479.

1477

Novgorod is annexed by Moscow after a renewed attack.

1480

Ivan III overthrows the Mongol Tatar rule.

1488

Russian Church again installed its own Metropolitan, showing independence from Constantinople.

1503

Condemnation of Judaizer heresy by the Church Council. Conflict in the Church between pro- and anti-property factions.

1521

Deposition of Metropolitan Varlaam by Basil III in Russia.

1525

Metropolitan Daniil authorizes divorce of Basil III.

1535

Edicts prohibit further acquisition of land by the monasteries.

1561

Disbandment of the Livonian Order.

1589

The Metropolitan Job is elected to the rank of Patriarch. Beginning of the Patriarchate of Moscow (fifth in honour in Orthodox world).

1619

Patriarch Filaret (Philaret) (the father of Michael Romanov, elected Tsar in 1613) is co-ruler until 1633.

1652

Election of Patriarch Nikon to lead Russian Orthodox Church. Programme of reforms gets under way, with innovations in ritual.

1654

Schism (*raskol*) in Russian Orthodoxy over adoption of Nikon's reforms by the Church Council. Dissenters excommunicated and thousands flee the country.

1658

Resignation of Nikon as Patriarch. He retires to the New Jerusalem monastery.

1665

Nikon deposed by the Church Council (which retains his reforms). Continuation of the schism in Russian orthodoxy.

1667

Condemnation of 'Old Believers' by the Church Council. Revolt of the Solovetsky Monastery.

1672

Orthodox Synod of Jerusalem.

1684

Formal persecution of the Old Believers is instituted.

1689

Expulsion of the Jesuits (return in 1691). Invitation to Huguenots to settle in Russia.

1700

Effective abolition of the Patriarchate by Peter the Great, substitution of Holy Synod from 1721 to govern the Church.

1702

Granting of religious toleration for non-Orthodox (but with a ban on proselytism).

1706

Independent Anglican community established in Moscow.

1708

Mazépa anathematized by church authorities.

1711

Only those selected from list approved by Senate can be chosen as bishops.

1713

St Alexander Névskii Monastery founded in St Petersburg.

1716

New oath for bishops instituted, with restriction on, for example, increasing number of clergy in their diocese. Relaxation of persecution of Old Believers. Introduction of compulsory confession.

1718

Attendance at church on Sundays and holidays compulsory.

1719

Expulsion of Jesuits from Russia.

1721

Patriarchate formally replaced by a 'spiritual college' (the eventual Holy Synod) by the *Spiritual Regulation*.

1723

Patriarchs of Antioch and Jerusalem recognize the Holy Synod.

1731

Overall responsibility for Muslim communities granted to the 'Commission for the Conversion of those of other faiths in Kazan, Nizhnii Novgorod and elsewhere'.

1740

Dukhobór sect begins to emerge.

1760

Restrictions on sale of serfs by monasteries and Church.

1762

Promulgation of Edict of Toleration for Old Believers.

CHRISTIANITY AND THE OTTOMAN EMPIRE, 1453–1763*

THE OTTOMAN ASCENDANCY, 1453–1571

1453

Fall of Constantinople to the Ottoman Turks under Mohammed II (Mahomet II, Mehmed II) ends the Eastern Roman Empire (29 May). Fall of Pera. Christians form a 'millet' (recognized religious group) of the Empire. The Union of Florence now effectively defunct.

1454

Ottomans permit election of a patriarch as millet-bachi (head of the millet, or ethnarch) with rights to tax, administer justice, etc. over Christians of the Empire (Jan.).

Phanariots (the Greek aristocracy of the Phanar district of Constantinople) gain effective monopoly of patriarchal elections. A *kharāj* required (tax demanded by the Sultan) at each patriarchal election.

1455

Moldavia becomes an Ottoman tributary (Oct.).

1456

Ottomans conquer Athens.

1458–60

Greece falls under Ottoman rule.

1459

Crusade against Turks is declared by Pius II. Serbia is overrun by the Ottoman Turks.

1460

Conquest of the Morea is completed.

1461

Empire of Trebizond finally falls to the Ottomans.

1462

Wallachia is invaded by Mohammed II.

1470

Euboea is conquered by Mohammed II.

1471

Coalition against the Ottomans includes the King of Cyprus, Venice and the Knights of St John.

1472

Pope Sixtus sends a fleet against the Ottomans.

1474

Transylvania is raided by the Ottomans.

1475

Genoese colonies in the Crimea are conquered.

1480

Ottoman capture of Otranto (on the Italian mainland) causes widespread panic. It is held by the Turks for a year.

1481

Death of Mohammed II. He is succeeded by Bayezid II. Ottomans in Otranto surrender (Sept.).

1484

Union of Florence formally condemned and terminated by Orthodox Council of Bishops.

1497

War of the Ottomans with Poland (until 1499).

1499

War of the Ottomans with Venice (until 1503). Ottoman successes include the naval victory at Navarino in August and the conquest of Lepanto.

1516

Egypt falls to Ottoman control after the defeat of the Mamelukes.

1517

Mecca submits to the Ottomans.

1520

Accession of Suleiman II (Süleyman) ('the Magnificent') following the death of Selim.

1521

Belgrade falls to Suleiman (Aug.).

1522

Rhodes is conquered by Suleiman (Jan.).

1526

Major Ottoman victory over the Hungarians at Mohács (29 Aug.).

1529

Suleiman captures Buda in his third campaign (Sept.). The first Ottoman siege of Vienna is repulsed (Oct.). Algiers becomes a vassal of the Ottomans.

1535

Ottoman fleet attacks Corfu.

1538

Major Ottoman naval victory at Prevesa (defeating the forces of the Pope, Venice and Charles V).

1541

Suleiman's campaign against Ferdinand of Austria. Annexation of most of Hungary by the Ottomans.

1543

Khairredin Barbarossa sacks Reggio (southern Italy) and captures Nice (southern France). Ottoman navy winters in Toulon.

1544

Ottoman conquest of Visegrad. Further conquests in western Hungary.

1551

Ottomans capture Tripoli from the Knights of Malta; beginning of a strong Ottoman naval presence in the western Mediterranean.

1565

Siege of Malta (May–Sept.). Ottomans forced to withdraw.

1566

Death of Suleiman during the siege of Szigetvár (6 Sept.). Accession of Selim II (24 Sept.). Occupation of Chios (taken from Genoa by the Ottomans).

1571

Ottomans complete the conquest of Cyprus from Venice (Aug.). Naval battle of Lepanto, a major Christian victory (7 Oct.).

THE ORTHODOX TORPOR

Note: Although the Ottoman Empire had reached its height with the reign of Suleiman the Magnificent, there were still some conquests to come from Christianity. For the Church, although not all was stagnation, the Patriarchate was in disarray. Although in a sense wielding more administrative authority (under the Ottoman millet system), its spiritual authority was in chaos. Patriarchs came and went (no less than four Patriarchs, Cyril I, Parthenius II, Parthenius III and Gabriel II, were put to death by the Turks on suspicion of treason).

1572

Patriarch Metrophanes deposed for alleged pro-Roman tendencies (restored 1579). Accession of Jeremias II.

1573–81

Lengthy correspondence of Patriarch Jeremias II with Lutherans in Germany (at Tübingen) only reveals the lack of understanding between them.

1595

Death of Patriarch Jeremias II, the 'ablest man to sit on the Patriarchal throne during the Captivity' (Runciman). His death was followed by a period of unprecedented chaos in the Patriarchate. Runciman calculated that inn the century from 1595, when Jeremias II ended his last Patriarchal reign, to 1695, there were sixty-one changes on the Patriarchal throne. (As many Patriarchs were reinstated after deposition, there were only thirty-one individual Patriarchs.)

1620–38

The era of Cyril Lucaris (elected and deposed five times between 1620 and 1638). His reign saw the amazingly Calvinistic *Confession of Faith* (1629).

1638–91

Six successive Orthodox Councils condemn the *Confession*.

1645

Venetian Crete is under siege by the Ottomans.

1657

Venetians lose Tenedos and Lemnos to the Ottomans.

1660

Beginning of the reduction of Transylvania by the Ottomans.

1669

Turks take Candia (Crete) from Venice (Sept.).

1683

Alliance between Poland and the Emperor against the Turks (March). Siege of Vienna by Mohammed IV; siege is relieved by John Sobieski of Poland and the Ottomans are routed (Sept.). A major turning point.

1684

Formation of Holy League (The Holy Roman Empire, Poland and Venice) against the Turks.

1686

Buda is taken by the Duke of Lorraine (Sept.) (after 145 years of Ottoman occupation).

1687

Important victory over the Turks at the Battle of Nagyharsány (near Mohács). Central Hungary comes under Austrian control and Transylvania is recovered. Suleiman III succeeds Mohammed IV as Sultan. Systematic attempts to convert Orthodox in Transylvania after Austria gained dominance in the region. Catholics found Romanian Greek Catholic Church (later forced to unite with Rome).

1688

Belgrade is taken from the Turks by Imperial forces who overrun Bosnia, Serbia and Wallachia. Religious toleration is confirmed in Transylvania.

1699

Peace of Carlowitz (Karlowitz) (26 Jan.). Major Ottoman territorial losses.

1718

Decline of Ottoman power is emphasized by the loss of Belgrade after the Peace of Passarowitz.

1739

Peace of Belgrade with Austria. Belgrade is ceded to the Austrians.

1748

Birth of St Nicodemus of the Holy Mountain (1748–1809). Famous for his translations and for his anthology *Philocalia*.

1755

Synod of Constantinople adopts strong anti-Western position declaring all Western sacraments, Latin or Protestant, to be invalid.

1766

Last remnants of Serbian church autonomy suppressed by Phanariot Patriarch Samuel Hantcherli.

1767

Remnants of Bulgarian Church autonomy likewise suppressed.

For the rise of nationalism in the Balkans, leading to the Greek insurrection of 1821, see p. 171.

---

*For a fuller chronology, see Chris Cook and Philip Broadhead, *The Routledge Companion to Early Modern Europe, 1453–1763* (2006).

CHRISTIANITY IN THE EIGHTEENTH CENTURY: THE AGE OF RATIONALISM

1685

Revocation of the Edict of Nantes (see p. 243).

1687

Newton publishes *Principia*. The discovery of laws governing natural phenomena will later stimulate thinkers during the Enlightenment to seek laws that govern society.

1688

The 'Glorious Revolution' in England (see p. 149).

1690

Locke publishes *Essay Concerning Human Understanding*, arguing that the human character is formed by experience in the world rather than supernatural forces.

1696

John Toland (1670–1722) publishes *Christianity not Mysterious*.

1702

The Jansenist (see p. 250) Schism of Utrecht. The revolt of the Protestant *Camisards* in France.

1704

The 'Malabar rites' of local Catholics in south India condemned.

1705

Condemnation of the Jansenists in bull *Vineam Domini*.

1708

Quesnel condemned.

1710

The monastery of Port-Royal destroyed.

1712

Leibniz publishes *Théodicée*. Christian Wolff publishes *Vernünftige Gedanken von den Kräften des menschlichen Verstandes*.

1713

Papal bull *Unigenitus* against Jansenists.

1714

Leibniz publishes *Monadologie*.

1715

Condemnation of the Chinese rites (see p. 198) in bull *Ex illa die* (missions barred from China in 1717 by Imperial Edict).

1718

Performance of *Œdipe*, the first play by Voltaire.

1719

Publication in Dutch Republic of Treatise of the Three Imposters (*Traité des Trois Imposteurs*) denouncing Moses, Jesus and Mohammed.

1720

Jansenist compromise as 'Accommodation' reached.

1721

Election of Pope Innocent XIII (Pope until 1724). Montesquieu publishes *Lettres persanes* which offer thinly veiled criticism of French society.

1722

Herrnhut founded by Zinzendorff.

1723

Wolff is accused of atheism, removed from his post of professor at Halle University and is banished from Prussia.

1724

Election of Pope Benedict XIII (Pope until 1730).

1728

The submission of Cardinal de Noailles.

1729

The *Parlement* supports the Jansenists, opposes the Bull *Unigenitus* and declares for liberty of conscience in France.

1730

The Redemptionists founded by St Alphonsus de Liguori. Election of Pope Clement XII

(Pope until 1740). Climax of the struggle between the Jesuits and the Jansenists.

1731

The Paris *Parlement* decrees that temporal power is to be independent of all other power (and clergy are to be under crown jurisdiction). The decree is annulled by Fleury in a crown versus *Parlement* clash (further clashes from 1738 to 1742).

1734

Voltaire publishes *Lettres philosophiques* which attack the methods of Descartes and praise a Newtonian approach to philosophical issues. Alexander Pope publishes the *Essay on Man*. Montesquieu publishes *Considérations sur les Causes de la Grandeur des Romains et de leur Décadence*.

1737

The Passionists founded by St Paul of the Cross.

1738

Condemnation of freemasonry in bull *In eminenti*. Hume publishes his *Treatise of Human Nature* (later revised as *Inquiry Concerning Human Nature*). It rejects the notion of divine causation regulating human affairs.

1740

Election of Pope Benedict XIV (Pope until 1758). Wolff returns to Halle following an invitation from Frederick II.

1741

Encyclical *Quanta Cura* forbids traffic in alms.

1744

Encouragement of the 'pariah' missions to India.

1746

Condillac publishes *Essai sur l'origine des connaissances humaines* (*Essay on the Origins of Human Understanding*). Frederick II writes *Histoire de mon temps*.

1747

Jean-Jacques Burlamaqui, *Principles of Natural Right*.

1748

Montesquieu publishes *L'Esprit des lois* (*The Spirit of the Laws*), an analysis of different forms of government. He calls among other things for checks on the power of the executive. Hume publishes *Essay on Miracles,* which attacks belief in religious miracles as being contrary to reason. La Mettrie publishes *L'Homme Machine*, which expresses atheistic opinions.

1749

Buffon publishes the first volume of *Histoire naturelle*, an account of natural history based on the observation of geological and other evidence, rather than on the biblical account of creation. (It is completed in 1778.)

1751

Diderot and d'Alembert publish the first volume of the *Encyclopédie*. (It is completed in 28 volumes in 1772.)

1752

Hume publishes *Political Discourses*.

1753

Spain and Pope Benedict XIV sign Concordat. Clerical power in France attacked by Paris *Parlement*. Long-standing dispute ensues.

1755

Rousseau publishes *Discourse on the Origins of Inequality Among Mankind*. Papal bull *Allatae Sunt* on the observance of Oriental rites by missionaries.

1756

Voltaire publishes *Essai sur l'histoire générale sur les moeurs et l'esprit des nations*.

1758

Helvétius published *Of Mind*. Election of Pope Clement XIII (Pope until 1769).

1759

Expulsion of Jesuits from Portugal ordered by Pombal. Voltaire's satirical *Candide*. Adam Smith's *Theory of Moral Sentiments*.

1761

Execution of Father Malagrida in Spain. Mary of the Immaculate Conception officially declared patroness of Spain. Hontheim publishes *On the Condition of the Church and the Legitimate Power of the Roman Pontiff.*

1762

Rousseau publishes *Du Contrat Social* (*The Social Contract*). Execution of Jean Calas, a French Protestant, who is charged with murdering his son to prevent him from converting to Catholicism. Louis XV forbids Jesuits to teach and recruit new members, and orders the sale of their property.

1763

Inspired by the Calas execution, Voltaire publishes *Traité sur la tolérance*, in which he calls for limited religious toleration to be granted in France.

1764

The Jesuit Order is suppressed in France. Pope Clement XIII issues a bull defending the Order. The Moravian Church is reformed by Spangenberg. Communication between Portugal and the papacy is broken off as a result of the execution of Malagrida as a heretic. Beginning of Pombal's work to suppress the Jesuits in Portugal.

1765

Cult of the Sacred Heart sanctioned by the Pope.

1766

Secular education, supervision of monasteries and tax on church lands introduced by D'Aranda in Spain.

1767

Jesuits expelled from Spain, the Sicilies and Parma.

1769

List of anti-papal grievances, the 'Coblenz Articles', presented by the Archbishops of Mainz, Cologne and Trier to Maria Theresa. Spain, France and Naples demand the abolition of the Jesuit Order. Election of Clement XIV as Pope.

1773

Dominus ac redemptor. Suppression of Jesuit Order by the papacy.

1774

Jesuits expelled from Poland.

1775

Election of Pope Pius VI (Pope until 1799).

1776

The Illuminati founded in Bavaria.

1781

The start of Josephism in Austria. Joseph II grants religious toleration to Protestants and members of the Greek Church. A total of 700 monasteries dissolved; papal bulls restricted; funds for Rome stopped, and six new bishoprics created without papal approval.

1782

Visit of Pope Pius VI to Vienna to protest at Joseph's actions, but to no effect.

1783

Joseph II makes marriage a civil contract and allows divorce. He proposes appointment of bishops without papal approval, suppresses diocesan seminaries and forms own schools for the education of clergy.

1786

The Synod of Pistoia held in Tuscany.

1787

Edict of toleration and legal civil status for Protestants in France. Leopold II of Tuscany dismisses national synod in Florence for failing to agree with his church reforms and sets about them himself. King of the

Two Sicilies refuses to pay annual tribute to the Pope.

1788

The revolt of the lower clergy (*curés*) in France.

1789

Opening of the States-General in France swiftly followed by the onset of the revolution (see p. 154).

THE ENGLISH CHURCH, 1689–1837

1688

Archbishop Sancroft and six bishops protest against James II's Declaration of Indulgence, suspending laws against Catholics and dissenters. Tried for seditious libel, but acquitted.

Invasion of England by William of Orange and flight of James II to France.

1689

The Protestant William and Mary take the throne. The Bill of Rights Act establishes that only a Protestant can become sovereign. Toleration Act allows dissenters to worship publicly on taking an oath and permits Quakers to affirm, but excludes Catholics and Unitarians. Archbishop Sancroft, nine bishops and more than 400 clergy, the non-jurors, refuse to take oaths of supremacy and allegiance to William and Mary and are deprived of their livings.

1690

Convention Parliament establishes Presbyterianism in Scotland.

1695

Locke's *Reasonableness of Christianity* published.

1696

Toland's *Christianity not Mysterious* founding the Deist movement in England is burnt by the public hangman.

1697

Lord Mayor of London, a dissenter, openly practises Occasional Conformity.

1698

The Society for Promoting Christian Knowledge is founded.

1701

Mission branch of the Society for Promoting Christian Knowledge is founded as the Society for the Propagation of the Gospel. Act of Settlement provided for Protestant Monarchy.

1703

Bill to prevent Occasional Conformity passes the House of Commons but is rejected by the Lords.

1704

Queen Anne's Bounty: Queen Anne surrenders the claim of the throne to first fruits and tenths to endow poorer clergy.

1707

Act of Security of Church of England excludes Presbyterians from holding office in England.

1709

Dr Sacheverell impeached after preaching against toleration of Dissenters and denouncing the Whig Ministers as traitors to the Anglican Church.

1710

Trial of Dr Sacheverell at Westminster Hall leads to rioting in London and attacks on dissenting chapels. Lords order Sacheverell's sermon to be burnt and silence him for three years.

1711

Occasional Conformity Act passed against Protestant Dissenters. Parliament votes £350,000 to build 52 churches in London.

1714

Schism Act introduced, forbidding Nonconformists from teaching.

1716

Negotiations between non-jurors and Greek Church for reunion.

1717

Convocation prorogued as a consequence of its censure of Hoadly, Bishop of Bangor, for his sermon declaring against tests of orthodoxy. Convocation does not reassemble again until 1852. Hoadly replies to the censure and the 'Bangorian controversy' ensues.

1719

Repeal of Occasional Conformity and Schism Acts.

1723

Francis Atterbury, Bishop of Rochester, exiled for part in pro-Jacobite plot. Penal levy of £100,000 placed on Catholics.

1727

Walpole introduces first annual Bill of Indemnity allowing Dissenters to escape penalties of the Test and Corporation Acts by taking the sacrament after rather than before election to office. Independent, Baptist and Presbyterian congregations form General Body of Protestant Dissenting Ministers.

1728

Moravian mission established.

1729

John Wesley, Junior Fellow of Lincoln College, Oxford, and friends begin to meet at Oxford in a strict religious society, Doddridge establishes a Presbyterian academy at Market Harborough.

1736

Bishop Warburton's *Alliance of Church and State* argues for the Established Church and a Test Act. Attempt to relieve Quakers from tithes fails.

1738

John Wesley returns from America, falls under the influence of Peter Bohler, a Moravian, and is converted on 24 May. George Whitefield undertakes missionary work in America.

1739

Wesley follows Whitefield's example of preaching in the open air. Methodist Society meets in Old Foundry, Moorfields, London.

1740

Wesley severs his connection with the Moravians. Begins to employ lay preachers and build chapels. Controversy with

Whitefield over Calvinist doctrine of predestination.

1742

Dodwell's *Christianity Not Founded on Argument* attacks both Deists and Christians.

1743

Methodists produce rules for 'classes'. Welsh Calvinistic Methodist body founded by Whitefield.

1744

First Methodist Conference held at Foundry Chapel, London.

1745

Many of the non-jurors implicated in the Jacobite rebellion.

1746

Persecution of Scottish episcopal clergy for Jacobitism.

1747

Methodist societies grouped into circuits.

1749

Calvinists under Whitefield desert Wesley; Whitefield becomes chaplain to Lady Huntingdon.

1756

Wesley's *Twelve Reasons Against a Separation from the Church* attempts to restrain breakaway tendencies among his followers.

1760

Wesley's lay preachers take out licences as dissenting teachers and administer the sacraments. Condemned by Charles Wesley. Board of Deputies of British Jews established.

1768

Lady Huntingdon founds a seminary at Trefecca.

1770

Wesley denounces Calvinism at conference; General Baptist New Communion established.

1771

Feathers Tavern petition against subscription to the Thirty-nine Articles; rejected by 217 to 17 in Parliament. Several clergy leave Established Church and become Unitarians.

1777

City Road Chapel, London, founded by Methodists.

1778

Sir George Savile obtains Catholic Relief Act. Roman Catholic worship permitted. New oath of allegiance. Protestant Association founded.

1779

Dissenting ministers and schoolmasters relieved from subscription to the Thirty-nine Articles.

1780

Gordon riots following campaign by Protestant Association against Catholic Relief Act of 1778. Mass petition of Parliament leads to riots in London with attacks on houses, chapels and embassies of Catholics. Raikes founds Sunday schools at Gloucester.

1781

Lady Huntingdon's Connexion separates from Church of England.

1782

Charles Simeon ordained curate of Trinity Church, Cambridge; introduces evangelical movement into the University.

1784

Wesley ordains Coke and Asbury as 'Superintendents' in America.

1787

Beaufoy's motion for repeal of the Test and Corporation Acts is defeated in the House of Commons. Beilby Porteus becomes Bishop of London and leads the Evangelical Revival within the Church of England, assisted by what became known as the 'Clapham Sect'.

1789

Dr Richard Price, Unitarian preacher and theologian, preaches sermon at the annual dinner of the London Revolution Society (4 Nov.), welcoming the French Revolution for its stimulus to reform in civil and ecclesiastical affairs.

1790

Motions for repeal of Test and Corporation Acts withdrawn from Parliament without a division.

1791

Attacks on Dissenters at Birmingham, Priestley's house destroyed by mob. Death of Wesley.

1794

Paley's *Evidence of Christianity* assumes the existence of a personal God and infers the probability of revelation. Paine's *Age of Reason* attacks Christianity.

Stonyhurst College founded for Roman Catholic students.

1795

Separation of Methodist and Anglican Churches made final as a result of breakdown of plans for reconciliation. Maynooth College founded in Ireland to provide seminary for Catholic priests other than in France.

1797

Methodist New Connexion secedes from main Wesleyan body.

1799

Church Missionary Society agreed on in principle by evangelical group (fully established in 1801).

1801

Pitt's proposals for Catholic relief blocked by opposition of the King.

1804

British and Foreign Bible Society founded.

1807

William Wilberforce, Henry Thornton, Sir James Stephen, Lord Teignmouth, Granville Sharp and John Venn form the 'Clapham

Sect' and campaign for various philanthropic causes, including the end of the slave trade.

1808

Expulsion of Hugh Bourne from Wesleyan Methodist Conference for open-air preaching.

1811

Welsh Calvinistic Methodists leave Church of England. Sidmouth's Bill to limit itinerant preaching defeated after protests from dissenting groups.

1812

Grattan's proposal for Catholic relief defeated. Unitarian Relief Act passed; Conventicle and Five-Mile Acts repealed. Primitive Methodist Connexion formed by Hugh Bourne and William Clowes.

1814

Wesleyan Missionary Society organized. Death of prophetess Joanna Southcott; followers, known as the New Israelites, found chapel in London.

1815

Bryanites or 'Bible Christians' separate from Methodists.

1816

Motion for Catholic relief defeated in the Lords.

1817

Military and Naval Officers' Oath Bill opens all ranks in the army and navy to Catholics.

1818

Church Building Society founded. At its instigation Parliament grants £1 million for church building and appoints a Commission to superintend its distribution.

1820

Revd Darby leaves Church of England and founds Plymouth Brethren, teaching a rigid Calvinism and the priesthood of all believers.

1826

Rose preaches at Cambridge on duties of the clergy and founds modern High Churchmanship.

THE CHURCH, THE FRENCH REVOLUTION AND THE NAPOLEONIC ERA, 1789–1815

Note: At the French Revolution Catholicism was the official religion of France. The clergy numbered 130,000, of whom 70,000 were regulars and 60,000 seculars. The Church was the biggest landowner. It received tithes, paid no direct tax, but voted a fiscal contribution every five years (the *don gratuit*). The Church supported nearly 2,200 hospitals, 600 colleges and 25,000 primary schools. Bishops of the 135 dioceses were recruited from the older aristocracy. The Church constituted one of the three 'Estates' of *ancien régime* France.

1787

Paris *Parlement* passes Edict of Toleration for Protestants in France (Nov.).

1788

Reduction of the *don gratuit* by the Assembly of Clergy, an indication of its support for the aristocratic revolt.

1789

Opening of the Estates-General (5 May). Title of 'The National Assembly' assumed by the Third Estate (17 June). Clergy and nobility ordered by the King to join the Commons (27 June). Decrees abolishing feudal privileges (4–11 Aug.). Declaration of Rights (26 Aug.). The principle of freedom of religion was stated in the Declaration of the Rights of Man. Protestants could hold all public appointments from September 1789, Jews from September 1791. National Assembly meets (19 Oct.). The Assembly abolished annates and tithes, and authorizes the transfer of all church property to the State (2 Nov.).

1790

Abolition of monastic vows together with suppression of many religious orders (13 Feb.). Parish priests required to read out the newly passed laws to their congregations (23 Feb.). Motion to make Catholicism the sole state religion rejected (April). The debate began on the hugely controversial civil constitution of the clergy (29 May). Avignon (a papal enclave within France) voted to be incorporated within France (11 June). Violent clashes between Protestants and Catholics in Nîmes (the *Bagarre*) and the Cévennes (June).

Civil Constitution adopted (July). The Civil Constitution of the clergy reduced the number of bishops to one for each department (83 not 160). Bishops to be chosen by the parliamentary electors and instituted by the Metropolitan. The clergy chosen by the electors to communal offices. Papal confirmation dispensed with. All clergy to take the oath to the Civil Constitution. Protestants become eligible for office and receive back property confiscated by Louis XIV. Jews also received civil rights.

Assertion by 16 bishops that Civil Constitution required papal endorsement (Oct.).

1791

First batch of 'constitutional' bishops consecrated by Talleyrand. Papal Bull *Caritas* condemns Civil Constitution (13 April). Crisis mounts with flight of King Louis XVI to Varennes (20 June) and convening of the Legislative Assembly (1 Oct.). The decree against non-juring priests (i.e. those who had refused to take the oath) (29 Nov.). Royal veto on decree against non-juring priests (19 Dec.).

1792

Religious dress suppressed (6 April). Clergy who refuse to take the oath to the Civil Constitution of the Clergy are given 14 days to leave after 10 August. The religious orders are dissolved (Aug.) and civil marriage and divorce are introduced (Sept.). Anti-clerical measures intensified and new oath required of clergy. Massacres of priests (225 in Paris) (Sept.). Paris Commune had earlier prohibited public religious processions and services. Growing dissent of non-juring priests, royalists, etc. in La Vendée. Constitutional clergy suffered when anti-Christian movement grew. All churches were secularized, many destroyed in the cult of Reason.

1793

Execution of Louis XVI (21 Jan.) and creation of the Revolutionary Tribunal (10 March). Discontent in La Vendée erupted into open revolt (March). Further wave of anti-clerical measures (the selling of episcopal palaces, melting of church bells to provide cannon for the war) (July). Dechristianization campaign begun by Fouché (Sept.) which later spreads from provinces to Paris. Revolutionary calendar introduced (Oct.). Convention abolishes Catholic faith and threatens recalcitrant clergy with death. Feast of Reason celebrated (10 Nov.) in Church of St Eustache. Notre Dame renamed the 'Temple of Reason'. Paris Commune ordered closure of all churches.

1794

Convention formally recognizes the existence of a Supreme Being and immortality (May). Robespierre presides over the Feast of the Supreme Being (June). Religion is banished from schools and replaced by moral education and civic training (Nov.).

1795

Formal separation of Church and State. State renounces any financial liability for public worship. Freedom proclaimed for all religions (Feb.). Use of church buildings allowed, but all priests to swear oath of allegiance to the Republic (May). New regulations restricting worship (Sept.). The Constitutional Church (now more commonly called Gallican Church) reconstituted.

1796–97

Gradual rightward move by the authorities aids church recovery. Armistice with papal states (June 1796) and Peace of Tolentino with papacy (Feb. 1797). Repeal of legislation against refractory priests (Aug. 1797).

1798

Roman Republic proclaimed, and Pope a prisoner of the French, after French overthrow papal government (Feb.). Insurrection in Belgium (following the 'Jourdan Law' on prescription). Several thousand priests in Belgium sentenced to deportation.

1799

Death of Pope Pius VI as a French prisoner in Valence.

1801

Concordat between France and the papacy (16 July). Under its main provisions, France acknowledges that the 'Catholic, Apostolic and Roman religion' is that of the 'majority of French citizens'. Public worship is guaranteed. New bishops to be nominated by the First Consul, the Pope conferring spiritual powers. Bishops to appoint parish priests from lists approved by the government. Before consecration they must take an oath to obey 'the government established by the constitution'. The government to pay the clergy, Catholic, Protestant or Jewish, a 'reasonable salary', and foundations with land or money allowed. But 77 Organic Articles severely restrict the Holy See in France. Some bishops refuse to recognize the Concordat and form *La Petite Eglise*.

1802

Concordat promulgated, but with Organic Articles which have not been discussed by the Pope. Papal bulls and representatives not allowed into France without government permission, nor synods held. Chateaubriand's *Genius of Christianity* published. It asserts the irrational and aesthetic values of Christianity in opposition to the criticism of the *philosophes*.

1804

Napoleon tightens control over Church, restoring laws against perpetual vows.

1805

Napoleon brings Jews under state control.

1806

Following a series of disputes with Napoleon, principally over the extension of the *Code Napoléon* to Italy and Napoleon's seizure of papal territory, the Pope refuses to expel French enemies from his territory, observe the continental system and appoint to the Venetian bishoprics under Napoleon's control.

1808

Rome occupied by French troops. Napoleon abolishes the Inquisition in Spain and suppresses most of the monasteries. Napoleon abolishes Italian Inquisition.

1809

Rome formally added to French Empire (17 May). Pius VII excommunicates Napoleon (11 June). Pius ˙ arrested and imprisoned in Savona (6 July). The Pope refuses to institute French bishops. Napoleon calls an Ecclesiastical Commission for France to seek a solution to the deadlock, but it fails to offer a solution acceptable to Napoleon and is suppressed (Jan. 1810).

1810

Senate decrees that all future popes and all the clergy of the Empire must accept the Gallican articles of 1682.

1811

Napoleon calls a Council in Paris to sanction a scheme for the institution of bishops. Although securing papal approval, Napoleon dissolves the Council because of the restrictions he requests.

1813

Napoleon brings Pope to France and forces a new Concordat giving Napoleon the nomination of bishops in France and Italy and the Metropolitan the power to institute if the Pope has not done so within six months. The Pope, however, later repudiates the agreement.

1814

Pope freed by Napoleon.

1815

The Congress of Vienna followed defeat of Napoleon (see p. 157).

THE PAPACY IN THE AGE OF REVOLUTION, 1789–1848

1790

Pope Pius VI strongly opposes Gallicanism and condemns the French Assembly's Civil Constitution of the Clergy.

1796

Democratic revolution in Rome encouraged by the French, who set up puppet republic.

1797

By Treaty of Tolentino the Pope gives up the legations of Ferrara, Bologna and Romagna to Cisalpine Republic, and Avignon to France.

1798

Pius VI deported by French to Siena and later to Valence, where he died.

1800

Pope Pius VII elected by Sacred College, meeting at Venice. Napoleon, seeking support of Catholics, restores Papal States.

1801

Concordat, extracted by Napoleon, reconciled papacy and France (see p. 155).

1804

Pius VII summoned to crown Napoleon in Notre Dame, Paris.

1806

Pius ignores Napoleon's orders to close Papal States to British trade.

1807

Napoleon occupies Papal States.

1809

Papal States annexed. Pius taken as prisoner to Savona, near Genoa, and (1812) to Fontainebleau. This encouraged many Catholics to oppose Napoleon and later support the Bourbons.

1814

Napoleon frees Pius before his first abdication. Pius re-establishes the Jesuit order, suppressed in 1773 by Pope Clement XIV.

1815

Congress of Vienna confirms the 1797 transfer of Avignon to France but, because of efforts by Cardinal Ercole Consalvi (1757–1824), Secretary of State until 1823, the Pope regains other territories – the legations of Bologna, Urbino, Ravenna and Ferrara, Spoleto, the Marches of Ancona, etc. Severe repression and reaction.

1817, 1828

Concordats made by Count Barbaroux, Minister of Clerical Affairs (d. 1843), in Sardinia.

1818

Concordat with Two Sicilies signed at Terracina (16 Feb.). The 109 dioceses were to be restored to the Church. Church to regain property not already sold. Many monasteries and religious orders restored.

1820

Concordat concluded between Prussia and the papacy.

1823

Death of Pius VII. Election of Leo XII (1823–29).

1824

Encyclical condemns liberty of faith and anathematizes bible societies (5 May). Encyclicals denounce liberalism, condemn indifferentism and de-Christianization of society, freemasonry, secret societies. Lamennais visits Rome and on his return advocates the political supremacy of the Pope.

1825

To demonstrate papacy's strength, jubilee held, first since 1775, when Pius moved from Quirinal to Vatican.

1827

Louis XVIII and the Pope restore principles of Concordat in France.

1829

Election of Pope Pius VIII (1829–30).

1830

Election of Gregory XVI (1830–46) after conclave of 50 days (2 Feb.). Bologna declared the temporal power of the Pope

at an end (8 Feb.). Widespread uprisings throughout Italy. Austrians, answering papal appeal for help, occupy Bologna (21 March), followed by second Austrian intervention (1832).

1832

Occupation of Ancona by French forces. Gregory XVI issues an encyclical condemning freedom of conscience and of the press in reaction to the new Belgian Constitution.

1834

Suppression of the monasteries in Portugal.

1837

French and Austrian troops withdrew from Papal States.

1843

Abbé Gioberti's *Del Primato morale e civile degli Italiani*, suggesting a federation of Italian states with the Pope as President.

1846

Election of Pius IX. Begins reform of Papal States, including an amnesty for 1,000 prisoners and reform of courts (July). Encyclical declaring Pius to be on the conservative side in all matters of dogma and faith (Nov.).

1847

Pope grants limited freedom of the press in Papal States (15 March) and becomes focus of anti-Austrian feeling after protest to Austria over violation of the Papal States.

1848

The 'Year of Revolutions' in Europe. Roman crowds demand lay ministers in Papal

States (8 Feb.). Papal armies cross into Austrian Italy. Pius IX states his unwillingness to declare war on Austrians and denies instigation of revolution (29 April). Effectively ended hopes of the Pope as champion of war against Austrian domination. Pope flees to Gaeta after demonstrations in Rome (24 Nov.). Jesuits expelled from Kingdom of Sardinia and influence of clergy on education restricted.

Note: For the revolutions and the Church elsewhere in 1848, see p. 160.

CHURCH AND STATE IN WESTERN EUROPE, 1848–1914

1848

Separation of Church and State decreed by Frankfurt Parliament (March) Meeting of German Bishops at Würzburg resolves to work for full independence from secular control of ecclesiastical legislation, administration and control of education. These are incorporated in concordats with several of the southern German States. Five hundred clergy meet at Wittenberg to celebrate success against revolution.

Falloux, French Minister of Education, introduces a bill permitting Catholics to be educated at Catholic primary and secondary schools, but only obtain degrees at secular universities. The numbers receiving clerical education greatly increase.

Dutch Reformed Church disestablished.

1849

Rome recaptured for the Pope. The Pope issues an encyclical to the Italian bishops condemning socialism and communism. He also issues an encyclical inviting views on the immaculate conception.

By the constitution, the Evangelical Lutheran Church in Denmark is supported by the state, parliament acting as legislative and money-voting authority, but full religious toleration also established.

1850

Prussian Constitution provides that all religious associations should administer their affairs independently and remain in possession of their property and funds for religious, educational and charity purposes. Communication with superiors and publication of ordinances largely unfettered. But nomination, election and confirmation of ecclesiastical posts governed by the state.

Pius IX protests against law in Belgium making secondary education subject to state control. Bishops insist on there being only Catholic chaplains in state establishments.

Siccardi Laws suppress ecclesiastical immunities in Kingdom of Sardinia. Archbishops of Turin and Sardinia imprisoned.

1851

Prussian Evangelical Churches placed under control of a Church Council instead of the King.

Church's jurisdiction over heresy and sacrilege taken by civil power in Kingdom of Sardinia.

Concordat signed with the papacy by Spain in which Catholicism is declared sole religion of the state. Church to supervise education and have sole jurisdiction over marriage disputes. Papacy guarantees the right of the Crown to appoint bishops and recognizes loss of church lands already secularized.

1852

The Eisenach biennial conference in Germany is instituted, made up of representatives of the

Protestants of each state. Under its direction a revision of Luther's Bible is instituted.

Church property secularized and civil marriage introduced in Sardinia.

Catholic hierarchy re-established in Holland in spite of protests.

1854

The New Lutherans in Germany attack pietism and individualism. Jewish seminary established at Breslau.

The Immaculate Conception of the Virgin is declared an article of faith for Roman Catholics. The Curia is reformed, and the Sacred College. Greater centralization of papal power.

Kierkegaard-Martensen controversy on Christianity in Denmark.

1855

Concordat with the papacy. Austrian Catholic bishops empowered to issue ordinances without the approval of the civil power, set penalties and supervise education, marriage and the press. State control of the Church abolished.

A Monastic Law abolishes all religious orders in the Kingdom of Sardinia except those employed in preaching, education and the care of the sick.

Obligatory communion for public office holders ended in Sweden.

Spiritualist movement spreads from the USA to England and later to Europe.

1859

Pope refuses to renounce temporal power.

Members of non-Lutheran faiths allowed to practise freely in Sweden.

1860

Encyclical *Nullis Certe* threatens to excommunicate all who attack papal domains. Papal army defeated by Austrians and Rome only saved by French troops.

Prota-Giurleo, a Dominican, attempts to found a National Church in Italy, with radical changes in organization and liturgy. Monastic orders partially suppressed in Kingdom of Two Sicilies.

1863

Protestant Union founded, seeking federation into a German National Church, with greater power for the laity, and greater latitude in doctrinal matters.

1863

Concordat between Russia and Holy See repudiated by Tsar following the Russian repression of Polish rising.

1864

Catholic monasteries dissolved and control of Catholic affairs given to Minister of Worship in Poland.

Pope issues encyclical *Quanta Cura*, a syllabus of 80 errors, including Liberalism. Religious toleration, freedom of conscience and press, free discussion and secularist legislation are challenged.

Diplomatic relations between Russia and Holy See broken off.

1866

Pope condemns attempts at Anglican–Catholic reunion.

Monasteries and congregations suppressed by law. Land held in mortmain sold by the state. Cathedral chapters and bishops forced to surrender their capital to the state. Seminarists made liable for military service and civil marriage made obligatory in Italy.

1867

The Pope announces his intention to hold an Ecumenical Council. The doctrine of Papal infallibility is widely canvassed.

Anglican Church in Ireland disestablished.

Civil marriage is restored in Austria and the schools are freed from clerical control. The Church can only open new ones. Jews granted full civil liberty and Jewish immigration increases substantially from neighbouring states. Pope condemns the new laws.

1868

White Fathers founded by Lavigerie for missionary and educational work.

Following Liberal Revolution, the Spanish Cortes proclaims freedom of worship and teaching, and introduces civil marriage. Religious houses suppressed and clergy deprived of salaries.

1869

Vatican Council meets and begins discussion of papal infallibility.

Prince Hohenlohe, Minister President of Bavaria, invites powers to confer on the prospect of decree of papal infallibility. German bishops at Fulda produce a pastoral to allay fears of a new dogma.

1870

Vatican Council declares papal *ex cathedra* definitions of faith and morals infallible by 533 votes to 2 (July). Rome falls to Piedmontese troops of Victor Emmanuel. Romans decide by plebiscite to become part of Italy. Decree of 9 October declares Rome and Roman provinces part of Kingdom of Italy. The Pope loses all temporal power.

Austrian government forbids promulgation of Council's decree and cancels Concordat with papacy.

After first producing a memorial against the new dogma (Jan.), the German bishops accept the dogma of infallibility. Archbishop of Cologne orders theological professors of Bonn to accept the dogma on pain of being forbidden to lecture to Roman Catholic students or exercise their priestly function. Bavaria refuses to accept papal bull on infallibility. Clergy and bishops accept and attempt to coerce opponents. Some German Catholics, now known as Old Catholics, prefer to secede from Rome rather than accept the decree. Several states give active support to the Old Catholic movement and its leaders Dr Dollinger and Dr Reinkens.

Communards enact separation of Church and State, the abolition of a budget for religious affairs, and execute 24 clergy, including the Archbishop of Paris.

Swiss Federal government breaks off relations with papacy after disputes over mixed marriages, education, freedom of the press, and the doctrine of infallibility.

Sunday Schools introduced by Home Mission Movement (*Indre Misjon*) in Denmark.

1871

Centre Party in Germany founded to defend Catholic interests and wins 63 seats in Diet. Congress of Old Catholics held at Munich. Catholic members of the Prussian Landtag petition the Emperor to restore the temporal power of the Pope. He refuses to assist. When some Catholic bishops attempt to excommunicate those not accepting infallibility, the government declares them still Catholics with full civil rights. Political pronouncements from pulpit made a criminal offence and Roman Catholic Department of Spiritual Affairs abolished.

The Law of Guarantees declares the Pope's person inviolable, accords the honours of a sovereign prince, allows the possession of the Vatican and other palaces, and grants an annuity (rejected by the Pope). Church and State separated in Italy and church property secularized, though religious orders once again allowed to own property. Restrictions on Church lifted.

Prime Minister Frère-Orban obtains law creating free 'neutral' schools in Belgium in which the Catholic faith may only be taught outside class hours. Catholic bishops protest and diplomatic relations with the papacy ended. Private Catholic schools organized. *Congrès des Oeuvres Sociales* founded by Bishop of Liège.

1872

The Prussian government reduces 'clerical influence' in schools. The bishops protest and the Pope excommunicates the authors of the law. Bismarck banishes the Jesuits and forces clergy to swear allegiance before appointment.

1873

May Laws in Prussia give state control in the education of the clergy, jurisdiction over church cases, excommunication, and the appointment and dismissal of ministers. Catholic bishops vote to oppose the laws and three are imprisoned and over 400 clergy dismissed.

1873

1866 law in Italy extended to Rome. Proceeds of property of religious corporations divided between Holy See and charitable activities.

By decree of toleration, Swedes allowed to leave Lutheran Church to join another.

1874

Civil marriage made compulsory in Prussia. German Old Catholics permit use of vernacular, allow marriage of priests, and abolish compulsory confession.

The May Laws replace Concordat of 1855 in Austria. Powers of Church restricted. Bishops say they will only obey the laws in so far as in agreement with old Concordat.

Church declares it 'inexpedient' to vote in Italian General Election, though many Catholics disobey.

Civil marriage made obligatory in Switzerland. No new monasteries to be founded, but religious freedom ensured.

1875

Pope declares recent anti-Catholic legislation in Germany invalid. The Prussian government refuses payment to clergy who will not obey; two-thirds of Prussian bishoprics and 1,400 curacies become vacant. Civil marriage made obligatory throughout the Empire. All religious orders suppressed in Prussia except those engaged in nursing.

Pope institutes the cult of the Sacred Heart.

1876

Alfonso XII takes throne. Church property in Spain restored, Catholic schools reopened, diplomatic relations with papacy restored. Catholicism once again official religion though recognized the existence of 'non-Catholic cults'. State takes responsibility for maintaining the Church. Civil marriage abolished and Protestant chapels closed.

1877

Eight Roman Catholic archbishops and bishops removed in Prussia, leaving only four.

1878

Roman Catholic seminaries closed in Germany.

1879

Bismarck lessens persecution of Catholic Church after accession of Leo XIII. Jules Ferry's education bill forbids members of unauthorized communities to teach in France.

1880

The Jesuit Order is dissolved, military chaplains are abolished, and candidates for the ministry are compelled to serve in the army for a year. State primary education made free and compulsory, and religious teaching abolished in France.

Diplomatic relations between the papacy and Belgian government broken off over the School Law of 1879.

Bismarck relaxes application of the May Laws and reinstates clergy.

1881

Ferry expels the unauthorized congregations in France.

1884

The Pope calls on the French bishops not to show hostility to the Republic. In Belgium, Catholic government elected. New education law makes many public schools Catholic and restores relations with papacy. First worker priests among miners.

1886

Concordat with Vatican in Portugal. Bishops to be nominated by the government, appointed by the Pope, and paid by the state. Parish clergy appointed by the state. Teachers belonging to religious orders removed from state schools in France.

State examination and control of seminaries given up in Germany.

1887

Bismarck ends the *Kulturkampf.*

1888

Papal encyclical *De libertate humana,* on human liberty.

1889

In Italy, penalties increased for clergy who use pulpit for political purposes.

1890

Pope Leo XIII's *'Ralliement'* policy encourages Catholics in France to accept the Republic through encyclical *Sapientiae christianae.* Right-wing and anti-Jewish Assumptionist Order dissolved. Compulsory tithes abolished and church charities taken over by state in Italy.

1891

Five French cardinals indict the government for its past anti-clerical legislation.

Encyclical *Rerum novarum* condemns condition of workers, advocates just wage, right of association and right of peasants to land; missions encouraged and Vatican archives opened; but modernism and rationalism also condemned.

1892

Further papal encyclical declares that 'acceptance of the new regime is not only permitted but demanded' in France.

Revision of Luther's Bible completed in Germany.

164

1894

Civil marriage made obligatory and declared sufficient without religious ceremony. Freedom of worship also proclaimed in Austria.

Discussion of reunion of Roman and Armenian Churches.

Religious instruction made obligatory in all state schools in Belgium.

Many Catholics support the prosecution of Dreyfus, intensifying anti-clerical feeling on the left in France.

Papal encyclical states that Polish Catholic clergy will no longer oppose Russia.

Los von Rom (Freedom from Rome) movement grows in Austria.

1898

Violence in Milan leads to suppression of 3,000 Catholic organizations.

1901

Law allows associations to be formed, but congregations in France have to be licensed.

1903

Congregational councils of clergy and laity set up in each parish to manage church fabric and funds and elect clergy and bishops in Denmark.

1904

Law suppressing teaching orders in France Quarrel over choice of bishops between French government and papacy.

1905

Separation of Church and State in France. Napoleon's concordat and organic articles repealed. Churches remain property of state but at the disposal of the ministers and orders.

In Italy, Bishops allowed to decide if Catholics of diocese can participate in political life.

1906

Pius X refuses to recognize the separation of Church and State in France.

Catholic Social Weeks started in the Netherlands.

1908

New Portuguese republic expels religious congregations, parish administration is taken over by lay committees, and financed solely from contributions. Religious teaching in schools abolished and religious oaths for university and other courses.

1909

Pope condemns modernism in encyclical *Pascendi gregis.*

During *'Semana Tragica'* in Barcelona over 50 religious buildings destroyed by the populace during socialist uprising.

1910

Prelates in Portugal publish a pastoral censuring government. Minister of Justice orders its suspension. When defied, the Bishop of Oporto is deposed.

1911

Law of separation. Church disestablished in Portugal.

Clergy forbidden to criticize the government or laws of the republic.

Boards of laymen to take charge of Catholic worship. Ministers permitted to marry.

HOLY RUSSIA: THE ORTHODOX CHURCH, 1762–1917

1762

Return of church land to the Church.

1764

Confiscation by Catherine the Great of some church estates.

1767

'Prudent toleration of other Religions' the theme of Empress Catherine the Great's *Instruction*.

1769

Courts can accept testimony of Old Believers. Theological academy opened at Moscow (followed by St Petersburg in 1809, Kiev 1819, and Kazan 1842).

1771

Communities of Old Believers set up in Moscow.

1772

Ban on publication of papal bulls or ordinances in Belorussia unless authorized by the Russian authorities.

1773

Catholic bishopric of Mogilëv created (to take charge of Catholics throughout Russia).

1777

Jesuit novitiate in Pólotsk receives authorization.

1782

Relaxation of rules on Old Believers: no longer designated schismatics, forced to pay double taxes or wear distinctive dress. Uniat Bishopric of Pólotsk created. Catholic see of Mogilëv created an archbishopric (by Catherine acting unilaterally).

1785

Old Believers now eligible for public office.

1786

Catholic Church in Russia forbidden from acquiring landed estates. Building of Muslim schools allowed.

1795

Uniat bishoprics of Pinsk, Luck and Brest abolished as 'unnecessary'.

1804

Land in Crimea designated for the Doukhobor community.

1811–12

Alexander I, under the influence of Prince Alexander Golítsyn, the Procurator, undergoes religious conversion. Briefly, toleration of other sects allowed and persecution halted.

1812

Founding of Russian Bible Society.

1814

Jesuits ordered to close their schools in Moscow and St Petersburg, and exiled to the provinces, being allowed to stay there if proselytizing stops.

1815

Pact of the Holy Alliance signed between the Emperor Francis I of Austria, King William I of Prussia and Tsar Alexander I.

1816

Jesuits expelled from St Petersburg and Moscow (2 Jan.).

1817

Alexander's religious enlightenment policy. The Ministry of Education united with the Ministry of Spiritual Affairs under Prince Alexander Golítsyn. All religions, including the Russian Orthodox faith, to be treated equally.

1818

Concordat between Russia and the Holy See establishing the canonical position of Catholics in Poland.

1819–21

Alexander's policy of religious toleration denounced by the monk, Photius, as an insult to pure Orthodoxy. Campaign successful and repressive measures were introduced.

1820

Jesuits expelled from the Russian Empire for continuing to proselytize (March).

1825

Accession of Nicholas I, whose reign saw rise of the Slavophiles believing in an orthodox Christianity uncorrupted by the West. Renewed repression of Old Believers.

1826

Suppression of Bible Society.

1827

Introduction of 25-year military service for Jews.

1830

Polish rising, powerfully supported by the Catholic clergy.

1832

Encyclical *Superiori Anno*, in which Pope Gregory directed Polish Catholics to 'obey their mighty Emperor who would show them every kindness' (9 June). This was published in Poland just as the Russian occupying forces were persecuting the Catholic Church.

1835–37

Various measures against old Believers. Their Moscow schools were closed (March 1835) and they were forbidden to take state employment (April). Some designated criminals and liable to transportation to Siberia (1837).

1839

Greek Uniat Church, which had been linked to the Catholic Church, united with the Russian Orthodox Church.

1840

Dispute over Holy Places. Greek lamps in chapel of the Holy Sepulchre in Jerusalem broken by Latin monks.

1841

Dispute over Holy Places. France suggests making Jerusalem a free city.

1842

Gregory XVI published a denunciation of Russian persecution of Catholics in Poland (July).

1846

Dispute over the Holy Places. Bishop of Bethlehem assaulted.

Concordat between Russia and the Holy See arranging a method of appointing Roman Catholic bishops in Russia.

1853

Dispute over the Holy Places led to Russian declaration of war with Ottoman Empire and subsequent Crimean War.

1858

Opposition to the proposed emancipation of serfs. The Church still owns about 3 million serfs attached to its monastic estates. Most bishops against reform, but Bishop Gregory of Kaluga preaches that Christianity and slavery are incompatible.

1863

Catholic rising in Poland. Priests executed, Catholics deported, churches and religious houses sacked. Bismarck hands back to the Tsar Polish refugees who had escaped to Prussia. Pope Pius IX denounces the persecution. The concordat between Russia and the Holy See repudiated by the Tsar.

1866

Diplomatic relations between Russia and the Holy See broken off.

1867

Panslav Congress in Moscow.

1875

Last Apostolic See of Roman Catholic Church suppressed in Russia.

1876–77

Holy War against the Ottoman Empire to 'liberate Balkan Christians' and re-establish Constantinople as a great Christian centre following Bulgarian Massacres (see p. 172).

1880

Constantine Petrovich Pobedonostsev becomes Procurator of the Holy Synod. An active promoter of Russian Orthodoxy, he sanctions the persecution or conversion of other religious groups.

1881

Pobedonostsev begins a widespread persecution of the Jews following the assassination of Alexander II. Many Jews leave Russia for other parts of Europe and America. Pobedonostsev calls on Tsar Alexander III to reassert autocratic rule and opposes talks to improve the position of Catholics in Russia.

1882

Diplomatic relations between Russia and Holy See resumed. May Laws restrict Jews to the south-west of Russia; forbid Jews from becoming lawyers, owning land, holding administrative posts, appealing against court sentence or marrying Christians without conversion. Jewish schools closed and Hebrew books banned.

1883

Pobedonostsev launches drive to establish parish schools throughout European Russia. Publishes Moscow Collection, which sees religion as the foundation of a civilized life and threatened by modernism and democracy.

1884

Lord Radstock and other Plymouth Brethren expelled from Russia. More parish schools established under direction of Holy Synod.

1885

Holy Synod forbids mixed marriages in largely Lutheran Baltic Provinces (Estonia and Latvia) unless children raised in Orthodox faith. Widespread protest.

1892

Salaries of clergy increased and training streamlined in Russia. Anti-Jewish pogrom in Moscow forces thousands to flee.

1894

Pobedonostsev prevents appointment of papal nuncio to St Petersburg and frustrates Church of England efforts to establish relations with the Orthodox Church. Protestant sects are persecuted.

1905

Fr Gapon leads ill-fated 'Bloody Sunday' procession. Group of 32 formed by St Petersburg priests and petition for church reform. Their leader Fr Petrov elected to the second Duma, but sentenced by the Synod to three months' confinement and unfrocked. Group of 32 produce a declaration, approved by Metropolitan Antoni, calling for freedom from state control, the restoration of the patriarchate abolished in 1700, and local religious councils. Religious tolerance law passed. Nonetheless persecution of evangelicals, Old Believers, Jews and Roman Catholics (especially in Poland) continues. Pobedonostsev replaced by Lukyanov.

1906

Fr Gapon assassinated.

1907

Holy Synod declares it incompatible with priestly office to belong to parties opposed to the state and the Tsar.

1908

Holy Synod tells bishops to encourage the participation of the Orthodox clergy in the right-wing League of the Russian People and other conservative societies. Russian Evangelical League founded, calling for moral regeneration to replace class struggle.

1910

Protestant conferences to be vetted by Minister of Interior. They are not allowed to educate their children in their faith.

1911

Rasputin, whose influence at court is very great, causes increasing embarrassment to ecclesiastical and political authorities, and is forced to make pilgrimage to the Holy Land, but returns and causes fresh scandals.

1912

Forty conservative clergy elected to the fourth Duma.

1914

Attempted assassination of Rasputin at the same time as the Archduke Ferdinand was murdered at Sarajevo. Protestants suspected of German affiliations are persecuted. As a result the Old Believers and Evangelicals ceased to support the monarchy.

1916

Rasputin assassinated (30 Dec.).

1917

Synod refuses to condemn the Revolution (Feb.). Provisional government withdraws church schools from church administration and puts them under the Ministry of Education. (June).

CHRISTIANITY AND THE OTTOMAN EMPIRE, 1774–1923

1774

By the Treaty of Kutchuk Kainarji, Russia allowed to build and protect a Christian Church in Galata (Constantinople) and Turkey promises to protect Christian religion in its territories.

1820

London Missionary Society for Promoting Christianity among the Jews founded.

1821

Beginning of Greek revolt. Orthodox clergy headed by Archbishop Germanos of Patras proclaim war of extermination. Orthodox Patriarch Gregory of Constantinople hanged by Sultan as reprisal. Turks massacre 40,000 Greeks in Chios. Sultan proclaims Holy War but the powers intervene and Greece becomes independent. In Cyprus, Archbishop Kyprianos executed for allegedly aiding insurgents.

1828

Greek government refuses to treat with Patriarch of Constantinople who had refused to sanction revolt; 300 smaller monasteries closed and revenues secularized.

1830

Independence of Greece recognized.

1832

Ecclesiastical autonomy for Serbia recognized following independence.

1833

Greek clergy at Navplion establish themselves as an autocephalous church. The Synod decides that the Orthodox Church of Greece is dependent on no external authority. In administration it acknowledges the King of Greece as supreme head. Permanent synod of bishops, who were selected by King, proclaimed the highest ecclesiastical authority.

1840

Dispute between Latin monks and Greeks over Holy Places (see p. 168).

1841

Dispute over the Holy Places. France suggests making Jerusalem a free city.

1846

Renewed dispute over the Holy Places. Bishop of Bethlehem assaulted. Samuel Gobat Bishop of Jerusalem (until 1879).

1847

Pope Pius IX appointed a Catholic Patriarch of Jerusalem.

1849

To forestall Russian claims, Christians admitted to office in Ottoman Empire and guaranteed free exercise of religion.

1850

Patriarch of Constantinople finally forced to recognize Greek Orthodox Church as autocephalous. Metropolitan of Attica *ex-officio* President of the Holy Synod, composed of five bishops and two laymen.

1853

Dispute over Holy Places. Tsar intervenes to protect Christians in Turkey and to confirm Russian rights over the Holy Places. The Western European powers see Russian imperialism at work and ally themselves with Turkey. On 1 November Russia declares war on Turkey (the Crimean War). Britain and France, concerned at the vulnerability of the Ottoman Empire to continued Russian advance, fight to guarantee Ottoman integrity. Seen by Russian Orthodox Church as a complete betrayal.

1856

The Hatt-i Humayun (18 Feb.). The Turkish government forced to make substantial guarantees of the property and rights of Christian minorities. Turkey promises church reform, with Bulgarian bishops and recognition of Bulgarian language in church and school. Promises not implemented.

1860

Bulgaria refuses to recognize any longer the patriarchate of Constantinople. Russia opposes move to bring the Church in Bulgaria under Rome. Massacre of the Maronite Christians in the Lebanon and Damascus by the Druze.

1861

Following Romanian independence, monasteries which had acquired a fifth of country's land were secularized (1863) and transferred to the state. For 30 years no provision made for clergy.

1864

Romanian Church, which had been under the patriarchate of Constantinople, unilaterally proclaims itself national and autocephalous. The patriarchate recognized this independence in 1885.

1866–68

Cretan revolt against Turks (again in 1878, 1889 and 1896–97).

1870

Turks promised to make Bulgarian Church free and national. Bulgarian Exarchate established at Constantinople (1872).

1876

In reply to civil disorders, the Turks massacre at least 12,000 Bulgarian Christians. Outburst of anger in England. Gladstone, in pamphlet *The Bulgarian Horrors and the Question of the East*, which sold 40,000 copies in four days, demands that the Turks should go 'bag and baggage … from the province they have desolated and profaned'.

1879

Serbian Orthodox Church officially recognized as autocephalous under Metropolitan of Belgrade.

1885

Romanian autocephaly officially recognized. Repeated revolts in Armenia (and in 1909 and 1914) receive little assistance from Christian countries.

1893

Romanian priests incorporated as government officials. Maintenance of church and clergy included in general budget.

1894

Turkey agrees to two bishops of the Bulgarian (exarchist) Church working in Macedonia. This lessens the power of the Greek patriarchate at Constantinople and also favours the Bulgarian claim to Macedonia, disputed by Greeks and Serbs.

1895

More than 200,000 Gregorian Armenians massacred. Orthodox protected by Russia, Roman Catholics by France.

1915

Armenians massacred in attempt at extermination to stifle bid for autonomy.

1923

Exchange of Greek and Turkish populations as agreed by the Treaty of Lausanne.

Postscript: In 1926 government recognized Mt Athos, with its 20 monasteries, as self-governing community.

THE GROWTH OF RELIGIOUS TOLERATION IN CONTINENTAL EUROPE, 1782–1905

1782

Edict of Toleration for Austrian Jews.

1787

Edict of Toleration for Huguenots and other non-Catholics in France relieves some civil disabilities of French Protestants.

1789

Outbreak of the French Revolution sees political emancipation (see p. 154).

1790–91

Emancipation in France of the Sephardic Jews (28 Jan. 1790) and the Ashkenazic Jews (27 Sept. 1791).

1798

French invasion of Italy produces legal equality regardless of religious belief by the Turin provisional government. Period of 'First Emancipation' for Jews.

1798

French invasion and occupation of German territories granted Jews civic equality (these rights lost in the reaction after 1814/15).

1802

The 'Organic Articles' promulgated in France (see p. 156).

1805

Emancipation of the Jews following creation of Kingdom of Italy.

1807–13

Series of 'Jew Laws' passed by various German states. Some improvements, some regressive measures, concerning Jewish rights.

1808

Reorganization of French Jewry by the three edicts of Napoleon; notorious for the constraints imposed by the third edict on Jewish economic activity in eastern France.

1812

Edict of Emancipation in Prussia.

1815

Wave of reaction across Europe after defeat of Napoleon and restoration of the pre-revolutionary order. Emancipation abolished in much of Italy (except Tuscany and the Habsburg-controlled lands).

1831

Equality of treatment in France for Catholics, Protestants and Jews where salaries for priests and rabbis paid for by the state (Feb.).

1837

Disturbances in Cologne following arrest of Archbishop of Cologne by Prussian authorities.

1848

The 'Year of Revolutions'. In Germany the Frankfurt National Assembly proclaims civic rights with no regard for religious creed (this was overturned in the reaction in 1850). The *Statuto Albertino* granted similar rights in Piedmont and Tuscany.

1850

Wide-ranging freedom granted to Catholic Church under Prussian constitution.

1862

Baden becomes first German state to complete emancipation of Jews.

1869

Complete religious emancipation declared in the constitution of the North German Confederation.

1870

Jewish and Protestant emancipation completed in Italy following fall of Rome and end of temporal power.

1871

Emancipation set out in the 1869 law adopted throughout the new German Empire (but rapidly followed by the *Kulturkampf* with its attack on church rights, dissolution of Catholic religious orders and expulsion of the Jesuits).

1905

Church and State separated in France.

1911

Separation of Church and State in Portugal following overthrow of the monarchy.

RELIGION IN AMERICA, 1776–1914

1776–83

The American Revolution. Civil and religious liberty secured in some key areas.

1776

Virginia begins to disestablish Anglican Church. Its legislature passes Jefferson's Bill for establishing religious freedom.

1777

New York becomes first state to grant religious freedom and to enfranchise Jews completely. Catholics barred from office.

1784

'Christmas Conference' held at Baltimore. Maryland heralds beginning of Methodist Church in America and period of rapid expansion.

1787

Quakers take lead in rejecting slavery.

1789

Protestant Episcopal Church founded. John Carroll becomes first Roman Catholic Bishop of Baltimore.

1791

Ratification of the Bill of Rights. Article I regarding freedom of religion states that 'Congress shall make no law respecting an establishment of religion'. Number of Methodists exceeds 43,000.

1792

First consecration on American soil (of Rev. Thomas John Claggett as Bishop of Maryland) by the four existing bishops.

1793

Roman Catholic diocese of Louisiana and the Two Floridas created (see 1803 below).

1798–1810

Period of the 'Second Great Awakening' (in Connecticut River Valley). Important leaders include Timothy Dwight (1752–1817), President of Yale, and Lyman Beecher (1775–1863).

1801

Cane Ridge revival in the West and onset of 'camp meetings'. Flourishing of missionary societies and new denominations.

1803

Under the Louisiana Purchase, diocese of New Orleans brought into America (all of the Mississippi Delta added). Numerous French and Spanish missions now added.

1804

Church of Christ (Disciples) emerges among evangelical Presbyterians in Kentucky and later (1809) in Pennsylvania.

1806–19

Split between Unitarian Congregationalists and Trinitarian Congregationalists.

1808

Baltimore elevated to Metropolitan rank by Pope Pius VII; new suffragans for Boston, New York, Philadelphia and Bardstown (subsequently Louisville).

1809

First native American sisterhood established by Mother Elizabeth Bayley Seton in Maryland.

1811

Massachusetts Religious Freedom Act exempts members of non-Congregational churches from taxation for support of establishment.

1815

Death of Archbishop Carroll. American Catholic Church estimated at 125 priests and *c.* 125,000 members. New Jersey elects its first bishop.

1818

Disestablishment in Connecticut of Congregationalists. Ohio first Western state to be organized.

1819

Toleration Act in New Hampshire. Unitarian Christianity preached by William Ellery Channing. The Dedham Case (control of church property now given to the township, not the congregation).

1820

Catholic numbers estimated at 195,000.

1822

First Roman Catholic newspaper founded at Charleston, *United States Catholic Miscellany*.

1823

New Carolina elects first bishop.

1827

Origin of Mormons. Joseph Smith receives revelation of *The Book of Mormon*.

1830

Launch of the *Protestant* (by Protestant ministers), which acts as rallying call for nativist anti-Catholicism.

1830s

A further 'Great Awakening' provides impulse for reform crusades – education, prisons, women's rights and against slavery.

1832

Church of Christ (Disciples) organized.

1833

Massachusetts disestablishes Congregationalism, the end of last remnant of 'establishment'.

1834

Nativist crowd burned down Ursuline Convent at Charlestown, Massachusetts.

1835

First domestic missionary bishop organized – Jackson Kemper (1789–1870) to cover much of the North-West.

1840s

Anti-Catholic feeling fuelled by mass immigration.

1844

Divisions in Methodist ranks over slavery cause three-way split into Methodist Episcopal Church, Methodist Episcopal Church South and the anti-slavery Wesleyan Methodist Connection (founded 1843). Anti-Catholic riots in Philadelphia (13 killed).

1845

Split in Baptist Churches, largely over slavery. Birth of Southern Baptist Convention.

1847

Christian Nurture published by Horace Bushnell. Salt Lake City founded by Mormons.

1848

USA and Papal States establish diplomatic relations. Ending of the US–Mexican War, whereby Mexico abandoned its claims to Texas, New Mexico and California. Influx of Catholics within US borders.

1850

Methodism is largest Protestant denomination. Immigration makes Roman Catholicism largest single religious group in America. Jewish population estimated at 50,000. New Catholic archbishoprics at Cincinnati, New Orleans and New York.

1853

Congregationalists in USA ordain first woman, Antoinette Brown.

1854

Rise of the 'Know-Nothing' party organized to keep Catholics (among others) out of public office.

1858

Paulist Fathers founded, first native religious community for men.

1860

Presbyterian numbers estimated at *c*. 292,000, Methodists at 1,661,000 and Southern Baptists at 650,000.

1873

The liberal Union of American Hebrew Congregations organized by Rabbi Isaac Mayer Wise.

1875

Founder of Christian Science, Mary Baker Eddy, publishes *Science and Health with a Key to the Scriptures*. John McCloskey, Archbishop of New York, becomes first American cardinal. Hebrew Union College organized.

1877

New Hampshire becomes last state to enfranchise Jews.

1879

Case of *Reynolds vs US*. Supreme Court upholds congressional ban on plural marriage.

1880s

Some theological colleges begin to admit women to prepare for non-ordained ministries.

1880

Rise of Afro-American Baptists reflected in formation of National Baptist Convention of America.

1884

Third Plenary Council of Baltimore gives major impetus to Catholic educational efforts.

1889

Central Conference of American Rabbis organized. Opening of the Catholic University of America.

1889

The 'errors' of Americanism condemned by Leo XIII in apostolic letter *Testem benevolentiae*.

1901

Emergence of Pentecostalism, at first in Topeka (Kansas) (see p. 220).

1907

Northern Baptist Convention formed. The same year sees split of National Baptist Convention of America with majority faction becoming Nationalist Convention, USA (Inc.). Publication of *Christianity and the Social Crisis* by Walter Rauschenbusch marks rethinking of Christian ethics. Followed by his *Christianity and the Social Order* (1912) and *A Theology for the Social Gospel* (1917).

1908

Search for Christian unity reflected in foundation of Federal Council of Churches of Christ. Methodist Social Creed adopted as its statement of social principles. Roman Catholic Church granted fully independent status (removed from control of the Congregation of Propaganda).

1909

First publication of best-selling *Scofield Reference Bible*.

1910

Opponents of Darwinian evolution theories pledge themselves to 'The Fundamentals'.

THE RISE OF BLACK RELIGION IN AMERICA, 1787–1918

1787

Foundation of African Methodist Episcopal (AME) Church.

1793

The 'Mother Bethel' Church founded in Philadelphia by breakaway led by Richard Allen (1760–1831).

1805

Birth of Union American Methodist Episcopal Church.

1816

First General Conference held of AME Church.

1821

AME Zion Church begun in New York, founded by James Varick (1750–1827).

1866

African Union Methodist Protestant Church founded.

1869

Foundation of Colored Cumberland Presbyterian Church.

1870

The Christian Methodist Episcopal (CME) Church founded.

1886

United Holy Church founded.

1895

Emergence of National Baptist Convention Inc. In the same year Booker T. Washington's Atlanta Exposition Addresses put forward the 'separate but equal' philosophy of development.

1896

Two new churches founded: the Church of Christ (Holiness) and the Church of God and Saints of Christ.

1901

Emergence of United Free Will Baptist Churches.

1902

Foundation of Triumph the Church and Kingdom of God in Christ.

1905

Free Christian Zion Church of Christ founded.

1906

Niagara Movement organized by W. E. B. DuBois.

1907

National Primitive Baptist Convention founded.

1909

Foundation of the National Association for the Advancement of Colored People (NAACP).

1915

The National Baptist Convention emerged.

THE SPREAD OF NEW RELIGIOUS MOVEMENTS IN AMERICA (TO 1940)

1792

Church of the New Jerusalem founded in Baltimore.

1817

General Convention of the New Jerusalem founded at Boston.

1830

Church of God in North America founded in Harrisburg.

1831

Plymouth Brethren founded.

1840s

Emergence of Seventh Day Adventists.

1847

Establishment of the Mormons (The Church of Jesus Christ of Latterday Saints) at Salt Lake by Brigham Young (1801–77). Various splinter movements later developed.

1854

Christian Union founded in Chicago.

1872

The Jehovah's Witnesses founded in Pittsburgh by Charles Taze Russell (1852–1916).

The original name (until 1931) was International Bible Students.

1875

The founder of Christian Science, Mary Baker Eddy (1821–1910), publishes *Science and Health*.

1876

American Ethical Union founded.

1877

General Church of the New Jerusalem founded in Philadelphia.

1879

Christian Science founded.

1881

Church of God founded at Anderson.

1883

Monthly *Christian Science Journal* founded by Mary Baker Eddy.

1895

Christian National Church founded at Marion.

1898

Weekly *Christian Science Sentinel* founded.

1899

New Thought founded.

1900

Mazdaznan Movement founded in Chicago.

1904

Christ's Sanctified Holy Church founded in Los Angeles.

1908

Christian Science Monitor founded.

1901

Christian Catholic Apostolic Church founded.

1919

Father Divine's Peace Mission Movement established in Sayville.

1921

Oxford Group Movement founded in Philadelphia.

1927

Institute of Religious Science founded in Los Angeles.

1936

Moral Rearmament founded in Philadelphia.

1940

Order of the Cross founded in Los Angeles.

THE RELIGIOUS QUESTION IN IRELAND, 1691–1871

The issue of Catholic Emancipation (or relief) was one of the great political divides of the later part of this period. It involved freeing Catholics from disabilities that prevented them from holding office, voting or serving in Parliament. Unlike Protestant Dissenters, Catholics had received no freedom of worship under the 1689 Toleration Act. Though in practice they did receive a degree of toleration, they were formally excluded from ministerial and administrative office, commissions in the armed services and from universities under a series of Acts known collectively as the Penal Laws.

From 1807, when Sydney Smith, Canon of St Paul's, took up the Protestant Dissenters' cause, agitation grew for the repeal of the Test and Corporation Acts of Charles II. In 1828 they were repealed and the remaining discriminatory legislation against Catholics was shown to be an anachronism. There were only 60,000 Catholics in England, but the majority of the Irish population was Catholic.

1691

Surrender of Limerick. Penal Laws excluded Roman Catholics, three-quarters of the population, from professions, education, civil office, juries, vote, right to arms and horse. Priests proscribed.

1721

Toleration Act passed by Irish parliament.

1747

Wesley's first visit to Ireland; made 42 visits altogether.

First Methodist church, Whitefriars Street, Dublin.

1750

Roman Catholics admitted to lower grades of army.

1771

Bogland Act enabled Roman Catholics to take lease for 61 years of not more than 50 acres of unprofitable land, free of taxes for 7 years.

1774

Act denying the Pope had any civil or temporal authority in Ireland, following declaration by Munster bishops, accepted by most Roman Catholics.

1778

Act to allow Roman Catholics on simple oath to inherit land and take leases.

1779

Roman Catholics supported the Volunteers with equipment and upkeep.

Irish Protestant Dissenters relieved from Test Act.

1782

Protestant Volunteers' congress at Dungannon, Ulster, supported freedom of conscience and declared sympathy with Roman Catholics.

Catholics allowed to purchase land freely and have own schools.

1791

Society of United Irishmen, started by Protestant Theobald Wolfe Tone (1763–98), welcomed Roman Catholics.

1793

Act by Irish Parliament conferred franchise on Roman Catholics on same terms as Protestants. But Catholics could not be MPs nor hold most important offices. They could receive degrees and fellowships at Dublin University.

1795

Religious disorders, e.g. at Armagh. Coalition between Roman Catholics and Presbyterians. Catholics harried.

1798

Insurrection in Wicklow, Wexford. Catholics led by priests.

1800

Catholic Emancipation, with commutation of tithe and provision for Roman Catholic clergy, expected as price of Union with England, but not granted owing to the opposition of George III.

1808

Grattan's motion for Catholic Emancipation defeated in the Commons by 281 votes to 128.

1810

Catholic Committee set up to campaign for Catholic Emancipation. Reconstituted in 1811 as the Catholic Board.

1812

Motion to consider Catholic claims passed by 225 votes to 106.

1813

Emancipation Bill defeated in committee.

1814

Catholic Board dissolved by government order.

1819

Catholic Emancipation Bill defeated in the Commons.

1821

Catholic Emancipation defeated in the House of Lords.

1823

Catholic Association founded by O'Connell to campaign for political and other rights.

1825

O'Connell unsuccessfully prosecuted for incitement to rebellion. Catholic Association suppressed but refounded under new name.

1828

Election of O'Connell for County Clare.

1829

Catholic Emancipation Act. Roman Catholics made eligible for all offices of state except

Regent, Lord Lieutenant and Lord Chancellor. No oath of supremacy required to sit in either house of Parliament. Catholic Association and similar organizations suppressed. £10 franchise replaced 40s franchise in counties.

1833

Irish Church Temporalities Act suppressed 10 sees and reduced the revenues of the rest. Surplus revenues to be administered for purely ecclesiastical purposes.

1838

Tithe Act removes a popular source of grievances.

1845

Grant to Irish Catholic college at Maynooth increased in spite of bitter opposition in Parliament. Irish National Education Board formed.

1845–50

Great famine due to successive failures of potato crop as a result of blight.

Irish population fell from 8,178,124 in 1841 to 6,552,386 in 1851 as a result of deaths and emigration.

1849

Serious affray between Catholics and Protestants at Dolly's Brae.

1862

Catholic University College founded in Dublin.

1869

Disestablishment and Disendowment of the Irish Church. From January 1871 the Church of Ireland was disestablished; all property except churches in use was vested in a body of commissioners for Irish Church temporalities. Compensation set at £16 million, half of the capital of confiscated property, the remainder to be used for public benefit.

THE ENGLISH CHURCH, 1828–1939

1828

Repeal of Test and Corporation Acts, hence admitting Nonconformists to Parliament. Church Building Act passed.

1829

Catholic Emancipation passed; Catholics permitted to sit in Parliament.

1831

Formation of Congregational Union of England and Wales.

1832

Palmer's *Origines Liturgicae* prepares the way for the Oxford Movement and Rose founds *British Magazine* for defence of High Church principles. Church Inquiry: Commissioners appointed.

1833

Keble's Assize Sermon on 'National Apostasy' denounces suppression of 10 Irish bishoprics and is later declared by Newman to have inaugurated the Oxford Movement. *Tracts for the Times* begin to appear. Nonconformists allowed to celebrate marriages in their chapels.

1834

Lords defeat admission of Nonconformists to university degrees. Wesleyan Methodist Association founded.

1835

Wiseman returns to England to lecture on the beliefs and system of Catholicism. Pusey joins the High Church movement.

1836

Tithes paid in kind commuted into a rent charge to vary with the price of corn. Ecclesiastical Commissioners incorporated. Newman's *Prophetical Office of the Church* defines the theory of the Oxford Movement. Church Pastoral Aid Society founded. Solemnization of Marriages Act permits licences to be issued for marriage in register offices and Nonconformist chapels.

1837

Additional Curates Society founded to provide extra clergy.

1838

Pluralities Act and Acts for building and enlarging churches passed. Froude's *Remains,* edited by Newman and Keble, condemns the Reformation.

1840

New Church Discipline Act. Jewish Reform Movement founded.

1841

Tait and three other Oxford tutors issue protest against Tract 90, in which Newman explained the Thirty-nine Articles in a Catholic sense.

Newman censured and persuaded to end the Tracts. Miall founds *The Nonconformist*.

1843

Newman resigns as vicar of St Mary's Oxford. Pusey forbidden to preach for two years. New Parishes Act. 'Disruption' in Scotland and formation of Free Church of Scotland.

1844

Ward's *Ideal of a Christian Church* condemned by Oxford authorities. Nonconformists found Liberation Society.

1845

Ward joins the Roman Catholic Church; Newman follows. Pusey, Marriott and Mozley lead the Anglo-Catholic Party.

1846

The Evangelical Alliance formed to oppose Romanism, Puseyism and rationalism.

1847

United Presbyterian Church of Scotland formed.

1849

Wesleyan Methodist Reformers formed after 'Fly-sheets' controversy leads to expulsion from main body.

1850

Re-establishment of Catholic hierarchy in English sees. Manning (later Cardinal) joins Roman Catholic Church. Pusey censured for use of Catholic devotional literature. Beginning of 'papal aggression' scare in England.

1851

Census of church attendance reveals only half the population regularly attend Sunday worship.

Archdeacon Henry Edward Manning (1808–92) joined Church of Rome (Cardinal 1875).

1854

Act for extending licences of dissenting places of worship.

1859

Darwin publishes the *Origin of Species by Natural Selection*, starting controversy about the literal truth of the Bible.

1860

At meeting of British Association in Oxford, Bishop Wilberforce attacks and Huxley defends Darwin's theory of evolution. English Church Union founded to organize High Church movement. *Essays and Reviews* published and arouse considerable controversy over their 'broad church' views, attaching little importance to nicety of dogma but stressing Christian virtues. Act for opening grammar schools to Dissenters.

1861

Convocation condemns *Essays and Reviews*.

1862

The Pentateuch, by Dr Colenso, Bishop of Natal, asserts the Bible contains 'unhistorical parts'. Condemned by Convocation and excommunicated.

1863

Bishop of London's fund for remedying spiritual destitution founded.

1864

Newman publishes his spiritual autobiography, *Apologia pro Vita Sua.*

1865

'General' William Booth assumes leadership of a Christian Mission for the 'evangelization of the very lowest classes', later called the Salvation Army. Church Association formed to oppose ritualism. Manning appointed Catholic Archbishop of Westminster.

1866

Pope condemns efforts to promote Anglican and Catholic reunion. Act for removing religious oaths for public offices.

1868

Compulsory church rates abolished by Gladstone. Irish Church Disestablishment Bill introduced by Gladstone.

1869

Irish Church Disestablishment passed, effective from 1 Jan. 1871. See p. 186.

1870

Suffragan bishops appointed. Keble College, Oxford, founded. Declaration of papal infallibility by Vatican Council.

1871

Motion for disestablishment of English Church obtains 96 votes. Act for abolition of religious tests at the universities.

1874

Gladstone's pamphlets on Vaticanism declare papal decree of 1870 inconsistent with civil allegiance.

1876

Presbyterian Church of England formed.

1877

Methodist Conference admits laity.

1878

General William Booth formally constituted as superintendent of Salvation Army with control over funds, property and the power to nominate successor. Catholic hierarchy restored in Scotland.

1880

Burials Act allows Christian Dissenters to hold services in the churchyard of the parish.

1881

Revised version of the New Testament appears.

1882

General Booth sets forth his principles in the *Contemporary Review*, upholding the gospel, opposing sectarianism and requiring implicit obedience from his 'soldiers', aiming at the reformation of 'drunkards and other reprobates'.

1888

Lux Mundi, a collection of essays, defines the position of the new Oxford Movement.

1889

Mansfield Congregational College, Oxford, founded.

1890

General Booth publishes *In Darkest England, and the Way Out*, an exposé of destitution and poverty among the 'submerged tenth'. Bishop of Lincoln prosecuted in the Archbishop's Court for High Church practices. First Mosque opened at Woking, Surrey.

1891

Church's *History of the Oxford Movement* published.

1892

Conference held at Grindelwald discusses reunion of Established Church and Nonconformist bodies.

1894

Informal discussions begin about Catholic and Anglican reunion. Bill for disestablishment of Anglican Church in Wales fails to reach second reading in Parliament.

1895

Construction of Catholic Cathedral at Westminster begun.

1896

Pope condemns Anglican Orders and attempt at reconciliation comes to an end.

1898

Benefices Act forbids the public sale of advowsons (see p. 231) and increases the power of bishops. Renewed attacks by Low Church Anglicans upon the ritualist party.

1899

Protestant agitation continues and archbishops pronounce against use of incense and processional lights. Balfour declares in favour of a Catholic university in Ireland.

1900

Free Church of Scotland and United Presbyterian Church of Scotland unite.

1901

Jewish Progressive Movement founded.

1904–5

Great Welsh revival. Large increases in membership of Nonconformist churches.

1906

Royal Commission appointed to consider Welsh Disestablishment.

1907

United Methodist Church formed from several of existing separate Methodist churches.

1910

World Missionary Conference at Edinburgh sees beginning of modern ecumenical movement. See p. 223.

1914

Disestablishment of the Anglican Church in Wales (effective 1920).

1921

Church of Scotland Act confirms its complete independence in all spiritual matters.

1924

Inter-denominational conference held at Birmingham urges churchmen to pay greater attention to social questions.

1927–28

Revised Prayer Book controversy. House of Commons rejects attempt by Church of England to modernize the Prayer Book.

1932

Following a conference at the Albert Hall in London, the Wesleyan Methodists, the Primitive Methodists and the United Methodists join to become the Methodist Church.

THE MISSIONARIES AND AFRICA, 1752–1913

1752

Society for the Propagation of the Gospel (SPG) at work in Gold Coast (Ghana).

1787

Sierra Leone acquired by Britain and used to resettle freed slaves.

1799

London Missionary Society at work (under Robert Moffat) in South Africa.

1806

Church Missionary Society active in Sierra Leone.

1811

Wesleyans begin work in Sierra Leone.

1813

Birth of David Livingstone, the Scottish Christian whose expeditions in Africa captured the Victorian imagination. First Wesleyan mission to Kaffraria (South Africa).

1821

Wesleyans at work in Gambia.

1823

Foundation of Liberia as a place of resettlement for freed American slaves.

1830

Church Missionary Society (CMS) mission to Abyssinia (Ethiopia).

1833

Slave trade suppressed throughout British Empire.

1834

Wesleyans active in Gold Coast.

1840

United Presbyterian Mission of Scotland active in Nigeria.

1840s

Church Missionary Society active in Zanzibar.

1841

Baptists at work in Fernando Po.

1842

Wesleyans and Church Missionary Society active in Nigeria.

1848

Baptists active in Cameroon.

1854

London Missionary Society active among the Matabele of southern Rhodesia (Zimbabwe).

1862

United Methodist Free Churches active in Kenya.

1868

Charles Martial Lavigerie (1825–92) founded Society of Missionaries of Our Lady of Africa (the 'White Fathers').

1874

Stanley in Uganda (CMS mission in 1877).

1876

Universities Mission to Central Africa (UMCA) and Livingstonia Mission (Church of Scotland) active in Nyasaland (Malawi).

1878

Pope assigns White Fathers to mission work in Africa. Livingstone Inland Mission to Congo. Baptists active in Angola.

1880s

Church Missionary Society active in Kenya.

1900

Christianity could claim rapid expansion in the Congo, Nigeria, Uganda and South Africa.

1910

Wesleyans begin activity in northern Rhodesia (Zambia).

1913

Sudan United Missions active.

For the proliferation of breakaway independent African churches, see p. 203.

THE MISSIONARIES AND INDIA, 1698–1857*

1698

Renewal of East India Company's Charter, including instructions to provide chaplains.

1705

King of Denmark sends first Protestant missionaries (Ziegenbalg and Plutscho) to India.

1749

C. F. Schwartz SPCK missionary in South India.

1758

Clive invites Kiernander to Calcutta.

1771

Kiernander builds the 'Old Church', Calcutta.

1786

Colonial Bishoprics Act passed. David Brown arrives at Calcutta. Charles Grant plans a Church and State India Mission. Schwartz in Tinnevelly.

1792

Carey founds the Baptist Missionary Society.

1793

East India Company's Charter renewed. Wilberforce fails to get 'pious clauses' inserted.

Carey arrives in Bengal.

1795

London Missionary Society founded.

1797

Claudius Buchanan at Calcutta.

1798

Death of Schwartz.

1799

Church Missionary Society (CMS) established (12 April). Thomas Scott first Secretary.

1812

First great CMS public meeting, on India Question (24 April).

1812

Claudius Buchanan, at request of CMS, prepares an appeal for an Indian episcopate.

1813

East India Charter renewed. Door opened for Missions in India. Agra Mission begun by Abdul Masih under Corrie's auspices.

1814

Consecration of first Bishop of Calcutta (Middleton) (8 May). Madras Mission begun.

1816

Travancore Mission begun.

1817

Benares Mission begun.

1818

Mission begun in Ceylon (modern Sri Lanka).

1820

Tinnevelly Mission (CMS) begun by Rhenius. Bombay Mission begun.

1823–26

Reginald Heber Bishop of Calcutta.

1824

CMS Mission in Gorakhpur begins.

1825

Abdul Masih ordained, first Native clergyman in India (30 Nov.).

1828

The Hindu Brahmo Samaj founded to reform Hinduism and counter expansion of Christianity.

1829

Abolition of *suttee* by Lord William Bentinck.

1832

Daniel Wilson consecrated Bishop of Calcutta.

1835

Bishopric of Madras established.

1836

Mission to Travancore begun.

1837

Bishopric of Bombay established. Jesuits arrive in India.

1841

Telugu Mission begun by CMS.

1850

Sindh Mission begun by CMS.

1851

Harding Bishop of Bombay.

1854

Sir Charles Wood's Despatch on Education in India.

1855

North India Missionary Conference held at Calcutta.

1857

Indian Revolt (the 'Mutiny') begins at Meerut (10 March).

1858

Suppression of Indian Mutiny. Death of Bishop Daniel Wilson of Calcutta (Cotton succeeds him). Lucknow CMS Mission begun.

1859

Allahabad Mission begun by CMS.

*For the earlier Portuguese missions in India, see p. 126.

195

THE MISSIONARIES IN AUSTRALASIA
AND THE PACIFIC

1788

Establishment of first penal settlement in Australia in New South Wales.

1795

Foundation of London Missionary Society (LMS).

1797

LMS mission ship *Duff* lands in Tahiti. Netherlands Missionary Society begins work in Dutch East Indies (modern Indonesia).

1803

Presbyterianism already established among Scottish immigrants in Sydney.

1814

LMS active in Java. First worship among Maoris in New Zealand.

1815

Tahiti Chief Pomare II accepts Christianity.

1820

American Baptist Church (ABC) arrives in Hawaii (Picpus Fathers follow in 1828).

1821

Protestant missionaries at work in Cook Islands.

1822

English Wesleyan Methodists active in Tonga and among Maoris in New Zealand.

1825

Responsibility given to the Picpus Fathers to evangelize Oceania.

1830

Arrival of Christianity in Fiji by native Protestants from Tahiti. Christianity introduced to Samoa from Tonga.

1834

Christianity arrived in Wallis Islands.

1835

Beginning of Methodist missionary work in Fiji.

1836

William Grant Broughton becomes first (and only) Anglican Bishop in Australia. The Picpus Fathers joined in mission field by Marists who were responsible for West Pacific and New Zealand.

1839

Christianity arrived in New Hebrides from Samoa (LMS arrived 1842).

1840

New Zealand annexed as a British colony. Criticism by such Anglican missionaries as Octavius Hadfield soon disappeared.

1841–67

George Augustus Selwyn served as first Anglican Bishop of New Zealand.

1843

Marists arrive in New Caledonia.

1845

Marists arrive in Solomon Islands. Estimates that around half of Maoris now converted.

1847

Anglican Mission begins work in Sarawak. Netherlands Mennonite Missionary Society arrives in Java.

1857

ABC arrives in Gilbert Islands.

1859

Jesuits arrive in Sumatra.

1871

London Missionary Society begins work in New Guinea.

1874

Australian Methodists begin work in Bismarck Archipelago.

1895

Society of Divine Word active in New Guinea.

THE MISSIONARIES AND THE FAR EAST

CHINA

Early missions (to 1727)

635

Mission from independent Nestorian Church of Persia of senior priest Araben to China. Mission based at Chang'an (now Xi'an). Chapels constructed and preaching undertaken. During later reign of Wu Zong, Christianity banned alongside Buddhism. Christianity extinct in inland China.

1245–53

Two missions of Franciscan Friars reach Mongol capital Qaraqorum (in present-day Mongolia).

1312

Catholic Franciscan friars despatched by Pope Nicholas IV and dioceses created (1312).

1333

Death of Giovanni de Monte Corvino, Archbishop of Peking.

Note: After the fall of the Yuan dynasty, Christianity again became extinct until the sixteenth century Jesuit missions.

Sixteenth–seventeenth century

Jesuit missions begin to penetrate China at end of Ming dynasty. These included MatteoRicci (1552–1610), Julio Aleni (1551–1649), and, later, Jean François Gerbillon (1654–1707).

1715

Condemnation of the 'Chinese rites' (i.e. emphasis on ancestor worship) in the bull *Ex illa die*.

1717

Missions to China banned by edict of Kang-Hsi.

1727

Russo-China Treaty followed by despatch of official Orthodox missionaries from Russia.

The modern era

1773

Suppression of activities of Society of Jesus.

1785

Persecution of Christians.

1800s

Growing attempts at trade with China and introduction of Protestant churches.

1805–11

Renewed period of persecution (in Beijing).

1807

Arrival of London Missionary Society and Robert Morrison (1782–1834) at Canton.

1830

First missionaries of ABC.

1834

Jesuits began work in China.

1839–42

Opium War. Hong Kong acquired by Britain.

1857–58

Taiping Rebellion (major uprising against imperial government).

1865

Formation of the very influential interdenominational China Inland Mission by J. Hudson Taylor (1832–1905). It soon became the largest mission in China and a model for other missionary work.

1870

Anti-foreign, anti-Western outbreak at Tientsin.

1875

Missionary work in Manchuria by Sisters of Providence of Portieux.

1877

First China Missionary Conference at Shanghai (repeated in 1890 and 1907).

1900

The Boxer Rebellion. Major uprising against Western influence. Missionaries were a prime target.

1911

Revolution in China led by Sun Yat-sen.

Postscript

1948

Communists come to power in China. Crisis for Christians.

JAPAN AND KOREA

Note: For sixteenth and seventeenth century early Christian contacts see p. 127.

1785

Jesuit Father Peter Grammont secretly enters Korea. Converts and baptisms follow.

1859

Arrival of Roman Catholic Paris Foreign Missionary Society in Japan. Also arrival of American Presbyterians, American Episcopal Mission and the American Dutch Reformed Church Mission.

1863–76

Twelve Korean priests and a community of 23,000 believers when persecution begins under xenophobic Prince Regent, Taewongun. Emergence of Ch'ondogyo, outspoken nationalist and anti-Western religion. Major series of martyrdoms of Christian missionaries in Korea. National Bible Society of Scotland active (1865).

1872

First of Japan Missionary Conferences (at Yokohama). Followed by Tokyo (1878), Osaka (1883) and Tokyo again (1900).

1876

Korean persecution ceased when Western powers force treaties on Korea. Influx of Protestant missionaries begins, led by Horace N. Allen, US medical doctor.

1909

Bavarian Benedictines begin work in Korea.

1910

Korea annexed by Japan.

1925

Beatification of 79 Koreans martyred during the Choson Dynasty persecution.

1940

Expulsion of foreign missionaries by Japan.

1950–53

Korean War sees major increase in Catholic relief work and other Christian missions.

1962

Catholic hierarchy established in Korea.

1984

Canonization of 93 Korean and 10 French missionary martyrs by Pope John Paul II. First canonization ceremony outside the Vatican (giving Korea fourth largest number of Catholic saints in the world).

1991

Protestants 34 per cent of the religious population (54 per cent declare a religion), Catholics 10.6 per cent and Buddhists 51.2 per cent.

THE MISSIONARIES AND SOUTH AMERICA, 1815–1914

1819

Despatch of 500 Bibles by American Bible Society for school use in Brazil.

1822

British and Foreign Bible Society active in Peru.

1835

American Methodist Mission in Brazil.

1836

American Methodist missionary in Buenos Aires. Franciscan missionary group from Europe entered Bolivia and also Chile.

1849

Moravians began work in Nicaragua.

1853

Arrival of 19 Franciscan missionaries in Argentina.

1855

First Protestant Church at Valparaiso (Chile).

1856

Presbyterian mission at work in Bogotá (Colombia).

1858

American Bible Society begins work in Argentina.

1860

Renewal of work by Franciscans in Ecuador.

1865

American and Foreign Christian Union begins work in Mexico at Monterey.

1869

First Anglican Bishop of the Falkland Islands (Waite H. Stirling, 1829–1923).

1872

Renewal of Roman Catholic missions in Mexico.

1882

Protestant missionaries active in Guatemala City.

1894

Capuchin mission begins work in Venezuela.

1897

Caracas receives Northern Presbyterian mission.

1900

Renewal of missionary work by Jesuits among Mexican Indians.

1901

American Methodist Mission begins work in Bolivia.

1903

Chaco Indians begin to be converted by Protestant San Pedro Mission in Paraguay.

1910

Missions to Paraguay by Society of the Divine Word.

Source: Littell, *Illustrated History of Christianity* (2nd edn, 2003).

THE GROWTH OF INDEPENDENT AFRICAN CHRISTIAN MOVEMENTS, 1872–1966

Note: From the late nineteenth century, a feature of Christianity in Africa was the proliferation of breakaway splinter churches often under local leadership. Many of these independent churches adopted forms of worship and other activities not always approved by the more traditional churches.

1872

Kiyoka secession (Congo).

1884

Tembu Church (South Africa).

1888

Native Baptist Church founded (Nigeria).
Native Baptist Church founded (Cameroon).

1891

United Native Africa Church (Nigeria).

1892

Ethiopian Church (South Africa).

1898

African Presbyterian Church founded (South Africa).

1899

Schism in Dahomey Methodist Church.

1901

Africa Church Inc. founded (Nigeria).

1911

Nazirite movement (Zulu Independent Church) founded by Zulu prophet Isaiah Shembe (1870–1935). Interpreted Christianity in a specifically Zulu way relating to traditional African society.

1913–15

Ivory Coast witnesses first great African native revival led by William Wade Harris (repressed by colonial rulers). Birth of the 'Harris Church'.

1914

Society of the One Almighty God formed (Uganda).

1921

Foundation of Church of Jesus Christ on Earth by the prophet Simon Kimbangu in Congo (see Kimbanguism, p. 251). It became the largest independent church in Africa.

1923

Church of Ashes of Purification (Ivory Coast).
Army of the Cross of Christ Church (Ghana).

1930

Church of the Lord formed (Nigeria). The prophet Mayange secedes (Cabinda).

1931

Christ Apostolic Church formed (Nigeria).

1935

African Orthodox Church founded (Kenya).

1937

Creation of Bantu Independent Churches' Union links breakaway churches with charismatic native prophet movements (South Africa).

1939

Church of the Blacks founded (Congo). Apostolic Revelation Society (Ghana).

1942

Africa Israel Church founded (Kenya).

1945

African Brotherhood Church established (Kenya).

1949

The Red Star Cult (Angola).

1953

Church of the Holy Spirit founded in Tanganyika (modern Tanzania).

1954

Lumpa Church formed (Zambia).

1955

Kambatta Evangelical Church (Ethiopia).

1956

Tanganyika Africa Church founded.

1957

Church of Christ in Africa begins in Kenya with around 75,000 former Anglicans.

1963

Church of God established (Burundi). Legio Maria Church begun by former Roman Catholics (Kenya).

1966

God's All Times Association (Ethiopia).

For explosion in the number of churches and followers, see p. 320.

THE CHURCH IN THE AGE OF THE DICTATORS, 1918–45

1918

Conservative regime of Sidonia Pais in Portugal revokes anti-clerical measures and reopens diplomatic relations with the papacy. Cult of Our Lady of Fatima becomes increasingly popular after three children claim to have seen the Virgin on a hillside in Extremadura.

1919

Catholic *Partito Popolare* formed (Jan.) in Italy. Pope lifts ban on Catholic participation in political life and in following elections (Nov.) Catholics strongly represented.

United Evangelical Protestant National Church reorganized in Germany.

1920

Moves towards reconciliation with papacy in France.

Canonization of Joan of Arc.

Cardinal Pacelli, later Pius XII, becomes papal nuncio in Berlin.

1929

Lateran treaties with papacy recognizing the Vatican as a state and the Pontiff as its head. The Church assumes privileged status in Italy and formal reconciliation between the papacy and Kingdom of Italy takes place.

1931

Constitution of Republic separates Church and State; reduces clerical salaries; forbids Orders to teach and suppresses the Jesuits in Spain.

Pius XI publishes encyclical *Quadragesimo Anno* on his ideas of the corporate state.

1932

Widespread attacks on church property in Madrid, Barcelona and southern Spain. Over 55 churches or convents destroyed. Protestant group founds pro-Nazi 'German Christians'.

1933

Pope Pius XI protests in encyclical *Dilectissima nobis* about anti-clerical measures in Spain.

Publicly praises Hitler for his stand against communism and German bishops withdraw their opposition. Hitler and chairman of German Catholic Centre Party hold discussions and Centre Party supports Enabling Act (March). Centre Party dissolves itself (July). Concordat signed between Nazi Germany and Holy See (July); ratified in September. Ludwig Muller of German Christians becomes Bishop of the Reich. Protestant churches amalgamate as German Evangelical Church.

1934

Priests and religious in Oviedo murdered during Asturias rising in Spain.

The Protestant Barmen Synod accuses German Christians of departing from the Gospels and abandoning the legal basis of the Protestant churches.

1935

Nuremberg Laws deprive Jews of citizen rights and forbid sexual relations and inter-marriage. Hitler sets up ministry of church affairs.

1936

Attacks on church property following election of Popular Front; 160 churches or convents destroyed and 269 clergy killed. Renewed attacks and atrocities in Spain following the outbreak of war: 12 bishops and over 7,000 religious and clergy killed. Pius XI denounces 'the satanic enterprise' and blesses Franco's cause. Franco declares 'Spain shall be an empire turned towards God'.

1937

Protestant Church deprived of control of its finances. Protestant opposition in Germany forbidden. Pastor Niemöller and other Protestant pastors arrested and sent to concentration camps.

Papal encyclical on atheistic communism.

1938

Diplomatic relations renewed in Spain between papacy and Nationalists. The Pope calls for the re-establishment of a Catholic Spain. Anti-Jewish pogrom on 9–10 November, the *Kristallnacht*, arouses protests from some church groups in Germany.

1939

Cardinal Pacelli becomes Pope Pius XII.

1941

Germans begin extermination of Jews in occupied territories of Poland and Russia.

Beginning of construction of camps primarily for the systematic murder of Jews. Mass deportations of Jews from Germany to camps in the east begin.

Cardinal Galen of Munster condemns Nazi euthanasia programme.

1942

Heydrich chairs 'Wannsee Conference' of Nazi officials in Berlin which adopts the 'final solution' of deportation and extermination of European Jewry. Hitler closes diplomatic channels with the Vatican.

Dutch bishops issue a public protest against the deportation of Jews to Germany.

1943

Archbishop Suchard of Paris founds worker-priest movement.

Continuation of mass extermination programme by the Nazis. Belsen concentration camp opened. Destruction of Jewish Ghetto in Warsaw.

1945

Mass extermination of European Jews continues until the last days of the war.

CHRISTIANITY UNDER COMMUNISM, 1917–90

1917

The February Revolution, followed by abdication of Tsar Nicholas II and formation of a provisional government (March). Synod refuses to condemn revolution. Communists led by Lenin seize power in 'October Revolution' (Oct.). Patriarch Tikhon (elected in Nov.) and synod oppose Communists. Liberal clergy support.

1918

Separation of Church and State (Jan.). Abolition of religious teaching and publications, censorship of sermons, and ban on church youth groups. Clergy deprived of vote, have to pay higher taxes, and children debarred from higher education. Churches may be used for secular purposes.

1921

Anti-Soviet clergy call a *Sobor* (church council) at Karlovtsy in Yugoslavia endorsing anti-Bolshevik cause and calling for return of the monarchy.

1922

Trial and execution of Metropolitan Veniamin for resistance to seizure of church treasure decreed by state for famine relief in Volga region. Patriarch Tikhon put under house arrest.

1923

Reformist clergy of so-called 'Living Church' hold *Sobor*, strip Patriarch Tikhon of titles and clerical status, pass resolutions in favour of socialist reconstruction of society; also give more influence to clergy in church administration and make married priests eligible to become bishops. Produces split among faithful and eventually among the 'Living Church'. Patriarch Tikhon offers muted support for Soviet State and is released from house arrest.

1927

After period of uneasy compromise, Metropolitan Sergei proclaims full support for Soviet State. Beginnings of widespread persecution of Islam and Islamic customs; mosques closed, mullahs displaced, veils banned and Islamic courts and schools closed. Polygamy, bride-money and Ramadan stopped or discouraged.

1929

Legislation on 'religious associations'. Religious activity only permitted to registered congregations each of which has to consist of at least 20 people over eighteen, who can hire church buildings and engage a priest. All outside religious activity prohibited. Evangelism banned.

1936

Widespread purge of clergy and bishops. Of 163 bishops active in 1930 only 12 still at liberty in 1939.

1941

German invasion of Russia. Russian Orthodox Church pledges support for war with Germany.

1943

Patriarchate and ecclesiastical administration re-established. Seminaries and theological academies opened, and churches permitted to reopen. Government appoints special Council for Church Affairs to supervise.

1945

Election of Patriarch Alexy. Victory of Soviet Russia in World War II followed by Communist takeover of Eastern Europe.

1946

The 'Living Church' abolished in Russia and the Uniat Church also banned.

1948

Trial of Cardinal Stepinac, Archbishop of Zagreb and Primate of Croatia, on charges of wartime collaboration (Sept.). Crackdown in Romania requires all clergy to take an oath of loyalty to the state (Aug.).

1949

Cardinal Josef Mindszenty, Archbishop of Esztergom and Roman Catholic Primate of Hungary, together with six others, is found guilty in Budapest on charges of high treason (Feb.). Vatican excommunicated all those involved in his trial. Anti-clergy trials in Bulgaria (false accusations of espionage).

1950

Nationalization without compensation of church estates in Poland. Monasteries nationalized in Czechoslovakia. Renewed attacks on Church in Hungary.

1951

Virulent oppression of churches in Czechoslovakia provokes papal excommunication.

Ten Romanian Roman Catholic priests and laymen, including the Bishop of Timisoara, are found guilty by a military court in Bucharest on charges of espionage and anti-state activities. Four are sentenced to hard labour for life and the Bishop (aged 81) to 18 years' solitary confinement. The Vatican excommunicates all Romanians who have persecuted, or helped persecute.

1952

Crackdown in East Germany of connections of churches to the West.

1953

Death of Stalin.

1958–64

Anti-Religious Campaign launched by Khrushchev (lasts until 1964) in Russia.

1961

Synod of bishops removes priests' function as legal administrator of parish and explicitly confines them to spiritual function. In next three years over half of existing parishes are disbanded, 10,000 churches and most monasteries closed in Soviet Union, including Monastery of the Caves in Kiev. Orthodox Churches join World Council of Churches.

1964

Khrushchev replaced as Soviet leader by Brezhnev (Oct.).

1965

Letter to Supreme Soviet by Eshliman and Yakunin criticizes Council for Affairs of Church.

1966

Demonstration at Supreme Soviet building in Moscow by Baptist protester.

1968

'Chronicle of Current Events' first issued.

1969

Initiative Group for Defence of Civil Rights formed (Jan.).

1972

'Chronicle of Lithuanian Catholic Church' first appears.

1976

Formation of Helsinki Watch Groups in USSR.

1987

President Gorbachev indicates a major relaxation towards the Russian Orthodox Church, the training of priests, and opening of places of worship.

1988

Russian Orthodox Church openly allowed to celebrate its millennium and three seminaries opened.

1989

President Gorbachev meets the Pope in Rome and reaches agreement in principle on the opening of diplomatic relations with the Vatican and the ending of the ban on the Catholic Church (Uniat) of the Ukraine in force since 1946.

Postscript

1990

The law on Freedom of Religions passed, declaring for first time in Russian history that religious freedom is an 'inalienable right of Russian citizens'.

1992

Kremlin cathedrals returned to Orthodox Church by state.

1997

Tensions increase over proselytization by non-Orthodox. New law on Freedom of Conscience and Religious Associations seriously restricts activities of new religious associations and those from abroad.

2000

Canonization of Tsar Nicholas II, the last tsar.

2003

Number of dioceses now 128 in Russia (compared to 67 in 1989).

THE CATHOLIC CHURCH AND THE MODERN WORLD

1945

Roman Catholicism becomes state religion in Spain under Franco. Eastern Europe falls under Soviet influence.

1948–49

Expulsion of Western missionaries from China.

1950

Papal decree *Humani Generis* against Existentialism and erroneous scientific theories. Pius XII pronounces dogma on Bodily Assumption of the Virgin Mary.

1951

Communist China severs links with the Vatican.

1953

Spain signs concordat with papacy entrenching position of Catholic Church in Spain.

1954

Worker-priest crisis in France.

1955

General Conference of the Latin American Episcopate (CELAM) organized in Rio de Janeiro.

1958

Death of Pius XII. Election of Pope John XXIII. Consecration of bishops in China without Vatican approval.

1959

Pope John XXIII announces the calling of the first Vatican Council since 1870. Vatican orders French worker-priest movement to discontinue. Oppression of Church in Cuba.

1960

Pope receives Anglican Archbishop of Canterbury at Rome.

1961

Papal encyclicals on Catholic social doctrine and for Christian reconciliation under Rome's primacy.

1962

John XXIII insists on retention of Latin as the language of the Roman Catholic Church. Second Vatican Council (see p. 307) opens with observer delegates from other Christian churches.

1963

Death of Pope John XXIII. Accession of Pope Paul VI. Vatican Council approves use of vernacular liturgies. Encyclical *Pacem in Terris* deals with peaceful settlement of disputes and with relations with non-Catholics and communists.

1964

Paul VI makes pilgrimage to Holy Land. Sudan expels missionaries.

1965

Vatican Council promulgates documents exonerating the Jews from the death of Christ.

The Catholic Church and the Eastern Orthodox Church agree to retract the excommunication put on each other in 1054. Worker-priests allowed to resume work in France.

1966

All churches in China closed during Cultural Revolution.

1967

Rights granted to non-Catholic denominations in Spain.

1968

Papal encyclical *Humanae Vitae* reaffirms Catholic doctrine of opposition to artificial birth control. Second General Conference of Latin American bishops (CELAM) at Medellin, Colombia, attended by Paul VI, first pope to visit South America.

1970

Pope reaffirms celibacy of clergy as a law of the Church.

1972

Reorientation of Catholic Church in Latin America gathered pace at CELAM meeting in Sucre, Bolivia.

1973

Sacred Congregation for the Doctrine of the Faith reaffirms papal infallibility and the Church's unique claim to be the authentic Church of Christ. Persecution of radical Christians in Chile.

1975

Suspension of rebel Archbishop Lefebvre in France.

1976

Roman Catholic Sacred Congregation for the Doctrine of the Faith rejects women's ordination in *On the Question of the Admission of Women to the Ministerial Priesthood.*

1978

Death of Pope Paul VI, followed by sudden death of his successor, Pope John Paul I. Election of Cardinal Karol Wojtyla of Cracow, who became first non-Italian pope since election of Adrian of Utrecht in 1522. In Spain, a new constitution promulgated.

1979

Liberal theology attacked by John Paul II at Puebla, Mexico. Reopening of churches in China. Nobel Peace Prize awarded to Catholic nun Mother Theresa (famous for her work in Calcutta). Papal visit to Poland marks first visit of a pope to a communist country since World War II. First papal visit to Ireland.

1980

In Poland, Gdansk agreement with striking shipyard workers includes permission for religious broadcasts (Aug.); Polish Roman Catholic hierarchy pledge support for newly formed Solidarity organization (Oct.). Murder of Archbishop Romero of San Salvador.

1981

Pope John Paul II is seriously wounded by a Turkish gunman in Rome (13 May).

Legalization of divorce in Spain. Archbishop Glemp criticizes introduction of martial law (Dec.) but urges Poles to refrain from violence.

1982

Pope attempts to mediate in dispute between Argentina and Great Britain after Argentina invades the Falkland Islands. First papal visit to Britain since the Reformation is followed by papal visit to Argentina.

1983

Revised Code of Canon Law issued. Pope meets Lech Walesa during visit to Poland (June) and defends right to join free trade unions.

1984

Spanish socialist government introduces law requiring private schools in receipt of state funds to accept pupils without regard for religious views of the parents; mass demonstrations by Catholics who fear loss of control over church schools. Pro-Solidarity priest Father Jerzy Popieluszko kidnapped and killed by policemen. Major outcry leads to imprisonment of the perpetrators.

1985

Spain introduces limited availability of abortion.

1986

Irish referendum votes against changes in the law on divorce following clerical opposition to the measure. First ever visit by a pope to a Jewish synagogue.

1989

Beginning of collapse of Communism in Eastern Europe. New era of liberation for churches in former Soviet bloc. Excommunication of rebel French Archbishop Lefebvre.

1990

Diplomatic relations re-established with many former East European communist states by the Vatican.

1992

Publication of Catechism of the Catholic Church. Vatican recognizes Russian Federation. Diplomatic relations established with Croatia, Slovenia and Ukraine.

1993

Papal encyclical *Veritatis Splendor*. Formal diplomatic relations established between Vatican and State of Israel.

1995

Encyclical *Evangelium Vitae* against artificial birth control and abortion. Catholics in Ireland embroiled in scandal over pay-offs of ex-mistresses of priests.

1996

Catholics in Scotland in crisis after desertion of bishop to live with his mistress raises question of celibacy.

1997

Pope visits Bosnia, preaching reconciliation of religious and ethnic groups. Also visits Poland. Catholic Church accepts responsibility for its part in wartime deportation of Jews in France (Sept.).

1998

Polish National Assembly ratifies concordat with Roman Catholic Church. Visit of Pope John Paul II to Cuba.

2000

Vladimir Putin, President of the Russian Federation, received in audience with Pope.

2003

Beatification of Mother Theresa of Calcutta. Apostolic visit to Bosnia and Herzegovina.

2004

Papacy sent gift of icon of Mother of God of Kazan to Patriarch Alexy II. Switzerland agrees to appoint Ambassador to the Holy See for first time. Gay rights debate in Spain angers Catholics. Spain passes law allowing embryonic stem cell research.

2005

Historic visit of President of Israel to the Vatican heralds reconciliation between Catholics and Jews. Death of Pope John Paul II (2 April). Election of Cardinal Joseph Ratzinger as Pope Benedict XVI. Number of Christians in China reported to exceed membership of Communist Party.

2006

First encyclical of Pope Benedict XVI, *Deus Caritas Est* (God is Love). Tensions between liberal Jesuits and conservatives leads to resignation of the Jesuit head, the Dutch Father Peter-Hans Kolvenbach. Outcry in Muslim world after Pope quotes remarks of Byzantine Emperor on Islam (Sept.).

THE ANGLICAN CHURCH SINCE 1939

1940

In letter to *The Times*, leading churchmen urge creation of a more egalitarian and just society as a postwar objective.

1942

William Temple becomes Archbishop of Canterbury. His *Christianity and the Social Order* outlines advances in social welfare as necessary to a Christian society.

1944

Geoffrey Fisher appointed Archbishop of Canterbury. Florence Li Tim-Oi (1907–92) ordained first woman priest in the Anglican Communion (25 Jan.).

1960

Geoffrey Fisher, Archbishop of Canterbury, visits Rome and meets the Pope. First to do so since the Reformation.

1961

Michael Ramsey becomes Archbishop of Canterbury.

1962

Consecration of new Coventry Cathedral.

1963

Controversy aroused by the radical theology of the Bishop of Woolwich's (John Robinson) *Honest to God*. Sales reach 300,000 copies.

Anglican–Methodist 'Conversations' about unification.

1964

Dr Coggan, Archbishop of York, advocates 'marriage' between Anglican and Methodist churches.

1965

Dr Heenan, Roman Catholic Archbishop of Westminster, created Cardinal.

1969

The Sharing of Church Buildings Act enables agreements to be made by two or more churches for the sharing of church buildings.

1970

Translation of the New English Bible completed.

1972

United Reformed Church formed from the merger of the Congregational Church of England and Wales and the English Presbyterian Church. General Synod of the Church of England fails to approve a scheme for Anglican–Methodist unity already approved by Methodists.

1975

Resolution passed by General Synod of Church of England that there were no fundamental objections to the ordination of women.

1979

Revised Prayer Book introduced for Anglican services.

1981

Anglican General Synod votes overwhelmingly to admit women to Holy Orders as deacons. Further merger of Free Churches as Reformed Association of the Churches of Christ.

1982

Pope John Paul II visits Britain.

1985

Church of England report 'Faith in the City' criticized by the government for depiction of inner-city problems.

1986

Church of England passes measure allowing women to become deacons.

1990

George Carey enthroned as 103rd Archbishop of Canterbury (April).

1992

Decision taken at General Synod of Church of England to allow ordination of women to the priesthood, subject to approval in Parliament.

1994

First 32 women priests ordained in Bristol Cathedral (12 March). First 42 women priests ordained in Scottish Episcopal Church (Dec.).

Several prominent defections from the Anglican Church to Roman Catholicism.

1995

Turnbull Commission report recommends sweeping changes in administrative structure of Church of England. Opening of Hindu temple in Neasden, north London – the largest centre for Hindu worship outside India itself.

1996

Movement for the Ordination of Women Bishops founded. Question of gay clergy in Anglican orders continues to cause dissension in Church of England.

1997

Around 10 per cent of Anglican priests now women. First women Anglican priests ordained in Wales.

1998

Changes to central structure of the Anglican Church with creation of a new Archbishops Council. Formal conversations between the Anglican and Methodist churches about unity scheduled for 1999; also informal trilateral talks between Anglicans, Methodists and the United Reform Church to begin. Lambeth Conference rejects homosexual practice as 'incompatible with scripture' and advises against the 'legitimising or blessing of same-sex unions' and of 'ordaining those involved in same-gender unions'.

2003

Consecration of 'Gene' Robinson (an openly gay father) as Bishop of New Hampshire in the USA reignites controversy. Lambeth Commission set up.

2004

Windsor Report, published by Lambeth Commission, calls for repentance from US Church and moratoria on future gay consecrations and same-sex blessings.

2006

Further consternation among conservative Anglicans as Episcopal Church in the USA elects first woman, Bishop Katharine Jefferts Schori, as Presiding Bishop, equal in status to an archbishop. Delegates in uproar. ECUSA also decides its future name will be the Episcopal Church.

2007

Conference in Tanzania of leaders of the Anglican Communion effectively gives US Episcopal Church seven months to curb gay rights or face possible eviction.

Prime Minister Gordon Brown abandons role in selection of senior bishops.

RELIGION IN AMERICA SINCE 1914

1916

Apostolic Overcoming Church of God formed (a Black Foundation).

1918

Merger forms United Lutheran Church.

1919

Father Divine's Peace Mission Movement established in Sayville. Apostolic Faith Inc. organized (a Black Church).

1921

Oxford Group Movement founded in Philadelphia.

1925

The infamous Scopes Trial takes place in Dayton, Tennessee. Supreme Court accepts parental right to send children to parochial or private schools (*Pierce v. Society of Sisters*).

1927

Institute of Religious Science founded in Los Angeles.

1928

Strong anti-Catholic sentiment aroused to defeat Democratic presidential candidate Alfred E. Smith.

1930

American Lutheran Church formed.

1932

Northern Baptists split over beliefs (and again in 1947). Christ Church Union formed.

1936

Morel Rearmament founded in Philadelphia.

1939

Methodist divisions begin to heal. Merger of Methodist Episcopal Church, Methodist Episcopal Church South and Methodist Protestant Church.

1940

Order of the Cross founded in Los Angeles.

1945

Four American Roman Catholics become cardinals.

1948

POAU founded (Protestants and Other Americans for Separation of Church and State). Opposed establishment of diplomatic relations with the Vatican and federal aid to private religious schools.

1949

Billy Graham (probably the best-known of all evangelists) commences work.

1950

National Council of Churches succeeds earlier Federal Council of Churches of Christ. Northern Baptist Convention becomes American Baptist Convention.

1956

Ordination of women by Methodists and Presbyterians. Number of Roman Catholic dioceses reaches 134 (after sees created in Atlanta, Jefferson City, etc.).

1957

United Church of Christ formed from merger of Congregational Christian with Evangelical and Reformed churches.

1958

Southern Christian Leadership Conference (SCLC) organized by Martin Luther King.

1959

Catholics become largest religious group in Congress (12 Senators and 91 Representatives), followed by Methodists.

1960

John F. Kennedy the first Catholic to become US President.

1962

Consultation on Church Unity (COCU) convened, attempting to unite nine major denominations.

1962–65

Major changes to Catholic Church following Second Vatican Council.

1963

School prayers banned in ruling by Supreme Court. The speech of Martin Luther King at the Lincoln Memorial ('I have a dream') (28 Aug.). Seen by many as the pinnacle of Christian teaching in modern America. Elizabeth Seton (founder in 1809 of first native Catholic sisterhood) becomes first American to be beatified.

1967

Roman Catholic dioceses in USA now 154.

1968

Union of the Methodist churches which merged in 1939 with the Evangelical United Brethren to form the United Methodist Church. Assassination of Martin Luther King in Memphis, Tennessee. Publication of Mary Daly's *The Church and the Second Sex.*

1970s

Beginnings of emergence of Christian Right popular movements.

1973

American Baptist Churches in the USA formed from American Baptist Convention. *Roe v. Wade* recognizes women's constitutional right to an abortion in certain circumstances.

1974

First woman ordained Episcopal priest in USA (Betty Bone Schiess).

1977

Growth in support for Christian Right following the Dale County, Florida, referendum on a gay rights ordinance. New organization, Save our Children, formed.

1978

The Christian Right–National Christian Action Coalition formed.

1979

Formation of Moral Majority (by Rev. Jerry Falwell), Christian Voice, Religious Roundtable (all Christian Right).

1980

Strength of fundamentalism demonstrated in the 'Washington for Jesus' rally.

1983

American Coalition for Tradition Values (ACTV) founded.

1984

Full US diplomatic relations with the Vatican established (first time in 117 years). United Methodist Church grants women's ordination to the episcopacy.

1986

Christian Right Liberty Federation founded.

1987

Christian Right–American Freedom Coalition founded. Continuing debate over Creationism v. Darwinism (e.g. *Edwards v. Aguillard* in the Supreme Court).

1988

Foundation of Christian Right Family Research Council.

1989

US Episcopal Church grants ordination of women to the episcopacy. First woman black Episcopal bishop appointed (Barbara Harris). Conservatives issue Danvers statement.

1992

In Supreme Court, *Planned Parenthood v. Casey* effectively upholds *Roe v. Wade* decision. Evangelical Lutheran Church in America grants ordination of women to episcopacy.

1993

The Religious Freedom Restoration Act becomes law (declared unconstitutional in 1997 by Supreme Court).

1998

Number of Catholics estimated at 68 million.

1999

Largest Lutheran denomination narrowly in favour of uniting with Episcopalians.

2001

Establishment of a White House Office of Faith-Based and Community Initiatives.

2003

Election of Vicky Imogene (Gene) Robinson, a gay divorced father of two, as Bishop of New Hampshire. Major divisions follow in Anglian Communion and schism threatens, see pp. 215–16.

MODERN PENTECOSTALISM

Note: Pentecostalism had been a feature of such movements as the Montanists, Shakers, Irvingites, Mormons and so forth long before the twentieth century. But its astounding growth in the last 100 years has been phenomenal since its traditional starting date in Kansas in 1901.

PENTECOSTALISM IN THE USA AND CANADA

1873

Birth of Charles Parham (1873–1929), generally recognized as founder of the Pentecostal Movement.

c. 1886

The Latter Rain Movement in Tennessee, an early manifestation of Pentecostalism.

1901

Traditional date for origins of the movement at the Bethel Bible School, Topeka, Kansas when Agnes Ozman, a pupil of Parham, spoke in tongues (1 Jan.).

1906

Founding of the Azusa Street Apostolic Faith Mission in Los Angeles by William Seymour (1870–1922), a black son of former slaves and one-time pupil of Parham, begins religious revival. Part of the 'Classical Pentecostal' group.

c. 1908

Introduction of the 'Finished Work of Calvary' doctrine by William H. Durham.

This declared conversion and sanctification a single act of grace. Most American Pentecostalists went along with this doctrine.

1914

The 'Finished Work' denomination organized into the Assemblies of God. But the 'Finished Work' denomination itself already divided by 'Oneness' or 'Jesus Only' Pentecostals.

1916

Pentecostalism now clearly split into three major strands.

1930s

Divisions among Pentecostalists reflected in splits along racial divides.

1943

Formation of National Association of Evangelicals by various Pentecostal groups.

1945

Oneness Pentecostals come together in the United Pentecostal Church.

1948

Pentecostal Fellowship of North America organized by the largest white-only denominations. Revival of New Order of the Latter Rain in Saskatchewan rapidly spreads worldwide.

1953

The Full Gospel Business Men's Fellowship founded by Demos Shakarian on encouragement of Oral Roberts (b. 1918).

1960s

Neo-Pentecostal charismatic movement takes off (following Father Dennis Bennett's 'Baptism in the Spirit') in California.

1967

Charismatic movements attract large numbers of Catholic students at such campuses as Duquesne, Notre Dame and Michigan State.

1970s

Pentecostalists attracted politically to the New Right in its reaction to 1960s radicalism.

1972

First of General Conferences on Charismatic Renewal held in Kansas City.

1973

Beginning of annual conference of Roman Catholic Pentecostals at University of Notre Dame.

1975

Teaching of C. Peter Wagner and John Wimber at Fuller Theological Seminary on 'Signs and Wonders' as the key to evangelism.

1985

Association of Vineyard Churches organized by John Wimber.

1994

Extreme manifestations of Pentecostalism at the Toronto Airport Vineyard Church. The old Pentecostal Fellowship of North America disbanded and replaced with a racially integrated organization.

1996

New Apostolic Church movement founded by Wagner.

THE SPREAD OF GLOBAL PENTECOSTALISM

1907

Rapid spread of Pentecostalism in Scandinavia by Thomas Ball Barratt from his church Kristiania (Oslo) Bymission. Barratt, an English-born Methodist minister, had been converted to Pentecostalism in New York in 1906.

In Britain, Pentecostalist centre established at All Saints Church, Sunderland, by the Anglican clergyman Alexander A. Boddy. Movement soon led by Welsh miners.

Pentecostalist revival in Germany in Hesse-Kassel. Pentecostalism reaches India (little impact until 1940s) and Chile.

1908

Pentecostalism takes root in Italy led by Italian-Americans from Chicago. Emergence of the segregationist Apostolic Faith Mission in South Africa. Pentecostalism reaches China.

1910

Establishment of Pentecostal movement in Brazil and subsequent spread elsewhere in Latin America.

1913

Beginning of the movement (but no real success until the 1950s) in Japan.

1921

Widespread popularity of preaching of Simon Kimbangu in the Congo.

(Early) 1920s

Growth of the Aladura (the 'Praying People') in Nigeria inspired by Pentecostal literature.

1920s

Spread of Pentecostalism in Eastern Europe (Russia, Romania etc.). Pentecostalism established on Bali.

1939

The first All-Europe Pentecostal Conference held.

1947

The first Pentecostal World Conference held.

1960s–70s

Period of massive expansion of Pentecostals in Asia, Africa and Latin America where the American-led evangelising campaigns of the 'Prosperity Gospel' find a ready audience. Not all these Pentecostal outpourings are accepted as Christian.

1980

Total Pentecostal numbers globally estimated at over 100 million (*World Christian Encyclopaedia*).

1995

Total Pentecostal numbers estimated at 400 million.

c. **2000**

Global 'Pentecostal' numbers estimated at 535 million by *World Christian Encyclopaedia* (total includes Pentecostals, charismatics and 'Third Wavers').

THE MODERN ECUMENICAL MOVEMENT

ORIGINS AND PRECURSORS

1844

YMCA founded (Young Men's Christian Association) by George Williams (1821–1905) in London. Its leaders were later to become prominent in the ecumenical movement.

1854

Beginning of Anglo-American Missionary Conferences demonstrated advantages of cooperation.

1886

Northfield Conference (Massachusetts) under leadership of Dwight L. Moody (1837–90) and Ira David Sankey (1840–1908) influences both missions and ecumenism.

1888

Lambeth Conference proposes four-fold basis for endeavours to bring about Christian unity (known as the Lambeth Quadrilateral). London Conference of 55 (missionary) societies in England and the colonies.

1893

The World Parliament of Religions held in Chicago.

1895

Foundation of World Student Christian Federation.

ECUMENISM AFTER EDINBURGH

1910

The landmark Edinburgh Missionary Conference.

1914

World Alliance for the Promotion of International Friendship through the Churches formed at Constance, Switzerland (Aug.).

1914–18

Series of international bodies established (e.g. World Alliance of Reformed and Presbyterian Churches) and national ecumenical bodies (e.g. the US Federal Council of Churches and the British Council of Churches).

1920

'Faith and Order Movement' begins on initiative of American Anglican Bishop Charles Brent.

1921

Formation of the International Missionary Council, a major initiative in the ecumenical movement. Start of the Malines Conversations between a group of leading Roman Catholic and Anglican theologians on areas of possible agreement. On the Catholic side, the leading figure was the Cardinal Archbishop of Malines, Désiré Joseph Mercier, and on the Anglican side Lord Halifax. Although there were some important areas of agreement, no lasting achievement resulted.

1925

'Life and Work' gathering at Stockholm under leadership of Swedish Archbishop Nathan Soederblom.

1927

First World Conference on Faith and Order at Lausanne, presided over by Episcopalian Bishop Charles Henry Brent (1862–1929).

1928

The gathering of the International Missionary Council at Jerusalem stresses partnership of churches. Papal bull *Mortalium Animos* stresses religious unity and the pre-eminence of Rome. Widely seen as a setback for the ecumenical movement.

1929

World Conference of Lutherans held at Copenhagen.

1931

Anglican Communion agrees to full inter-communion with the Old Catholic churches of the 1889 Union of Utrecht, a concordat that served as basis for intercommunion with non-Anglican Episcopal churches.

1934

Opposition to Hitler brings Reformed and Lutheran Churches together in the Barmen Declaration.

1937

Life and Work gathering at Oxford.

1938

Important ecumenical gathering of the International Missionary Council at Madras discusses relationship to other world religions.

1939

Union among American Methodists.

1940

Taizé (ecumenical religious order) founded by Swiss layman Roger Schutz.

1942

Council of Christians and Jews formed in the UK.

1946

Committee of World Council of Churches (WCC) drafts plan for a reconstructed World International Assembly. International Christian Conference at Cambridge aims at closer relations between Protestant and Orthodox Churches.

1947

Church of South India formed (from Congregationalists, Methodists and Presbyterians, but also incorporating Anglicans and accepting bishops).

1948

Representatives of 147 churches from 44 countries meet in Amsterdam to inaugurate World Council of Churches. First General Secretary is Dutchman W. A. Visser't Hooft. Merging of Faith and Order, and Life and Work Movements.

1952

International Missionary Council gathering at Willingen (Germany) stresses urgency of Christian unity.

1954

Second Assembly of World Council of Churches meets at Illinois (160 churches from 44 countries).

1958

Lambeth Conference first to invite representatives from other churches. The Presbyterian Church (USA) created.

1960

Vatican establishes Secretariat for Promoting Christian Unity under German Cardinal Augustin Bea.

1961

Meeting of World Council of Churches at New Delhi is joined by members of the Russian Orthodox Church and by five Roman Catholic observers. The International Missionary Council is integrated with the World Council of Churches. The entry of the Russian Orthodox Church into the WCC. This ensured that the issue of Christian presence within a Marxist state would be under continual scrutiny. Full intercommunion established between Anglican Communion and Philippine Independent Catholic Church.

1962

Major Protestant, Anglican and Orthodox bodies invited to send observers to Second Vatican Council by Pope John XXIII.

1963

Founding of the *Journal of Ecumenical Studies*, a major instrument in ecumenical movement.

1964

Meeting of Pope Paul VI and Ecumenical Patriarch Athenagoras I in Jerusalem.

1965

Lifting of mutual excommunication of Rome and Orthodox Church. From 1965 to 1972 local union of churches of two or more confessions in such countries as Zambia, Jamaica, North India and Pakistan.

1966

Official visit of Anglican Archbishop Ramsey to Rome to meet Pope Paul VI (March).

1970

Church of North India formed (on similar lines to the 1947 Church of South India and including Baptists, Brethren and Disciples of Christ).

1970s

Ecumenical Association of Third World Theologians (EATWOT) develops.

1981–82

Publication of areas of substantial Anglican–Roman Catholic agreement by ARCIC (Anglican-Roman Catholic International Commission) in its *Final Report*. A next stage agreed on Pope John Paul II's visit to England (the 'Common Declaration').

1982

Lutheran–Episcopal dialogue in USA agrees to celebrate an interim shared Eucharist.

1995

The Porvoo Declaration, an agreement uniting the Anglican Church in England with Protestant Churches in mainland Europe, effectively healing the 460-year-old rift between the Anglican Church and the Lutheran Churches of northern Europe. The agreement allows Lutherans in Scandinavia and the Baltic (and Anglicans in England) to regard themselves as members of each other's churches, and to receive communion across the board. Each Church mutually recognizes priests and bishops.

1995

Papal encyclical *Ut Unum Sint* states Catholic position on dialogue with other Christian churches, including both Protestant and Orthodox.

1998

Bulgarian Orthodox Church withdraws from WCC (in protest at what it saw as a dominant Protestant liberal agenda).

1999

Lutheran World Federation and the Vatican agree historic 'Common Statement' on doctrine of justification.

2000

Anglican concordat with Lutherans in USA.

2001

Anglican concordat with Lutherans in Canada.

2006

Visit of Pope Benedict XVI to Patriarch Bartholomew I (head of Greek Orthodox Church) in Turkey.

DIALOGUE AND DEBATE: CHRISTIANITY AND THE NON-CHRISTIAN WORLD

1893

The World Parliament of Religions assembled in Chicago on the initiative of the Swedenborgians.

1901–13

International Council of Unitarian and Other Liberal Religious Thinkers and Writers active, with its declared aim of introducing believers to one another and stressing the 'universal elements' in all religions.

1910

Seminal event when first World Missionary Conference (see p. 223) meets at Edinburgh.

1913

Publication of J. N. Farquhar's *The Crown of Hinduism.*

1921

Foundation by Rudolf Otto of the *Religioser Menschheitsbund* (Interreligious League), again aiming to link all believers.

1923

First campus inter-faith programme (Cornell United Religious Work).

1928

Second World Missionary Conference (held at Jerusalem). In USA, National Conference of Christians and Jews founded.

1929

World Fellowship of Faiths founded, a culmination of growing internationalism after World War I.

1932

Publication of W. E. Hocking's *Rethinking Missions.*

1933

Report of the Commission of Appraisal of the Laymen's Foreign Mission Enquiry (edited by W. E. Hocking) published in USA. Publication by the Hindu Sarvepalli Radhakrishnan of *East and West in Religion.*

1938

Third Missionary Conference held at Tambaram (near Madras). Written as a background for this is Hendrik Kraemer's *The Christian Message in a Non-Christian World.*

1946

International Council of Christians and Jews established (after the full horror of the Holocaust was revealed).

1959

In USA, Association for the Coordination of University Religious Affairs founded to promote dialogue.

1963

Vatican Secretariat for Non-Christians established (one of the achievements of the Second Vatican Council).

1964

Papal encyclical *Ecclesiam suam*.

1965

Vatican II declaration 'The Relationship of the Church to Non-Christian Religions'.

1971

Creation of WCC's sub-unit Dialogue with People of Living Faiths and Ideologies.

1974

Roman Catholic Commission for Religious Relations with the Jews established. New guidelines on preaching about Judaism.

1975

Nairobi Assembly of World Council of Churches a watershed development.

1977

Conference at Chiang Mai, Thailand, organized by World Council of Churches opens more doors.

1983

Vancouver Assembly of World Council of Churches, followed by Canberra Assembly in 1991.

1992

Reorganization of World Council of Churches.

2001

Pope John Paul II became first pope to set foot inside a mosque (in Damascus).

2005

Controversy with Islam over publication in Danish newspaper *Jyllands-Posten* (Sept.) of 12 cartoons depicting Mohammed as a stereotypal Islamic extremist.

2006

Controversy over Pope Benedict XVI's quotation from the fourteenth century Byzantine Emperor Manuel II Palaeologus, which was seen as portraying everything that the Prophet Mohammed had promulgated was both evil and inhuman.

II
GLOSSARY OF TERMS AND EVENTS

A

ABECEDARIANS Anabaptist (*q.v.*) sect founded in sixteenth-century Germany by Stork, a disciple of Luther. Its members held all human knowledge to be valueless and declined to learn even the alphabet.

ADVOWSON In Britain, right of presentation to a clerical benefice by either clerical or lay patrons. Dating from the eighth century, it became subject to many abuses after the 1164 Constitutions of Clarendon when it was recognized as a right of property. It still exists today as a property right tenable by non-Catholics.

ALASCANS Foreign Protestant refugees in England in the reign of Edward VI (1547–53) named after Laski, the superintendent of foreign church communities.

ALBIGENSIANS (*also* Albigenses) The medieval heretic Cathars (*q.v.*) of southern France. The name is derived from the Albi region of Provence, where many Cathars were located under the protection of Raymond, Count of Toulouse. The sect appeared in the eleventh century. Its beliefs largely reflected and were ultimately derived from those of Manichaeism. Like Manichaeism, the Albigensian heresy challenged orthodox Catholicism on two levels. First, it held that matter was evil, the domain of Satan, and that the spiritual alone was godly. God was locked in perpetual combat with the forces of evil which dominated the material world. Only by the rejection of the material world (e.g. the denial of sensual desires) was salvation to be reached. This belief constituted a direct denial of the orthodox doctrine of the nature of Christ, who became incarnate (i.e. material) and yet remained God. Moreover, the heresy implied that God was not the creator and master of all things both spiritual and material, and suggested that the path to salvation lay not in the sacraments of the Church but in the strict pursuit of an ascetic life.

Second, the sect had its own organization separate from that of the Church. Those following a rigidly ascetic life were known as the 'perfect', while those living under less severe discipline were 'believers'. The 'perfect' were held to have direct access to heaven when they died. This concept of a hierarchical elite was a direct affront to orthodox teaching.

The sect was condemned for heresy by Pope Innocent III (1198–1216), who inaugurated the Albigensian Crusade, the first crusade against Christians. See p. 72.

ALUMBRADOS (Span., enlightened) Groups of mystics which emerged in Spain *c.* 1510 and attacked by the Inquisition (*q.v.*). They were the spiritual forefathers of the better-known Illuminati (*q.v.*) of Germany.

AMALRICIANS (*also* Amalricini) Twelfth-century pantheist sect, the somewhat confused followers of Amaury of Bène, condemned by the Pope for heresy in 1210.

ANABAPTISTS An extreme religious sect which arose in Switzerland and Germany and became famous for their seizure of the city of Münster in 1534.

ANGLO-CATHOLIC That strand in the Church of England which stresses the Church's Catholic heritage, rejects the term 'Protestant' and espouses much of Roman Catholic ritual and dogma. Many Anglo-Catholics have found it impossible to accept women priests in the Anglican Church.

ANNATE (deriv. Lat. annus, year) A fee or tax paid to the Pope in respect of ecclesiastical preferment, consisting originally of the whole of the first year's income from the office. Annates, introduced into England in the thirteenth century, were annexed to the Crown under Henry VIII and transferred in 1704 to a perpetual fund for the benefit of the poorer clergy (known as

Queen Anne's Bounty (*q.v.*)). On 1 April 1948 Queen Anne's Bounty was abolished and the Ecclesiastical Commissioners administering it were embodied in the Church Commissioners for England.

ANTI-CLERICALISM Opposition to organized religion, particularly the power and privileges of the Roman Catholic Church. Anti-clericalism, though not a coherent political doctrine, has a long history. In England it is traceable to the fourteenth century, when Wycliffe insisted that all men had a right of access to the scriptures. In Tudor times, anti-clericalism arose from a variety of motives ranging from greed and a desire to plunder the monasteries to a genuine dislike of priestly powers and abuses. Modern anti-clericalism was prevalent in revolutionary France and remained characteristic of French radicalism during the nineteenth century. Anti-clericalism has broken out sporadically in Spain (notably in 1873, 1909–13 and 1931–36) and in Latin America. In Germany it was confined to the *Kulturkampf* (*q.v.*) and the later Nazi persecution of individual church leaders. In Italy there has been a long history of anti-clericalism stemming from opposition to the territorial claims of the Pope and, more recently, over the Catholic Church's attitude to divorce and contraception. In some communist states, anti-clericalism developed from the government's identification of the clergy with former fascist regimes and as part of an ideological battle for the loyalty of the masses.

ANTINOMIANISM The belief that the law expounded in the Old Testament is no longer relevant and binding upon Christians.

ANTI-SEMITISM Term first applied in the mid-nineteenth century to denote animosity towards the Jews. Throughout the Middle Ages the Jews faced hostility on religious grounds and because, unlike Catholics, they were allowed to practise usury. Modern anti-Semitism differs in being largely politically and economically motivated, doctrinaire, and based on a pseudo-scientific rationale devised by, for example, Gobineau (1816–82), Houston Stewart Chamberlain (1855–1927) and Nazi 'philosophers'. In the 1870s a group of German writers, using the linguistic distinctions 'Semitic' and 'Aryan' as racial terms, began speaking of the Jews as a distinct and inferior race. Anti-Semitic political parties were active in both Germany and Austria–Hungary in the 1880s while pogroms (*q.v.*) began in Russia in 1882. In France, the 1894 Dreyfus case revealed a large core of anti-Semitic feeling. Between 1905 and 1909 anti-Jewish violence on a large scale again broke out in Tsarist Russia, particularly in Lithuania and Poland. In the late nineteenth and early twentieth centuries thousands of Jews from eastern Europe fled to Britain and the USA. From 1920 to 1933 Hitler expounded theories of Aryan racial supremacy and blamed the Jews for Germany's misfortunes. The Nuremberg Laws of 1935 codified Nazi theories of race, denied Jews German citizenship and forbade them to marry Aryans; in 1938 Jewish property was confiscated. During World War II over five million Jews were murdered in 'Concentration Camps'. Since 1945 anti-Semitism has usually been a reaction to Zionism (*q.v.*) and the State of Israel. In the former USSR anti-Semitism re-emerged in 1953 and there was serious violence against Jewish communities in 1958–59. In 1962–63 Jews were executed for 'economic crimes' and before 1990 many Jews seeking to emigrate to Israel were imprisoned.

APOSTLE OF ROME Title given to St Philip Neri (1515–95). The founder of the Oratorians (*q.v.*), he was canonized in 1622.

APOSTOLIC BRETHREN (*also* Apostolics) An order founded by Gerard Segarelli in Parma in 1260, holding heretical doctrines on perfection and poverty in exaggerated imitation of the Franciscans (*q.v.*). They were responsible for a rebellion under the leadership of Dolcino di Novara, who was burnt in 1307.

APOSTOLIC FATHERS Term for those early Christian writers who were contemporary with the orginal apostles. Those usually cited are Barnabas, Clement of Rome, Ignatius, Polycarp, Hermas and Papias.

ARMENIAN MASSACRES Massacres of Armenians, a Monophysite (those who claim that Christ had only one, Divine, nature after the Incarnation) Christian people living within the Ottoman (*q.v.*) Empire, by Turks between 1894 and 1895. They led to outrage in Britain and ended Britain's attempts to preserve the integrity of the empire. In 1914–15 the Turks exterminated a large part of the Armenian population and deported the remainder from Armenia in 1915.

ARMINIANS Followers of Jacob Arminius (1560–1609), a Leyden professor who in the early seventeenth century dissented from the strict Calvinism of Dutch Protestantism. They rejected the doctrine of Predestination (*q.v.*), emphasizing instead the teachings of the early Church on free will. In 1618 the Synod of Dort issued a decree banishing the Arminian preachers; the Great Pensioner, Barneveldt, their chief lay supporter, was executed. In mid-seventeenth-century England, Archbishop Laud was accused by his opponents of Arminianism – i.e. of favouring the doctrine of free will above that of predestination, but the latter remained part of Anglican orthodoxy. For the enemies of James I and Charles I, the appellation 'Arminian' served as a term of abuse for the Court and those divines who implemented its religious policies. Parliament, mainly Puritan and Calvinist, used it as a pejorative label for any holder of views that it disliked and suspected.

ARNOLDISTS Members of a twelfth-century north Italian movement which attempted to impose a form of apostolic poverty upon the Church. They were followers of Arnold of Brescia (*c.* 1100–55), who held Donatist (*q.v.*) and anti-clerical views. After condemnation at the Synod of Verona in 1184, the influence of the heresy waned, although it remained one of a number of manifestations of discontent with the state of the established Church.

AUGMENTATIONS, COURT OF Institution established by Thomas Cromwell (1485–1540) in 1536 to collect revenues from the estates confiscated by the English Crown during the dissolution of the monasteries between 1536 and 1540. Some 800 institutions were dissolved and their lands possessed by the King; Henry VIII augmented his income by £90,000 a year as a result. The Court was also responsible for selling former church property to the English gentry; in 1547 it was reconstituted and took charge of all crown lands until 1554, when it was abolished and its duties transferred to the Exchequer.

AUTO DA FÉ (*auto da fé* Span., act of faith) Ceremony accompanying the execution of condemned heretics during the Inquisition (*q.v.*) in Spain and Portugal. Pope Sixtus IV first authorized the Spanish monarchy to name inquisitors in a bull of 1478. The Inquisition lasted until 1813, when it was suppressed by the Cortes de Cádiz. Restored by Ferdinand VII in 1814, it was suppressed again in 1820, only to be reinstated three years later. The last *auto da fé* took place in 1826; the Inquisition was finally abolished in 1834.

B

BABYLONIAN CAPTIVITY (1) The exile of the Jews in Babylon following the capture of Jerusalem by Nebuchadnezzar's Babylonian Empire in 586 BC, which according to tradition lasted for 70 years, although the Jews were allowed to return when Babylon fell to Cyrus of Persia in 538 BC.

(2) Metaphorically, the period 1309–78 when the papacy moved to Avignon and was under the control of the French monarchy.

BAPTISTS Members of an English Christian denomination founded by John Smyth (d. 1612), a minister of the Church of England who came under Arminian (*q.v.*) influence in Holland. They base their doctrine upon the teaching of the apostles and hold that members can only be received into the faith by baptism as adults. The first Baptist Church, built at Newgate in 1612, saw the start of the General Baptist Church, which rejected Calvinism (*q.v.*) in favour of the Arminian belief in redemption open to all. A later split caused the formation of the Particular Baptist Church, which was Calvinistic. In 1891 the two bodies were reunited in the Baptist Union; today the Church is spread all over the world and is particularly strong in the USA.

BARROWISTS Congregational sect active in the sixteenth century led by Henry Barrow and John Greenwood, who preached views similar to those of the Brownists (*q.v.*). They held that, contrary to Elizabethan doctrine, the Church had no relationship to the State; its only statute-book was the Bible; the Articles of Religion and Book of Common Prayer were mere acts of parliament and each congregation was independent, with the power to choose its own ministers. Barrow and Greenwood were hanged at Tyburn in 1593 under an act of the previous year which sought to punish 'persons obstinately refusing to come to church'. Their followers fled in large numbers, first to Holland and later to America.

BEATIFICATION In the Roman Catholic Church, the prefixing of 'Blessed' to the name of one of the faithful departed, which usually preceeds Canonization (*q.v.*).

BEGHARDS In the thirteenth and fourteenth centuries, men who pursued a religious life without rules or vows, similar to that of the female Béguines (*q.v.*).

BÉGUINES (Fr.) Pious women who belonged to a sisterhood founded in Liège in the twelfth century, pursuing a religious life without rules or vows. They lived singly or in convents which were often linked to the mendicant orders. The movement was popular from the early thirteenth century, but its growth was restricted in the fourteenth century by prejudice and accusation of heresy.

BENEFICE (OFr. deriv. Lat., favour) An ecclesiastical living or preferment. Clerical benefices originated in the twelfth century as an imitation of the lay system of fiefs; until then priests had been supported by alms and oblations.

BENEFIT OF CLERGY The right claimed by the medieval Church to withdraw its members from the jurisdiction of the secular courts to that of ecclesiastical courts. The term 'clerk', held to carry the right to ecclesiastical trial, was applied to all who could read. The spread of lay education consequent upon the Renaissance brought increasing abuse and in 1532 the right to plead benefit of clergy in cases of felony was limited to the rank of sub-deacon and above.

BIANCHI (Ital., white) The members of a fanatical sect which appeared in Italy in 1399; they wore long white garments and ate only bread and water.

BIBLE BELT Southern states of the USA where fundamentalist (*q.v.*) Christianity retains a strong popularity.

BISHOP'S BOOK An Anglican doctrinal statement, *The Institution of a Christian Man*, drawn up with Henry VIII's approval by a committee of bishops in 1537, as part of an attempt to construct a consistent set of beliefs and practices for the English Reformed Church.

BISHOPS' WARS Hostilities between England and Scotland, 1638–40, so called because they arose from Charles I's attempt to impose Anglicanism and the Episcopacy (*q.v.*) on the Scots. James I had re-established the episcopacy in Scotland and Charles I had at the beginning of his reign (1625–49) sought to wrest back from the Scottish nobles the church lands they had seized in the past. In 1637 he introduced a modified version of the English Prayer Book to Scotland which provoked the Covenanters (*q.v.*) into abolishing the episcopacy. An army was raised by the Scots and in 1638 war broke out. Charles raised an army to oppose them but did not have the finance to pay his troops. As a result he was forced to sign the Treaty of Berwick in June 1638 but he refused to agree to the abolition of the episcopacy in Scotland. He then summoned the 'Short Parliament' to secure finance, but it refused to vote supplies for a resumption of the war. He turned to the convocation (*q.v.*) who gave him £20,000 as a benevolence. With further aid from the Irish parliament, war was resumed but the discipline and morale of the army was poor, and it was routed near Newcastle. On 26 October 1640 Charles signed the Treaty of Ripon, which was virtually a surrender. He was forced to summon parliament and had to pay £850 a day to the Scots who were to retain possession of Durham and Northumberland until the religious issue was settled.

BLACK FRIARS *See* Dominicans.

BOGOMILS Members of a heretical movement, founded by Bogomil, a priest of the tenth century, which opposed the Greek Church and believed that all matter is evil. Initially active in Byzantium and the Balkans, they spread to western Europe and were responsible for founding the Cathars (*q.v.*). The movement died out in the fifteenth century.

BOHEMIAN BRETHREN *See* Unitas Fratrum.

BOY POPE Benedict IX, a layman whose family purchased the office of Pope in 1032; reputedly aged 12, it is more likely that he was in his late twenties. Benedict held the office until 1044, in 1045, and again in 1047–48 when he was finally ousted for his vices.

BROWNISTS Followers of Robert Browne (1550–1633), an early Congregationalist (*q.v.*) who rejected the authority of the Episcopacy (*q.v.*). In 1580 he formed an independent congregation in Norwich but was forced to flee to Middleburg in Holland in the following year. He moved to Scotland, where for a time he was imprisoned by the church authorities; he returned to England in 1584.

BULL (deriv. Lat. *bulla*, seal) Seal affixed to a papal edict; by extension, the edict itself. Papal bulls have statutory authority within the Roman Catholic Church.

BYZANTINE EMPIRE The eastern half of the Roman Empire which, when it fell to the Turks in 1453, had survived the Western empire by a thousand years.

C

CALIXTINES (deriv. Lat. chalice) The more moderate of the two sections into which the Hussite (*q.v.*) sect was divided after the death of Jerome of Prague in 1416. Their name derived from their claim that lay communicants should be allowed to take the wine as well as the bread. The more fanatical Hussite group was that led by John Zisca, known as the Taborites (*q.v.*).

CALVINISM Branch of Protestantism (*q.v.*) founded on the teaching of the French reformer Jean Chauvin (1509–64), known as Calvin from the Latin form of his name. Calvin gave the first systematic justification of Protestantism in *Institutions of the Christian Religion* (1536) and thus became the intellectual leader of the Reformation. Calvinism is marked by its dogma of predestination, the belief that God has unalterably destined some souls to salvation and others to eternal damnation. Its harsh, logical beliefs inspired

English Puritans (*q.v.*), French Huguenots (*q.v.*) and some of the Dutch in their fight against the domination of Catholic Spain. The sect has been established in the Reformed or Presbyterian churches of France, Holland and Scotland; Calvinist rule was also ruthlessly enforced under Calvin himself in Geneva by the Consistorium (*q.v.*). The Calvinist beliefs that labour is a command of God and material success a mark of his favour – contradicting the medieval ideas of the virtue of poverty and the evil of usury – may have contributed to the rise of capitalism.

CAMISSARDS *See* Enfants de Dieu.

CANONIZATION Procedure for putting one of the faithful departed on the list of saints of the Roman Catholic Church. The rules which govern it were simplified by papal decree in 1969. Beatification (*q.v.*), by which a person is called blessed, is usually, but not necessarily, followed eventually by canonization.

CANON LAW Ecclesiastical law in the areas of faith, morals and discipline.

CAPUCHIN Member of a mendicant order of Franciscans (*q.v.*) founded in the sixteenth century with the aim of restoring the primitive and stricter observance of the rule of St Francis; their name is derived from their capuces or pointed cowls.

CARMELITES Members of a body of mendicant friars founded at Mount Carmel in the Holy Land in the twelfth century. Their severe original rule, requiring absolute poverty, abstinence from meat and an eremitical life, was mitigated by Pope Innocent IV (1243–54). They are also known as White Friars on account of their white mantles. An order of Carmelite nuns was instituted in the fifteenth century.

CARTHUSIANS Order of monks founded by St Bruno in 1084 at Grande Chartreuse near Grenoble in France. The chief characteristics of the order are a separate dwelling-house for each monk and a general assembly in the church twice each day and once at night. The order invented and still holds the secret of the liqueur Chartreuse, from which it derives a large revenue. An order of Carthusian nuns was instituted in the twelfth century.

CATHARS Heretical Christian movement whose name derived from the Greek word meaning 'pure' and which spread from the Byzantine Empire to Italy and southern France in the twelfth century. Persecuted for denying Christ's humanity and rejecting divine incarnation, the Cathar settlements in France were destroyed in the Albigensian (*q.v.*) crusades of 1209–29.

CATHOLIC EMANCIPATION Movement in Britain and Ireland to secure full political and civil rights for Roman Catholics. Unlike Protestant Dissenters, Catholics had received no freedom of worship under the 1689 Toleration Act. Though in practice they did receive a degree of toleration, they were formally excluded from ministerial and administrative office, commissions in the armed services and from universities under a series of acts known collectively as the Penal Laws. A Roman Catholic Relief Act applying to England and Wales was passed in 1778 and one applying to Scotland in 1793. But for most of the eighteenth century, opinion remained fiercely anti-Catholic.

From 1807, when Sydney Smith, Canon of St Paul's, took up the Protestant Dissenters' cause, agitation grew for the repeal of the Test and Corporation Acts of Charles II. In 1828 they were repealed and the remaining discriminatory legislation against Catholics was shown to be an anachronism. There were only 60,000 Catholics in England, but the majority of the Irish population was Catholic and was beginning to refuse to accept the Protestant ascendancy.

In May 1823, Daniel O'Connell (1775–1847) revived an old Catholic association which raised a rent of 1*d* a month from the Irish Catholic community. Within the year it had £22,700 to fight for emancipation. Its aim was to promote Protestant MPs sworn to Catholic emancipation. In 1829 the association was suppressed. O'Connell was elected an MP but as a Catholic could not take his seat. In the face of constitutional deadlock and increasing agitation, the Prime Minister, Wellington and the Home Secretary, Peel, renounced their opposition and in 1829 steered the Catholic Emancipation Act through parliament. In 1832 a Roman Catholic Charities Act regularized the position of Catholic charities.

CATHOLIC MAJESTIES Titles used of the Spanish monarchs, continuously after the time of Ferdinand the Catholic.

CHAMBRE ARDENTE Court of devout Roman Catholics, charged with the trial of heretics, established by Henry II in the *Parlement* of Paris in 1551.

CHANTRY (ME deriv. AFr., singing) Endowment founded to celebrate masses for the souls of the founder and others; also the place – an altar in a specially reserved chapel or a separate building – where masses were sung for the dead. From the thirteenth century onwards, chantry foundations to intercede for both the living and the dead were common. They often had independent financial provisions and were sometimes linked with the founding of schools (e.g. Winchester and Eton). In England the chantries themselves, though not their associated institutions, were dissolved in 1545–47.

CHRISTIAN SOCIALISM (1) In Britain, a movement which began in the mid-nineteenth century with the object of emphasizing the social principles found in the New Testament. It opposed *laissez-faire* and sought to establish industrial co-operatives. To further the education of the poorer classes, it founded the Working Men's College in 1854. The movement's leaders were John Malcolm Forbes Ludlow (1821–1911), Charles Kingsley (1819–75), F.D. Maurice (1805–72), and Thomas Hughes (1822–96), whose novel *Tom Brown's Schooldays* displays many of the tenets of the movement.

(2) Name given to the beliefs of many political parties in Europe, founded in response to the challenge of socialism. The first was formed in Austria in the late nineteenth century. Two papal encyclicals (*q.v.*) (*Rerum novarum* and *Quadragesimo Anno*), anti-socialist but in favour of a Christian corporate state with protection for labour, encouraged their efforts. Today the Christian Socialist parties are essentially conservative but may have quite advanced programmes of social reform. After World War II the Austrian Christian Socialist Party was renamed the People's Party.

CHURCH SCOT In early Anglo-Saxon England, payment of grain and hens to support parish priests, levied on all free men according to their holdings; it was originally known as 'food rent'. The peasantry found it a heavy burden and although it continued after the development of the tithe (*q.v.*), it gradually declined to a modest payment of eggs and hens.

CIRCUMSPECTA AGATIS (Lat.) Royal writ issued by Edward I in June 1286, directing the justices to 'deal circumspectly' with the Bishop of Norwich and his clergy and to allow the Church to hear certain pleas such as moral offences, tithe (*q.v.*) disputes and cases of defamation of the clergy. The writ, Edward's response to complaints by the clergy that royal courts were encroaching on matters which properly related to ecclesiastical jurisdiction, provided a much-needed definition of the judicial sphere of church courts and came to be regarded as a statute. It was repealed by the 1963 Ecclesiastical Jurisdiction Measure.

CISTERCIANS Religious order for men and women founded at Cîteaux, near Dijon, in 1098, noted for the rigidity and uniformity of its rule. The golden age of the order was the twelfth century, when its fortunes were closely tied to those of St Bernard of Clairvaux (1090–1153). Bernard entered Cîteaux as a novice in 1112 and in 1115 left to found a Cistercian monastery at Clairvaux.

He was extremely active in encouraging the foundation of further houses, and monks from Clairvaux alone were responsible for establishing 68 houses by the end of the century; by the time of his death the order had 338 abbeys from Sweden to the eastern Mediterranean.

Between 1130 and 1145 Bernard was a member of numerous ecclesiastical and civil councils, had been adviser to five popes and was instrumental in launching the Second Crusade. In theological matters he combined a Christian mysticism with a desire to serve others, but he remained a strong adherent to the institutionalized church. His beliefs brought him into direct conflict with the rationalist dialectics of Peter Abelard (1079–1144), a founder of scholastic moral theology, whose rationalism led him to publish *Sic et Non* ('Yes and No'), a collection of quotations aimed at showing inconsistencies in the position of the Church, and whose *Theologia* was declared to be heretical in 1121. Bernard was canonized in 1174.

The architectural achievements of the Cistercians in the twelfth century are considerable. Notable buildings were constructed at Pontigny, Burgundy (1140); Rievaulx and Fountains (1131 and 1135); Kercz, Hungary (1202); Beirut, Lebanon (1155); Alcobaca, Portugal (1158); Vieta, Sweden (1100) and Fossanova, Italy (1187).

From having been noted for their austere and strict rules, the Cistercians were notorious for laxity and greed by the fifteenth century. After the Reformation (*q.v.*) they disappeared from northern Europe and were struggling to survive elsewhere. However, the seventeenth century saw successful attempts at reform. In 1664 Armand Jean Le Bouthillier de Rancé became abbot of La Trappe and commenced restoration of a rule of seclusion, silence, prayer and manual labour: his followers became known as Trappists. Trappists adopted the title 'Order of Cistercians of the Strict Observance' (OCSO). The rest of the order, which underwent moderate reform in 1666, are known as Cistercians of Common Observance.

CLAPHAM SECT A strand of the Anglican Evangelical Movement, stressing the importance of good works, moral earnestness and salvation by faith. The Sect – whose leading members worshipped in Clapham Parish Church, South London – was involved in the campaign to abolish the slave trade, missionary work in India and ameliorating the plight of the poor.

CLARENDON CODE Series of acts passed in the English parliament between 1661 and 1665 with the aim of destroying the power of the Protestant Dissenters by restricting their religious freedom and excluding them from secular office. Edward Hyde, 1st Earl of Clarendon (1609–74), was not in fact the driving force behind the legislation; more accurately it was the extremist Anglican House of Commons that was returned in 1660. In 1661 the Corporation Act was passed, barring Dissenters from municipal office; in 1662 the Act of Uniformity excluded them from church offices. Finally the Conventicle Act of 1664 and the Five Mile Act of 1665 restricted their freedom of public worship.

CLERICOS LAICOS (Lat.) Bull (*q.v.*) issued by Pope Boniface VIII in 1296 fobidding the clergy to pay tribute to temporal sovereigns without papal assent on pain of excommunication (*q.v.*). In England the clergy complied with the bull and were outlawed by Edward I in 1297 and their property confiscated. However, the Pope allowed Philip IV of France the right to levy taxes on the clergy in cases of emergency. This precedent, together with the Scottish victory at the Battle of Stirling in 1297, led the English clergy to agree to a subsidy for Edward I, though only for use against the Scots. The King consequently abandoned his claim to tax the clergy as of right.

CLUNIACS Monastic order founded by the Benedictines at Cluny, near Mâcon in Burgundy, in 910, marking the first real attempt at closer organization of the Benedictine order. The order had a strict rule and observed exacting liturgical services. Cluny Abbey was increasingly approached for advice on the reform of other monasteries and a succession of Cluniac abbots developed a network of client monasteries throughout western Europe. The monks were usually nobles and the order prided itself on the eminence of its princely patrons and the numerous former Cluniacs who became bishops and even popes.

CODINI (Ital., pigtails) Name given to the papal party by the House of Savoy in the late nineteenth century, implying that supporters of the papacy were reactionary and conservative.

COMMONWEALTH Generally, the period between the execution of Charles I on 30 January 1649 and the Restoration on 8 May 1660; specifically, the period from the declaration of the English republic on 19 May 1649 to the establishment of the Protectorate by the Instrument of Government on 16 December 1653, which made Cromwell Lord Protector. Under the Commonwealth, severe censorship was enforced by a high court of justice which conducted treason trials without a jury. Revenues were derived from taxation, victimization of royalists and the sale of crown and church lands.

CONCILIAR THEORY A body of opinion in the fifteenth century which held that supreme authority in the Catholic Church lay with the General Council rather than the Pope.

CONCLAVE Assembly of the cardinals of the Roman Catholic Church, meeting in seclusion for the purpose of electing a new pope. A conclave must be convoked within three weeks after the death of a pope. All cardinals are invited, but only half need to be present for the conclave to act. Each accompanied by a secretary and attendant, they meet in the Vatican – usually about 300 persons are present and they are pledged to secrecy for life as to what occurs. They have no communication with the outside world until a pope is chosen. A two-thirds majority is needed for

the papal election and if this is not achieved the ballot papers are burned with straw.

CONCORDAT (deriv. Lat. pactum concordatum, agreed pact) Agreement between the Pope and a secular government regarding the status and rights of the Roman Catholic Church within that country. Where State–Church relations preclude a concordat, a modus vivendi may be reached instead.

CONFESSIONAL PARTY Political party declaring a relationship, either formal or intentional, between its principles and its religious faith, creed or denomination. The Italian Christian Democrats professed a connection between their politics and Catholicism, while several Lebanese parties revolve around their adherence to Christianity.

CONGÉ D'ÉLIRE (AFr., permission to elect) In England, a royal writ to a cathedral chapter inviting it to elect the person named to the vacant see of the diocese (q.v.). First introduced as part of the process of Reformation in 1533, it marked the victory of the state over the chapters and the papacy in determining the outcome of episcopal elections.

CONGREGATIONALISM In England, the oldest tradition of Nonconformism (q.v.), originating with the Brownists (q.v.) and the Barrowists (q.v.) and represented in the ranks of the Independents (q.v.), which was finally given liberty of worship under William III in 1689. Common to its various manifestations is the insistence on the right of each local congregation to choose its own minister and forms of worship independently of a central church government. In 1833 its members formed the Congregational Union of England and Wales, but this was without prescriptive powers over its component congregations and ministers remained responsible to their own churches and to no one else. The sect is widespread in England and the USA, where it is held in special honour since Congregationalists were among the Pilgrim Fathers (q.v.) who set sail for America in

1620 in search of religious liberty. In 1972 the Congregational Church in England and Wales and the Presbyterian Church of England formed the United Reform Church; the majority of members who did not join comprise the Congregational Federation.

CONSISTORIUM (deriv. Lat., hold firm) Tribunal established by Calvin in Geneva in 1541 to maintain religious and moral standards. It acted with great severity, proscribing all amusements and vigorously repressing criticism of Calvinist doctrine. Within five years it was responsible for 58 executions and 800 imprisonments.

CONSISTORY An assembly of cardinals called by the Pope. In the Church of England the word is used to describe a diocesan bishop's court.

CONSUBSTANTIATION The belief of German Protestant reformer Martin Luther (1483–1546) that although the bread and wine remain unchanged at the Eucharist, Christ's body and blood are physically present, a concept that divided the reform movement.

CONVENTICLE (Lat., assembly) In Scotland, an open-air meeting for public worship held by ministers dispossessed when the Restoration established the Episcopal Church in Scotland in 1660. Conventicles were declared illegal in 1662, then permitted by Indulgence in 1664, before being finally declared illegal and suppressed.

In England, the Conventicle Act of 1593 penalized those persons who declined to attend Church of England services and went to conventicles. An act of 1664 (part of the Clarendon Code (q.v.)) was more lenient, prohibiting only those conventicles attended by more than five persons not from the same household. The act expired in 1668, was renewed in 1670, but moderated by the Declaration of Indulgence in 1672 and 1688.

CONVERSOS Term applied in Spain to those Jews who had converted.

CONVOCATION Assembly summoned to deliberate upon ecclesiastical affairs.

In the Church of England the provinces of Canterbury and York each have their own convocation, whose history dates back to Archbishop Theodore's occupation of office (668–90). Under the Angevins, convocations dealt not only with ecclesiastical affairs but also acted as a clerical parliament, claiming the right to tax the clergy and make payments to the royal exchequer. From the fifteenth century both convocations have had two houses, an upper house of the archbishop and diocesan bishops, and a lower of inferior clergy. In 1533 the Act of Submission of the Clergy prohibited convocations without the King's permission; in 1660 the clergy renounced its claim to the right to tax itself and since 1663 has been taxed by Parliament. For a time after 1688 the convocations displayed an independent turn of mind which proved an embarrassment to the government. In 1716 the convocation censured Benjamin Moadly, Bishop of Bangor, for his work *A Preservative against the Principles and Practices of the Non-Jurors both in Church and State,* defending the secular power's right to deprive the Non-jurors (q.v.) of office. The following year, George I suspended convocation which then met only rarely until the mid-nineteenth century.

Since then they have met two or three times a year and are concerned mainly with reform of the canons of ecclesiastical law.

COUNCIL OF BLOOD The notorious court established in the Netherlands by the Duke of Alva to suppress religious and political opposition to Philip II. From its opening session on 20 September 1567, it became a byword for tyranny. Among its most prominent victims were the counts of Egmont and Hoorn in 1568.

COUNTER-REFORMATION Term for the renaissance in Roman Catholicism after the Reformation. One aspect of this was the Council of Trent. *See also* Jesuits.

240

COVENANTERS Name given to supporters of the National Covenant of 1638, drawn up by the Tables (*q.v.*) in opposition to Charles I's attempts to Anglicanize the Scottish Church by enforcing the use of a new Prayer Book. In 1581, the Scottish Protestant leaders, the Lords of the Congregation, had entered into a covenant designed to protect the Protestant religion which was signed by James VI. The National Covenant led to the Bishops' Wars (*q.v.*) and, in 1640, the calling of the Long Parliament.

On 25 September 1643, Parliament adopted the Solemn League and Covenant between the English and Scots parliamentarians in opposition to Charles I. This attempted to pledge the signatories to the establishment of Presbyterianism (*q.v.*) in England, although a sentence added by Sir Henry Vane to the effect that the form of religious organization to be adopted should be 'according to the word of God' allowed greater religious liberty than was originally intended. Under the terms of the Covenant, the Scots received £30,000 a month and in return undertook to provide an army to fight the Royalists. The Covenant was accepted by Charles Prince of Wales in the early 1650s in his efforts to secure Scots help to put him on the English throne. After his restoration in 1660, the Covenant was declared illegal by Parliament in 1661 and all copies of it were ordered to be burnt.

CRUSADE (deriv. Lat. *cruciata*, cross) Generally, a fight, either spiritual or physical, against evil, anti-Christian beliefs or the enemies of Christianity. More specifically, the military campaigns of feudal Christendom against the Islamic peoples in the Near East between 1096 and 1254. The continuous warfare between the seventh and twelfth centuries and the actions of the Teutonic Knights (*q.v.*) in East Prussia might also be called crusades. Finally, in 1208, a crusade was launched against the heretic Albigensians (*q.v.*).

Religious fervour pervaded all these activities. Popes promised that Christians killed on crusade would go to heaven and St Bernard of Clairvaux (*see* Cistercians) urged criminals to join the crusades and thus gain forgiveness for their sins. The crusades were also the result of social-economic conditions in western Europe: the feudal system was becoming more rigid and lands in the East were available for conquest by the younger landless sons of the European nobility. The prospect of trade with the East drew many merchants to the Holy Land in later crusades, while plunder and higher living standards were also an attraction. Finally, in these years the concept of the knight carrying out 'great deeds' was emerging to capture the imagination of the feudal nobility, making adventure and chivalry further reasons for 'taking the cross'.

CUIUS REGIO, EIUS RELIGIO The principle provided for at the religious peace of Augsburg of 1555. It provided that, within the Holy Roman Empire, in the secular territories of princes and imperial knights, the ruler had the right to determine the religion of his subjects.

CULDEES Monks in the eighth-century Irish Church and in the ninth-century Scottish Church who later developed into the secular clergy. Culdees survived in Scotland until the fourteenth century.

D

DARWINISM The evolutionary theories of Charles Darwin (1806–82) set out in *On the Origin of Species by Means of Natural Selection* (1859) and *The Descent of Man* (1871). Darwinism's central concepts are the struggle for existence, the survival of the fittest, and natural selection.

DEFENESTRATION OF PRAGUE Incident at the start of the Thirty Years War. When the Austrian monarch Ferdinand II threatened the religious liberties of Bohemian Protestants, Count von Thürn led Protestant nobles to the palace in Prague on 23 May 1618 and threw two Roman Catholic governors and a secretary out of a window. Their fall was broken by a rubbish heap.

DEFENSOR FIDEI (Lat., defender of the faith; *abbr.* Fid. Def.) Title conferred on Henry VIII of England by Pope Leo X in 1521 for his defence of the seven sacraments in opposition to Luther. After Henry broke with Rome and assumed headship of the Church of England in 1534, Pope Paul III withdrew the title but Parliament confirmed it in 1544 and it has been used ever since by English monarchs, who are head of the church of England.

DÉVOTS Term for those zealous Catholics who opposed any toleration for Huguenots and who opposed Richelieu's foreign policy. Dévots wanted a pro-Spanish, pro-Catholic policy.

DEVSHIRMEH (deriv. Turk., levy of boys) The 'tribute of children' levied on Christian people, particularly the Slavs in the Balkans who were subject to Ottoman (*q.v.*) rule, established by Bayezed I (1389–1403). It lapsed after the Battle of Ankara (1402) but was revived by Murad II (1421–51). Many became Janissaries (*q.v*), while the most able were trained for high administrative posts. The devshirmeh was only intermittently applied in the sixteenth and seventeenth centuries, and was last imposed in 1705.

DIOCESE (deriv. Lat., governor's district) Territorial area administered by a bishop in the Roman Catholic and Anglican churches, and by a patriarch in the Eastern Orthodox churches of Greece and Russia. It was initially an administrative division of the Roman Empire, itself being subdivided into provinces. The early Christian Church reversed this order; they made the province the larger unit, under the control of a metropolitan bishop, and the dioceses subdivisions of the province. From the ninth to the thirteenth centuries, church organization was in a state of flux but by the thirteenth century two distinct patterns had emerged. In the Orthodox Church the basic unit of administration was and is the parish, administered by a bishop. The diocese is a larger area comprising a number of parishes and under the control of a patriarch. In the Catholic Church dioceses are administered by bishops but are also subdivided into parishes (each having its own church) or into rural deaneries containing several parishes. The Pope alone can abolish, merge or create new dioceses. In the Church of England, Parliament has created new dioceses (in the sixteenth, nineteenth and twentieth centuries) by dividing existing ones. Dioceses are subdivided into rural deaneries which are in turn divided into parishes.

DISSENTERS *See* Nonconformists.

DIVINE RIGHT OF KINGS Doctrine which holds that monarchs in direct line of succession have a divine or God-given right to the throne and that rebellion against their will is a sin. The doctrine originated in France, where it reached its apogee in the seventeenth century. In England it first appeared in 1569 in a 'Homily against Wilful Rebellion'. The English clergy accepted the doctrine on the whole, and were prepared to comply with the ecclesiastical canons of 1640 that required them to remind their congregations of the doctrine four times a year. The doctrine was most popular during the reign of Charles I (1625–49). Where obedience was impossible non-resistance (*q.v.*) was prescribed. The Civil War (1642–46) broke the doctrine, though the position of the Non-jurors (*q.v.*) reflected a late manifestation of it.

DOMINICANS Order of mendicant preaching friars founded by St Dominic in Languedoc in 1215 and confirmed by the Pope in 1216. Their official name is Friars Preachers; they are also called Black Friars on account of their long black mantles.

DONATISTS Members of a heretical sect in Numidia (modern Algeria) from the fourth to the eighth centuries who originally called

242

themselves the Church of the Martyrs, but were more commonly known after Donatus, the bishop they elected in Carthage in 312. Their strength lay in powerful and rigid organization and the simplicity of their dogma, the main tenets of which were that God's church was a society of saints which no sinner could enter and that only the priests of this pure church had the power to administer the sacraments. In 412 they were crushed as an organized church by the Emperor Honorius, but their influence persisted until Islam reached Africa in the seventh and eighth centuries. Their most lasting influence on Christianity stems from the reaction they provoked. St Augustine of Hippo (354–430) spent many years combating the heresy and, though he was initially hostile to secular intervention in church affairs, he eventually recognized the need for the State to interest itself in the Church and vice versa.

DOPPERS (Afrikaans) Members of the strict Calvinist Separatist Reformed Church in the Orange Free State and Transvaal, established in 1859.

E

EDICT OF NANTES The edict issued on 13 April 1598 by Henry IV of France which ended the religious wars (see p. 108). Its grant of toleration to the Huguenots (*q.v.*) lasted until the famous revocation of the Edict by Louis XIV on 22 October 1685. For further details, see pp. 108–109.

EDICT OF RESTITUTION The edict issued on 6 March 1629 by the Emperor Ferdinand II which ordered Protestants to restore to Roman Catholics the sees and ecclesiastical property taken since the 1552 Treaty of Passau. The Protestant reaction to this edict was a major factor in the Thirty Years War (see p. 267).

ENCYCLICAL (deriv. Lat. bulla encyclica, circular letter) Letter defining papal policy from the Pope to the Catholic bishops on matters of religious and political doctrine or discipline. The contents do not have the status of dogma, but nonetheless carry great authority and influence. Issued only on matters of importance, they are known by their opening words, e.g. Leo XIII's *Rerum Novarum* ('on new matters') which criticized the idea of a socialist state; Pius XI's *Mit Brennender Sorge* (written in German and criticizing Nazi excesses) and John XXIII's *Pacem in Terris* on nuclear weapons and the need for peace.

ENFANTS DE DIEU (Fr., children of God) Name used by the Camissards, the Protestants of the Cévennes whose 1702 rebellion against the French Crown was suppressed in 1704.

ENTRADA (Span., entry) Term used in Spain's South American colonies to denote a military expedition into previously unexplored or unconquered regions; in Brazil, any exploratory expedition into the interior and also, occasionally, the conversion of Indians to Christianity by military force.

EPISCOPACY (deriv. Lat., bishop) The government of the church by bishops, a form of organization which was retained in England by Elizabeth I (1558–1603) distinguishing the Anglican from most other 'reformed' churches. Archbishops Parker and Whitgift checked early attempts by Calvinists (*q.v.*) to introduce a Presbyterian (*q.v.*) system but the struggle continued under James I and Charles I when the Puritans (*q.v.*) attacked episcopacy. It was abolished by Parliament in 1643 but reinstated at the Restoration and confirmed at the Savoy Conference of 1661. The episcopacy was not seriously questioned again until the rise of Methodism (*q.v.*) in the eighteenth century. The Scottish Reformation created a Presbyterian system after 1560. Despite James I's gradual reintroduction of episcopacy, it was abolished by the Covenanters (*q.v.*) in 1638. Reinstated in

1661, it was finally abolished in the Scottish Church in 1689.

ERASTIANISM Theory, wrongly attributed to Erastus of Switzerland (1524–83), that the state has the right to decide the religion of its members. The term has usually been used in a derogatory sense: the Scottish churches, for example, held that the 'call' of the congregation was the only way to elect ministers and considered that the advocates of Episcopacy (*q.v.*) were practising Erastianism.

ETHIOPIANISM An early form of Pan-Africanism based on the establishment by Africans and people of the African diaspora of their own Christian churches as a reaction to the racism of white churches. The term derives from Ethiopia, the Greek word for Africa. The earliest examples are the Ethiopian Baptist Church, established in Jamaica in 1784, and the American Methodist Episcopal Church, founded in the USA in 1797. In central Africa, churches formed by John Chilembwe in 1915 and Simon Kimbangu in 1920 became a focus for anti-colonial agitation. *See also* Kimbanguism.

EVANGELISM (deriv. Gk., gospel) Preaching of the gospel with emphasis on the need for a new birth or conversion. In England, the evangelistic fervour of John Wesley and George Whitefield (*see* Methodism) aroused the great missionary spirit of the late eighteenth and the nineteenth centuries. George Fox, founder of the Society of Friends (*see* Quakers), was also an evangelist.

EXARCHATE An ecclesiastical province in the Orthodox Church enjoying autonomous status under a patriarchate.

EX CATHEDRA (Lat., from the throne) Term used to describe pronouncements made by the Pope in Consistory (*q.v.*) (*see* papal infallibility).

EXCOMMUNICATION Censure by most Christian churches, by which someone is excluded from the communion of the faithful according to canon law. It does not exclude a person from church membership, but from the sacraments and from church burial. An excommunicant can be absolved if he confesses his sin and does penance. In the Roman Catholic Church there are two types of excommunication: *toleratus* ('tolerated') and *vitandus* ('to be avoided') Only the gravest sins are punished by *vitandus* excommunication, which is announced in public, usually by the Vatican.

F

FALK LAWS Series of laws introduced in Prussia by the Minister of Public Worship, Dr Falk, between 1872 and 1879, which were extremely oppressive to Roman Catholics. Passed in pursuance of the *Kulturkampf* (*q.v.*), the more important of them date from May 1873 and are known as the May laws.

FIFTH MONARCHY MEN Members of a seventeenth-century fanatical sect with great influence among the supporters of Cromwell in the English Civil War. They believed that the Commonwealth (*q.v.*) signalled the coming of the fifth monarchy, prophesied in Dan. 2:44, which they identified with the Millennium as predicted in the Apocalypse.

FILIOQUE (Lat., and from the Son) Clause in the Nicene Creed claiming that the Holy Ghost proceeds from the Son as well as the Father. It is not accepted by the Eastern Orthodox churches.

FLAGELLANTS Members of the fanatical medieval religious movements, usually laymen, who engaged in mass public flagellations as a form of penance. They were stimulated in Italy from 1260 by the spread of the prophetic works of Joachim of Fiore which were often distorted to predict the coming of the end of the world. In the following century, the Black Death again produced flagellant movements, particularly in Germany. They were condemned by Pope Clement VI in 1349, and again by the Council of Constance in 1411–18.

FRANCISCANS Order of mendicant friars, founded by St Francis of Assisi, authorized by Pope Innocent II in 1215. Unlike earlier orders, they were not confined to monasteries but lived among the community caring for the poor; in addition to their ordinary monastic vows they took a vow of poverty.

FRATICELLI (Ital., humble friars) Spiritual Franciscans (*q.v.*) in Italy who left the order and attempted to follow a rigorous observance, with an exaggerated emphasis on the role of poverty in religious life. They were condemned for heresy by Pope John XXII in 1317. The name was also given generally to orthodox members of religious orders and to hermits.

FREEWILLERS An heretical Protestant sect led by Henry Harte in south-east England during the reign of Edward VI. Its followers believed in free will and religious toleration and were opposed by other Protestants. Freewillers were persecuted under the Catholic Mary I.

FRIARS Members of certain mendicant orders of the Roman Catholic Church. The four main orders are Franciscans (*q.v.*) (Grey Friars); Dominicans (*q.v.*) (Black Friars); Carmelites (*q.v.*) (White Friars) and Augustinians (Austin Friars).

FRIARS PREACHERS *See* Dominicans.

FUNDAMENTALIST One who believes that the Bible contains only literal truths which need not be the subject of interpretation: the description of creation in Genesis, for example, leads to a refusal to accept Darwinism (*q.v.*). Fundamentalism is popular in the southern states of the USA, hence the description of those states as the 'Bible Belt' (*q.v.*).

Muslim fundamentalists, such as the Ayatollah Khomeini in Iran, desire that their countries be ruled in strict accordance with Islamic law and reject non-Islamic Western or communist influences.

G

GALLICANISM Term coined in the nineteenth century for the position opposed to Ultramontanism (*q.v.*) in France, also denoting a more general complex of doctrines favouring restriction of papal power. It has three main strands: the assertion of the independence of the French king from the papacy; the collaboration of clergy and secular powers to limit papal intervention in the French state; and the superiority of an ecumenical council over the papacy. It first manifested itself in a thirteenth-century dispute between Philip IV and Pope Boniface VIII; by the sixteenth century a conciliar theory of church hierarchy had arisen which held that the Pope is subject to the general council of the Church. In 1398, following a national synod of French bishops, Charles VI withdrew his obedience to Benedict XIII, the Pope at Avignon, yet did not recognize his rival Boniface IX in Rome. In 1438 Charles VII issued the *Pragmatic Sanction of Bourges*, stating that the Pope's secular jurisdiction was dependent on the king and that the Pope was subject to a general council of the Church. The papacy secured its revocation in 1516.

The best exposition of Gallicanism was the *Gallican Articles* issued by a synod of the French clergy in 1682. These held (1) that the Pope has no secular power though he is spiritually supreme; (2) that he is subject to ecumenical councils; (3) that papal infallibility in matters of doctrine is conditional on confirmation of the papal position by the whole church, and (4) that the Pope must recognize the inviolability of the immemorial customs of the church in France, such as the right of the Crown to appoint bishops and receive the revenues of vacant bishoprics. The articles were condemned by Pope Alexander VIII in 1690 and revoked by Louis XIV in 1693. However, not all the French clergy accepted the Gallican position. The French Jesuits did not and Napoleon took no real interest in the matter. The first Vatican Council (1869–70) formally declared the Ultramontanist position to be the correct one, but by this time the emergence of the modern state had rendered disputes about papal intervention anachronistic.

GHIBELLINES (Ital., deriv. Germ. *Waiblingen*) Party in medieval Italian and German politics whose name is said to be derived from that of an estate belonging to the Hohenstaufens. Their feud with the Guelphs (*q.v.*), occurring during the campaigns of Emperor Frederick I, developed in thirteenth-century Italy into a bitter conflict between the Ghibellines supporting the Emperor, and the Guelphs, supporting the Pope.

GOLDEN LEAGUE League formed by the Catholic states of Switzerland in 1586 to defend their faith.

GOMARISTS Followers of Gomarus, professor of theology at Utrecht, and opponents of the Arminians (*q.v.*). Gomarus favoured the severe doctrine of Calvin, Arminius a milder and broader form of religious belief. In 1604 their differences divided the Dutch Church and led to the convening of the Synod of Dort in 1618.

GRAND REMONSTRANCE Statement of Parliament's demands of King Charles I prepared in 1641 by John Pym (1584–1643) and other parliamentary leaders. It was largely a propaganda exercise, listing reforms enacted by the Long Parliament, accusing 'Jesuited Papists' of a 'malignant and pernicious design' for subverting the constitution, and demanding resolution by the King of parliamentary grievances, the appointment of crown ministers approved by Parliament, the curbing of the powers of the Episcopacy

(*q.v.*) and Protestant reform of the clergy. The highly controversial proposal was passed only by eleven votes and rejected outright by Charles. Its real significance lay in its startling assertion of parliamentary demands and it drove many moderates into Charles's camp, marking a hardening of lines as civil war approached.

GREAT AWAKENING Evangelical, Protestant religious reform movement which began in the mid-Atlantic colonies in the 1720s and continued for some 20 years. It was marked by an emotional emphasis on the need for personal salvation and by criticism of the established churches. A second Great Awakening occurred in the frontier region and New England in the period 1800–30 and led to the establishment of the Mormon Church in 1830.

GREAT SCHISM The election of Pope Urban VI in 1378 was disputed by the French party in the Catholic Church which elected a rival in Clement VII. Papal rivalry continued until 1417 when the election of Martin V as Pope in Rome proved acceptable to both parties.

GREGORIAN Religious chant named after Pope Gregory I (560–604) which added extra tones to the hitherto traditional Ambrosian chants.

GUELPH (Ital., deriv. Germ. *Welf*) Party in medieval Italian politics whose name is said to be derived from that of the founder of the House of Brunswick. *See also* Ghibellines.

H

HEADS OF PROPOSALS The proposals set out on 1 August 1647 in England that Bishops and all other ecclesiastical officers should be deprived of any coercive powers. All the laws that enabled the civil magistrate to administer civil penalties for ecclesiastical censures should be repealed. All acts enjoining the use of the Prayer Book and imposing penalties for neglecting them should be repealed, as also the acts imposing penalties for not attending church. Roman Catholics should be disabled and Jesuits and Roman priests prevented from disturbing the state. The Covenant should not be forced on anyone. There should be religious toleration for all but Roman Catholics.

HENRICIANS Heretical followers of Henry the Monk, active in the French-speaking areas of Europe during the early twelfth century. They preached penance, argued for the rejection of the sacraments and denied the doctrine of original sin.

HERMANDAD (Span., brotherhood; also *Santa Hermandad*, holy brotherhood) Confederation of the major cities of medieval Castile, formed as a source of mutual protection against brigands. It gradually usurped the functions of a legislative body and used force to secure obedience to its rule.

HIGH CHURCH An expression – once virtually synonymous with Tory – first used in England in 1703 to describe the church party which insisted upon the enforcement of laws against the Dissenters (*see* Nonconformists). Since the early nineteenth century the term has chiefly referred to the Anglo-Catholic (*q.v.*) wing of the Church of England. *See also* Low Church.

HIGH COMMISSION, COURT OF Ecclesiastical court, established after Henry VIII declared himself head of the Church of England in 1534, to investigate and punish transgressions against the Acts of Supremacy and later of Uniformity. Its actions were often arbitrary and it was strongly opposed by Puritans (*q.v.*) and conscientious members of the legal profession. In the early seventeenth century the Stuart kings used it to enforce the royal prerogative in secular matters. In the sixteenth and seventeenth centuries its jurisdiction was challenged by common-law courts by means of writs of prohibition to get cases transferred to superior courts. It was abolished by Parliament in 1641.

HOLOCAUST (deriv. Gk., a whole burnt offering) Term applied to the attempted annihilation of the Jews in Europe by the Nazis in World War II. The culmination of centuries of anti-Semitism (*q.v.*), the attempted planned extermination was carried into effect in concentration camps and by *Einsatzgruppen* execution squads in conquered Russia. It destroyed an east European Jewish culture 1,000 years old, and carried out the murder of around 6 million Jews, half of them from Poland. It convinced many Jews that they could no longer live in Europe, or indeed anywhere except in their own state, and was thus the major impetus to Zionism (*q.v.*).

HOLY ALLIANCE Alliance concluded in September 1815 between Russia, Austria and Prussia, whose sovereigns agreed that their policies would be guided by Christian principles. In fact, the alliance was directed against the democratic and nationalist movements spawned all over Europe by the French Revolution.

HOLY EXPERIMENT William Penn's description for his own Quaker (*q.v.*) colony of Pennsylvania, founded in 1681.

HOLY PLACES Centre of conflicting claims between France, Russia and Turkey over the protection of the Holy Sepulchre in Jerusalem and the Church of the Nativity in Bethlehem, partially provoking the Crimean War in 1854. In 1852 Turkey recognized French claims to administer the Holy Places. Russia's attempt to secure equivalent rights for the Orthodox Church encouraged fears that it intended to extend its influence in the Near East.

HOLY ROMAN EMPIRE Major European institution from the ninth century to 1806. The old imperial title of 'Roman Emperor' was revived in AD 800 when Pope Leo III conferred it on Charlemagne (742–814), King of the Franks. From the mid-tenth century when the Carolingian line died out, it was borne by the kings of a succession of German dynasties. The term 'Holy Empire' was first used in 1034 to describe the territories held by Conrad II, and the use of the name 'Holy Roman Empire' (*'sacrum Romanum imperium'*) dated from 1157.

Initially the allies of the popes, the emperors were involved in a continual struggle with the papacy for supremacy in Europe from the eleventh to the thirteenth centuries.

In 1806 the last Holy Roman Emperor, Francis II (one of the Habsburgs) resigned the title, adopting instead that of Emperor of Austria.

HOLY SEE The papal seat. As Bishop of Rome, the Pope is head of the Roman Catholic Church and claims to be the lawful successor to St Peter.

HOLY SYNOD Council created by Peter the Great (1672–1725) in 1720 to exercise state control over the Orthodox Church. It was closely based on the Lutheran model.

HOSPITALLERS, KNIGHTS The military monks of the Order of St John of Jerusalem. Founded *c.* 1048 to help the sick, they played a prominent part in the twelfth century during the Crusades (*q.v.*). In 1309 they captured Rhodes, which they held until expelled by the Ottomans (*q.v.*) in 1522. In 1530 Emperor Charles V gave them the island of Malta which, as Knights of Malta, they held until Napoleon dislodged them in 1798. They still survive as a sovereign order with headquarters in Rome, and their medieval Benedictine habit of black with an eight-pointed cross is similar to that worn today by the St John Ambulance Brigade. *See also* Templar.

HOT GOSPELLER Originally the name given to the Protestant Edward Underhill, imprisoned in 1553 for his attack on Roman Catholicism on the accession of Queen Mary. After the Restoration in 1660 the term was applied to Puritans (*q.v.*). It survives today as a description of evangelists in the USA.

HUGUENOTS French Protestants of the sixteenth and seventeenth centuries. On 24 August 1572 thousands were killed in the massacre of St Bartholomew. In 1598 Henry IV, their

former leader, who had become a Catholic, granted them religious toleration by the Edict of Nantes (*q.v.*). When this was revoked by Louis XIV in 1685, thousands left France illegally for exile in England, Holland, America and Germany.

HUMBLE PETITION AND ADVICE Document of 25 May 1657 proposing that a confession of faith be drawn up. It contained the idea that it was possible to agree on the essentials of religion while differing on matters of detail. Subscription to the confession was to be a qualification for office-holding. One clause about disturbing assemblies was directed against the Quakers (*q.v.*). It marks a definite reaction against toleration.

HUMILIATI (Lat., humble ones) In medieval northern Italy, loosely organized religious congregations who led a penitential life based on manual labour and preaching. After Pope Alexander III had refused laymen amongst them the right to preach, they fell into heresy, but in 1201 Pope Innocent III gave regulations to those prepared to return to the Church.

HUSSITES Followers of John Hus, rector of Prague University and a pupil of John Wycliffe, who was excommunicated by Pope Alexander V in 1412. He continued disseminating his doctrine and was summoned to the Council of Constance. Having been assured of safe conduct by the Emperor Sigismund of Hungary, he attended but was imprisoned and burned as a heretic in 1415. Sigismund argued that he had no obligation to keep faith with heretics; his action was prompted by the contempt Hus held for all forms of authority. In 1416 Hus's principal disciple, Jerome of Prague, was also executed. Led by John of Zisca, the Hussites became a formidable body in Moravia and Bohemia, where they took up arms against the Church and the Emperor. In 1424 John of Zisca died and the movement splintered. However, the Hussites remained in insurrection until 1436 when their revolt was ended by the Treaty of Iglau.

HUTTERITES An Anabaptist sect named after Jakob Hutter. Distinguished by their withdrawal from the world and the establishment of communities in which all property was held in common.

I

ICONOCLASTS (deriv. Gk., breaker of images) Name originally given to the followers of Leo III, Emperor of the eastern Roman Empire, who forbade the worship of images in 726. The interdiction met great opposition and led to the Iconoclast War. The same name was given in 1560–61 to militant Huguenots (*q.v.*) in France who destroyed the religious statues adorning churches and monasteries wherever they could. During the English Civil War the Parliamentarians were also accused of iconoclasm.

ILLUMINATI (Lat., enlightened ones) Members of a secret society founded in 1776 by Adam Weishaupt, a Bavarian professor of canon law at Ingolstadt. He hoped to combat superstition and ignorance by establishing an association for rational enlightenment and the regeneration of the world. Under conditions of secrecy, the Illuminati, whose members included Goethe and Schiller, sought to penetrate and control lodges of Freemasons for subversive purposes. They spread over Austria, Hungary and Italy but were condemned by the papacy and dissolved by the Bavarian government in 1785. The same term was also applied to a sect of Spanish heretics in the sixteenth century (*see* Alumbrados).

IMPROPRIATIONS Tithes and patronage rights re-allocated by the Crown to lay rectors or impropriators in the sixteenth century, following the dissolution of the monasteries in the reign of Henry VIII. A consequence was that tithes (*q.v.*) tended to become simply rent tributes to absentee landlords, while the impropriators usually passed on only a small fraction of the revenue to the actual incumbents, for whose maintenance it was originally intended. It became increasingly difficult for the Church to provide adequate stipends for the upkeep of the clergy before Queen Anne's Bounty (*q.v.*), particularly since the gentry frustrated attempts in the sixteenth and seventeenth centuries to remedy the situation.

INDEPENDENTS Originally the Barrowists (*q.v.*) and Brownists (*q.v.*) of Elizabeth I's reign; later, with the English Civil War, any of a multiplication of separatist religious movements, the main ones being Baptists (*q.v.*) and Congregationalists (*q.v.*). They maintained that each congregation should be autonomous and free to choose its own minister and form of worship, thus rejecting both Episcopacy (*q.v.*) and Presbyterianism (*q.v.*). Cromwell, while curtailing their political activities, tolerated them; with the aid of the army of which they comprised an important element, they became one of the most influential groups in the state. The term was also applied loosely to certain political groups in the Long Parliament, particularly in the Rump. Their policies are well summarized in the Heads of the Proposals (*q.v.*).

INDEX EXPURGATORIUS (Lat., index of expurgations; also *index librorum prohibitorum,* index of prohibited books) List of books which the Roman Catholic Church forbids its members to read on grounds of immorality or heresy. The first papal Index was commissioned by Pope Paul IV in 1559 but was largely ignored by the Council of Trent (1545–63). Pope Pius IV commissioned a new list in 1564. Originally part of the Counter-Reformation, the Index attempted to halt the diffusion of heretical opinions; it is still in existence. Its severity varied from country to country.

INDULGENCES (deriv. Lat., allow time for) In the Roman Catholic Church, the remission granted by an ecclesiastical authority of the temporal punishment still due to a repentant sinner. Indiscriminate and corrupt sale of indulgences by Tetzel and other papal agents in the sixteenth century was one of the grievances against the Catholic Church which fuelled the Reformation (*q.v.*).

INJUNCTION In England, a prohibitive writ by which a party is commanded not to do, or to cease from doing, an act that does not amount to a crime. Ecclesiastical injunctions, requiring the observance of church law and customs, were common during the Reformation (*q.v.*). They declined in importance after 1571 when the canons of the convocation (*q.v.*) began to replace them.

INQUISITION Ecclesiastical court of the Roman Catholic Church made into a very formidable weapon for stamping out heresy by Pope Innocent III in the thirteenth century. It was established in various Catholic countries in Europe but obtained its most extensive power and organization in Spain under the rule of Ferdinand V of Aragon (1452–1516) and his wife Isabella of Castile (1451–1516). The Grand Inquisitor Torquemada exercised his duties with terrible cruelty and harshness (*see* auto da fé). Not until the eighteenth century did the Inquisition's authority and influence start to decline; its jurisdiction then became restricted to the suppression of heretical literature.

INTERDICT (deriv. Lat., forbid by decree) A decree of the Roman Catholic Church to withhold services and comforts from an individual or community. Its main function was to put pressure on offenders against canon law or on secular powers with whom the papacy was in dispute. In 1208 Pope Innocent III issued an interdict against King John and the realm of England under which all church sacraments were withheld except baptism and extreme unction. The dead, for example, could be buried only in unconsecrated ground. *See* excommunication.

IRVINGITES Name given to members of the Catholic Apostolic Church founded in 1832 by a Scottish minister, Edward Irving (1792–1834) and the MP Henry Drummond (1786–1860). The sect's main tenet was the imminence of Christ's second coming. Initially it attempted to organize itself on the lines of the early Church but later it adopted increasingly Catholic practices. By the end of the nineteenth century it had little influence.

J

JACOBITES Name applied to a Monophysite heretical sect in sixth-century Syria, called after their leader Jacobus Baradaeus.

JANISSARIES The elite band of Ottoman foot soldiers who acted as the Sultan's bodyguard, first recruited under Bayezed I in the fourteenth century from Christian children taken from the conquered countries of Serbia and Albania. They were brought up as Muslims and were not allowed to marry. They gained great power in the empire.

JANSENISTS Members of a Roman Catholic sect in seventeenth-century France, whose doctrines were based on the *Augustinus* of Cornelius Jansen, Bishop of Ypres, published posthumously in 1638. They were strongly opposed to the doctrinal and ethical teachings of the Jesuits (*q.v.*) and counted Arnauld, Pascal and Racine among their adherents. In 1653 the papal bull *Cum occasione* declared five of the main Jansenist propositions regarding grace and the freedom of choice to be heretical; the condemnation was repeated in 1705 with the bull *Unigenitus*.

JESUITS Members of the Roman Catholic teaching order, the Society of Jesus, founded in Paris by Ignatius Loyola in 1540 as a spearheading force in the Counter-Reformation. Its strict organization made it very powerful and at various times it has played an important part in politics. A long and rigorous course of study is prescribed before an applicant is admitted into the privileges of full membership.

JUMPER Expression used by Irish Catholic peasants to describe a person who changed their religion from Catholic to Protestant. In some cases (as in the famine of 1845–49) starving peasants were forced to convert in exchange for food.

K

KIMBANGUISM An independent African Christian church formed in the Belgian Congo (now the Democratic Republic of the Congo, formerly Zaïre) by Simon Kimbangu, a Bakongo peasant and Baptist priest, in 1921. Kimbanguism, which, with several million members, was the largest religious movement in Africa, absorbed Christianity into traditional African culture. Persecution by the Belgian authorities, and the sentencing of Kimbangu to life imprisonment, encouraged the Church's followers to take up anti-colonial resistance. In the 1950s, following Kimbangu's death in prison, his son established the Church of Jesus Christ on Earth through the Prophet Simon Kimbangu; this was the first independent African Church to be recognized by the World Council of Churches.

KNIGHTS HOSPITALLERS See Hospitallers, Knights.

KNIGHTS TEMPLARS See Templar.

KULTURKAMPF (Germ., culture struggle) Conflict of beliefs between Bismarck and the Roman Catholic Church between 1871 and 1887. Bismarck, alarmed at decrees of the Vatican which implied that the Church and not the State had prior claim on the citizens' obedience (see Ultramontanism), and at the

creation of an anti-Prussian Catholic Centre Party, passed the Falk laws (q.v.) in May 1873 subjecting the Church to state regimentation. However, negotiations with Pope Leo XIII led to the restoration of Catholic rights by 1887.

L

LATERAN TREATIES Agreements reached on 11 February 1929 between Mussolini and Pope Pius XI (pontiff 1922–29), under which the sovereignty of the Vatican City State was recognized and a substantial indemnity paid to it in respect of papal possessions confiscated during Italian unification in 1870. A concordat (q.v.) was established between the Church and the Fascist government of Italy.

LATITUDINARIAN During seventeenth- and eighteenth-century England, a member of that section of the Church of England favouring breadth of thought in religious belief and practice. In the seventeenth century they stood roughly mid-way between the extreme Puritans (q.v.) and the advocates of Episcopacy (q.v.); later their criticism of both ritual and episcopacy promoted laxity of worship and opportunism. In the eighteenth century there was a danger of the Church becoming simply an adjunct of government, when latitudinarians were given preferment by successive Whig administrations as a means of weakening the 'High Church' (q.v.) and hence the Tory Party. In the nineteenth century the influence of latitudinarianism was challenged by both Evangelism (q.v.) and the Puseyites (q.v.).

LATTER DAY SAINTS See Mormons.

LAUDIAN Supporter of the policies of William Laud (Archbishop of Canterbury 1633–45) in the seventeenth-century Church of England. Laudians were influenced by the

Arminians (*q.v.*), and strove to enforce discipline and uniformity of worship on the basis of the Prayer Book. They also emphasized the essential catholicism of the Anglican Church and the desirability of ritual and the use of vestments. Supporters of the Stuart claims to the supremacy of the Crown, they recruited royal aid in their attempts to anglicanize the Scottish Church in the 1630s (*see* Bishops' wars). In their efforts to suppress the Puritans (*q.v.*) they made full use of the law and prerogative courts, while the Puritans charged them with seeking to eliminate Protestantism (*q.v.*) from the Church. Laud was executed by attainder in 1645. The restoration of the Church of England in the 1660s in some ways represented the triumph of Laudianism in liturgical and doctrinal terms though the social policy advocated by Laud himself was abandoned.

LAUREANISTAS Right-wing Catholic conservatives, led by Laureano Gómez, who sought to spiritualize Colombia in the 1930s through the Catholic faith, giving the clergy the task of administering social services and paternalistic government programmes. In the countryside the masses were to be freed of the Liberal caudillismo by the establishment of local collective and co-operative associations run by the clergy. Rural society was to be reconstructed on a corporative basis and parliamentary democracy was to be discarded.

LAY IMPROPRIATOR In sixteenth-century England and later, a layman in receipt of tithes (*q.v.*), i.e. ecclesiastical revenues. Lay impropriators originated partly from the grants of land made by abbeys and other church communities to powerful laymen in return for their protection, but mainly from the impropriations (*q.v.*) made at the dissolution of the monasteries by Henry VIII.

LEGATIONS Name given to the provinces of Bologna, Ferrara and Romagna, over which the papacy claimed rights, but which were surrendered to France in 1797 by the Treaty of Tolentino.

LEGATUS A LATERE (Lat., legate from the side of the Pope) In the Roman Catholic Church, a cardinal legate with plenipotentiary powers e.g. Thomas Wolsey under Henry VIII.

LEONISTS *See* Lyonists.

LIBERATION THEOLOGY The belief and practice of some Central and South American Roman Catholic priests who attempt to combine Marxist social and economic analysis with Christian theology and argue that the Church should have a 'bias to the poor'.

LIBERTINS (Fr.) In Switzerland, those who opposed the extreme stringency of Calvinism (*q.v.*) in Geneva in 1541. They were repressed by the Consistorium (*q.v.*).

LIGUEUR A supporter of the anti-Huguenot Catholic Party in France in the 1570s.

LOLLARD (deriv. Dutch *lollaerd,* mumbler) Member of a group of religious reformers and followers of John Wycliffe (*c.* 1320–84). They were reviled and persecuted during the reign of Richard II (1377–99) and again under Henry IV (1399–1414) who had a friend, the Lollard leader Sir John Oldcastle, burnt at the stake. *See* Wycliffite.

LORDS SPIRITUAL Bishops who sit in the House of Lords, i.e. the Archbishops of Canterbury and York, the Bishops of London, Durham and Winchester and 21 other Anglican bishops.

LOS VON ROM (Germ., away from Rome) Movement started *c.* 1899 in the German areas of Austria–Hungary by the Austrian Pan-German Deputies, whose aim was to detach their followers from the Roman Catholic Church so that, in the event of the Austro-Hungarian Empire breaking up, the German states of Austria would be more acceptable as members of the German Empire.

LOW CHURCH The latitudinarian (*q.v.*) wing of the Church of England, close to Protestant nonconformity, which in the seventeenth and eighteenth centuries attached less importance than the High Church (*q.v.*) to the sacraments and the priesthood. The term was revived in the mid-nineteenth century to refer to Evangelism (*q.v.*) within the Church of England.

LYONISTS In late twelfth-century Europe, moderate Waldensians (*q.v.*) who took their name from the movement's original centre, Lyons. After splitting from the Waldensians and, in 1205, from the Poor Lombards (*q.v.*), they survived for some time in France and its neighbouring areas.

M

MALCONTENTS Catholic nobles in the Netherlands, opposed to William of Orange after 1578, who desired the supremacy of the Catholic religion. They placed themselves under the leadership of the French Duke of Alençon; their ranks included Montigny, Hèze and Lalaing. Originally anti-Spanish, their dislike of Calvinism (*q.v.*) caused them to return to allegiance to Spain.

MANICHAEISM Asiatic religion founded by Mani, a Persian born in AD 216 in Babylonia, who obtained the permission of his ruler Shapur I to found a religion which would have the same impact on Babylonia as Christianity had on the West. It was a development of Zoroastrianism, influenced also by Buddhism and Gnosticism. With 12 disciples, Mani represented himself as a paraclete or comforter, equivalent to the Holy Spirit in Christianity. The rapid expansion of Manichaeism in Persia antagonized the Zoroastrian priests, who resented Mani's reforms of their religion and regarded him as a dangerous heretic; in 276 he was crucified.

Manichaeist beliefs were extremely complicated, but their underlying tenet was one of dualism, i.e. that there is an eternal struggle between God as the spiritual or light and matter as darkness. The religion spread to India and China, where it flourished until the eleventh century. In the West its influence was felt in Spain and North Africa, where it had an effect on the Christian Bishops of Alexandria and Carthage. St Augustine of Hippo (AD 354–430) was for a time a believer. Manichaeism was eventually suppressed as a heresy in the West during the fourth and fifth centuries, but its name continued to be used in connection with dualist heresies, such as that of the Albigensians (*q.v.*).

MARONITE Member of the Maronite Church, an Orthodox Christian Church in union with the Holy See (*q.v.*). The Pope is head of the Church but immediately below him is the Patriarch of Antioch and all the East, in residence at Bkirki near Beirut. The Maronite Church is one of the largest practising the Eastern rite but in communion with the Roman Catholic Church. It was founded by a Syrian hermit, St Maron, in the late fourth century but owes its survival to St John Maron, Patriarch of Antioch, 685–707, who in 684 had defeated the Byzantine army and made the Maronites independent. There are 400,000 Maronites in Lebanon, Syria, Israel and Egypt, and about half a million more scattered through the Americas and southern Europe, descendants of those forced to migrate to avoid Ottoman (*q.v.*) persecution in the nineteenth century.

MARRANOS Term used offensively of those Jews in Spain and Portugal who, although they were converted to Christianity (*conversos*), secretly continued to practise their Jewish beliefs.

MASSACRE OF ST BARTHOLOMEW'S DAY The massacre of the Huguenots in Paris on the night of 23–24 August 1572.

MENNONITES Anabaptists (*q.v.*) who followed the teachings of Menno Simons. Distinguished by their pacifism and separation from secular authority.

METHODISM English religious movement founded in 1738 by John Wesley (1703–91) with the aim of spreading scriptural holiness. Wesley was greatly influenced by the Moravians (*q.v.*) whom he had encountered in North America. He organized the movement (described as 'People called Methodists') into 'societies', united into 'circuits' under ministers. The circuits in turn were united into 'districts' and all brought together into a single body by a conference of ministers which has met annually since 1744. Local lay preachers were also employed and moved from circuit to circuit each year. Chapel services were designed to supplement, rather than conflict with, the Church of England, of which Wesley always considered himself a member. Methodists were to attend church in the morning and chapel in the evening; they met regularly at class-meetings and at the end of every quarter. If their attendance had been regular, they received a ticket entitling them to come to monthly sacramental services. If a member's attendance was inadequate, his or her name was removed from the list. Wesley started Sunday Schools, composed many hymns and revived the Agape or 'love feast' of the early Church in meetings designed to increase the society's sense of brotherhood. Copying the open-air meetings of the Calvinist preacher, George Whitefield, he found that his sermons caused religious ecstasies among the congregation. Similar groans, tears and fainting-fits were produced by other Methodist preachers, including lay speakers, leading the Church of England to claim that its services would be 'without enthusiasm' of the type manifested by Methodism.

From 1784 onwards, Wesley personally consecrated clergy to go as missionaries to America; the movement finally broke with the Church of England in 1795. Differences arose within the movement regarding the status of the laity and the relationship of the movement to the Church of England. In 1797 the Methodist New Connection emerged, giving the laity equal representation with ministers, and in 1810 a more important schism occurred with the formation of the Primitive Methodists, who gave the laity even more power and reintroduced camp-meeting-style services. In 1811 there was a split between the Calvinists (*q.v.*), who accepted the doctrine of predestination, and the Arminians (*q.v.*), who did not. In 1815 the Bible Christians ('Bryanites') were formed and a further schism, ostensibly over the foundation of a theological college, led to actions in the law courts. The movement remained divided until 1932 when a conference at the Albert Hall, London, led to the unification of the Wesleyan Methodists, the Primitive Methodists and the United Methodists in the Methodist Church. In recent years talks aimed at union with the Church of England have been held.

METROPOLITAN Title bestowed in Russia and elsewhere on the Orthodox bishops in the historic cities of Moscow, St Petersburg, Kiev, Minsk and Novosibirsk.

MILLENARIANISM The belief that the Millennium will begin in the 6001st year after the Creation, computed by Archbishop Ussher (1581–1650) as having taken place in 4004 BC. Associated with the notion of the second coming of Christ and similar eschatological beliefs, it was very popular during the English Civil War and Interregnum (1642–60). The term is now used in the wider connotation.

MILLENARY PETITION Puritan (*q.v.*) appeal to James I in 1603 for changes in the liturgy and form of worship, including discontinuance of the ring in marriage and the sign of the cross in baptism, a request for stricter sabbath observance and a greater emphasis on preaching. The authors of the petition claimed that it bore the signatures of 1,000 Puritan ministers; hence the name. James promised to consider the matter at the 1604 Hampton Court Conference, but by then he had allied himself with the Anglican bishops and told the Puritans that if they did not conform he would 'harry them out of the land'.

MOLINISTS In seventeenth-century Europe, followers of the Spanish Jesuit (*q.v.*) Luis de Molina (1535–1600), a principal antagonist of the Jansenists (*q.v.*).

MORAL MAJORITY A right-wing pressure group influential in American politics since the 1980s which takes a Christian fundamentalist position on such issues as family life, abortion, gay rights and pornography.

MORAVIANS Members of the Moravian Church, a revival of the 'Bohemian Brethren' (*see* Unitas Fratrum) in 1722. As a Protestant sect it was persecuted by Emperor Ferdinand II and barely survived. But in the eighteenth century it was re-established by Count Zinzendorf in Saxony and built the town of Herrnhut ('God's protection'), which became the centre from which Moravian missionaries spread their doctrine all over the world. Their central tenet (which strongly influenced John Wesley, the founder of Methodism (*q.v.*)) was that goodness of behaviour, piety and orthodoxy are of no avail without faith, the 'sufficient sovereign saving grace' that comes as a direct illumination from God.

MORISCOS Moors in Spain who converted to Christianity.

MORMONS American religious sect founded in 1830 by Joseph Smith (1805–44) after a vision of two heavenly messengers who forbade him to join an existing church but told him to become the prophet of a new one. He also claimed to have been told of two hidden gold plates which he uncovered in 1827 and translated with the aid of the 'angels' from 'reformed Egyptian' into English. The resulting *Book of Mormon* was published in 1830 and a small church founded in New York State. The *Book* identified the American Indians as the ten lost tribes of Israel and alleged that Christ had appeared in America after his ascension.

The sect encountered hostility from the local community for styling themselves the 'Chosen People' and participating in politics as Smith directed. In 1844 Smith was murdered and became a martyr for his Church. He was succeeded as leader by Brigham Young, who led the sect across a thousand miles of desert to Salt Lake, Utah in July 1847. By 1851, 30,000 Mormons had arrived and Salt Lake City was built as their headquarters. In 1852 the reorganized Church of Jesus Christ of Latter Day Saints, with its headquarters at Independence, Missouri, became a separate and distinct body though it holds similar beliefs.

The Mormons have two orders of priests or leaders: the Melchizedeks, or high order, who attend to the spiritual affairs of the Church and include the apostles or ruling elders and the high priest; the Aaronic priesthood, or lower order, who attend to temporal affairs. Polygamy, sanctioned by Brigham Young, was renounced in 1890. The Mormons are believers in Millenarianism (*q.v.*), abstain from alcohol, coffee, tea and tobacco, and lay stress on community welfare and the importance of revelation through visions.

MORTMAIN (OFr. deriv. Lat., dead hand) In medieval England, lands held by the Church which were not liable to the feudal dues, such as reliefs and escheats, that were obligatory on land held in frankalmoin. It became common practice for laymen to give land to the Church and then receive it back as tenants, in order to avoid their feudal obligations. The Statute of Mortmain, introduced in 1279, forbade the gift of land to the Church without the prior consent of the Crown.

MORTUARY (ME deriv. Lat.) A gift from the estate of a deceased man at the time of his death to the parish clergy. The practice developed from the soul scot (*q.v.*); the gift was originally the second-best beast, and later the second-best possession. Eventually cash sums were paid instead, which opened the way to abuse and was a source of anti-clerical feeling in late medieval England. In 1529 Parliament set a limit to the size of mortuary fees. They continued to be collected up to the eighteenth century.

MUGGLETONIANS Members of an English religious sect founded c. 1651 by two journeymen tailors, Ludowicke Muggleton and John Reeve. Unlike most sects of the period they had no political interests but were purely religious. They rejected the doctrine of the Trinity; asserted that God had a human body; maintained that the Father, not the Son, died on the cross and that he left Elijah in control. Muggleton and Reeve believed that they represented Aaron and Moses (Rev. 11: 3–6).

N

NEW CHRISTIANS In Portugal, after the royal decree of 1499, those Jews and their descendants who were forcibly converted to Christianity.

NEW PURITANISM A radical and often authoritarian rejection of the permissive society of the 1960s which emerged in the 1980s, encouraged by the spread of Aids. See Moral Majority.

NEW RIGHT Term embracing conservative, Christian-based politics, an increasingly important section of the right, in the late 1970s. Later based around the Moral Majority (q.v.) organization founded by Rev. Jerry Falwell in 1979. Often fundamentalist and evangelical, it bitterly opposed abortion, pornography, gay rights, etc., and supported school prayers, anti-communism, traditional values etc.

NONCONFORMIST Member of those Christian bodies which do not conform to the doctrines

of the Church of England. Until the 1662 Act of Uniformity they were usually termed 'Puritans' or 'Dissenters', and were often persecuted. The oldest bodies of nonconformists are the Baptists (q.v.), Independents (q.v.) and (in England) the Presbyterians (q.v.). In Scotland the Presbyterians are the official Church of Scotland and hence it is the Anglicans who are 'Nonconformists'. The Methodists (q.v.) date from 1738 but refused to consider themselves Nonconformists until some time later.

NON-JURORS The High Church clergymen, 300–400 in number, who refused to swear the oaths of allegiance and supremacy on the accession to the English throne of William III and Mary in 1689.

NON-RESISTANCE Doctrine, also known as the 'doctrine of Passive Obedience', which held it to be a deadly sin to oppose the will of the King. The roots of the doctrine lay in theories of Divine Right of Kings and it was much preached by the Anglican clergy during the reign of Charles I (1625–49).

NUNCIO (Ital. deriv. Lat. nuntius, messenger) Title given to papal envoys in foreign capitals.

O

OFFICIAL REFORMATION Term used to describe the means used by Henry VIII in England to break with the jurisdiction of Rome, as opposed to the wider reforms of doctrine and worship undertaken by the Protestants (q.v.).

OLD BELIEVERS Russian dissenters who in the seventeenth century refused to accept patriarch Nikon's reform of the services of the Russian Orthodox Church.

OLD CATHOLICS Dissident Catholics in Austria, Germany, Holland and Switzerland who broke with Rome in the eighteenth and nineteenth centuries, rejected the 1870 Doctrine of Papal Infallibility (*q.v.*) and united in the 1889 Declaration of Utrecht.

OPUS DEI A Roman Catholic organization dedicated to the progress of faith and reform in its members' professional spheres. Founded in 1928 by a Spanish priest, Josemaria Escriyá de Baláguer (1902–75).

ORANGE ORDER The society, an influential and bitterly anti-Catholic body, largely maintained the Unionist Party of Northern Ireland which ruled from 1921 to 1972. Although it chiefly flourishes in Ulster, the Order has branches in many English-speaking countries, particularly in mainland Britain in cities associated with Ulster such as Glasgow and Liverpool.

ORATORIANS A secular order of Catholic priests founded by Philip Neri in 1556 to undertake moral and religious teaching work. Cardinal Newman introduced the order to Britain in 1847.

OREBITES (*also* Horebites) Sect of radical Hussites (*q.v.*) from Hrade Králové (Königgrätz) in eastern Bohemia. They founded a community and formed a military force comparable to that of the Taborites (*q.v.*). Their name is derived from their town, renamed after the scriptural Mount Horeb.

OTTOMAN (deriv. Turk. *Osman*) Dynasty, founded by Osman, which ruled the Turkish Empire until the abolition of the sultanate in 1922. The name was given first to the Turkish state which was formed *c.* 1300 and later to the Ottoman Empire. The expansion of the Ottoman state, based on the morale of *jihad* and the administrative skills acquired by Islam, reached a peak in the late sixteenth and early seventeenth centuries.

OUTREMER Crusader kingdoms established in the Middle East at the end of the eleventh century, including the principality of Antioch (1098–1263); the counties of Edessa (1098–1144) and Tripoli (1109–1289); the Kingdom of Cyprus (1191–1489, then a Venetian colony until 1571) and the Kingdom of Jerusalem (1100–87) and then the Kingdom of Acre until 1291. These states were run on the lines of European feudalism, though their European population was always in the minority. It was only successive crusades (*q.v.*) and the establishment of military orders such as the Templars (*q.v.*) and Hospitallers (*q.v.*) which enabled them to exist for 200 years amidst hostile Muslim states and a subject Muslim population. Internal power struggles among the ruling families, treachery and disregard for the native populations, both Muslim and Christian, helped weaken them. As interest in the Holy Land declined in Europe it became impossible to attract sufficient Europeans to Outremer to enable it to survive. One by one, the states gradually collapsed under Muslim pressure.

OXFORD MOVEMENT Group within Church of England from 1830s seeking to restore the High Church (*q.v.*) traditions of the seventeenth century. The movement arose out of anxiety over the implications of Catholic emancipation (*q.v.*) and the Parliamentary Reform Act of 1832. It was led by three Fellows of Oriel College, Oxford, and led to a strong Anglo-Catholic revival Though Keble and Pusey remained in the Church of England, Newman became a Roman Catholic. *See* Puseyism.

P

PALLIUM (Lat.) Robe of office sent by the Pope to high dignitaries of the Catholic Church, signifying that they have received authorization.

PAPAL INFALLIBILITY Doctrine of the Roman Catholic Church proclaimed in July 1870 by the Vatican Council summoned by Pope Pius IX, claiming that the Pope, when speaking in his official capacity on questions of morals or faith, is protected by God from any possibility of error. It has been suggested that the new dogma was intended to counter the Church's loss of temporal power in the nineteenth century by increasing the Pope's authority. Many people, including the German priest and historian Döllinger, were excommunicated for refusing to accept it.

Its basis is that the Bible does not contain answers to every question of morals and faith and that a sure and final court of appeal is provided by the Church as Christ's temporal teaching authority. After studying a problem carefully and receiving all possible help from the Church, the answer given by a pope to the question at issue must be correct and not open to doubt. Superhuman intelligence is not attributed to the Pope, nor is it suggested that God gives him an answer to every conceivable question. The Pope may, of course, be wrong in a personal capacity and his sphere of infallibility is strictly limited.

Only when speaking officially (*ex cathedra*) as supreme leader of the Church and definer of doctrine does his decision have to be accepted by all Catholics; furthermore, pronouncements are only infallible if specifically so defined. The vast majority of statements on matters of ethics and doctrine, such as the 1968 encyclical on birth control (*Humanae Vitae*), do not involve infallibility. In July 1973 the Sacred Congregation for the Doctrine of the Faith published a strong reaffirmation of the doctrine of infallibility.

PASSAGIANS Small sect of Christian heretics, centred in Lombardy, condemned by Pope Lucius II in 1184. They followed a literal observance of Old Testament precepts, including circumcision.

PASTARENE (Ital.) Heretics, particularly Cathars (*q.v.*). The term became current after the third Lateran Council of 1179.

PASTOUREAUX Spontaneous rising of a group of peasants and shepherds in north-east France in 1251, with the primary object of rescuing King Louis IX, captured on crusade in Egypt, and the subsidiary aims of reforming church abuse and liberating the Holy Land. Led by a Hungarian styling himself 'the Master of Hungary', their campaign soon degenerated into local pillaging and excesses against priests and scholars and was soon suppressed.

PATARIA (Ital.) Name given to an eleventh-century reform movement in Milan, possibly derived from the Milan rag-market. The movement aimed to reform abuses in the Church and had papal support.

PATRIARCH The chief bishop in some Orthodox churches, particularly used to describe those presiding in Alexandria and Antioch.

PATRIMONIUM PETRI (Lat., 'Patrimony of St Peter') A medieval expression for the estates held by the Church in Rome.

PATRONATO REAL (Span., royal patronage) Right granted to Spanish and Portuguese kings by the papacy to appoint candidates to ecclesiastical benefices in South America, placing the Latin American Church effectively under crown control.

PENAL LAWS *See* Catholic emancipation.

PETER'S PENCE In England, a tribute to the Pope paid first by Offa in the eighth century; that paid by Ethelwulf in the ninth century was to provide funds for the support of a Saxon college at Rome. A tribute also paid to Rome in the time of King Alfred (871–899) later came to be regarded by the Pope as a right and was standardized as hearth money of £200 a year from the whole country. Peter's Pence was abolished by Parliament in 1534. It was also to be found in other European states.

PETROBUSIANS Followers of Peter of Bruis, a French village priest from the Embrun region who preached in south-west France between *c.* 1120 and 1140, who rejected all external forms of worship.

PFFAFENBRIEF (Germ., priests' charter) Ordinance issued in 1370 by the Federal States of Switzerland, declaring that clerics were subject to state authority and could claim no special privileges in relation to secular rule.

PIKARTS Medieval term of abuse for heretics.

PILGRIM FATHERS The 101 English Puritans (*q.v.*) and other Congregationalists (*q.v.*) who, after living for some years in exile in Holland, sailed for America in the *Mayflower* on 6 September 1620. They landed at Plymouth, Massachusetts, on 4 December, where they founded a settlement. They are regarded as the pioneers of American colonization, although a small colony had been founded in Virginia 13 years earlier.

PILGRIMAGE OF GRACE Name given to insurrections in Cumberland, Durham, Lincolnshire, Lancashire, Northumberland, Westmorland and Yorkshire in 1536–37 against the ecclesiastical and other reforms of Henry VIII. The rebels, led by Lord Thomas Darcy, the Archbishop of York, and Robert Aske, were suppressed following the imposition of martial law in the north and Aske, Darcy and 20 other leaders were executed.

PLACADES The 'Affaire des Placades' was an attempt by French Protestant evangelicals in October 1534 to force Francis I to take up a defined religious position. The attempt went badly wrong. The leading reformers were arrested. Others (including Calvin) fled from Paris.

PLACES DE SÛRETÉ Towns in France allowed, under the Edict of Nantes (*q.v.*), to have a Huguenot (*q.v.*) garrison.

PLURALISM The simultaneous holding of more than one ecclesiastical office or benefice which continued despite a papal bull of 1317 and strenuous efforts to prevent it at the sixteenth-century Council of Trent. Pluralism was forbidden in England by successive Acts of Parliament in 1529, 1838, 1850 and 1885.

POGROM (Russ., destruction) Term used to denote anti-Jewish violence, first used to describe attacks on the Jews authorized by the tsarist authorities in 1881. Pogroms in eastern Europe forced many Jews to emigrate to Britain and the USA in the late nineteenth and early twentieth centuries. In 1938, Hitler ordered a general pogrom in Germany which led to the destruction of all synagogues and nearly all Jewish shops, homes and hospitals.

POLITIQUES (Fr.) French Catholic party, led by the Montmorency family and formed after the massacre of St Bartholomew's Day (*q.v.*) of Parisian Huguenots (*q.v.*) in 1572, which wished to put an end to such religious persecution.

PONTIFEX MAXIMUS (Lat., chief priest) In ancient Rome, the official head of Roman religion; after the rise of Christianity the title, abbreviated to Pontiff, was adopted by the popes.

PONTIFF *See* Pontifex maximus.

PONTIFICALIA (Lat.) Ecclesiastical term for the vestments of a pope or bishop.

POOR LOMBARDS A wing of the medieval Waldensians (*q.v.*), initially based in northern Italy, who were influenced by radical and anti-church opinions and followed the trend of the region by forming congregations supported by manual labour. They split from the Lyonists (*q.v.*) in 1205 and were active missionaries, particularly in the German-speaking areas of Europe.

POPISH PLOT So-called Jesuit plot, 'exposed' in August 1678 by Titus Oates and Israel Tonge, to assassinate Charles II of England, install his Catholic brother James on the throne and massacre Protestants. French forces were also to invade Ireland. This nonsense resulted in a frenzy of anti-Catholicism, and even the more responsible elements were alarmed to learn of the unexplained death in October 1678 of Sir Edmund Berry Godfrey, the magistrate who had first heard Oates's dispositions. On 31 October the House of

Commons resolved 'that there has been and still is a damnable and hellish plot, contrived and carried on by popish recusants for the assassinating and murdering the King, and for subverting the government and rooting out and destroying the Protestant religion'.

A number of suspects were executed and tension mounted further when it was discovered that Edward Coleman, secretary to the Duchess of York, was corresponding with the Jesuit La Chaise, adviser to Louis XIV of France. Finally, it was revealed that the King was obtaining subsidies from France and a movement grew to exclude James from the succession to the throne and replace him by Charles's natural son, the Duke of Monmouth. Charles responded by dissolving the Cavalier Parliament and declaring Monmouth illegitimate. James Duke of York went voluntarily into temporary exile in the Spanish Netherlands.

PRAEMUNIRE, STATUTE OF English statute passed in 1392 confirming the earlier Statute of Provisors which declared the English realm to be free of all earthly subjection. The procurement of bulls (*q.v.*) or other papal instruments was made punishable by outlawry and forfeiture.

PRECARIAE In medieval England, grants of church land to laymen, generally only for the life of the grantee, but occasionally renewed to his successor. They were often extorted from the Church by force.

PREDESTINATION Doctrine of Calvinism (*q.v.*) and other Protestant faiths which holds that God has destined some souls to salvation and others to damnation and that nothing individual people can do will change their allotted destinies.

PRESBYTERIANISM (deriv. Gk., elder) A system of church government by presbyters who are all of equal rank. Its doctrinal standards, generally accepted by Scottish, English and Americans as a thorough and logical statement of Calvinism (*q.v.*), are contained in the 1647 Westminster Confession of Faith.

In Britain, the leading Presbyterian church is the Church of Scotland. At the Reformation (*q.v.*) the Scots demanded a fundamental change of doctrine, discipline and worship. The leading Scottish Protestant John Knox had worked with Calvin in Geneva, and Calvinism was to be the system introduced into Scotland. The Reformed Kirk was based on the *Scots Confession*, drawn up and signed by Knox, the *Book of Discipline* and the *Book of Common Order*, the so-called 'Knox's Liturgy', an English translation of the liturgy used by Calvinists in Geneva. However, Laud's attempts in the 1630s to force a prayer book on the Scottish Church led to the abandonment of these liturgies in favour of 'free prayer'.

Under James I and Charles I the episcopacy (*q.v.*) was re-established but was abolished by the 1638 Glasgow Assembly. Cromwell abolished General Assemblies and at the restoration Charles II re-established the episcopacy. Those Covenanters (*q.v.*) who opposed episcopacy were persecuted until in 1690 William III re-instituted Presbyterianism.

Presbyterianism laid uncompromising stress on the word of God, revealed in the Old and New Testaments, as the supreme rule of faith and life, and emphasized the value of a highly trained ministry. The Church of Scotland provides for democratic representation through a hierarchy of courts. Ministers are elected by their congregations. A local kirk session comprises the minister and lay church elders, also elected, who assist the ministers. Above the kirk session is the court of the presbytery which has jurisdiction over a specified area. The court of synod rules over a large number of presbyteries and finally the General Assembly is presided over by the Moderator: it acts as the supreme court of the Church with both judicial and legislative powers. In 1972 the Presbyterian and Congregationalist (*q.v.*) churches in England merged to form the United Reformed Church.

PRESIDIOS (Span) Frontier blockhouses of Latin America, extensively used by the Spaniards in the colonial period. Staffed by small bodies of soldiers, they were usually run in conjunction with a church mission, the idea being both to pacify and convert the natives of northern Mexico and the south-west of North America.

PRIMITIVE METHODISTS *See* Methodists.

PROTECTORATE The period of the Interregnum from 16 December 1653 to 25 May 1659, when England was governed by a Protector. Following the expulsion of the Rump and the failure of the Barebones Parliament to act effectively and in compliance with the desires of the army leaders, Parliament's powers were transferred to Oliver Cromwell (1599–1658). The Instrument of Government was drafted and Cromwell appointed Lord Protector.

PROTESTANT ASCENDANCY The religious and political dominance of the Protestant minority in Ireland from the seventeenth to the nineteenth centuries.

PROTESTANTISM Collective term applied to that part of Western Christianity which denies the authority of the Pope and emphasizes Christians' responsibility to God rather than to the Church and its sacraments. The term was first applied to the supporters of Martin Luther (1483–1546) who were critical of the intolerance of reform that was displayed by the Roman Catholic Church at the second Diet of Speyer (1529), which reversed the decision of the first Diet of Speyer (1526) that reform was needed. Most Protestant churches severed their links with the Catholic Church at the time of the Reformation (*q.v.*).

PROVISOR Originally, one who was appointed to an ecclesiastical living by the Pope before the existing incumbent was dead; later, any right of patronage usurped by the Pope. In 1351 the English Crown passed the Statute of Provisors, directed against the papal claim to appoint men to benefices, which enacted that the king and the lords were to appoint to benefices of their own and their ancestors' creation. Papal bulls (*q.v.*) were thereby made illegal and crown patronage increased.

PURITANS Extreme Protestants (*q.v.*) of the sixteenth and seventeenth centuries, including Presbyterians (*q.v.*) and Independents (*q.v.*). The Puritans emphasized individualism in religion, had a strict code of morality, a high sense of public duty and were opposed to certain forms of art and amusement. They came into dispute with Arminians (*q.v.*) over ritual and later over the episcopacy (*q.v.*). Elizabethan persecutions drove many of them to Holland and despite a show of strength in the Millenary Petition (*q.v.*), many emigrated to America during the reigns of the first two Stuarts. Charles I and the Laudians (*q.v.*) pushed them into violent opposition and they were a dominant political force in the struggle between Parliament and the Crown. Following the Restoration (*q.v.*), the Act of Uniformity (1662) ejected Puritan ministers from their livings. Those who conformed came to be known as the Low Church (*q.v.*) party in the Church of England; those who did not became Dissenters or Nonconformists (*q.v.*).

PUSEYITE Follower of Dr Edward Pusey (1800–82), one of the leaders of the Oxford Movement (*q.v.*), so called because its leaders were members of Oxford University. Its adherents sought to reassert the authority of the Anglican Church to counter the spread of 'liberal theology' in the nineteenth century. One motive force was the fear that the 1832 Reform Act would take power out of the hands of the Tories and Churchmen and place it in those of Liberals and Dissenters (*q.v.*).

The movement dated from July 1833 when John Keble preached a sermon criticizing a bill for the suppression of 10 Irish bishoprics. Between 1833 and 1841 Keble, Newman and Hurrell Froude issued a series of pamphlets, *Tracts for the Times,* stating their position. (From the title, adherents also became styled Tractarians.)

The movement saw the Church of England as threatened by secular power. Emphasis was laid on it as a divine institution and on ritual and the continuity of the Catholic faith. In Tract 90 Newman showed that the Thirty-nine Articles (*q.v.*) could be made to square with Roman doctrine. In October 1845 Newman, followed by many of his supporters, was received into the Roman Catholic Church, while Pusey and Keble persisted in their efforts to secure recognition of Catholic liturgy and doctrine in the Anglican Church by emphasizing ministry, worship, ceremonial and religious community life.

Q

QUAKERS Society of Friends, a religious body founded in seventeenth-century England by George Fox whose central tenet is that each believer communicates with God and is directly guided by him in the ways of truth. Quakers do not have ordained ministers, prepared sermons or ritual; much reliance is put on the Holy Spirit moving members of the congregation to speak. Speaking in tongues and physical 'shaking' in religious ecstasies earned the movement its nickname.

To escape persecution, many Quakers emigrated to Pennsylvania, which William Penn had founded in 1682. From there missionaries were sent all over the world. Quakers championed the movement for the abolition of slavery and helped in prison and educational reform.

QUEEN ANNE'S BOUNTY Fund established in 1704 by Queen Anne for the augmentation of the maintenance of poor clergy from her revenues from first fruits and tithes (*q.v.*). In the nineteenth century parliamentary grants and private donations supplemented the fund, which was administered by ecclesiastical commissioners. On 1 April 1948 they and the Bounty became embodied in the Church Commissioners for England.

QUIETIST Exponent of quietism, a doctrine of extreme asceticism and contemplative devotion embodied in the works of Miguel Molinos, a seventeenth-century Spanish priest condemned by the papacy.

R

RALLIEMENT (Fr.) In France, policy initiated in an encyclical of Pope Leo XIII in 1892, which attempted to end the estrangement of Catholics from the Republic. However, most Catholics and monarchists remained hostile to the Republic; the monarchist right wing proved to have a considerable nuisance value in French politics.

RADICAL REFORMATION Term for the large group of separatist churches, sects, conventicles and individuals which proliferated in the period after the Reformation. They include the Anabaptists.

RANTERS (1) In Commonwealth England, fanatical sect of pantheists and 'antinomians' who did not believe that Christians were bound to keep the law of God.

(2) Primitive Methodists (*q.v.*), so called because of their noisy preaching.

RASKOL Great religious schism in the seventeenth-century Russian Church, which arose because of attempts by the Patriarch Nikon to introduce innovations in ritual for the purpose of correcting errors that had arisen from careless copying of the liturgies and other religious books. Dissenters were excommunicated and thousands fled the country.

RECONQUISTA (Span., reconquest) The 800-year struggle to drive the Moorish occupiers from Spain. The final Arab kingdom in Spain, that of Granada, was defeated and subdued in a campaign waged from 1482 to 1492 by Ferdinand II and Isabella I, leaving the whole of the Spanish peninsula under their control.

RECUSANTS (deriv. Lat., refuse) Those who refused to attend the services of the Church of England, most commonly Roman Catholics. Recusants were first fined under the Acts of Uniformity of 1552 and 1559. Elizabeth I fined both Catholics and recusant Protestants.

REDUCCIONES (Span.) Mission villages in Spanish colonial South America where natives were concentrated or 'reduced' to receive religious instruction and training. The most famous were organized in Paraguay by the Jesuits (*q.v.*). In Portuguese colonies they were called *reduçoẽs.*

REFORMATION Great religious reform movement of the sixteenth century which led to the establishment of Protestantism (*q.v.*). In the fourteenth and fifteenth centuries John Wycliffe and John Hus had acted as forerunners; when Luther (1483–1546) in Germany and Zwingli in Switzerland took up the case for the reform of Catholicism, adherents became numerous. Abuses such as the sale of indulgences (*q.v.*) by papal agents had incensed many and Luther's denunciation of such acts in 1517 found a receptive climate of opinion.

Amidst much controversy, the reformers evolved new doctrines based on principles which produced a variety of strands of Protestantism. They claimed justification (salvation) by faith and the direct use by the faithful of the scriptures. They rejected the Catholic doctrine of transubstantiation (*q.v.*), the adoration of the Virgin and the saints, and the supremacy of the Pope. Luther was excommunicated, but the principles of the Reformation spread, converting large parts of Germany, Switzerland, the Low Countries, England and Scotland. *See also* Calvinism.

RÉGALE (Fr.) Right claimed by French kings to present to benefices (*q.v.*) that fell vacant when the bishop's see of the same diocese

was also vacant and to collect the revenues of vacant sees. The papacy disputed the claim and a conflict arose between Louis XIV and Pope Innocent XI in 1681.

REGIUM DONUM (Lat., gift of the king) Annual grant from the English Crown, introduced by Charles II, for the maintenance of Presbyterian (*q.v.*) ministers in Ulster. James II allowed it to lapse, but it was revived by William III. It was finally abolished at the time of the disestablishment of the Irish Church in 1869.

RELIGIOUS Term used to describe members of the clergy who lived in monasteries and convents as, for example, Benedictines or Dominicans, until the dissolution of both the orders and the religious houses in the sixteenth century. Historians have sought to discover what happened to what became known as the ex-religious following the dissolution.

REMONSTRANTS (1) In the Netherlands, name given to those Arminians (*q.v.*) who, in 1610, presented a remonstrance to the States-General against the charges of heresy made against them. The document contained the *Five Articles of Arminianism.*

(2) In Scotland, name given to those Covenanters (*q.v.*) who, after the defeat of Dunbar in 1650, remonstrated to the Committee of Estates against the alliance of Argyle and others with the Royalists. They refused to acknowledge Charles II until he proved himself true to the Covenant. The remonstrance was in turn condemned by a resolution of the Estates, which caused opponents of the remonstrants to be nicknamed 'resolutioners'.

RESOLUTIONERS *See* Remonstrants.

ROMANISM An expression, often used pejoratively, and now very-dated, for the Roman Catholic Church.

ROME SCOT Another name for Peter's Pence (*q.v.*).

S

SALADIN TITHE A tax levied in 1188 in England and France to raise money to wage a crusade against Saladin, the Saracen leader. The tithe, which was levied at a tenth of income and the value of capital, represented the first attempt to tax personal property and was levied on the laity and clergy alike. Juries were appointed to question difficult cases.

SANBENITO (Span.) Long garment of yellow cloth enforced on penitent heretics by the Spanish Inquisition (q.v.).

SANCTUARY In England, the right claimed by the Church since Anglo-Saxon times to afford protection to criminals and others seeking refuge in churches and consecrated precincts. After 40 days the coroner would enter the sanctuary and impose an oath on the fugitive that he would abjure the realm. Some sanctuaries, however, such as those at Ripon, Durham and Beverley, provided a permanent refuge that allowed a fugitive to defy the law indefinitely. In 1486 judges ruled that sanctuary could not protect second offenders and those accused of treason. The powers of sanctuaries were further drastically curtailed in the reign of Henry VIII (1509–47). Sanctuary in criminal cases was abolished in 1623 and in civil cases by acts of 1697 and 1723. Sanctuary was also a common practice in, for example, Spain and Latin America.

SANFEDISTI Secret society established in Naples in the early nineteenth century with papal approval, to support the Catholic Church and to oppose the carbonari.

SARACENS Name given in the first three centuries AD to Arab tribes in Syria and adjacent territories. By Christians it was applied to Arabs in general and later to Muslims, especially those fighting in the crusades (q.v.) in Syria, Palestine and Egypt in the eleventh, twelfth and thirteenth centuries.

SCHMALKALDIC LEAGUE The League of the Protestant princes which was formed in Germany in 1531.

SCHOOLMEN Those who, from the mid-ninth century onwards, attempted to reconcile Christian beliefs with the philosophy of Aristotle and Plato. From the time of Augustine, philosophy, like science, had received little attention, but interest in Greek philosophy revived in the ninth century in an attempt to use it to justify church teaching. Interest increased in later centuries as western Europeans came into contact with the Islamic world which had already absorbed Greek science and philosophy. Among the more famous Schoolmen are the Irish-born John Scotus Erigena (c. 800–877); St Anselm, Archbishop of Canterbury (1033–1109); Peter Abelard (1079–1142) who had a school in Paris; his contemporary, Bernard of Chartres; and St Thomas Aquinas of Naples (1225–74).

The philosophies of the Schoolmen, closely integrated because limited by the Church, are known as 'scholasticism'. Some of their great internal arguments were those between the orthodox Realists, headed by Aquinas (who held that the world of appearance is illusory and that ideas, forms or universals are the true realities beyond matter and appearance) and the Norminalists (who held 'universals' or abstract concepts to be mere names without any corresponding realities).

There were also arguments between the Ancients, comprising the Thomists who followed Aquinas, and the Scotists who followed John Duns Scotus (c. 1265–1308), and the Terminalists, followers of William Ockham, a Nominalist. In the late fifteenth century all became reconciled to meet the threat of the philosophy of humanism, expounded by Erasmus of Rotterdam (1466–1536).

SECTARIES Puritan extremists in the fragmented Church during the English Civil War who stressed their inner light and the hearing of divine voices, including Antinomians (*q.v.*), Baptists (*q.v.*), Fifth Monarchy Men (*q.v.*) and Ranters (*q.v.*).

'SECOND REFORMATION' The term, from the German '*Zweite Reformation*', for the spread of Calvinism after 1555 in some German principalities and cities.

SECULAR CLERGY Members of the clergy who did not come under the rule of a religious order. *See also* religious.

SEDE VACANTE (Lat.) Vacancy of a bishopric, used particularly of the papal see.

SHAKERS Members of a revivalist group, the United Society of Believers in Christ's Second Appearing, which seceded from the Quakers (*q.v.*) in 1747. In 1758 Ann Lee, a young convert from Manchester, claimed to have had 'revelations' that she was the female Christ. 'Mother Ann' became leader of the sect and in obedience to her prophetic visions set out with nine followers to find 'Emmanuel's land' in America. She located it in New York State near Albany, where the group lived communally, gaining prosperity and the reputation of good agriculturalists and craftsmen. They held that God had a dual role, the male principle becoming incarnate in Christ and the female in 'Mother Ann'. The sexes were equal and women preached as often as men. Their nickname was given to them in ridicule of their involuntary movements in moments of religious ecstasy. The movement declined after 1860.

SIMONY In medieval times, the presentation of a person to an ecclesiastical benefice in return for money, gift or other reward, named after Simon Magus who offered Peter and John money for the power of the Holy Spirit (Acts 8: 18–24). Although much condemned, simony was common. Since the Church itself controlled estates and derived profit from them, it could be argued that a lord with a right of presentation to a benefice (*q.v.*) was also entitled to a share in its profits.

SKOPTSI (Russ.) Schismatic religious sect in tsarist Russia whose members practised self-mutilation, interpreting literally the scriptural injunction, 'If thine eye offend thee, pluck it out'.

SOCINIANS Followers of Laelius Socinus, who founded a sect in 1560 with doctrines similar to those of the later Unitarians (*q.v.*). They attracted many adherents in Poland and in 1658 the Diet of Warsaw proscribed them, after which they gradually declined.

SOLEMN LEAGUE AND COVENANT *See* Covenanters.

SOUL SCOT In Anglo-Saxon England, the custom of making a gift from the goods of a deceased person to the parish priest. Later the term was used loosely to denote all bequests made for religious purposes.

SOUL TAX Tax introduced by Peter the Great in Russia. Also known as a poll tax.

SPERONISTS Followers of Ugo Speroni of Piacenza, who founded a minor sect preaching a heretical doctrine of predestination and rejecting the sacraments and doctrine of original sin. They were condemned by Pope Lucius III in 1184.

STRANNIKI (Russ.) Sect of religious ascetics, active in tsarist Russia, who emerged in the reign of Catherine II. They opposed military service, refused to recognize secular authority or to pay taxes, and believed the Tsar to be the Antichrist.

STUNDISTS (Russ.) Dissenting Russian religious sect which objected to the icon-worship of the Orthodox Church.

SUPPLICANTS In England, those who signed the Supplication in 1637 opposing attempts to force a new prayer book on the Scottish Church. After 1638 they were known as Covenanters (*q.v.*).

SUPREMACY, ACTS OF (1) Act of 1534 establishing Henry VIII as head of the Church of England in place of the Pope and giving him control of church doctrine, ecclesiastical appointments and church income. It was repealed during the Catholic 'reaction' in the reign of Queen Mary (1553–58).

(2) Act of 1559 establishing Elizabeth I as supreme head of the Church of England. The British monarch is still head of the Church of England although in March 1982 a joint Anglican–Roman Catholic Commission suggested that eventually the Pope might become 'universal primate' of both churches.

SWISS GUARD The papal Swiss Guard, the corps that has provided a special military force for popes and the Vatican palace continuously since 1505. The force is over 100 strong and is commanded by a colonel who is also a privy chamberlain.

T

TABLES, THE Group of four representative committees which virtually assumed control of Scotland in 1637 and organized the resistance to Charles I's religious innovations. They consisted of four members of each of the four classes of nobles, lesser barons, clergy and burgesses and were chosen originally with the object of bringing about agreement between Archbishop Laud and the Presbyterians (*q.v.*). See also Covenanters.

TABORITES Sect of militant Hussites, led by John of Zisca, whose name was taken from Tabor, their fortress and base south of Prague which was founded in 1420. They began as a religious movement with eschatological expectations, preaching the abolition of almost all the visible Church and practising a primitive communism. Drawing their strength from the rural areas and the lower orders,

they later developed a political and military organization that proved essential for Hussite success.

TEMPLAR A member of the Order of the Knights Templars, founded in Palestine in 1118 (confirmed by Pope Honorius II in 1128) to protect Christian pilgrims travelling to the Holy Sepulchre; the Order took its name from its headquarters on the site of Solomon's Temple in Jerusalem. It became very rich and powerful and spread widely over Europe, but was accused of heresy in the thirteenth century and proscribed by Pope Clement V and its property confiscated in 1312.

TEN ARTICLES An Act that set out the doctrine of the Church of England following Henry VIII's break with Rome. Under the terms of the articles, which were accepted by the convocation (*q.v.*) of the church in 1536, baptism, penance and the eucharist were retained as sacraments (although transubstantiation was not referred to), salvation was by contrition, faith and charity, the worship of images was forbidden but prayers of intercession to saints and masses and prayers for the dead were allowed.

TEST ACTS Acts designed to exclude members of churches other than the Church of England from certain positions of authority. The 1673 Test Act excluded Catholics and Nonconformists (*q.v.*) from military and civil office by requiring office holders to repudiate the doctrine of Transubstantiation (*q.v.*), receive Anglican communion and take an oath of allegiance to the monarch as head of state and of the Church of England. It was not repealed until 1829. An act of 1678, passed in the aftermath of the Popish Plot (*q.v.*), prohibited Roman Catholics (except for the Duke of York, future King James II) from entering Parliament. In Scotland an act of 1681 required all government office holders to subscribe to the Protestant faith.

TEUTONIC KNIGHTS The Teutonic Knights of the Hospital of St Mary of Jerusalem, a military fraternity established in 1198 that evolved from a hospital in the Holy Land established by German merchants in 1190 to care for German pilgrims at the siege of Acre. It was based on the orders of the Hospitallers (*q.v.*) and Templars (*q.v.*). Although it took part in major engagements in Palestine in the thirteenth century, its main activities were against the pagan tribes of eastern Europe. Between 1211 and 1225 it was active in Hungary, and between 1230 and 1288 it conquered Prussia in a series of bloody campaigns and established a sovereign state, the Ordenstaat. The papacy and the German Emperor confirmed its right to the Baltic lands. The order's headquarters officially remained at Acre until the city fell to the Muslims in 1291; they were then transferred to Venice and finally, in 1308 to Marienberg in Prussia.

The order continued to exist until 1809, when Napoleon confiscated its properties, but in 1840 it was revived as a semi-religious association in Austria. The exploits of the Teutonic Knights figured often in Nazi propaganda. Their habit was white with a black cross on the left shoulder and their banner a white field and plain black cross; the black cross remains part of Germany's national insignia.

THEATINS Religious order founded in 1524 by members of the Oratory of Divine Love, notably Gian Pietro Caraffa, Archbishop of Brindisi and later Pope Paul IV; their name comes from the Latin form of Chieti, one of Caraffa's bishoprics. Pastoral priests who lived and worked in society, they also took monastic vows and set an example to the regular clergy. They concentrated on preaching, and though few in number exerted a strong spiritual influence on the Roman Catholic Church in the mid-sixteenth century.

THIRTY-NINE ARTICLES Convocation's definition of the doctrine of the Church of England, first set out in 1563 and revised in 1571. The Articles were based on an original Forty-two

Articles of 1553. All members of the clergy were required to accept the doctrines.

TITHE (OE, tenth) Ecclesiastical tax, consisting of a tenth part of the annual produce of the laity, used to maintain the ministers of the Church. Known to the ancient Jews, tithes were first imposed by Christian authorities in the fourth century and were made compulsory in England after the ninth century. They were connected with the land and took three forms: praedial tithes such as corn, hops and wood; personal tithes, assessed on the profits of industry and labour; and mixed tithes, which combined the two. A tenth part of the gross amount had to be paid on praedial and mixed tithes, but only a tenth of clear profit on personal tithes, which were not always collected and which depended on local custom. The major praedial tithes were known as 'great tithes'.

THIRTY YEARS WAR A political-religious conflict lasting from 23 May 1618 to 25 Oct. 1648 which began in the Austrian Monarchy, spread into the German Holy Roman Empire and soon involved Denmark, France, Spain and Sweden. The resulting Treaty of Westphalia left Germany a patchwork of absolute monarchies in which Catholic counter-reformation had failed to eradicate Protestantism.

TITULAR BISHOP A member of the Roman Catholic hierarchy who is officially accepted as a bishop but who is unable to exercise rights of residence and authority because his nominal diocese lies outside the authority of the Church.

TRACTARIAN *See* Puseyite.

TRADITOR Term used in Christian North Africa in the great persecution of 303–305 to denote those who had surrendered the scriptures to the authorities and thus compromised their faith. They were deemed unworthy of readmittance to high ecclesiastical office.

TRANSUBSTANTIATION Roman Catholic doctrine which holds that the sacrament of the eucharist transforms bread and wine into Christ's flesh and blood. The Thirty-nine Articles (*q.v.*) regulating the Church of England (issued in 1563) deny the doctrine, pointing instead to a position somewhere in between consubstantiation (co-existence of bread and wine and Christ's flesh and blood) and virtualism (that communicants receive the 'virtue' of Christ's body and blood). Nonconformists (*q.v.*) prefer to see the eucharist simply as a memorial service.

TRIERS AND EJECTORS The 'Triers' were an examining body drawn from the ranks of the Independents (*q.v.*), Baptists (*q.v.*) and Presbyterians (*q.v.*) which was appointed by Cromwell in March 1654 to enquire into the qualifications of clergy to be appointed to benefices (*q.v.*) by lay patrons. In August, local commissions of 'Ejectors' were also set up to eject all 'scandalous, ignorant and insufficient' clergy and schoolmasters from their livings. Immorality and the Prayer Book were condemned, but generally both bodies were moderate and in practice almost anyone, other than a Catholic, whose creed was fundamentally orthodox was allowed to hold his post.

U

ULTRAMONTANISM (deriv. Lat. *ultra*, beyond + *mons*, mountain) Belief in the ultimate authority of the papacy above that of loyalty to the state, particularly evident in nineteenth-century France, and encouraged by Pope Pius IX's decree of 1870. In Germany it contributed to the Kulturkampf (*q.v.*). The long-term consequence of the Ultramontanist movement was to free the papacy from dependence on civil powers and to give the Catholic Church freedom of action.

UNIFORMITY, ACTS OF Series of Acts designed to provide the legal and doctrinal bases on which the Church of England stands. The first two were passed in the reign of Edward VI. That of 1549 specified that the moderately Protestant Book of Common Prayer, written by Archbishop Cranmer, should be used in church services. Penalties on the clergy for non-compliance were, however, light. That of 1552 marked a move towards a more clearly Protestant position. A more Protestant prayer book was to be used and stricter penalties were enforced for failure to do so. Both Acts were repealed in the reign of Queen Mary I (1553–58). However, in 1559, a third Act was introduced following the accession of Queen Elizabeth I. This required the use of a modified version of the 1552 Prayer Book and imposed fines of a shilling a week on persons who failed to attend church services using the new book. In 1662 a fourth Act was passed (*see* Clarendon Code), which required the use of yet another revised prayer book and a new liturgy. Over 2,000 members of the clergy who could not accept the provisions of the Act were obliged to resign their livings.

UNITARIANISM Religious movement, whose members believe in the single person of God, which is generally thought to be heretical and anti-trinitarian. They first appeared in England after the Reformation (*q.v.*) and increased in numbers under the Commonwealth (*q.v.*) and Protectorate (*q.v.*). They were excluded from the Toleration Act of 1689 and from the Dissenters' conference at Salter's Hall, London in 1719. From 1813 they were legally tolerated, but attempts were made to turn them out of their chapels on the grounds that their preachers did not hold the same views as the founders of the endowments. This conflict ended with the 1845 Dissenting Chapels Act. In 1825 the British and Foreign Unitarian Association was founded though it issued no authoritative confession of faith.

In the USA some New England Puritans (*q.v.*) developed along Unitarian lines and the movement influenced the Harvard Divinity School. In nineteenth-century Boston many literary figures, e.g. Longfellow and Lowell, were Unitarians. Ralph Waldo Emerson guided the movement towards humanitarianism and rationalism; in 1910 the American Unitarians joined the International Congress of Free Christians and other religious liberals. Today many deny a personal God and interpret their religion purely in moral terms, putting their faith in the value of love and brotherhood of man.

UNITAS FRATRUM The Bohemian Brotherhood, a small, rigorous Hussite (*q.v.*) sect influenced by the pacifist ideas of Peter Chelčický which split from the Utraquist (*q.v.*) Church in 1467. Its members were the forerunners of the Moravians (*q.v.*).

UTRAQUISTS Movement in Hungary, Bohemia and Poland in the fifteenth century which evolved from the moderate wing of the Hussites (*q.v.*). Their main demand was for communion in both kinds (*sub utraque specie*) for the laity, from which they take their name. Such a form of communion was initiated in Prague in 1414 but condemned by the Council of Constance the following year. In 1485 the Utraquist Church became the state church of Bohemia.

VALOR ECCLESIASTICUS (Lat.) Tax book in which all the ecclesiastical property in England was valued, with great speed and efficiency, by the commissioners appointed by Thomas Cromwell as a prelude to the dissolution of the monasteries in 1535.

VESTIARIAN CONTROVERSY A dispute within the Anglican Church in 1566–67 over details of ecclesiastical dress which focused Puritan

(*q.v.*) dissatisfaction with the Elizabethan church settlement.

VICAR-GENERAL The substitute – often a Chancellor of Diocese – appointed by a bishop to exercise his jurisdiction.

VICEREGENT Office held by Thomas Cromwell (1485–1540) in which he acted as deputy to Henry VIII in religious matters. Cromwell was appointed to the post by Henry as head of the Church in 1535 but the office lapsed following Cromwell's fall.

VULGATE Latin version of the scriptures, translated by St Jerome in the late fourth century and sanctioned by the Council of Trent in 1545. They remain the authorized Bible of the Roman Catholic faith.

WALDENSIANS Religious movement founded *c*. 1170 by Peter Waldo of Lyons which fell into heresy after being refused the right to preach and was subsequently condemned by Pope Lucius III in 1184. Split into two factions, the Lyonists (*q.v.*) and the Poor Lombards (*q.v.*), they survived in France, Germany and parts of Italy and eastern Europe into modern times.

WHITE FRIARS *See* Carmelites.

WYCLIFFITE Follower of John Wycliffe, or Wyclif (*c*. 1320–84), Master of Balliol College, Oxford, and rector of Lutterworth. He published *De dominio divino* and *De dominio civil* in 1376 in which he criticized the Church for holding temporal possessions and intervening in state affairs. Later he denied the authority of the pope and doctrine of transubstantiation (*q.v.*). His followers took up his attacks on ecclesiastical abuses and on transubstantiation. From about 1380 onwards they were known as Lollards (*q.v.*).

Z

ZENTRUM The conservative Roman Catholic Centre Party in Germany from 1871 to 1933. Developed in response to Bismarck's anti-Catholic policies, it was influential in early twentieth-century coalitions and again in the post-World War I Weimar Republic. Dissolved by the Nazis in July 1933.

ZIONISM Belief in the need to establish an autonomous Jewish homeland in Palestine which in its modern form originated with Theodor Herzl (1860–1904), a Hungarian journalist living in Vienna. The Dreyfus Affair and the pogroms (*q.v.*) of Eastern Europe convinced him that the Jews could have no real safety until they had a state of their own. They had always regarded Palestine as a spiritual homeland but had not up to then considered forming an actual state there. Herzl faced opposition from assimilated Jews who felt safe in the countries where they lived. Even after the 1917 Balfour Declaration supporting a Jewish homeland in Palestine, few Jews went to Palestine until the horrors of the Nazi regime and the Holocaust had led them to reassess their position in Europe.

The Jewish state was proclaimed in 1948 and today most Jewish communities support Zionism.

III
COMPENDIUM OF LISTS, TABLES
AND STATISTICS

THE SPREAD OF CHRISTIANITY

ESTIMATES OF EARLY CHRISTIAN MEMBERSHIP

There are no figures of any reliability of the growth of membership of the Church in the early years. The Church was frequently beset by persecution (see p. 281) and often forced underground. Some historians (beginning with Edward Gibbon) believed Christians numbered around 5 per cent of the population of the Roman Empire at the time of Constantine's conversion. Other historians prefer 10 per cent. The following figures (adapted from Stark) give an indication of the possible growth of the early Church.

Christian growth projected at 40 per cent per decade

Year	No. of Christians	% of population*
40	1,000	0.0
50	1,400	0.0
100	7,530	0.0
150	40,496	0.1
200	217,795	0.4
250	1,171,356	1.9
300	6,299,832	10.5
350	33,882,008	56.5

*Based on an estimated population of 60 million.

Growth would probably have been fastest in the largest cities. The following list of the nine largest cities of 100,000 population or more is provided by Stark.

Rome	650,000	Pergamum	120,000
Alexandria	400,000	Sardis	100,000
Ephesus	200,000	Corinth	100,000
Antioch	150,000	Gadir (Cadiz)	100,000
Apamea	125,000		

Source: Rodney Stark, *The Rise of Christianity: A Sociologist Reconsiders History* (Princeton University Press, 1996), pp. 6–7, 13.

THE EARLY MISSIONARY APOSTLES

Irenaeus, St	'Apostle of the Gauls'. A celebrated Greek church father, Irenaeus became Bishop of Lyons in 177. Died *c*. 202.
Denys, St	'Apostle of the French'. According to legend, beheaded in Paris in 272. Patron Saint of France.
Ninian, St	'Apostle of the Picts'. Missionary among the Southern Picts (fl. *c*. 400).
Patrick, St	'Apostle of Ireland'. Patron Saint of Ireland. Dates uncertain (perhaps *c*. 396–469).
Columba, St	'Apostle of Caledonia' (alternatively 'Apostle of the Highlanders'). Born *c*. 521 in Ireland; founded Iona monastery, 565, died at Iona, Scotland, 597.
Augustine, St	'Apostle of the Anglo-Saxons' (alternatively 'Apostle of the English'). The Benedictine monk despatched by Pope Gregory I in 597 as a missionary to Kent. First Archbishop of Canterbury (where he died in 604).
Killan, St	'Apostle of Franconia'. Irish-born, whose ministry was based at Würzburg. He died *c*. 689.
Hubert, St	'Apostle of the Ardennes and of Brabant'. Bishop of Liège (died 727).
Willibrord, St	'Apostle of the Friesians'. English missionary (spelling variations include Wilbrod and Wilbrord). Settled among the Friesians, *c*. 690. Born in Northumbria, *c*. 657. Died *c*. 738.
Boniface, St	'Apostle of Germany'. Famous English missionary (original name Winfrid or Winfrith). Born in Devon, died in Friesland, 755.
Magnus, St	'Apostle of the Allgau'. His mission was based on Fusen. Died *c*. 770.
Ansgar, St	'Apostle of the North'. Born near Amiens, 801. Missions to Denmark (827), Sweden (828–831) and northern Germany. First Bishop of Hamburg. Died at Bremen, 865.
Vicelin, St	'Apostle of Holstein'. Born *c*. 1090, died 1154. Worked first as missionary among the pagan Wagrians and later in Holstein.

EARLY WESTERN DIOCESES IN THE MISSIONARY AGE, 700–1000*

722	Boniface created Bishop of the German Frontier (without a fixed see). Early bishoprics created around this time included Passau, Ratisbon and Salzburg.
787	Bremen (with Willehad as first bishop)
c. 780	Minden
804	Hamburg
968	Magdeburg (as springboard for newly conquered lands)
968	Poznan (first see in Poland)
975	Prague (dependent on Mainz)

c. 996–997	Breslau
c. 995–1000	Cracow (date unsure, in existence 1000)
1000	Gnesen
1008	Bamberg

*For the creation of sees in England, see p. 276.

THE WEALTHIEST SEES IN WESTERN EUROPE, *c.* 1500*

12,000fl.	Rouen, Winchester
10,000fl.	Aquileia, Auch, Canterbury, Cologne, Mainz, Salzburg, Trier, York
9,000fl.	Durham, Langres, Narbonne
8,000fl.	Toledo
7,500fl.	Ely
7,200fl.	Liège
6,000fl.	Braga, Carcassonne, Exeter, Metz, Sens
5,000fl.	Gniezno, Nicosia, Norwich, Passau, Seville, Thérouanne, Toulouse, Tournai, Valencia, Zaragoza
4,600fl.	Beauvais, Utrecht
4,500fl.	Salisbury
4,400fl.	Bayeux, Verdun, Viviers
4,300fl.	Bath & Wells
4,200fl.	Amiens
4,000fl.	Autun, Arras, Bordeaux, Bourges, Bratislava, Cashel, Châlons-sur-Marne, Chartres, Cominges, Dol (Brittany), Esztergom, Freising, Laon, Lisieux, Maguelone, Ravenna, Rheims, Santiago de Compostela

*fl. = florin Stella (1fl. = ∼37p).
Source: Stella Fletcher, *The Longman Companion to Renaissance Europe, 1390–1530* (2000).

ECCLESIASTICAL STATES IN THE EMPIRE, 1500

Archbishoprics	Bremen	Mainz
	Cologne	Salzburg
	Magdeburg	Trier
Bishoprics	Augsburg	Eichstatt
	Bamberg	Freising
	Basel	Geneva
	Brixen	Gurk
	Cambrai	Halberstadt
	Chiemsee	Havelberg
	Chur	Hildersheim
	Constance	Lausanne

Liège	Regensburg/Ratisbon
Lübeck	Schwerin
Meissen	Seckau
Merseburg	Speyer
Metz	Strasbourg
Minden	Toul
Münster	Trento
Naumburg	Utrecht
Osnabrück	Verden
Paderborn	Verdun
Passau	Worms
Ratzeburg	Würzburg

Source: Mark Greengrass, *The Longman Companion to the European Reformation, c. 1500–1618* (1998).

FOUNDATION DATES FOR SELECTED SEES IN ENGLAND (to 1133)

597	Canterbury
604	Rochester
	London*
627	York**
630	Dunwich (Thetford after 1070)
635	Durham (formally from 997)
656	Mercia (Lichfield from 669, Coventry and Lichfield from 1148)
669	Lichfield (formerly Mercia)
673	Elmham (after 1070 Thetford)
676	Hereford
679	Winchester
	Worcester
680	Leicester (originally Lindine in 678, then Dorchester-on-Thames after 886)
681	Selsey (from 1075 Chichester)
705	Sherborne (from 1075 Salisbury)
886	Dorchester (transferred from Leicester) (transferred to Lincoln, 1072)
909	Wells (Bath and Wells from 1218)
	Crediton (transferred to Exeter, 1049)
	Ramsbury (after 1075 Salisbury)
1049/50	Exeter (transferred from Crediton)
1070	Thetford (originally Dunwich and Elmham) (transferred to Norwich, 1094)
1072/73	Lincoln (transferred from Dorchester)

1075   Chichester (formerly Selsey)
      Salisbury (transferred from Sherborne)
1094   Norwich (formerly Thetford)
1109   Ely
1133   Carlisle

*Technically a recreation of the see as the earliest bishops were appointed in the fourth century.
**Created an archbishopric in 735.

REVENUES FROM ENGLISH BISHOPRICS, 1760

See	Revenue p.a.
Canterbury	£ 7000
Durham	£ 6000
Winchester	£ 5000
York	£ 4500
London	£ 4000
Ely	£ 3400
Worcester	£ 3000
Salisbury	£ 3000
Oxford	£ 500 (+ £ 1800)
Norwich	£ 2000
Bath and Wells	£ 2000
Bristol	£ 450 (+ £ 1150)
Exeter	£ 1500
Chester	£ 900 (+ £ 600)
Rochester	£ 600 (+ £ 900)
Lincoln	£ 1500
Lichfield and Coventry	£ 1400
St Asaph	£ 1400
Bangor	£ 1400
Chichester	£ 1400
Carlisle	£ 1300
Hereford	£ 1200
Peterborough	£ 1000
Llandaff	£ 500 (+ £ 450)
Gloucester	£ 900 (+ rich Durham prebend)
St Davids	£ 900 (+ two livings)

Source: *A list of the Archbishops, Bishops, Deans and Prebendaries in England and Wales in His Majesty's Gift, with the Reputed Yearly Value of Their Respective Dignities* (1762).

LATER DIOCESES IN ENGLAND

Dioceses created at the Reformation

Diocese	Date of foundation	Area of jurisdiction
Bristol	1542	Bristol and part of Gloucestershire (from diocese of Worcester), Dorset (from diocese of Salisbury)
Chester	1541	Cheshire, Lancashire (from diocese of Coventry and Lichfield)
Gloucester	1541	Gloucestershire (from diocese of Worcester)
Oxford	1542	Oxfordshire (from diocese of Lincoln)
Peterborough	1541	Northamptonshire (from diocese of Lincoln)

Dioceses created during the period 1847–1918

1847	Manchester	1905	Birmingham
1877	Truro		Southwark
	St Albans	1914	Sheffield
1880	Liverpool		Chelmsford
1882	Newcastle		St Edmondsbury and Ipswich
1884	Southwell	1918	Coventry
1888	Wakefield		

CREATION OF ANGLICAN SEES IN THE BRITISH EMPIRE

Africa and Asia (to 1914)*

Asia

Calcutta	1814	Chota Nagpur	1890
Bombay	1832	Lucknow	1893
Madras	1835	New Guinea	1896
Colombo	1845	Hokkaido	1896
Victoria (Hong Kong)	1849	Osaka	1896
Labuan and Sarawak	1855	Nagpur	1902
Lahore	1877	Fukien	1905
Rangoon	1877	Dornakal	1912
North China	1880		

Africa

Sierra Leone	1852	Eastern Equatorial Africa	1884
Zanbeir (Zanzibar)	1861	Mombasa	1889
Nyasaland	1862	Bloemfontein	1890

278

| Transvaal | 1877 | Mashonaland | 1891 |
| Pretoria | 1877 | Accra | 1909 |

*Including China and Japan.

Australia and New Zealand: selected dioceses
Australia

Sydney	1847	Bathurst	1869
Adelaide	1847	Ballarat	1875
Perth	1857	North Queensland	1878
Brisbane	1859	Carpentaria	1900
Goulburn	1863	Bendigo	1902
Grafton and Armidale	1867		

New Zealand

Auckland	1841	Nelson	1858
Christchurch	1856	Dunedin	1866
Wellington	1858		

Canada: creation of Dioceses to 1900

1787	Nova Scotia	1873	Algoma
1793	Quebec	1874	Saskatchewan
1839	Toronto	1874	Athabasca
1839	Newfoundland	1875	Niagara
1845	Fredericton	1879	Caledonia
1849	Rupert's Land	1879	New Westminster (later Vancouver)
1850	Montreal	1884	Qu'Appelle (Assiniboia, later Regina)
1857	Huron	1884	Mackenzie River
1859	British Columbia	1887	Calgary
1862	Ontario	1891	Yukon (originally Selkirk)
1872	Moosonee	1896	Ottawa

Source: Philip Carrington, *The Anglican Church in Canada* (1963).

Provinces of the Anglican Church in Canada

1861	Canada
1875	Rupert's Land
1912	Ontario
1914	British Columbia

GROWTH OF ROMAN CATHOLIC DIOCESES IN THE USA

Creation of Metropolitan Provinces and Sees, 1880–1962

1888	St Paul	1944	Indianapolis
1893	Dubuque	1945	Omaha
1926	San Antonio	1951	Seattle
1936	Los Angeles	1952	Kansas City
1937	Detroit, Louisville, Newark	1953	Hartford
1941	Denver	1962	Atlanta

Source: John Tracy Ellis, *American Catholicism* (1955).

ROMAN CATHOLIC CATHEDRALS IN ENGLAND AND WALES

Cathedral	Opened	Consecrated
Birmingham	1808	1841
Brentwood	1836	1869
Cardiff	1836	1887
Clifton	1848	1848
Hexham and Newcastle	1844	1860
Lancaster	1799	1859
Leeds	1838	1904
Liverpool (old)	1807	1815
(new)	1933	1967
Menevia (Wrexham)	1857	1907
Middlesbrough	1868	1911
Northampton	1825	1864
Nottingham	1842	1844
Plymouth	1858	1880
Portsmouth	1882	1887
Salford	1848	1890
Shrewsbury	1856	1891
Southwark	1841	1894
Westminster	1903	1910

PERSECUTION AND MARTYRDOM

OVERVIEW

The statistics assembled in the *World Christian Encyclopaedia* estimate that nearly 70 million Christians of different persuasions have died for their faith. This total is broken down as follows:

Eastern Orthodox	37,444,000
East Syrians (Nestorians)	12,400,000
Roman Catholics (after AD 1000)	11,000,000
Protestants	3,170,000
Gregorians (Armenian Apostolic)	1,220,000
Coptic Orthodox	1,070,000
Anglicans	983,000
Catholics (before AD 1000)	838,000
Ethiopian Orthodox	651,000
West Syrians (Jacobites)	351,700
Maronites	153,000
Non-White indigenous Christians	140,000
Total all martyrs	69,420,000

Within this overall figure, the *World Christian Encyclopaedia* suggests there were some 600 major martyrdoms, including:

76 with over 100,000 martyrs each
27 with over 500,000 martyrs each
15 with over 1 million martyrs each

CALENDAR OF EARLY CHRISTIAN MARTYRS (before 380)

Note: Traditionally Stephen is held to be the first Christian martyr (stoned to death, perhaps *c*. 35). Another early martyr is held to be James, the first of the twelve apostles to suffer this fate (in *c*. 44).

In *c*. 62 James the Just, brother of Jesus and leader of the church in Jerusalem, was put to death (according to Hegesippus). Both Peter and Paul are traditionally held to have suffered martyrdom at Rome, with *c*. 64–67 possible dates.

Martyrs from 100 onwards

c. 107	Ignatius, Bishop of Antioch, at Rome.
c. 117	Cecilia (date very much questioned).
c. 156	Polycarp, Bishop of Smyrna. Burnt to death.
c. 163–165	Justin Martyr, author of First Apology (*c.* 155). Beheaded, with some disciples, after refusing to sacrifice.
177	Martyrdom of 48 Christians at Lyons and others at Vienne.
180	The 12 martyrs (7 men and 5 women) at Scillium (near Carthage in North Africa).
c. 203	Martyrdom of Perpetua and Felicitas, executed in the arena in Carthage. The *Passion of St Perpetua and St Felicitas* relates the account.
250	Fabian (under persecution of Decius). Agatha (in Sicily).
c. 251	Christopher.
c. 258	Cyprian of Carthage and Sixtus II. Lawrence.
c. 288	Sebastian.
c. 310	Catherine (in Alexandria).

The ten traditional periods of persecution

64–68	Under Emperor Nero (when Christians were blamed for the fire in Rome).
95	Under Emperor Domitian (ruled 81–96) in Rome and Asia.
106	Under Emperor Trajan.
166–177	Under Emperor Marcus Aurelius.
199–204	Under Emperor Septimus Severus.
235–238	Under Maximinus Thrax.
250–252	Under Decius (reportedly bloodier than any earlier persecution). The first empire-wide persecution. Seizures of Christians began in January 250. Victims included Pope Fabian and Bishop Babylas of Antioch.
258–260	Under Valerian, who had made a major effort to force Christians to accept Roman gods (summer 257). Execution of clergy ordered, August 258.
275	Under Aurelian. Details unclear.
303–313	Under Diocletian. The great persecution which saw enormous suffering.

MARTYRS OF THE REFORMATION ERA IN ENGLAND

Protestant

Celebrated Protestant martyrs in England included Thomas Bilney and Robert Barnes (in the reign of Henry VIII) and over 300 in the short reign of Mary. These included Thomas Cranmer (21 March 1556), Latimer, Ridley and Hooper. They are catalogued in John Foxe's *Book of Martyrs* (on which he began work in 1563).

Roman Catholic

Among Roman Catholics who were put to death in England, the most famous are the so-called '40 Martyrs' (put to death between 1535 and 1680). They were beatified in 1970.

MARTYRS AND PERSECUTIONS OF THE MODERN ERA

1876	Bulgaria	The 'Bulgarian Massacres' by the Ottoman Turks which aroused huge protests in England, led by Gladstone. See p. 172.
1894–95, 1915–16	Armenia	The massacres of 1895 and again in 1915–16. This terrible holocaust (still denied by some in Turkey) effectively wiped out Armenian Christians. Millions died.
1917	Russian Revolution	Following the Bolshevik Revolution of October 1917, there was intense persecution of the Orthodox Church (see p. 207). Among the victims was Metropolitan Veniamin (1874–1922) of Petrograd (St Petersburg), executed on 12 August 1922.
1917	Mexico	Anti-clerical persecution following the revolution of 1917.
1931–39	Spain	Anti-clericalism in the 1930s, including the killing of priests, nuns, etc. in the bloody Spanish Civil War, 1936–39.
1933–45	Nazi Germany	Anti-church persecution in the Hitler era. The most famous single martyr was Dietrich Bonhoeffer (1906–45). Bonhoeffer was a founder, with Martin Niemoller, of the Pastors' Emergency League. Among famous martyrs of the concentration camps was the Polish priest, Maximilian Kolbe (1894–1944). World War II saw extensive persecution of Orthodox believers in Bosnia by the pro-Nazi Ustashi government in Croatia.
1945–89	Eastern Europe	Widespread repression and persecution throughout the Soviet-controlled countries of the Eastern bloc. Among its Catholic victims were the Romanian Cardinal Alexandru Todea and the Czech Cardinal Stepan Trochta (1905–74). A famous victim in Poland was Father Jerzy Popieluszko (1947–84).
1945–85	Albania	Under the communist dictatorship of Enver Hoxha, a ferocious and sustained attack was launched on the Church. Among early victims was the Metropolitan Archbishop of Durres in February 1949. A final attack

		was ordered in 1967 and the New Constitution of December 1976 formally outlawed religion, making Albania an atheist state.
1966–67	China	The 'Cultural Revolution' in communist China. Described as 'the most systematic attempt ever, by a single nation, to eradicate and destroy Christianity'.
1963–99	Sudan	Anti-Christian massacres in the Sudan, particularly in the south of the country, amounted in some areas to a holocaust.
1971	Uganda	Massacres in Uganda (including the assassination of Archbishop Janani Luwum in 1977).
1994	Rwanda	The Rwanda genocide.

Postscript: Among current persecutions of Christians, and attacks on Christians by other faiths, prominent examples include Nigeria, Indonesia and Burma.

THE ORTHODOX 'NEW MARTYRS', 1453–1821

The Orthodox Church remembers the 'New Martyrs' of the period of Ottoman domination – the 'Great Captivity'. These names are largely unfamiliar in the West. They include:

1507	Makarios, an Orthodox monk and zealot. Put to death for preaching Christianity in public.
1526	John of Ioannina, also put to death for proclaiming Christianity in public.
1589	Philothei, put to death for leading a revival movement.
1657	Demetrios of Philadelphia, executed for openly returning to Christianity.
1716	Anthimos the Georgian, apparently executed for 'political intrigue'.
1779	Kosmas Aitolos, executed for disturbing the peace.
1788	Theodore Sladich, also executed for disturbing the peace.
1821	Patriarchs Cyril VI and Gregory V (in reprisal for the insurrection against Ottoman rule in Greece).

THE RELIGIOUS ORDERS

EARLY MONASTIC FOUNDATIONS IN WESTERN EUROPE (BEFORE CLUNY)

528/529	Monte Cassino (the first in Western Europe)
561	St Médard (Soissons)
c. 590	Luxeuil (by St Columbanus)
614	Bobbio
c. 625	St Denis (near Paris)
c. 660	Corbie (founded from Luxeuil)
714	Reichenau (by Pirminius)
744	Fulda
802	Münster (by Charlemagne)
880	Montserrat (in Catalonia)

EUROPEAN MONASTIC FOUNDATIONS (FROM CLUNY TO CLAIRVAUX)

909–910	Cluny
917	Souvigny
928	Sauxillanges
930	Brogne
934	Einsiedeln
940	Jumièges
959	Gorze
966	Mt St Michel
989	Dijon
1001	Fécamp (reorganized)
1005	Verdun
1030	Cérisy
c. 1035	Conches
By 1050	Fontenay
1055	La Charité
1067	Moissac
1075	Molesme
1079	Hirsau; St Martin
1084	La Grande Chartreuse (in Dauphin Alps, by St Bruno)
1085	Vézelay
1098	Cîteaux

1105	Altkisch, Savigny
1113	La Ferté
1114	Pontigny
1115	Morimond; Clairvaux (by St Bernard)

THE CISTERCIANS: FIRST FOUNDATIONS OF THE CISTERCIANS OUTSIDE FRANCE

1120	Italy	1142	Ireland
1123	Germany	1143	Denmark, Sweden, Bohemia
1129	England	1146	Norway
1135	Slovenia	1153	Portugal
1136	Scotland	1179	Poland and Hungary
1140	Spain and Wales		

THE INTRODUCTION OF SELECTED ORDERS INTO ENGLAND

Order	First House in England
Cluniac	1077
Augustinian canons	c. 1100
Canons of the Holy Sepulchre	c. 1120
Savigniac	1124
Cistercian	1128
Gilbertine	c. 1131
Victorine	c. 1133
Premonstratensian	1143
Fontevrault	c. 1154
Carthusian	1178–79
Grandmont	c. 1204

Source: David Knowles, *The Monastic Orders in England*
(2nd ed., 1963).

MONASTIC FOUNDATIONS IN ENGLAND

Crowland	716
Fountains	1132 (Cistercian)
Garendon	1133 (Cistercian)
Glastonbury	708 (originally a Celtic foundation)
Gloucester	681
Iona	(after) 563
Jarrow	681

Lewes	1077
Lindisfarne	(after) 635
Milton Abbey (Dorset)	938 (founded by Athelstan)
Peterborough	654
Rievaulx	1132 (Cistercian)
Ripon	661
St Albans	793
Selsey	681
Thorney	662
Tintern	1131 (Cistercian)
Waverley	1128 (Cistercian)
Wearmouth	675
Westminster	1065 (rebuilding dedicated) (first founded, 604)
Whitby	657
Wimborne	713
Winchester	646

THE 12 RICHEST MONASTERIES, 1066

Value of the holdings of selected
monasteries in Domesday (gross income)

House	Gross, £
Glastonbury	827
Ely	768
Christ Church, Canterbury	687
Bury St Edmunds	639
St Augustine's, Canterbury	635
Winchester, Old Minster	600
Westminster	583
Abingdon	462
Winchester, New Minster	390
Ramsey	358
Peterborough	323
St Albans	269

Principal source: David Knowles, *The
Monastic Orders in England* (2nd edn, 1963).

THE DISSOLUTION OF THE MONASTERIES, 1525–59

Note: The wealth of the monasteries soon proved an irresistible attraction for the
Tudor monarchy. Following the Acts of 1536 and 1539 the monastic foundations
were swiftly dissolved.

1525	Wolsey completes the suppression of 29 religious houses: their revenues are transferred to Cardinal College, Oxford.
1530	Twenty-two abbots sign petition to the Pope in support of the Royal Divorce.
1534	The Oath of Supremacy administered to all houses.
	Houses of Observant Friars closed.
	Visitation of all friaries by John Hilsey and George Browne.
1535	Compilation of *Valor Ecclesiasticus*.
	Execution of Prior Houghton and other monks.
	Visitation of all religious houses begins.
1536	Visitation continues under Dr Richard Layton (later Dean of York), Dr Thomas Legh, John Price, Dr John Tregonwell and Thomas Bedyll, Archdeacon of London.
	Act for the Dissolution of the Lesser Monasteries (27 Hen. VIII, cap. 28): all houses with an annual income of under £200 to become the King's, on account of the 'manifest sin, vicious, carnal and abominable living' they have produced.
1537	Execution of further Carthusians.
1538	Surrender of the friaries under the supervision of Richard Ingworth, Suffragan Bishop of Dover, and Dr John London, Warden of New College, Oxford (the latter now a prominent royal agent).
1538–39	Surrender of many great houses under official pressure.
1539	Act for the Dissolution of the Greater Monasteries (31 Hen. VIII, cap. 13). Closure of remaining houses.
	Execution of Thomas Beche, Abbot of Colchester, Hugh Cook, Abbot of Reading and Richard Whiting, Abbot of Glastonbury on charges of treason.
1539–42	Foundation of six new episcopal sees based on former monastic churches: Peterborough, Gloucester, Oxford, Chester, Bristol, Westminster.
1555	Appointment of a committee by Mary to consider refoundation of certain religious houses.
	Reopening of monasteries at Greenwich (Observant Friars), Smithfield (Dominican Friars), Sheen (Carthusians), Syon (Bridgettine Nuns) and King's Langley (Dominicanesses).
1556	Refoundation of Benedictine house at Westminster under John Feckenham, Dean of St Paul's.
1559	Suppression of refounded houses by Elizabeth I.

Source: Powell, K. and Cook, C., *English Historical Facts, 1485–1603* (1977).

288

THE MILITARY ORDERS

c. 1070	Foundation of Knights Hospitaller at Jerusalem by merchants from Amalfi to care for the Hospital of St John. The Order is militarized around 1130 on the lines of the Templars.
c. 1120	Foundation of Knights Templar by Hugh of Pajens to guide and protect pilgrims in the Holy Land.
1128	Confirmation of Knights Templar by the Synod of Troyes.
1130	Knights Hospitaller militarized (see above).
1164	The Spanish Knights of Calatrava founded.
1166	Portuguese Order of Avis founded.
1175	Spanish Order of St James of Compostela founded.
1183	Spanish Order of Alcantara founded.
1189	Start of the Third Crusade.
c. 1190	Founding at Acre of the Knights of the Hospital of St Mary of the Teutons, Jerusalem (the Teutonic Knights). See p. 75.
1191	New headquarters established by the Templars at Acre.
1191–92	Occupation of Cyprus by Templars. Beginnings of intermittent war with Leo of Armenia over the Amanus March.
c. 1202	Livonian Knights founded to Christianise Baltic region.
1217	Construction of Atlit begun by Knights Templar (completed 1221).
1218	Start of Fifth Crusade (see p. 69).
1228–40	Various new crusades (Frederick II, 1228–29, Theobald of Champagne, 1239–40, Richard of Cornwall, 1240–41).
1240	Beginning of rebuilding of Safad by Templars (which subsequently falls to Mamelukes in 1266).
1248	Crusade of St Louis (see p. 70).
1274	The Council of Lyons (see p. 305).
1291	Fall of Acre to the Mamelukes. The Templars evacuate Atlit and Tortosa and transfer to Cyprus.
1307	Attack on the Templars by Philip of France.
1310	Knights Hospitaller transfer to Rhodes (the Knights of Rhodes). Over 50 Templars burnt as relapsed heretics near Paris.

1312	Dissolution of Order of the Templars follows the Council of Vienne. Its property passed to the Knights Hospitaller (except in Spain and in France, where it passed to the Crown).
1314	Execution of James of Molay, Grand Master of the Templars.
1522	Knights Hospitaller forced from Rhodes to Malta.
1571	The Templar archive in Cyprus destroyed by the Ottomans after their seizure of the island.

THE MODERN MISSIONARY AGE

CATHOLIC MISSIONS TO THE NEW WORLD, 1502–1767

Franciscans

1502	Santo Domingo
1509	Darién
1523	Mexico
1534	Quito

Dominicans

1510	Santo Domingo
1526	Mexico
1529	Santa Maria and Venezuela
1541	Quito
1549	Bogotá

Augustinians

1523	Mexico
1570	Quito
1575	Bogotá
1595	Chile

Jesuits

1566	Florida
1567	Peru
1572	Mexico
1589	New Granada
1593	Chile
1605	Asunción
1607	The Paraguayan Missions become independent of Peru

1628   Venezuela
1650   Santo Domingo
1767   Expulsion of the Company

Principal source: G. Arciniegas, *Latin America: A Cultural History* (New York, 1967).

ESTABLISHMENT OF PORTUGUESE OVERSEAS BISHOPRICS

The early Portuguese Catholic bishoprics created in Asia were as follows:

1534   Sá Salvador de Agra (India)
1534   Goa (Archbishopric in 1557) (India)
1557   Cochin (India)
1557   Malacca (Malaya)
1576   Macao (China)
1588   Funai (Japan)
1600   Angamale (India)*
1606   Mailapur (India)

*Raised to an archbishopric in 1608 and transfered to Cranganur in 1609.

DATES OF FOUNDATION OF SELECTED BRITISH MISSIONARY SOCIETIES, 1815–1914

From the eighteenth century onwards a tide of Protestant missions went out from the British Isles to all parts of the globe. Most of the major missionary societies had been founded by 1815. The Society for the Promotion of Christian Knowledge (SPCK) had been founded back in 1698, the United Society for the Propagation of the Gospel (USPG) in 1701. Other major early foundations were the Baptist Missionary Society (founded 1792 as the Particular Society for Propagating the Gospel Among the Heathen), the British and Foreign Bible Society (1804); the Church Missionary Society (1799); the London Missionary Society (1795) and the Edinburgh Missionary Society (1796).

1824   Church of Scotland Foreign Missions Committee
1834   Female Education Society
1836   Colonial Missionary Society
1841   Jerusalem and the East Mission
1843   Loochow Naval Mission
1844   Patagonian Missionary Society (after 1852 the South American Missionary Society)
1847   Presbyterian Church of England Foreign Missions Committee
1848   Melanesian Mission

1853	Anglo-Continental Society (Anglican and Foreign Church Society in 1904)
1858	Christian Vernacular Education Society for India
1859	Universities Mission to Central Africa
1865	China Inland Mission
1867	Baptist Zenana Mission
1868	Friends Foreign Mission Association (Quaker)
1877	Cambridge Mission to Delhi
	School and Tract Book Society (for China)
1878	Livingstone Inland Mission
1880	Church of England Zenana Missionary Society
1889	Cape General Mission (became the South African General Mission in 1894)
1895	Africa Inland Mission
1900	United Free Church of Scotland Foreign Mission
1910	Conference of British Missionary Societies formed following the World Missionary Conference in Edinburgh
1912	Conference for World Mission

THE EXPLOSION OF CONTINENTAL EUROPEAN MISSIONS

During the nineteenth century a vast number of missionary societies was formed in mainland Europe to parallel those being formed in the British Isles (see p. 292). Not only the major colonial powers (such as France, Germany or Belgium) witnessed this phenomenon, but countries (as in Scandinavia) with few pretensions to empire. They are best listed under Catholic and Protestant.

Protestant

1780	Basel Society for Christianity
1793	Herrnhuter Missions (Dutch)
1797	Netherlands Missionary Society
1800	Jänicke Mission School (Berlin)
1815	Basel Mission
1821	Danish Missionary Society
1822	Paris Evangelical Missionary Society
1824	Berlin Missionary Society
1830	Swiss Evangelical Hebrew Mission
1835	Swedish Missionary Society
1836	Bremen Missionary Society; North German Missionary Society
1842	Norwegian Missionary Society
1859	Finnish Missionary Society
1866	Continental Missionary Conferences begin at Bremen
1887	Start of Dutch Missionary Conferences

Catholic

1805	Picpus Fathers (Italian)
1812	Sisters of Providence of Portieux (French)
1816	Society of Mary (Marists); Oblates of Immaculate Virgin Mary (both Italian)
1829	Leopold Foundation (Austrian)
1830	Oblates of St Francis de Sales (Swiss)
1838	Ludwig Missionary Union (German)
1839	Holy Ghost Fathers (Dutch)
1843	Association of the Holy Childhood (Italian)
1845	Sisterhood of Our Lady of Sion (French)
1855	Salesians of Don Bosco (Italian)
1856	Society of the Orient (French)
1857	Congregation of the Immaculate Heart of Mary (Belgian)
1868	'White Fathers' (Society of Missionaries of Our Lady of Africa)
1875	Society of the Divine Word (German)
1887	Society of St Charles Borromeo (Italian)

THE ADVENT OF AMERICAN MISSIONS

Modern American missions began their work in earnest with the foundation in 1810 of the American Board of Commissioners for Foreign Missions. Some key dates prior to 1914 are as follows:

1810	Foundation of American Board of Commissioners for Foreign Missions (ABC)
1816	American Bible Society founded
1817	American Colonisation Society founded
1817	United Foreign Missionary Society founded
1818	Foundation of Baptist Convention to promote foreign missions
1825	American Tract Society established
1826	American Home Missionary Society founded
1886	Northfield, Massachusetts, Student Conference sets aside 'Mount Hermon Hundred' for mission field
1902	Missionary Education Movement founded

THE DEVELOPMENT OF CHRISTIAN DOCTRINE

THE MAKING OF THE NEW TESTAMENT

There is no consensus among historians or theologians as to the precise dates when many of the books of the New Testament were compiled. Excluding the Gospels and Acts (and the later Revelation) there is a broader consensus on the *order* in which they may have been written. One possible list is as follows:

Galatians	Philemon
1 and 2 James	Philippians
1 and 2 Thessalonians	1 Peter
1 and 2 Corinthians	Jude
Romans	Timothy
Ephesians	2 Peter
Colossians	Hebrews

No agreed consensus exists for the dates of the writing of the four canonical gospels, but Mark is agreed to be first and John the last. Possible dates might be as follows:

c. 70	Gospel of Mark
c. 80–85	Gospel of Matthew
c. 85–90	Gospel of Luke
c. 90–100	Gospel of John

Nor was the final list of books making up the New Testament canon agreed at any early date by all Christians. Seven books of the New Testament were still in dispute *c.* 300. These were:

Hebrews
James
2 Peter
2 John
3 John
Jude
Revelation

SELECTED EARLY CHURCH FATHERS

Athanasius (c. 296–373)
Theologian who made a major contribution at Nicaea in 325. Patriarch of Alexandria (but frequently expelled by Emperors who sympathized with the Arian cause).

Augustine of Hippo (354–430)
Regarded as the greatest of the Latin Fathers of the Church. Born in Tagaste in Numidia (present-day Algeria). Converted to Christianity and baptized in 386 by St Ambrose. Bishop of Hippo after 396. His great works include *Confessions* (400) and *The City of God* (22 books, 412–427).

Chrysostom, St John (c. 347–407)
Famous as the greatest orator of the early Church. Born at Antioch. Became Archbishop of Constantinople in 398 but deposed and banished by the Empress Eudoxia.

Cyril of Alexandria (376–444)
Patriarch of Alexandria after 412. He expelled the Jews (415) and instituted a relentless persecution of Nestorius.

Cyril of Jerusalem (c. 315–386)
Bishop of Jerusalem (though twice expelled). Theologian who played a major part in the controversies over Arian.

Gregory the Great (c. 540–604)
Pope from 590 to 604. He wrote the enormously influential *Pastoral Care*.

Gregory of Nyssa (c. 331–395)
Bishop of Nyssa in Cappadocia, after c. 371 a staunch defender of orthodoxy. Deposed by Arian Emperor Valens in 376. Regained office, 378. Brother of Basil the Great. Along with Gregory of Nazianzus and Basil of Caesarea, one of the Cappadocian Fathers.

Irenaeus (c. 125–c. 202)
Bishop of Lyons who developed the important theory of apostolic succession through bishops.

Jerome (c. 342–420)
Scholar and ascetic. A hermit who later became secretary to Pope Damasus. Moved to Bethlehem, 386. Best known for his Vulgate, the first translation of the Bible from Hebrew into Latin.

Maximus the Confessor (c. 580–662)
The most influential Byzantine theologian of the seventh century. In 90 major works he counselled Christian humanism and had considerable influence on the mysticism of the Middle Ages.

Origen (c. 185–254)
A Greek author from Alexandria, his major treatise *On First Principles* set out a systematic account of Christian theology for the first time.

Severus of Antioch (c. 465–538)
A monk–theologian who was a leader of the Monophysites. Patriarch of Antioch after 512, but forced to flee under Emperor Justin I and again in 535.

Tertullian (c. 160–225)
The first important Latin Christian author. He set out the main outlines of Latin theology.

CHRONOLOGY OF EARLY CHRISTIAN WRITINGS

96	The *Epistle of Clement*
c. 100–130	The *Shepherd* of Hermas
c. 115	The *Epistles* of Ignatius (disputed)
c. 116	Polycarp, *Epistle to the Philippians*
c. 125	Quadratus, *Apology*
c. 130	*Epistle of Barnabas* (or perhaps much earlier)
c. 140	Aristides, *Apology*
c. 150	*Letter to Diognetus*; Justin, *Apology*; *Pistis Sophia*
152	Tatian, *Oration to the Greeks*
c. 157	*Martyrium Polycarpi*
c. 160	Ptolemaeus, *Letter to Flora*
c. 173	Tatian, *Diatessaron*
175	Melito, *Apology*
c. 175	Celsus, *True Word*
177	Athenagoras, *Legatio pro Christianis*
180	Theophilus, *Ad Autolycum*
185	Irenaeus, *Adversus Haereses*
190	Clement, *Address to the Greeks*
c. 195	Clement, *Tutor*
197	Tertullian, *Apology*
200	Tertullian, *De Praescriptione*
c. 220	Hippolytus, *Apostolic Tradition*
220	Tertullian, *Adversus Praxean*
c. 230	Origen, *Hexapla: De Principiis*
c. 230	Hippolytus, *Refutation*
c. 250	Origen, *Contra Celsum*
c. 250	*Didascalia*
251	Cyprian, *De Unitate*
c. 260	Dionysius Alex, *Refutation and Defence*
c. 275	*Apostolic Church Order*
311	Eusebius, *Martyrs of Palestine*
317	Athanasius, *De Incarnatione*

THE APOSTOLIC FATHERS*

Clement of Rome (n.a.)	Possibly the third Bishop of Rome, either *c.* 88–97 or 92–101. The first epistle attributed to him is generally accepted as his. His martyrdom is legendary.
Ignatius (*c.* 35–107)	Second Bishop of Antioch. His authorship of *The Ignatian Epistles* is controversial.
Hermas (second century)	Known only through his work, the *Shepherd*. Possibly a brother of Pope Pius I (d. 155). His work was popular in the East.

Polycarp (*c.* 69–155)   Bishop of Smyrna and author of the Epistle to the Philippians (his only extant writing).

Papias (early second century)   Bishop of Hierapolis, Phrygia. His work (only fragments survive) includes 'Explanations of the Sayings of the Lord'.

* Epistle of Barnabas
* Epistle to Diognetus
* 2 Clement
* The Didache

*Authors of the works indicated with an asterisk are not known.

DOCTORS OF THE CHURCH

In order of creation, the Doctors of the Church (i.e. those saints officially recognized by the Pope or an ecumenical council as eminent teachers of the faith) were:

1298	Ambrose
	Jerome
	Augustine of Hippo
	Gregory the Great
by 1568	Athanasius
	John Chrysostom
	Basil the Great
	Gregory of Nazianzus

Additions to these original eight were:

1567	Thomas Aquinas
1588	Bonaventure
1720	Anselm of Canterbury
1722	Isidore of Seville
1729	Peter Chrysologus
1754	Leo the Great
1828	Peter Damian
1830	Bernard of Clairvaux
1851	Hilary of Poitiers
1871	Alphonsus Liguori
1877	Francis de Sales
1882	Cyril of Alexandria
	Cyril of Jerusalem
1890	John of Damascus
1899	The Venerable Bede
1920	Ephraem the Syrian

1925	Peter Canisius	
1926	John of the Cross	
1931	Robert Bellarmine	
1932	Albertus Magnus	
1946	Anthony of Padua	
1959	Lawrence of Brindisi	
1970	Teresa of Avila	
	Catherine of Siena	
1997	Thérèse of Lisieux	

THE ECUMENICAL COUNCILS

Introductory note: Not all of the 21 Ecumenical Councils as enumerated by the Roman Catholic Church are recognized by the Orthodox or Eastern churches. Only the first two are recognized by the Assyrian Church of the East (commonly but incorrectly called Nestorian), while only the first three are recognized by the Monophysite Armenians, Syrians and Copts. Most of the Orthodox Churches recognize the first seven councils (up to Nicaea II in 787).

Of the 21 Ecumenical Councils, the first eight were held in the East, the last 13 in the West.

1. Nicaea I	Sylvester I	May to June, 325
2. Constantinople I	St Damasus I	May to July, 381
3. Ephesus	Celestine I	June to July, 431
4. Chalcedon	St Leo the Great	Oct. to Nov., 451
5. Constantinople II	Vigilius	May to June, 553
6. Constantinople III	St Agatho; Leo II	Nov. 680 to Sept., 681
7. Nicaea II	Hadrian I	Sept. to Oct., 787
8. Constantinople IV	Nicholas I; Hadrian II	Oct. 869 to Feb., 870
9. Lateran I	Callistus II	March to April, 1123
10. Lateran II	Innocent II	April 1139
11. Lateran III	Alexander III	March 1179
12. Lateran IV	Innocent III	Nov. 1215
13. Lyons I	Innocent IV	June to July, 1245
14. Lyons II	Gregory X	May to July, 1274
15. Vienne	Clement V	Oct. 1311 to May, 1312
16. Constance	Martin V	Nov. 1414 to April, 1418
17. Florence	Eugene IV	Dec. 1431 to Aug., 1445
18. Lateran V	Julius II; Leo X	May 1512 to March, 1517
19. Trent	Paul III; Pius IV	Dec. 1545 to Dec.,1563
20. Vatican I	Pius IX	Dec. 1869 to July, 1870
21. Vatican II	John XXIII; Paul VI	Oct. 1962 to Dec., 1965

Councils to 870

325   *First Council of Nicaea* (May–July 325) in the presence of Emperor Constantine with 318 bishops attending. Its main achievements were to formulate the Nicene Creed; condemn Arianism (which denied the divinity of Christ); fix the date for Easter; and adopt as the model of the Church's organization the civil division of the Empire (20 canons).

381   *First Council of Constantinople* A gathering of 150 bishops under Emperor Theodosius I and Pope Damasus I. Among its achievements were the condemnation of Macedonianism and Appollinarianism, a reaffirmation of the Nicene Creed and attempts to heal the Antiochene Schism. It designated the Bishop of Constantinople as the top-ranking prelate of the East, with primacy next to the Pope (4 canons).

431   *Council of Ephesus* (22 June–17 July 431, over 5 sessions) A gathering of 200 bishops presided over by St Cyril of Alexandria (representing Pope Celestine I). Among its achievements, it condemned Nestorianism and Pelagianism, and the title *Theotokos* (Bearer of God) was given to Mary. Cyprus was made independent of Antioch (6 canons).

451   *Council of Chalcedon* (8 Oct.–1 Nov. 451 over 17 sessions) A gathering of *c.* 150 bishops convened under Pope Leo I and Emperor Marcion. Its highly important doctrine of the two natures in the one person of Christ (divine and human) was defined. Diascorus was condemned and deposed, the Tome of Leo approved as dogma and the division of Christendom into 5 patriarchates completed (28 canons).

553   *Second Council of Constantinople* (May–June 553) A gathering of *c.* 165 bishops convened by Pope Vigilius and Emperor Justinian. Its main achievements were to reinforce the controversial decisions agreed at Chalcedon and to condemn the Nestorian 'Three Chapters' of Theodoret of Cyrus.

680–681   *Third Council of Constantinople* (Nov. 680–Sept. 681, 16 sessions) A gathering of 174 bishops which condemned Monotheletism (the doctrine of one will in Christ) and also condemned the letter of Pope Honorius I to Bishop Sergius of Constantinople for its ambiguity on this question.

787   *Second Council of Nicaea* (Sept.–Oct. 787, 8 sessions) A gathering of over 300 bishops, preoccupied with the question of Iconoclasm (which was strongly condemned). Adoptionism was also condemned (this doctrine maintained that Christ was the Son of God by adoption rather than by nature) (20 canons).

869–870   *Fourth Council of Constantinople* (Oct. 869–Feb. 870) A gathering of 102 bishops, but not regarded as ecumenical until the eleventh century and never recognized by most of the Orthodox East. This last Council to be held in the East attempted to end the schism of Patriarch Photius and restore Ignatius as Patriarch (27 canons).

Principal sources: Hubert Jedin, *Ecumenical Councils of the Catholic Church* (1960); *The Encyclopaedia of Catholicism.*

THE GROWTH OF HERESY

From its earliest days, Christianity was beset by sects and factions often deemed heretical. The more important sects are listed below.

To the conversion of Constantine

70–120	Dosithæans
	Menandrians
	Nazarenes
	Cerinthians
	Docetæ
	Ebionites
	Ophites
	Adamites, or Prodicians
	Sethians
	Cainites
	Cleobians
120–130	Basilidians
	Saturninians
	Carpocratians
	Marcellinians
130–140	Cerdonians
	Marcionites
	Lucianists
	Apellianists
138–158	Valentinians
	Heracleonites
	Marcosites
	Colorbasians
	Secundians
150–170	Florinians
	Quartodecimans
	Encratites
	Tatianists
	Severians

	Hydroparastatæ
	Archontics
	Apotactics
170–200	Hermogenians
	Seleucians
	Montanists
	Theodotians
	Tertullianists
	Artemonites
	Bardesanians
	Ascodrugytæ
205	Noëtians
	Praxeans
	Melchisedechians
	Arabici
220	Sabellians
224	Elchasaites
250	Origenists
251	Novatians
264–325	Audians
280	Manichæans
	Samosatenes
	Metangismonitæ
300	Artotyritæ
	Ascitæ
306	Meletian Schism

Source: This outline follows the classification in the old, but monumental, work of John Henry Blunt, *Dictionary of Sects, Heresies, Ecclesiastical Parties and Schools of Religious Thought* (1874).

From the fourth to the seventh centuries

320–350	Arians
	Eusebians
	Semi-Arians
	Aëtians
	Anomœans, or Eunomians
	Acacians
	Eudoxians
	Psathyrians
	Photinians

	Aërians
	Donatists
	Circumcellions
	Marcellians
	Macedonians
350–400	Luciferians
	Apollinarians
	Synusiastæ
	Bonosians
	Collyridians
	Jovinianists
	Euchites, or Messalians
	Hypsistarians
	Antidicomarianites
	Tropitæ
428 onwards	Nestorians
448	Eutychians
450–500	Pelagians
	Hieracites
	Helvidians
	Esaianites
	Barsanians
	Barsanuphites
	Eunomio-Theophronians
	Theosebites
	Timotheans
451	Monophysites, or Jacobites
482	Acephali
520–600	Aphthartodocetæ
	Gaianitæ
	Actistetes, or Ctistolatræ
	Phthartolatræ, Severians, or Theodosians
	Xenaians
	Theopaschites
	Triphysites
	Tritheists, or Philoponists
	Cononites
	Damianists
Seventh century	Monothelites
	Paulicians
	Athingani
	Agynians
	Agoniclites

Medieval heresies

Some of the more important medieval heresies can be found in Part II (Glossary) (See pp. 229–70). For the Albigensians, Wycliffites and Hussites, see separate chronologies.

ORTHODOX DOCTRINE SINCE 787

The major Orthodox statements of doctrine since 787, once referred to as the 'Symbolical Books' of the Orthodox Church, are as follows:

867	The Encyclical Letter of St Photius
1054	The First Letter of Michael Cerularius to Peter of Antioch
1341 and 1351	The decisions of the Councils of Constantinople on the Hesychast Controversy
1440–41	The Encyclical Letter of St Mark of Ephesus
1455–56	The Confession of Faith by Gennadius, Patriarch of Constantinople
1573–81	The Replies of Jeremias II to the Lutherans
1625	The Confession of Faith by Metrophanes Kritopoulos
1642	The Orthodox Confession by Peter of Moghila, in its revised form (ratified by the Council of Jassy)
1672	The Confession of Dositheus (ratified by the Council of Jerusalem)
1718 and 1723	The Answers of the Orthodox Patriarchs to the Non-Jurors
1848	The Reply of the Orthodox Patriarchs to Pope Pius IX
1895	The Reply of the Synod of Constantinople to Pope Leo XIII
1920 and 1952	The Encyclical Letters by the Patriarchate of Constantinople on Christian unity and on the 'Ecumenical Movement'

Source: Timothy Ware, *The Orthodox Church* (1982).

CHURCH COUNCILS OF THE WEST (to 1563)

9*   1123   ***First Lateran Council*** (18 March–6 April 1123) The first Ecumenical Council since 870 and the first ever to be held in Rome. Convened by Pope Callistus II (1129–34), it confirmed the Concordat of Worms, abolishing the right of lay princes to investiture with ring and crosier, passed 25 reforming canons and focused on the Crusades.

10   1139   ***Second Lateran Council*** (April 1139) A gathering of 1,000 bishops summoned by Pope Innocent II. It ended the schism of Anacletus II and among its 30 canons it precluded holy orders to married men.

304

11	1179	***Third Lateran Council*** (5–19 March 1179) A gathering of 302 bishops summoned by Pope Alexander III. It was noted for its condemnation of the Waldensians and the Albigensian heresy (see p. 72). Among its many reforms was the rule that a two-thirds vote of the cardinals was necessary for the election of a new pope.
12	1215	***Fourth Lateran Council*** (11–30 Nov. 1215) A major gathering (the most important medieval council) summoned by Pope Innocent III and attended by 71 archbishops and over 400 bishops. Among major doctrinal decisions were the definition of the term transubstantiation and the requirement of annual confession and communion.
13	1245	***First Council of Lyons*** (28 June–17 July 1245) A gathering of 140 bishops and three patriarchs, presided over by Pope Innocent IV. Among the main business of the council was the launching of a new crusade under King Louis of France, the excommunication of Emperor Frederick II and approval of over 20 new canons.
14	1274	***Second Council of Lyons*** (7 May–17 July 1274) A major gathering attended by over 500 bishops and the patriarchs of Constantinople and Antioch. The reunion with the Greek Church achieved at Lyons was only short-lived. Rules for conducting papal elections were approved and further debate took place on ways to take back the Holy Land (31 chapters).
15	1311–12	***Council of Vienne*** (13 Oct. 1311–6 May 1312) A gathering called by Pope Clement V which is chiefly remembered for the debate and subsequent repression of the military order of the Knights Templar (see p. 266). It also enacted some clerical reforms and was involved with the controversy over Franciscan poverty.
16	1414–18	***Council of Constance*** (45 sessions over 4 years) (5 Nov. 1414–22 April 1418) One of the greatest gatherings in the history of the Church (forced on the Pope by Emperor Sigismund). Called to restore unity to the Church, it finally accomplished this (John XXIII was deposed, Gregory XII resigned and Benedict XIII was also deposed). Decrees were issued against Wycliffe (see p. 95) and Hus (see p. 96), who was later burnt at the stake. Among its decrees were *Sacrosancta* (1415), asserting that a council is superior to a pope; and *Frequens* (1417), providing for stated meetings of general councils. The conclave elected Cardinal Colonna as Martin V.
17	1431–45	***Council of Florence*** (sometimes referred to as Basel–Ferrara–Florence) The Council first met at Basel in 1431 to attempt to solve the crisis in Bohemia (see p. 97). Following disputes with the Pope (Eugenius IV) the Council was moved to Ferrara and

then Florence. The eventual outcome was to reaffirm the primacy of the papacy over conciliarism. The reunion achieved with the Greek (July 1439), Armenian (November 1439) and Jacobite churches (February 1442) was only temporary.

18   1512–17   ***Fifth Lateran Council*** (12 sessions, 10 May 1512–16 March 1517) A gathering summoned by Pope Julius II in direct response to the anti-papal council at Pisa in 1511. The Council extended over the papacy of Leo X and condemned the Council of Pisa. With the death of Julius II, however, Louis XII of France ceased opposition to the Council and in 1516 the Concordat of Bologna was agreed.

19   1545–63   ***Council of Trent*** (13 Dec. 1545–4 Dec. 1563 in 25 sessions) The great reforming council of the Roman Catholic Counter-Reformation. The sessions were held at Trent (1–8, 1545–47), at Bologna (9–11, 1547), at Trent again (12–16, 1551–52, under Pope Julius III) and finally at Trent again (17–25, 1559–63, under Pope Pius IX). The Council issued numerous reform decrees and produced its Doctrine of Scripture and Tradition, Original Sin, the nature of the Mass, Veneration of the Saints, etc.

* Numbers refer to their place in the table of Ecumenical Councils.

MAJOR CONFESSIONS OF THE REFORMATION ERA

Date	Title	Denomination	Principal author
1527	Schleitheim Confession	Anabaptist	Michael Sattler
1530/31	Augsburg Confession	Lutheran	Martin Luther and Philipp Melanchthon
1530	Confession to Charles V	Reformed	Zwingli
1530	Tetrapolitan Confession	Reformed	Capito, Bucer, etc.
1534	First Confession of Basel	Reformed	Oecolampadius
1536	First Helvetic Confession	Reformed	Bullinger
1536	The Genevan Confession	Reformed	Farel and Calvin
1549	The Zurich Consensus	Reformed	Calvin and Bullinger
1557	The Hungarian Confession	Reformed	Various
1559	The Gallican Confession	Reformed	Calvin *et al*.
1561/62	The Belgic Confession	Reformed	Gui de Brès
1566	Second Helvetic Confession	Reformed	Bullinger
1575	Bohemian Confession	Reformed/ Lutheran	n.a.

| 1577/80 | The Formula of Concord | Lutheran | n.a. |
| 1619 | The Canons of Dordrecht | Reformed | n.a. |

Note: This table excludes developments in the Anglican Church. See pp. 110–14 for major doctrinal developments. For Scotland, see pp. 115–16.
Sources: Mark Greengrass, *The Longman Companion to the European Reformation. c. 1500–1618* (1998); Jaroslav Pelikan, *Credo* (2003).

VATICAN I AND VATICAN II

1869–70   *First Vatican Council* (8 Dec. 1869–18 July 1870, 4 sessions) This was the first ecumenical council of the Roman Catholic Church for 300 years, summoned by Pope Pius IX in 1869 to bolster confidence in the Church at a time when the faith was under attack from new doctrines and the papacy was losing its temporal possessions in Italy. The Council promulgated major definitions of Catholic doctrine, including the primacy of the Pope and papal infallibility.

1962   *Second Vatican Council* (11 Oct. 1962–Sept. 1965) This was the second ecumenical council of the Roman Catholic Church in modern times, summoned by Pope John XXIII in January 1959. Its purpose was to consider increased collaboration with other churches and renewal of the faith. Over 8,000 bishops attended in Rome when the Council opened on 11 October 1962, including many observers from other churches, especially the Anglican and Orthodox faiths. The council published 16 decrees pointing towards a closer relationship with non-Catholic churches, the use of the vernacular rather than Latin in the liturgy and a greater humanism in Catholic doctrine. Many people thought that the tone of the Council presaged a relaxation of the Church's position on birth control, but the 1968 encyclical *Humanae Vitae* condemned its use.

Chronology

25 Jan. 1959	Pope John XXIII announces his intention to summon a council. Convoked in the apostolic constitution 'Humanae Salutis' (25 Dec. 1961).
11 Oct. 1962	Formal opening of the Council.
8 Dec. 1962	Conclusion of First Session of Council.
3 June 1963	Death of Pope John XXIII.
21 June 1963	Election of Pope Paul VI.
29 Sept. 1963	Second Session of Council opened.
4 Dec. 1963	Second Session of Council closed.
17 May 1964	Secretariat for Non-Christian Religions established.
14 Sept. 1964	Opening of Third Session of Council.

21 Nov. 1964	Closing of Third Session, with the promulgation of the Dogmatic Constitution on the Church, the Decree on Ecumenism, and the Decree on Eastern Catholic Churches. Pope Paul proclaims the title of Mary as Mother of the Church.
14 Sept. 1965	Fourth and final session opened.
28 Oct. and 18 Nov. 1965	Documents promulgated on Council's decisions including the Declaration on the Relationship of the Church to Non-Christian Religions, reform of the Roman Curia and the introduction of the process for the beatification of Pope Pius XII and Pope John XXIII.
7 Dec. 1965	Promulgation of (among others) the Declaration on Religious Freedom and the Pastoral Constitution on the Church in the Modern World.
8 Dec. 1965	The Council closes.

PAPAL PRONOUNCEMENTS OF THE MODERN ERA

Some of the more important pastoral letters or encyclicals (see p. 243) of the modern papacy since 1849 are given below. They are important for the understanding of the development of Roman Catholic theology in the modern world.

1849	*Ubi Primum* pronounces on the Immaculate Conception of the Virgin Mary (Feb.).
1859	*Qui Nuper* on the protection of the Papal States (June).
1864	*Quanta Cura*, denouncing errors in modern society. Attached to this is the *Syllabus Errarum* of Pius IX in which 80 errors are listed and condemned. Widely interpreted as highly reactionary and a rejection of the modern state (Dec.).
1870	*Respicientes*, strong denunciation of the loss of sovereignty over the Papal States (Nov.). Followed by *Ubi Nos* on the Papal States (May).
1875	*Quod Numquam*, addressed to the bishops of Prussia on the problems in Bismarck's Germany.
1891	*Rerum Novarum*, a major pronouncement on the condition of the working class, on the rights of workers to organize in trade unions and on capital and labour and the defence of private property. A major contribution to modern Catholic social teaching.
1892	*Au Milieu des Sollicitudes*, issued on the problem of Church–State relations in France.
1899	*Testem Benevolentiae*, concerned with the 'errors' of Americanism and addressed to Cardinal Gibbons of Baltimore.
1906	*Vehementer Nos*, the response of the Catholic Church to the Law of Separation in France.
1907	*Pascendi Dominici Gregis*, effectively a new Syllabus of Errors, denouncing many aspects of modernism in the new century.

1911	*Iamdudum*, in response to the Law of Separation in Portugal.
1914	*Ad Beatissimi Apostolorum Principis*, an appeal for peace issued in November following the start of World War I.
1926	*Iniquis Afflictisque*, a response to the anti-clerical hostilities against the Church in Mexico.
1928	*Mortalium Animos*, stressing religious unity and the pre-eminence of Rome. It was widely seen as a setback for ecumenism.
1930	*Casti Connubii*, a conservative encyclical on the sanctity of Christian marriage and family life coupled with a denunciation of many aspects of theatre, cinema, publishing, etc.
1931	*Quadragesimo Anno*, issued to mark the 40th anniversary of *Rerum Novarum*. On the social order, capital and labour.
	Non Abbiamo Bisogno, a defence of the Catholic position in Italy and an attack on Mussolini's fascism.
1933	*Dilectissima Nobis*, in support of Catholics in Spain (under attack from the anti-clericalism of the Second Republic in Spain established in 1931).
1937	*Mit Brennender Sorge* ('With Burning Anxiety'), a condemnation of Nazi policy towards the German Church. This was one of the few encyclicals not written in Latin. Drafted by the Secretary of State, Cardinal Eugenio Pacelli, later Pius XII.
1950	*Humani Generis* (On the Human Race), setting out the Christian view of Darwin's theory of evolution, the encyclical of Pius XII unleashed a wave of repression against progressive theologians.
1963	*Pacem in Terris*, encyclical on the dangers of an East–West conflict and nuclear war as well as a discussion of human rights (and the right of the individual to worship according to conscience). Also called for a strengthening of a world body to solve the problems of the world.
1968	*Humanae Vitae*, a strongly traditional statement on birth control, repeating the Catholic Church's ban on the use of artificial contraceptives, and holding that 'every conjugal act must be open to the transmission of life'. The encyclical provoked a very major clash in the Roman Catholic Church with widespread opposition to the encyclical.
1981	*Laborem Exercens*, discussed human work and the 'indispensable element' provided by trade unions in the modern world.
1995	*Ut Unum Sint*, major statement on Catholic dialogue with other Christian churches, including the Orthodox and Protestant. It remains the basis of Catholic ecumenism.

Principal source: J. Deedy, *The Catholic Fact Book* (1992).

HISTORY OF THE ENGLISH BIBLE (from Wycliffe to the Reformation)

1382	First complete translation of the Bible into English by Wycliffe and his followers (see p. 95). Denounced by ecclesiastical conservative authorities and linked to social insurrection.
1388	An improved version of the Bible circulates in his name.
Fifteenth century	Despite prohibition on any translation of the Bible, the advent of printing by Gutenberg after 1455 and the dissemination of scholars after the fall of Constantinople in 1453 gives birth to new forces.
1488	Printing of whole of Old Testament in Hebrew.
c. 1492	Birth of William Tyndale.
1511–14	Intensive work by Erasmus at Cambridge on his Latin translation of the Greek New Testament.
1516	Erasmus's New Testament published.
1522	Martin Luther publishes his German New Testament (based on Erasmus's text) at Wittenberg.
1523	The first parts of the Old Testament in German appear at Wittenberg (the last was not completed until 1533).
1524	Tyndale leaves England for Germany.
1525	Work begins on printing Tyndale's English New Testament at Cologne (completed at Worms). By 1526 it was on sale in England and by 1528 there were prosecutions for possession of it.
1530	Tyndale's edition of the Pentateuch (the first five books of the Old Testament) printed by Hoochstraten at Antwerp.
1534	A complete German Bible published in Wittenberg. A new edition of Tyndale's New Testament published in Antwerp. Miles Coverdale begins work on his biblical translation at Antwerp.
1535	In May, Tyndale arrested and imprisoned at Vilvorde Castle near Brussels.
1536	Tyndale executed at Vilvorde (Aug.).
1557	The 'Mathew Bible' published. (Mathew was the pseudonym of John Rogers, a friend of Tyndale.)
1539	The 'Great Bible' finally appears (April).
1540	A second edition of the Great Bible appears (April), with a preface by Cranmer. The first cheap edition of the Great Bible appears (printed by Berthelet).
1543	The Act for the Advancement of True Religion severely curtails the right to read the Scriptures.
1553–58	Destruction of many bibles during the Marian reaction.
1557	Whittingham produces a version of the New Testament at Geneva.
1560	The 'Geneva Bible' appears (April), a massively influential work which was to go through 140 editions by 1644. It was the work of Whittingham, Anthony Gilby and Richard Sampson.
1563	An Act was passed ordering the translation of the Bible into Welsh.

1567	A Welsh New Testament, mainly the work of William Salesbury, appears.
1568	Parker's version (the 'Bishops' Bible) published.
1576	The Geneva Bible first published in England.
1582	Appearance for Catholics of Douai Bible (New Testament). The Old Testament appeared in 1609. The Douai Bible was the work of Gregory Martin, an English seminary priest.
1588	The first Welsh Bible published by William Morgan, Bishop of St Asaph.
1611	Final appearance of Authorized Version of the Bible (King James Version). This is not revised for over two centuries.

Source: Ken Powell and Chris Cook, *English Historical Facts 1485–1603* (1977).

THE MODERN BIBLE MOVEMENT IN ENGLAND (since 1611)

1611	Publication of King James Version of the Bible. A landmark event, this version remained unaltered in Britain for two centuries.
1698	Society for Promoting Christian Knowledge (SPCK) formed in England.
1701	Society for Propagating the Gospel in Foreign Parts founded in England.
1709	Society for Promoting Christian Knowledge in Scotland formed.
1710	Canstein Bible Institute in Halle, Germany, begins production of cheap bibles.
1730	Society for Promoting Religious Knowledge Among the Poor established in England.
1780	Naval and Military Bible Society founded to distribute bibles to soldiers and seamen.
1785	Sunday School Society set up in England.
1804	Foundation of the British and Foreign Bible Society, on an interdenominational basis (March), in order to encourage a wider circulation of the Holy Scriptures at home and abroad. Formed in response to an appeal for bibles for Wales, it soon widened its scope to supply the countries of Europe. During the nineteenth century it established its agencies all round the world, and inspired the formation of many other bible societies.
1806	Hibernian Bible Society formed.
1812	City of London Auxiliary Bible Society formed.
1816	Merger of local US Bible Societies to form the American Bible Society (ABS).

SELECTED MODERN VERSIONS OF THE BIBLE

1881	English Revised Version of the New Testament appears.
1885	English Revised Version of the Old Testament appears.
1942	Encyclical of Pius XII calls for new and more accurate bible translations.
1946	United Bible Societies created.
1956	One-volume edition of Jerusalem Bible published in France.

1961   The New English Bible, an entirely new translation, begins to appear in Britain (under chairmanship of Charles Harold Dodd). An Anglican/Free Church venture.

1965   American Roman Catholic hierarchy authorizes publication of the American *Revised Standard Version*.

Among a plethora of editions over the last 40 years have been the following:

1970   New American Bible (and subsequent revisions, Catholic).
1971   New American Standard Bible (revised 1901 version).
1976   Good News Bible (and updated 1995). Conservative, evangelical.
1978   New International Version (revised 1984). A popular modern-language version.
1982   New King James Version.
1988   New Century Version (revised 1991).
1989   New Revised Standard Version.
1995   Contemporary English Version (intended as an easy-to-read introduction for those new to the Bible).
1996   New Living Translation.
2002   The Message (an evangelical paraphrase).

PILGRIMAGE AND CULTS

SELECTED KEY DATES (TO THE SIXTEENTH CENTURY)

Second century	Evidence of earliest pilgrimages to Jerusalem and Rome.
325	Churches built by orders of Constantine on the Holy Sites in Jerusalem stimulate pilgrimages.
354	Listing in Roman liturgical calendar of 29 local saints' sanctuaries which witness annual pilgrimages.
397	Tours becomes eventual pilgrim destination following death of St Martin.
400	The travel memoir of Etheria testifies to arrangements for pilgrims to Palestine.
754	Pilgrims begin to make their way to Fulda after death of St Boniface.
1061	Emergence of Walsingham in England as Marian shrine.
Twelfth century	Among major Marian shrines in Europe to develop from the twelfth century onwards were Rocamadour (in central France), Chartres, Montserrat (in Catalonia), Mariazell (Austria), Einsiedeln (Switzerland) and Czestochowa in Poland.
1170	Canterbury becomes major medieval shrine after death of Thomas à Becket.
1226	Growing pilgrimages to Assisi following death of St Francis.
Thirteenth century	Rapid rise of pilgrimage centre of St James the Greater at Santiago de Compostela.
1531	Appearance of Virgin Mary at Guadalupe.
1552	Start of pilgrimages to Goa.

PRINCIPAL MEDIEVAL ENGLISH PILGRIMAGE CENTRES*

Beverley	Death of abbey founder, St John, in 721.
Bury St Edmunds	St Edmund, King of the East Angles, killed by Danes, 869.
Canterbury	Shrine of Thomas à Becket. Murdered 1170.
Chester	Shrine of Werberg (died 699).
Chichester	St Richard, died 1253.
Durham	Shrine of St Cuthbert, died 687.
Ely	Shrine of St Etheldreda, died 679.
Hereford	St Thomas Cantelupe, died 1282.
Lincoln	St Hugh, Bishop, died 1200.

Oxford	St Frideswide, nun and Anglo-Saxon princess, died *c*. 735.
St Albans	St Alban, protomartyr of England, died 303.
Salisbury	St Osmund, Bishop, died 1099.
Walsingham	Miracles and cult of Virgin Mary.
Winchester	St Wulfstan, Bishop, died 1095.
York	St William, Archbishop, died 1154.

*For a fuller list, see Roger Hudson, *Hudson's English History: A Compendium* (2005).

THE CULT OF THE VIRGIN MARY (SINCE THE REFORMATION)

1531	Vision of the Virgin Mary reported at Guadalupe, Mexico.
1558	Publication of the Litany of Loreto.
1563	The foundation of Sodality of Our Lady.
1568	Official introduction into the Breviary of present form of *Hail Mary*.
1573	Establishment of the Feasts of Expectation of the Virgin and of Our Lady of Victory and Rosary.
1577	Publication by Peter Canisius of *De Maria Virgine Incomparabili*.
1644	Establishment of Feast of the Purest Heart of Mary.
1680	Preaching of Jean Eudes establishes pattern of devotion to the Immaculate Heart of Mary.
1683	Extension to whole Church of the Feast of the Holy Name of Mary.
1716	The Feast of Rosary extended to the whole Church.
1754	Proclamation of Our Lady of Guadalupe as Patroness of Mexico.
1830	Vision of the Miraculous Medal by Catherine Labouré (at Paris).
1842	The Holy Slavery of Mary founded.
1846	Visions at La Salette (France). Declaration of Mary Immaculate as Patroness of the United States.
1854	Proclamation of the Dogma of the Immaculate Conception by the Pope.
1858	Famous first vision of Bernadette at Lourdes, France.
1871	Visions of the Virgin Mary at Pontmain (France).
1878	Beginning of papacy of Leo XIII, 'Pope of the Rosary'.
1879	Vision of the Virgin Mary at Knock (Ireland).
1900	Proclamation of Our Lady of Guadalupe as Patroness of the Americas.
1917	Vision of the Virgin Mary at Fatima (Portugal) by three girls.
1921	Foundation of Legion of Mary in Dublin.
1931	Establishment of the Feast of Divine Motherhood.
1932–33	Appearances in Belgium (at Beauraing and Banneux).
1942	Dedication of the world to the 'Immaculate Heart of Mary'.
1945	Proclamation of Marian Year.
1950	Proclamation of the Dogma of the Assumption of the Virgin Mary.
1950s	Visions at Necedah (USA).*
1954	Feast established after proclamation of the Queenship of the Virgin.

1958	Centennial of Lourdes apparition proclaimed.
1961–65	Vision at Garabandal (Spain).*
1964	Proclamation of Mary as *Mater Ecclesiae*.
1968–71	Vision at Zeitoun (Egypt).*
1970s	Vision at Bayside (New York).*
1974	Papal Encyclical *Marialis Cultae*.
1981	Appearance of the Virgin Mary (24 June) to six young people in Croatian village of Medjugorje.

*Not recognized by the Church.

Source: Michael P. Carroll: *The Cult of the Virgin Mary: Psychological Origins* (1986).

MAJOR MARIAN SHRINES IN EUROPE

Among the major Marian shrines of mainland Europe are the following (arranged by country):

Austria	Our Lady of the Bowed Head (Vienna)
Belgium	The Virgin of the Poor (Banneux)
	Our Lady with the Golden Heart (Beauraing)
Bosnia	The Virgin of Medjugorje
France	The Three Shrines of Chartres
	Our Lady of La Salette
	Our Lady of the Smile (Lisieux)
	St Bernadette (Lourdes)
	Our Lady of Hope (Pontmain)
	Our Lady of the Miraculous Medal (Paris)
Germany	Our Lady with the Golden Horse (Altötting)
	The Chapel of Mercy (Kevelaer)
Italy	Our Lady della Guardia (Genoa)
	Our Lady of the Rosary (Pompeii)
	Our Lady of Montallegro (Rapallo)
	Salus Populi Romani, Santa Maria Maggiore (Rome)
	The Weeping Madonna of Syracuse (Sicily)
Netherlands	Star of the Sea (Maastricht)
Poland	The Black Madonna (Częstochowa)
Portugal	The Virgin of Fatima
Spain	Our Lady of Mount Carmel (Garabandal)
	La Moreneta (Montserrat)
Switzerland	Our Lady of Einsiedeln

CHURCH MEMBERSHIP IN THE MODERN ERA

GLOBAL CHRISTIANITY

Membership of world religions, 1900 (estimates)

Religion	%	Millions
Christians	34.4	558
Hindus	12.5	203
Muslims	12.3	200
Buddhists	7.8	127
Tribal Religions	6.5	106
Shinto	3.7	60
Jews	0.7	12

Distribution of Christian membership, 1900 (by geographical area)

Geographical area	%	Millions
Africa	1.8	10
East Asia	0.4	2
Europe	49.8	278
Latin America	11.1	62
North America	14.1	79
Oceania	1.0	5
South Asia	3.0	17
Russia	18.8	105

Breakdown of Christian membership, 1900 (by denomination)

Denomination	%	Millions
Roman Catholic	48.7	272
Eastern Orthodox	21.7	121
Anglican	5.9	33
Protestant	21.5	120
Marginal Independents	2.2	12

Source for all tables: Extracted from D.B. Barrett, ed., *World Christian Encyclopaedia* (1982). Percentages calculated by author.

Total number of Christians, 2000 (by main branches) (1975 figures for comparison)

Branch	2000	1975
Roman Catholic	1,170	734
Protestant	357	280
Marginal Independents	258	122
Orthodox	153	118
Anglicans	82	62
Total	2,020	1,316

Distribution of Christians, 2000 (by geographical area) (in rank order, 1975 figures for comparison, millions)

Geographical area	2000	1975
Latin America	571	305
Europe	432	410
Africa	393	171
North America	254	212
South Asia	192	92
Russia/USSR	118	91
East Asia	32	16
Oceania	28	19
Total	2,020	1,316

Source: Barrett, *World Christian Encyclopaedia* (*op. cit.*) and *World Almanac*.

Countries with most Christians (*c.* 2000),* millions

USA	252
Brazil	167
Mexico	102
Russia	84
Philippines	74
India	68

*This list excludes China, where membership figures can only be very imprecise estimates.

Religious adherence, *c.* 2000 (by major faiths), millions

Christianity	2,020
Islam	1,200
Hinduism	860
Buddhism	360
Judaism	20
Sikhism	24
Shintoism	95
Others	13
New Religions	138
Tribal Religions	100

Source: Parrinder (*op.cit.*) quoting from D.B. Barrett, ed., *World Christian Encyclopaedia*, global table 4.

The areas of Roman Catholic Strength, *c.* 2000

Countries with most Catholics (thousands)

Brazil	151,200
Mexico	93,600
Philippines	66,400
USA	66,300
Italy	55,800
France	48,000
Spain	38,500
Poland	36,900

Roman Catholic Bishops and Diocesan Priests (by continent)

Continent	Diocesan priests	Bishops
Europe	148,595	1,464
America	73,495	1,659
Asia	23,789	617
Africa	14,873	562
Oceania	2,769	118
Total	263,521	4,420

Source: various.

Estimated membership of the Orthodox Church, *c.* 1995

The Ancient Patriarchates (thousands)

Constantinople	6,000
Alexandria	350
Antioch	750
Jerusalem	60

The 9 other autocephalous churches (thousands)

Russia	100–150,000*
Romania	23,000*
Greece	9,000
Serbia	8,000*
Bulgaria	8,000*
Georgia	5,000
Poland	750
Cyprus	450
Albania	160

*With the title Patriarch for head of the Church.

Autonomous (but not autocephalous) (although disputed in case of Czech/Slovaks)

Czech Republic & Slovakia	55,000
Sinai	900
Finland	56,000
Japan	25,000
China	n.a.

Source: Timothy Ware, *The Orthodox Church* (2001). In addition there is now a very substantial Orthodox diaspora in North America.

Decline of Christianity in the Middle East (selected countries/towns)

		%		%
Turkey	1920	15	2006	1
Syria	1920	33	2006	10
Iraq	1970	5.8	2006	2.6
Jerusalem	1922	53	2006	2
Bethlehem	1948	85	2006	12

AFRICAN CHRISTIANITY

The explosion of Christianity in Africa

Roman Catholic

	Churches
1960	32,690
1970	36,929
1980	60,447
1990	84,771
2000	100,913

1960–2000 percentage increase = 209%

Anglican

	Churches
1960	8,515
1970	20,059
1980	28,691
1990	40,021
2000	46,371

1960–2000 percentage increase = 445%

Indigenous

	Churches
1960	16,685
1970	28,082
1980	50,325
1990	74,536
2000	92,433

1960–2000 percentage increase = 454%

Pentecostal

	Churches
1960	8,785
1970	23,327
1980	43,286
1990	81,744
2000	108,632

1960–2000 percentage increase = 1147%

Note: Percentages calculated by author from figures in *World Christian Encyclopaedia*

The countries with the largest Christian population in Africa (*c.* 2000)*

Nigeria	69,000,000	Egypt	10,500,000
Congo	48,000,000	Zimbabwe	10,400,000
South Africa	40,700,000	Madagascar	9,800,000
Ethiopia	32,200,000	Zambia	9,600,000
Kenya	25,400,000	Rwanda	7,400,000
Uganda	20,400,000	Cameroon	7,300,000
Tanzania	18,000,000	Burundi	6,900,000
Ghana	15,800,000	Malawi	6,800,000
Angola	12,200,000		

*With memberships over 5 million. Table compiled from figures in Littell, *Illustrated History*.

CHRISTIANITY IN THE USA

Religious affiliation in the USA, *c.* 1790–1950

Church membership (thousands)

Methodist

1790	58
1830	478
1860	1,661
1891	3,511
1914	5,394
1950	8,936

Protestant Episcopal

1927	1,789
1957	3,163

Roman Catholics

1789	35
1830	318
1860	3,103
1891	8,297
1900	12,041
1914	16,068
1930	45,640

Southern Baptist

1845	352
1860	650
1891	1,282
1914	2,589
1950	7,080

Presbyterian

1826	127
1860	292
1891	790
1914	1,428
1950	2,364

Source: Chris Cook and David Waller, *The Longman Handbook of Modern American History, 1763–1996* (1998).

The Church in the USA, 1975

Church	Membership (thousands)
Roman Catholic	48,700
Baptists	27,705
Eastern Orthodox	4,070
Methodists	13,190
Presbyterian	3,787
Lutheran	8,248
Protestant Episcopal	2,917

Source: *World Almanac* (1976).

Number of Churches, 1995 (excluding Roman Catholic, which easily surpasses any other)

Baptist	115,800
Methodist	49,100
Pentecostal	36,700
Lutheran	18,400
Latter Day Saint	11,600
Presbyterian	12,700
Episcopal	7,400

Source: Littell, *Illustrated History of Christianity* (2nd edn, 2003).

THE CHURCH IN LATIN AMERICA

A major transformation in South America has been the erosion of the once totally dominant position of Roman Catholicism. The comparative table below shows the growth of other Protestant churches alongside Catholicism.

	Numbers of churches			
	Roman Catholic	*Anglican*	*Baptist*	*Methodist*
1960	14,183	279	1,676	1,419
1975	18,927	450	4,006	2,004
2000	25,513	624	10,793	3,303

In this period, whilst Catholic adherents have risen from *c*. 90,000,000 to over 175,000,000 (nearly doubled), Baptist numbers have risen from 228,000 to 1,362,000 (a five-fold increase).

Source: *World Christian Encyclopaedia; World Almanac.*

RELIGIOUS ADHERENCE IN SELECTED EU COUNTRIES, 2002

The following percentages, compiled by the 2002 European Social Survey, are for persons stating that they attended church at least once a month:

Country	% attendance	Country	% attendance
Poland	75.5	Netherlands	20.9
Ireland	67.2	Germany	20.1
Greece	54.6	Belgium	18.9
Portugal	46.9	UK	18.6
Italy	44.1	Hungary	18.2
Austria	35.3	France	14.2
Slovenia	30.0	Denmark	9.3
Spain	28.9		

RELIGIOUS AFFILIATION IN BRITAIN, 1851–2001

The census of 1851

Note: The government's Census of Religious Worship was a unique attempt to enumerate religious attendance in the nineteenth century. It was based on a return of all those attending places of worship for morning, afternoon or evening services on a given Sunday in 1851.

The 1851 Religious Census of England and Wales

	Persons present at church on census Sunday	% of total population	% of those 'at church' on census Sunday
Church of England	2,971,268	17	47
Nonconformist	3,110,782	17	49
Roman Catholic	249,389	1	4
Other	24,793	0.1	0.4
Total	6,356,222	35	100

The Church of England

There had been comparative stagnation in the Church of England in the eighteenth century. Little had been done to meet the needs of an expanding industrial population. Eventually this position changed after 1815. Anglicanism revived with grants for church building in 1818 and 1824, so that over 4,500 churches were built or rebuilt by 1875. Abuses were reformed by the Ecclesiastical Commissioners after 1840.

Even so, the 1851 Religious Census revealed that only half the population went to church and only half of these were Anglicans. The late nineteenth century saw church-going remaining high in the countryside but declining in urban areas. The scientific discoveries of the ninteenth century, especially Darwin's *The Origin of Species* (1859), had done a great deal to undermine fundamental religious attitudes by questioning the authority of the Bible. Church building failed to keep pace with population growth and movement. After World War I religious adherence was obviously on the decline.

	Clergy	Easter Day communicants (000s)
1801	–	535
1811	14,531	550
1821	–	570
1831	14,933	605
1841	15,730	755
1851	16,194	875
1861	17,966	995
1871	19,411	1,110
1881	20,341	1,225
1891	22,753	1,490
1901	23,670	1,945
1911	23,193	2,293
1921	22,579	2,236
1931	21,309	2,311

Church attendances in major cities in 1882 (% of total population)

Sheffield	23	Southampton	38
Nottingham	24	Hull	41
Liverpool	26	Portsmouth	41
Bristol	31	Bath	52

The Church of England: number of churches and chapels

1831	11,900	1871	15,500
1841	12,700	1881	16,300
1851	14,000	1891	16,900
1861	14,700	1901	17,400

The Roman Catholic Church

	Estimated Catholic population	Churches and chapels
1840	700,000	469
1851	900,000	597
1891	1,357,000	1,387
1911	1,710,000	1,773
1921	1,915,475	1,932
1941	2,414,002	2,580
1961	3,553,500	4,222

Nonconformity

Methodism grew rapidly from the mid-eighteenth century, especially in places where Anglicanism was weak, such as mining and industrial areas. By the early nineteenth century Methodism had separated from the Church of England and was the largest Nonconformist Church. By 1815, the Methodists had some 200,000 members. Other Dissenters, especially the Baptists and Congregationalists, grew in numbers in many areas. The Roman Catholics showed increased membership mainly due to Irish immigration.

Methodist membership in England and Wales, 1816–1914[1]

1816	189,777
1826	267,652
1836	364,641
1846	452,238
1856	443,493
1866	547,613
1876	610,846
1886	676,542
1896	702,411
1906	800,234
1914	777,886

[1] For complete statistics, the definitive source is A.D. Gilbert, *Religion and Society in Industrial England: Church, Chapel and Social Change, 1740–1914* (1976).

Recent trends

After World War II religious adherence was obviously on the decline, with the growth of affluence and the extension of the state's role in many areas traditionally occupied by the churches, such as education and social welfare. The result is that only 10 per cent or less of people are now regular church attenders, compared with nearly 50 per cent in 1851. There have been exceptions to this general pattern. The numbers of Roman Catholics have increased, while some smaller groups, such as the Salvation Army, Jehovah's Witnesses, and Seventh Day Adventists, have also maintained or improved their position.

The 2001 Census

The 2001 Census revealed that Britain is becoming a less Christian country, with a large rise in people who do not profess any religion or refuse to state their religion. Both Muslim, Hindu and Sikh adherents are growing.

Religion	Percentage
Christian	71.6
Muslim	2.7
Hindu	1.0
Sikh	0.6
Jewish	0.5
Buddhist	0.3
Other	0.3
None	15.4
Not stated	7.3

Source: Callum G. Brown, *Religion and Society in Twentieth Century Britain* (2006).

SELECTED OFFICES AND OFFICE HOLDERS

THE ROMAN CATHOLIC CHURCH

Landmarks in early papal history

c. 91–101	Papacy of Clement I, author of the document *I Clement* sent to Corinth to resolve a dispute about authority.
c. 125–136	Papacy of the Greek Telesphoros, the only second-century pope whose martyrdom can be confirmed.
c. 189–198	Papacy of the African Victor I, who insisted on the Roman date for the celebration of Easter.
217	The first disputed election for Bishop of Rome when Callistus I was opposed by Hippolytus (the first anti-pope).
235	Abdication of Pontian (28 Sept.). The first Bishop of Rome known to have abdicated (after his arrest and deportation by the new Emperor).
236–250	Papacy of Fabian, a major reformer and administrator.
260–268	Papacy of Dionysius. Like Fabian, an important administrator and reformer.
308	Election of Marcellus ended the longest vacancy (4 years) in papal history.
384–399	Papacy of Siricius. He ruled that no bishop could be consecrated without the knowledge of Rome. He was the first pope to issue decretals on the lines of Imperial edicts.

Sources: Richard P. McBrien (ed.) *The HarperCollins Encyclopaedia of Catholicism* (1995); Greg Tobin, *Selecting the Pope* (2004).

Key early popes (From Innocent I to Gregory the Great)

401–417	Papacy of Innocent I, whose claims for the supreme teaching authority of Rome were unprecedented.
419	The first Imperial intervention in papal elections when Emperor Honorius supported Boniface against the anti-pope Eulalius (3 April).
440–461	Papacy of Leo I (Leo the Great). A major supporter of the Council of Chalcedon and a leading early claimant for the supreme and universal authority of Rome.

483–492	Papacy of Felix III. Leading opponent of Monophysitism (which denied the human nature in Christ). His papacy saw the first schism with Constantinople when Acacius, the Patriarch of Constantinople, was excommunicated (the Acacian Schism).
492–496	Papacy of Gelasius I. Along with Leo I the most outstanding fifth-century Pope. He was the first to be called 'Vicar of Christ'.
523–526	Papacy of John I. His papacy saw the ratification of the Alexandrian date for Easter. He was also the first pope to leave Italy for Constantinople.
590–604	Papacy of Gregory I (Gregory the Great). His major papacy saw the despatch of Augustine's mission to England. The first pope who had been a monk, his writings included *Pastoral Care*.

The discrediting of the papacy

844–847	Sergius II	Notorious for simony and corruption.
872–882	John VIII	The first pope to be assassinated (16 Dec. 882).
891–896	Formosus	Subject to a mock trial *after* his death and exhumation (the 'Cadaver Synod'). Eventually (after being thrown in the Tiber) reburied by Pope Theodore II.
896	Boniface VI	A twice-defrocked priest whose papacy lasted 15 days.
896–897	Stephen VI	Having participated in the trial of Formosus, he was imprisoned and strangled to death.
903	Leo V	Imprisoned and murdered after 30 days in office.
904–911	Sergius III	Famous for having both Leo V and the anti-pope Christopher strangled to death.
914–928	John X	Deposed, imprisoned and suffocated to death in 929.
939–942	Stephen VIII	Imprisoned, mutilated and died in prison.
955–964	John XII	Elected at the age of 18.
973–974	Benedict VI	Imprisoned and strangled to death by order of the anti-pope Boniface.
983–984	John XIV	Appointed without consultation of people or clergy in Rome by Emperor Otto II. Died in prison of either starvation or poisoning.
985–996	John XV	Hated for his greed and nepotism.
996–999	Gregory V	A 24-year-old relative of Emperor Otto III.

The medieval papacy (from Urban II to Alexander VI)

1088–99	Urban II
1099–1118	Paschal II

[1100–1101	Theodoric]
[1101	Albert or Adalbert]
[1105–11	Silvester IV]
1118–19	Gelasius II
[1118–21	Gregory (VIII)]
1119–24	Callistus II
1124–30	Honorius II
[1124	Celestine (II)]
1130–43	Innocent II
[1130–38	Anacletus II]
[1138	Victor IV]
1143–44	Celestine II
1144–45	Lucius II
1145–53	Eugene III
1153–54	Anastasius IV
1154–59	Hadrian IV
1159–81	Alexander III
[1159–64	Victor IV]
[1164–68	Paschal III]
[1168–78	Callistus (III)]
[1179–80	Innocent (III)]
1181–85	Lucius III
1185–87	Urban III
1187	Gregory VIII
1187–91	Clement III
1191–98	Celestine III
1198–1216	Innocent III
1216–27	Honorius III
1227–41	Gregory IX
1241	Celestine IV
1243–54	Innocent IV
1254–61	Alexander IV
1261–64	Urban IV
1265–68	Clement IV
1271–76	Gregory X
1276	Innocent V
1276	Hadrian V
1276–77	John XXI
1277–80	Nicholas III
1281–85	Martin IV
1285–87	Honorius IV
1288–92	Nicholas IV
1294	Celestine V

1294–1303	Boniface VIII
1303–04	Benedict IX
1305–14	Clement V
1316–34	John XXII
[1328–30	Nicholas (V)]
1334–42	Benedict XII
1342–52	Clement VI
1352–62	Innocent VI
1362–70	Urban V
1370–78	Gregory XI
1378–89	Urban VI
[1378–94	Clement (VII)]
1389–1404	Boniface IX
[1394–1417	Benedict (XIII)]
1404–06	Innocent VII
1406–15	Gregory XII
[1409–10	Alexander V]
[1410–15	John (XXIII)]
1417–31	Martin V
[1423–29	Clement (VIII)]
[1425	Benedict (XIV)]
1431–47	Eugene IV
[1439–49	Felix V]
1447–55	Nicholas V
1455–58	Callistus III
1458–64	Pius II
1464–71	Paul II
1471–84	Sixtus IV
1484–92	Innocent VIII
1492–1503	Alexander VI

*Those in brackets were antipopes.

The modern papacy: popes since 1500

1492	Alexander VI
1503	Pius III
1503	Julius II
1513	Leo X
1522	Adrian VI
1523	Clement VII
1534	Paul III

1550	Julius III
1555	Marcellus II
1555	Paul IV
1559	Pius IV
1566	Pius V
1572	Gregory XIII
1585	Sixtus V
1590	Urban VII
1590	Gregory XIV
1591	Innocent IX
1592	Clement VIII
1605	Leo XI
1605	Paul V
1621	Gregory XV
1623	Urban VIII
1644	Innocent X
1655	Alexander VII
1667	Clement IX
1670	Clement X
1676	Innocent XI
1689	Alexander VIII
1691	Innocent XII
1700	Clement XI
1721	Innocent XIII
1724	Benedict XIII
1730	Clement XII
1740	Benedict XIV
1758	Clement XIII
1769	Clement XIV
1775	Pius VI
1800	Pius VII
1823	Leo XII
1829	Pius VIII
1831	Gregory XVI
1846	Pius IX
1878	Leo XIII
1903	Pius X
1914	Benedict XV
1922	Pius XI
1939	Pius XII
1958	John XXIII
1963	Paul VI
1978	John Paul I
1978	John Paul II
2005	Benedict XVI

The oldest popes (with age at death)

Leo XIII	93	1878–1903
Clement XII	87	1730–40
Clement X	86	1670–76
Pius IX	85	1846–78
Innocent XII	85	1691–1700
John Paul II	84	1978–2005
Gregory XIII	83	1572–85
Paul IV	83	1555–59
Benedict XIV	83	1740–58
Pius VII	83	1800–23

Longest-serving popes (in order of length of pontificate)

Pius IX	1846–78
John Paul II	1978–2005
Leo XIII	1878–1903
Pius VI	1775–99
Adrian I	772–795
Pius VII	1800–23
Alexander III	1159–81

Antipopes

If an antipope shares the same name and number as a legitimate pope, his number is given in parentheses. There are two Victor IVs among the antipopes. The second Victor IV took no note of the first one because he was in 'office' less than two months.

217–235	St Hippolytus
251–258	Novatian
355–365	Felix II
366–367	Ursinus
418–419	Eulalius
498–499, 501–506	Lawrence
530	Dioscorus
687	Paschal
687	Theodore
767–768	Constantine
768	Philip
844	John
855	Anastasius Bibliothecarius
903–904	Christopher
974, 984–985	Boniface VII
997–998	John XVI
1012	Gregory (VI)

1058–59	Benedict X
1061–64	Honorius (II)
1080, 1084–1100	Clement (III)
1100–01	Theodoric
1101	Albert
1105–11	Sylvester IV
1118–21	Gregory (VIII)
1124	Celestine (II)
1130–38	Anacletus II
1138	Victor IV
1159–64	Victor IV
1164–68	Paschal III
1168–78	Callistus (III)
1179–80	Innocent (III)
1328–30	Nicholas (V)
1378–94	Clement (VII)
1394–1417	Benedict (XIII)
1409–10	Alexander V
1410–15	John (XXIII)
1423–29	Clement (VIII)
1425–30	Benedict (XIV)
1439–49	Felix V

Leaders of Roman Catholicism in England (from the Reformation to the Restoration)

Archpriests

1599	George Blackwell
1608	George Birkhead
1615	William Harrison

Vicars Apostolic

1623	William Bishop
1625	Richard Smith
1685	John Leyburn
1703	Bonaventure Giffard
1734	Benjamin Petre
1758	Richard Challoner
1781	James Talbot
1790	John Douglas
1812	William Poynter
1827	James Yorke Bramston
1836	Thomas Griffiths
1848	Thomas Walsh
1849	Nicholas Wiseman

Roman Catholic Archbishops of Westminster*

1850	Nicholas Wiseman
1865	Henry Edward Manning
1892	Herbert Vaughan
1903	Francis Bourne
1935	Arthur Hinsley
1943	Bernard William Griffin
1956	William Godfrey
1963	John Carmel Heenan
1976	Basil Hume (d. 1999)
2000	Cormac Murphy O'Connor

*All became cardinals.

Generals of the Jesuit Order (until suppression of the Jesuits in 1773)

1541–56	St Ignatius Loyola
1558–65	James Laynez
1565–72	St Francis Borgia
1573–80	Everard Mercurian
1581–1615	Claudius Acquaviva (or Aquaviva)
1615–45	Mutius Vitelleschi
1646–49	Vincent Caraffa
1649–51	Francis Piccolomini
1652–52	Aloysius Gottfried (Jan.–March)
1652–64	Goswin Nickel
1664–81	John Paul Oliva
1682–86	Charles de Noyelle
1687–1705	Thyrsus González
1706–30	Michelangelo Tamburini
1730–50	Francis Retz
1751–55	Ignatius Visconti
1755–57	Aloysius Centurioni
1758–73	Lorenzo Ricci

THE ORTHODOX CHURCHES

Bishops of Constantinople (in 381 Constantinople created a patriarchate) up to 431

324–337	Alexander
337–339	Paul I
339–341	Eusebius
341–342	Paul I (again)
342–346	Macedonius I

346–351	Paul I (again)
351–360	Macedonius I (again)
360–370	Eudoxius of Antioch
370–379	Demophilus
379–381	Gregory I of Nazianzus
381–397	Nectarius I
398–404	John I Chrysostom
404–405	Arsacius
406–425	Atticus
426–427	Sisinnus I
428–431	Nestorius

Selected Patriarchs of Constantinople (to 1821)

381 — Bishop of Constantinople given 'primacy of honour'. **St Gregory of Nazianzus** (one of the Cappadocian Fathers) briefly Bishop. He wrote the 'Five Theological Orations'.

398–404 — Patriarchate of *St John Chrysostom*, one of the 'Doctors of the Church'. Famed as a preacher and perhaps the greatest Christian expositor. Exiled after 404.

428–431 — Patriarchate of *Nestorius*, from whom the Nestorian heresy (with its rejection of the term *theotokos*) took its name.

446–449 — Patriarchate of *Flavian* who played major role in Monophysite controversy (excommunicating Eutyches in 448).

458–471 — Patriarchate of *Gennadius I*. Author of many commentaries. In his early career a noted opponent of Cyril of Alexandria.

471–489 — Patriarchate of *Acacius*, remembered for the temporary schism with Rome arising from the Emperor Zeno's Henoticon.

582–595 — Patriarchate of *John the Faster*, the first to use the title Ecumenical Patriarch.

610–638 — Patriarchate of *Sergius I*. The *Ecthesis* was promulgated to set out his view that there was only one will in Christ. Trusted adviser of Emperor Heraclius and most influential exponent of Monothelitism.

715–730 — Patriarchate of *Germanus I*, who played an important part in the Quinisext Council. He was a staunch opponent of Emperor Leo III's iconoclasm.

784–806 — Patriarchate of *Tarasius*. Pursued good relations with the West and presided over the Council of Nicaea in 787 which he had helped convoke.

858–867
877–886 — Patriarchate of *Photius* (appointed after deposition of his predecessor Ignatius). Photius himself was declared deposed by Pope Nicholas I. In the ensuing conflict the Pope was also declared deposed.

1043–58 — Patriarchate of *Michael Cerularius*, remembered for the formal breach or schism with Rome in June 1054.

336

1454–*c*. 56	Patriarchate of **Gennadius II** (George Scholarius). A scholar, philosopher and theologian who was installed in 1454 by the new Muslim conquerors as Patriarch with civil authority over the Christians of the Ottoman Empire. He resigned within two years.
1572–95	Patriarchate (with interruptions) of **Jeremias II**. A scholar and reformer who served three terms in office (1572–79, 1580–84 and 1587–95).
1620–37 (various dates)	Patriarchate of **Cyril Lucaris**, known as the 'Calvinist Patriarch'. He was variously deposed and reinstated.
1748–57	Patriarchate (with interruptions) of **Cyril V**. He served 1748–51 and 1751–57. Important for his ruling that Roman Catholic and Armenian converts needed rebaptizing.
1821	Patriarchate of **Gregory V**, executed in reprisal for the uprising in Greece against Ottoman rule.

THE RUSSIAN ORTHODOX CHURCH

Procurators of the Holy Synod

1722–25	Colonel I.V. Boltín
1725–26	Captain A.P. Baskákov
1726	Captain R. Raévskii
1726–41	vacant
1741–53	Ia.P. Shakhovskói
1753–58	A.I. Lvov
1758–63	Major-General A.S. Kozlóvskii
1763–68	I.I. Melissino
1768–74	Brigadier P.P. Chébishev
1774–86	S.V. Akchúrin
1791	A.I. Naúmov
1791–97	A.I. Músin-Púshkin
1797–99	V.A. Khovánskii
1799–1803	D.I. Khvostóv
1803	A.A. Iákovlev
1803–17	A.N. Golítsyn
1817–33	P.S. Meshchérskii
1833–36	S.D. Necháev
1836–55	General N.A. Protásov
1855–56	A.I. Karasévskii
1856–62	A.P. Tolstoy
1862–65	General A.P. Akhmátov
1865–80	D.A. Tolstoy
1880–1905	K.P. Pobedonóstsev

1905–06	A.D. Obolénskii
1906 (April–July)	A.A. Shirínskii-Shikhmátov
1906–09	P.P. Izvólskii
1909–11	S.M. Lukiánov
1911–15	V.K. Sabler (Desiatovskii)
1915 (July–Sept.)	A.D. Samárin
1915–16	A.N. Vólzhin
1916–17	N.P. Ráev

Patriarchs (in the era of Lenin and Stalin; Russian Orthodox)

(1721)–1917	Patriarchate vacant
1917–25	Tikhon (Belavin)
1925–43	Locum tenentes
1943–44	Sergii (Stragorodsky)
1945–70	Alexy (Simansky)

The current (2007) Patriarch is Alexy II

Principal Source: David Longley, *The Longman Companion to Imperial Russia, 1688–1917* (2000) p. 91.

THE CHURCH OF ENGLAND

Archbishops of Canterbury

597–605	Augustine
605–619	Laurentius
619–624	Mellitus
624–617	Justus
627–653	Honorius
655–664	Deusdedit
668–690	Theodore
693–731	Berhtwald
731–734	Taetwine
734–740	Nothelm
740–758	Cuthbert
759–762	Breogwine
763–790	Jaenberht
790–803	Æthelheard
803–829	Wulfred
829–830	Fleogild
830–870	Ceolnoth
870–889	Æthelred

891–923	Plegemund
923–925	Æthelm
928–941	Wulfelm
941–958	Odo
958–959	Ælsine
959–988	Dunstan
988–989	Æthelgar
990–994	SIgeric
995–1005	Ælfric
1006–12	Ælfeah or Alphege
1013–20	Lyfing
1020–38	Æthelnoth
1038–50	Eadsige
1051–52	Robert of Jumièges
1052–70	Stigand
1070–89	Lanfranc
1093–1109	Anselm
1114–22	Ralph de Turbine
1123–36	William de Corbeuil
1139–61	Theobald
1162–70	Thomas à Becket
1174–84	Richard
1185–90	Baldwin
1191	Reginald Fitz-Jocelin
1193–1205	Hubert Walter
1207–28	Stephen Langton
1229–31	Richard Wethershed
1233–40	Edmund Rich
1240–70	Boniface of Savoy
1273–78	Robert Kilwardby
1279–92	John Peckham
1293–1313	Robert Winchelsea
1313–27	Walter Reynolds
1327–33	Simon de Meopham
1333–48	John Stratford
1348–49	John de Ufford
1349	Thomas Bradwardin
1349–66	Simon Islip
1366–68	Simon Langham
1368–74	William Wittlesey
1375–81	Simon Sudbury
1381–96	William Courtenay
1396–98	Thomas Fitzalan
1398	Roger Walden

1399–1414	Thomas Arundel
1414–43	Henry Chicheley
1443–52	John Stafford
1452–54	John Kemp
1454–86	Thomas Bourchier
1486–1500	John Morton
1501–1503	Henry Deane
1503–32	William Warham
1533–56	Thomas Cranmer
1556–58	Reginald Pole
1559–75	Matthew Parker
1575–83	Edmund Grindal
1583–1604	JohnWhitgift
1604–10	Richard Bancroft
1611–33	George Abbot
1633–45	William Laud
1660–63	William Juxon
1663–77	Gilbert Sheldon
1678–91	William Sancroft
1691–94	John Tillotson
1694–1715	Thomas Tenison
1716–37	William Wake
1737–47	John Potter
1747–57	Thomas Herring
1757–58	Matthew Hutton
1758–68	Thomas Ecker
1768–83	Frederick Cornwallis
1783–1805	John Moore
1805–28	Charles Manners-Sutton
1828–48	William Howley
1848–62	John Bird Sumner
1862–68	Charles T. Longley
1868–82	Archibald Campbell Tait
1882–96	Edward W. Benson
1896–1902	Frederick Temple
1903–28	Randall Davidson
1928–42	Cosmo Gordon Lang
1942–44	William Temple
1945–61	Geoffrey Francis Fisher
1961–74	Arthur Michael Ramsey
1974–79	Donald Coggan
1979–91	Robert Runcie
1991–2002	George Carey
2002–	Rowan Williams

Archbishops of York

The earliest Archbishops of York, 627–732

627–633	Paulinus
664–669	Chad (Ceadda)
669–677	Wilfrid I (St Wilfrid)
678–705	Bosa
705–714	John (St John of Beverley)
718–732	Wilfrid II

Medieval Archbishops, 1066–1464

1061–69	Ealdred
1070–1100	Thomas I
1101–08	Gerard
1109–14	Thomas II
1119–40	Thurstan
1143–47 and 1154	William Fitzherbert
1147–53	Henry Murdac
1154–81	Roger of Pont-L'Eveque
1181–91	Geoffrey Plantagenet
1215–55	Walter de Grey
1256–58	Sewal de Bovill
1258–65	Godfrey of Ludham (or Kineton)
1265–79	Walter Giffard
1279–85	William Wickwane
1286–96	John le Romeyn (Romanus)
1298–99	Henry of Newark
1300–04	Thomas of Corbridge
1306–16	William Greenfield
1317–40	William of Melton
1342–52	William le Zouche
1352–73	John of Thoresby
1374–88	Alexander Neville
1388–96	Thomas Arundel
1396–98	Robert Waldby
1398–1407	Richard le Scrope
1407–23	Henry Bowet
1425–52	John Kempe
1452–64	William Booth

Modern Archbishops

1847–60	Thomas Musgrave
1860–62	Charles Thomas Longley

1862–90	William Thomson		
1891	William Connor Magee		
1891–1908	William Dalrymple Maclagan		
1908–28	Cosmo Gordon Lang		
1929–42	William Temple		
1942–55	Cyril Forster Garbett		
1956–61	Arthur Michael Ramsey		
1961–74	Frederick Donald Coggan		
1975–83	Stuart Yarworth Blanch		
1983–95	John Stapylton Habgood		
1995–2004	David Hope		
2005–	John Sentamu		

Principal dioceses and their bishops, 1484–1603

Province of Canterbury

Canterbury

1454–86	Thomas Bourchier	1556–58	Reginald Pole, Cardinal
1486–1500	John Morton, Cardinal		
1501–03	Henry Deane	1559–75	Matthew Parker
1503–32	William Warham	1576–83	Edmund Grindal
1533–55	Thomas Cranmer	1583–1604	John Whitgift

Lincoln

1480–94	John Russell	1552–54	John Taylor
1495–1514	William Smith	1554–56	John White
1514	Thomas Wolsey, Cardinal	1557–59	Thomas Watson
		1559–71	Nicholas Bullingham
1514–21	William Atwater	1571–84	Thomas Cooper
1521–47	John Longland	1584–95	William Wickham
1547–51	Henry Holbeach	1595–1608	William Chaderton

London

1448–89	Thomas Kempe	1539–49	Edmund Bonner
1489–96	Richard Hill	1550–53	Nicholas Ridley
1496–1501	Thomas Savage	1553–59	Edmund Bonner
1501–03	William Warham	1559–70	Edmund Grindal
1504–05	William Barons	1570–77	Edwin Sandys
1506–22	Richard FitzJames	1577–94	John Aylmer
1522–30	Cuthbert Tunstal	1594–96	Richard Fletcher
1530–39	John Stokesley	1597–1604	Richard Bancroft

Winchester

1447–86	William Waynflete	1553–55	Stephen Gardiner
1487–92	Peter Courtenay	1556–59	John White
1493–1501	Thomas Langton	1560–80	Robert Horne
1501–28	Richard Fox	1580–84	John Watson
1529–30	Thomas Wolsey, Cardinal	1584–94	Thomas Cooper
		1594–95	William Wickham
1531–51	Stephen Gardiner	1596	William Day
1551–53	John Ponet	1597–1616	Thomas Bilson

St Davids

1485–96	Hugh Pavy	1548–53	Robert Ferrar
1496–1504	John Morgan	1554–59	Henry Morgan
1505–08	Robert Sherborn	1560–61	Thomas Young
1509–22	Edward Vaughan	1561–81	Richard Davies
1523–36	Richard Rawlins	1582–93	Marmaduke Middleton
1536–48	William Barlow	1594–1615	Anthony Rudd

Province of York

Durham

1484–94	John Shirwood	1523–29	Thomas Wolsey, Cardinal
1494–1501	Richard Fox		
1502–05	William Senhouse	1530–59	Cuthbert Tunstal
1507–08	Christopher Bainbridge, Cardinal	1560–76	James Pilkington
		1577–87	Richard Barnes
1509–23	Thomas Ruthall	1589–95	Matthew Hutton
		1595–1606	Tobias Matthew

York

1480–1500	Thomas Rotherham	1545–54	Robert Holgate
1501–07	Thomas Savage	1555–59	Nicholas Heath
1508–14	Christopher Bainbridge, Cardinal	1561–68	Thomas Young
		1570–76	Edmund Grindal
1514–30	Thomas Wolsey, Cardinal	1577–88	Edwin Sandys
		1589–94	John Piers
1531–44	Edward Lee	1595–1606	Matthew Hutton

RULERS AND MONARCHS

260–268	Gallienus*
268–270	Claudius II
270–275	Aurelian
275–276	Tacitus
276	Florianus
276–282	Probus
282–283	Carus
283–285	Carinus*
283–284	Numerianus*
284–305	Diocletian*
286–305	Maximian
305–306	Constantius I*
305–310	Galerius*
306–312	Maxentius
308–313	Maxinus
308–324	Licinius (E)
306–337	Constantine I

* = Joint.
E = East.

ROMAN BYZANTINE EMPERORS (to the fall of Constantinople in 1453)

306–337	Constantine I
337–340	Constantine II
337–350	Constans I
337–361	Constantius II
361–363	Julian (the Apostate)
363–364	Jovian
364–375	Valentinian I
364–378	Valens
375–383	Gratian
383–392	Valentinian II
379–395	Theodosius I (the Great)
395–423	Honorius
395–408	Arcadius
408–450	Theodosius II
423–425	John
425–455	Valentinian III
450–457	Marcian
457–474	Leo I
474–491	Zeno*
475–476	Basiliscus
491–518	Anastasius I

518–527	Justin I
527–565	Justinian I
565–578	Justin II
578–582	Tiberius II
582–602	Maurice
602–610	Phocas
610–641	Heraclius I
641	Constantine III
641	Heracleonas
641–648	Constans II
668–685	Constantine IV
685–695	Justinian II
695–698	Leontius
698–705	Tiberius III
705–711	Justinian III
711–713	Philippicus
713–715	Anastasius II
716–717	Theodosius III
717–741	Leo III
741–775	Constantine V
775–780	Leo IV
780–797	Constantine VI
797–802	Irene
802–811	Nicephorus I
811	Stauracius
811–813	Michael I
813–820	Leo V
820–829	Michael II
829–842	Theophilus
842–867	Michael III
867–886	Basil I
886–912	Leo VI
912–913	Alexander
913–919	Constantine VII
919–944	Romanus I
944–959	Constantine VII (again)
959–963	Romanus II
963	Basil II
963–969	Nicephorus II
969–976	John I
976–1025	Basil II
1025–28	Constantine VIII
1028–34	Romanus III
1034–41	Michael IV

1041–42	Michael V
1042	Zoe and Theodora
1042–55	Constantine IX
1055–56	Theodora
1056–57	Michael VI
1057–59	Isaac I
1059–67	Constantine X
1067–68	Michael VII
1068–71	Romanus IV
1071–78	Michael VII
1078–81	Nicephorus III
1081–1118	Alexius I
1118–43	John II
1143–80	Manuel I
1180–83	Alexius II
1183–85	Andronicus I
1185–95	Isaac II
1195–1203	Alexius III
1203–04	Alexius IV
1204	Alexius V
1204–22	Theodore I
1222–54	John III
1254–58	Theodore II
1258	John IV
1258–82	Michael VIII
1282–1328	Andronicus II
1328–41	Andronicus III
1341–76, 1379–91	John V
1347–54	John VI
1376–79	Andronicus IV
[1390	John VII]
1391–1425	Manuel II
1425–48	John VIII
1448–53	Constantine XI

*Strictly 474–475, 476–491.

RULERS OF THE LATIN EMPIRE (from its foundation in 1204 to its demise in 1261)

1204–05	Baldwin I
1206–16	Henry
1217	Peter of Courtenay
1218–28	Robert of Courtenay
1228–37	John of Brienne
1237–61	Baldwin II

GENERAL MISCELLANY

THE HOLY CITY: CHRONOLOGY OF JERUSALEM

c. 49–50   The Council of Jerusalem held, with James, the brother of Christ, a leading figure.

68–70   Jewish revolt briefly re-establishes Jewish sovereignty over Jerusalem. Destruction of the Temple (AD 70).

135   Romans reconquer Jerusalem after Second Jewish Revolt. Jews not allowed into city under penalty of death. Jerusalem renamed Aelia Capitolina.

250   Roman Xth Legion replaced by Moors loyal to Rome.

326   Jerusalem visited by Helena, mother of the Emperor Constantine, following Byzantine conquest of the city. Tradition says various sites and relics located.

335   Church of the Holy Sepulchre dedicated (on site of former Temple of Venus). Construction of Eleona Church on Mount of Olives.

438   Jews allowed to return to Jerusalem after first visit to city by Empress Eudocia.

451   Jerusalem elevated to status of patriarchate at the Council of Chalcedon.

614   Jerusalem handed over to Jews after Persian conquest.

629   Byzantine rule restored in Jerusalem. Renewed expulsion of Jews.

638   Fall of Jerusalem to advancing Muslims (who had already subjugated northern Syria, Aleppo and Antioch). Around 70 Jewish families allowed to return to Jerusalem (the Christian patriarchate opposed the Jewish return). Jerusalem is now third-holiest Muslim city after Mecca and Medina.

660   Construction begun of Al Aqsa Mosque on Temple Mount.

685–691   Construction of the Dome of the Rock (completed 691).

750   Decline of Jerusalem, now ruled from Baghdad, following the Abbasid conquest.

878   Egyptian Muslim dynasties rule Jerusalem. Periodic persecution of both Christians and Jews.

1016   Rebuilding of Dome of the Rock following its collapse.

1099   Crusaders enter Jerusalem (July). Massacres of both Muslims and Jews. All Jews not massacred were enslaved or ransomed. Jerusalem made capital of the Latin Kingdom.

348

1187	Crusaders ousted from Jerusalem by Saladin.
1210	Return of groups of Jews to Jerusalem following defeat of Crusaders.
1244	Final defeat of the Crusaders when Jerusalem sacked by the Kharezmian Tartars. Many Christians massacred.
1250–1517	Jerusalem under the rule of the Mamluks of Egypt.
1440	Heavy annual tax on all Jews imposed by the Mamluks.
1460	Chapel of the Holy Spirit on Mount Zion destroyed by Muslims.
1517	Beginning of Ottoman rule (which lasts four centuries until 1917).
1539–42	Suleiman restores and strengthens the city walls.
1586	Ottomans deprive Jewish community of use of their synagogues in Jerusalem.
1700	Jewish population estimated at 1,200 (around 300 families).
1720	Ashkenazi Synagogue seized by the Arabs.
1726	Local Muslim Arabs seize a Jewish synagogue (retained until 1816).
1775	Imposition of a head-tax on all Jews by Ottoman Turks.
1780	Massacre of monks of the Monastery of the Cross.
1831	Capture of Jerusalem from Ottomans by Mohamed Ali of Egypt.
1840	Restoration of Ottoman Turkish rule.
1854	Population of Jerusalem estimated at 9,000 Jews, 5,000 Muslims and 4,000 Christians. Jews a majority presence from the 1860s.
1892	Jerusalem linked by railway to Jaffa.
1914	Britain declares war on Ottoman Empire (Oct.).
1917	Jerusalem conquered by British forces (10 Dec.).
1922	British League of Nations Mandate comes into effect (continued until 14 May 1948).
1948	Independence of Israel. Jerusalem divided between Israel and Jordan.
1967	Israeli forces enter East Jerusalem and then city reunited but still much disputed.

FEAST DAYS AND HOLY DAYS OF THE CATHOLIC WEST (as celebrated at the Reformation)

Some of the most important dates and festivals of the Church's year varied according to factors such as the date of Easter, etc. The main variable dates and festivals were:

Advent	The four (or five) Sundays before Christmas
Ash Wednesday	The first day in Lent
Lent	The 40-day fast before Easter
Passion Week	The week before Easter, which included Good Friday
Easter Day	Fixed for the Sunday after the full moon on, or next after, 21 March
Ascension Day	The fifth Thursday after Easter
Corpus Christi	Held on the Thursday after Trinity Sunday

The principal fixed dates included:

1 Jan.	Circumcision
6 Jan.	Epiphany
2 Feb.	Candlemas (celebrating the purification of the Blessed Virgin Mary and the presentation of Christ in the Temple, 40 days after his birth)
25 March	Annunciation (Lady Day), the feast commemorating the announcement of the Incarnation by the angel Gabriel to Mary and the conception of Christ in her womb
24 June	John the Baptist (Feast of the Nativity of)
29 June	St Peter and St Paul
1 Aug.	Lammas
15 Aug.	Assumption of the Blessed Virgin Mary
29 Sept.	St Michael the Archangel (Michaelmas)
1 Nov.	All Saints' Day (All Hallows), the commemoration of all the Christian saints
2 Nov.	All Souls' Day, the commemoration of the souls of the faithful departed
25 Dec.	Christmas Day

Principal source: Greengrass, *op. cit.*

BIBLIOGRAPHY

INTRODUCTORY NOTE

This relatively concise bibliographical guide provides a short introduction to the enormous and ever-growing literature available on the history of Christianity. The list, of around 100 titles, has aimed to include not just those specific works of reference found most useful in compiling this volume, but also a selection of readily-available one-volume recent surveys of the history of Christianity, which readers new to the subject may find of value. Also included are some authoritative new books on areas of popular interest, such as the Crusades and the Reformation, now available in paperback.

Ahlstrom, Sydney, *A Religious History of the American People* (1972)
Anderson, Allan, *An Introduction to Pentecostalism: Global Charismatic Christianity* (2006)
Angold, Michael, *Eastern Christianity* (2006)
Armstrong, A., *The Church of England, the Methodists and Society, 1700–1850* (1973)
Armstrong, Karen, *The Battle for God* (2000)
Armstrong, Karen, *Holy War: The Crusades and Their Impact on Today's World* (2001)
Asbridge, Thomas, *The First Crusade: A New History* (2004)
Barraclough, Geoffrey, *The Medieval Papacy* (1968)
Barrett, D.B. (ed.), *World Christian Encyclopaedia* (1982)
Battle, Michael, *The Black Church in America* (2006)
Bebbington, D., *Evangelism in Modern Britain* (1989)
Behringer, Wolfgang, *Witches and Witch-hunts: A Global History* (2004)
Bossy, John, *Christianity in the West* (1985)
Bowden, John (ed.), *Christianity: The Complete Guide* (2005)
Boxer, C.R., *The Christian Century in Japan, 1549–1650* (1993)
Brooke, C.N.L., *The Monastic World* (1974)
Brown, Callum G., *Religion and Society in Twentieth Century Britain* (2006)
Brown, Peter, *The Rise of Western Christendom* (1996)
Butler, Jon and Stout, Harry S. (eds), *Religion in American History: A Reader* (1997)
Cameron, Euan, *The European Reformation* (1991)
Carmody, Denise, *Christian Feminist Theology* (1995)
Chadwick, Henry, *The Early Church* (1967)
Chadwick, Henry and Evans, G.R., *Atlas of the Christian Church* (1987)
Chadwick, Owen, *The Reformation* (1964)
Chadwick, Owen, *A History of Christianity* (1995)
Chadwick, Owen, *The Christian Church in the Cold War* (1992)
Chadwick, Owen, *The Victorian Church* (2 vols, 1966–70)
Chidester, David, *Christianity: A Global History* (2000)

Christiansen, Eric, *The Northern Crusades* (new edn, 1997)

Cohn, Norman, *The Pursuit of the Millennium* (1957)

Cohn-Sherbok, Dan, *Atlas of Jewish History* (1994)

Collinson, Patrick, *The Reformation* (2003)

Cookson, Catharine (ed.), *Encyclopaedia of Religious Freedom* (2003)

Corley, Felix, *Religion in the Soviet Union* (1996)

Cross, F.A. and Livingstone, E.A., *The Oxford Dictionary of the Christian Church* (rev. 3rd edn)

Dickens, A.G., *The English Reformation* (1967)

Duffy, Eamon, *Saints and Sinners* (1997)

Edwards, David L., *Christianity: The First Two Thousand Years* (1997)

Elliot, J.K., *The Apocryphal New Testament* (1993)

Elton, G.R. (ed.), *The Reformation* (1990)

Fossier, Robert, *Cambridge Illustrated History of the Middle Ages, Vol II, 950–1250* (1997); *Vol III, 1250–1520* (1986)

Frend, W.H.C., *The Rise of Christianity* (1984)

Frend, W.H.C., *Martydom and Persecution in the Early Church* (1965)

Gascoigne, Bamber, *A Brief History of Christianity* (rev. edn, 2003)

Gilbert, Alan, *Religion and Society in Industrial England: Church, Chapel and Social Change, 1740–1914* (1976)

Gilmore, Alec, *Dictionary of the English Bible and its Origins* (2001)

Green, V.H.H., *A New History of Christianity* (1996)

Greengrass, Mark, *The Longman Companion to the European Reformation, c. 1500–1618* (1998)

Hales, E.E.Y., *The Catholic Church and the Modern World* (1958)

Hastings, Adrian, *A World History of Christianity* (1999)

Hastings, Adrian, *The Church in Africa, 1450–1950* (1994)

Hillenbrand, Carole, *The Crusades: Islamic Perspectives* (2nd edn, 2000)

Hindley, Geoffrey, *The Crusades* (2003)

Jedin, Herbert and Dolan, John (eds), *A Handbook of Church History* (Vol I, 1965)

Johnson, Marshall D., *The Evolution of Christianity: Twelve Crises that Shaped the Church* (2006)

Johnson, Paul, *A History of Christianity* (1976)

Kelly, J.N.D., *The Oxford Dictionary of the Popes* (1988)

Knowles, David, *The Monastic Orders in England, 943–1216* (2nd edn 1963)

Knowles, David, *Christian Monasticism* (1969)

Lambert, Malcolm, *Medieval Heresy: Popular Movements from the Gregorian Reform to the Reformation* (1992)

Latourette, Kenneth Scott, *History of the Expansion of Christianity* (7 vols, 1937–45)

Lewis, Donald M., *Christianity Reborn: The Global Expansion of Evangelicanism in the 20th Century* (2005)

Littell, Franklin H., *Illustrated History of Christianity* (2nd edn, 2003)

Lock, Peter, *The Routledge Companion to the Crusades* (2006)

Lynch, Joseph, *The Medieval Church* (1992)

MacCulloch, Diarmaid, *Reformation: Europe's House Divided, 1490–1700* (2003)

McGrath, Alister E., *An Introduction to Christianity* (1997)

Mcleod, Hugh, *Religion and Society in England, 1850–1914* (1996)

Mcleod, Hugh, *World Christianities, c. 1914–c. 2000* (2006)

McManners, John, *The Oxford Illustrated History of Christianity* (1990)

Mango, Cyril, *Byzantium: The Empire of New Rome* (1980)

Martin, Janet, *Medieval Russia, 980–1584* (1995)

Maxwell-Stuart, P.G., *Chronicle of the Popes* (2nd edn, 2006)

Michel, Patrick, *Politics and Religion in Eastern Europe* (1991)

Mullett, M., *Radical Religious Movements in Early Modern Europe* (1980)

Mullett, M., *The Catholic Reformation* (1999)

Neill, Stephen, *A History of Christian Missions* (2nd edn, 1996)

Noll, Mark A., *America's God* (2002)

Norman, Edward R., *Church and Society in England, 1770–1970* (1976)

O'Shea, Stephen, *Sea of Faith: Islam and Christianity in the Medieval Mediterranean World* (2006)

Parrinder, Geoffrey, *A Concise Encyclopaedia of Christianity* (1998)

Parry, Ken (*et al.*) (eds), *The Blackwell Dictionary of Eastern Christianity* (1999)

Rassam, Suha, *Christianity in Iraq* (2006)

Read, Piers Paul, *The Templars* (1999)

Riley-Smith, Jonathan, *The Oxford Illustrated History of the Crusades* (1995)

Riley-Smith, Jonathan, *Atlas of the Crusades* (1991)

Runciman, Steven, *The Great Church in Captivity* (1968)

Tobin, Greg, *Selecting the Pope* (2004)

Treadgold, Warren, *A History of the Byzantine State and Society* (1997)

Tyerman, Christopher, *God's War: A New History of the Crusades* (2006)

Ward, Kevin, *A History of Global Anglicanism* (2006)

Walsh, Michael, *Dictionary of Christian Biography* (2001)

Ward, W.G., *Religion and Society in England, 1790–1850* (1972)

Warner, Marina, *Alone of All Her Sex: The Myth and Cult of the Virgin Mary* (1986)

Ware, Timothy, *The Orthodox Church* (1982)

Whitlow, Mark, *The Making of Orthodox Byzantium, 600–1025* (1996)

Williams, Peter, *American Religions: From Their Origins to the Twenty-First Century* (2002)

Zernov, Nicolas, *Church of the Eastern Christians* (1942)

INDEX

Babylonian captivity 233–4; Avignon
1309–76 78–9, 234
Baker, Mary 178
Baltic 39, 75–7
Baptists 234, 249; African 192; American
178, 179, 180, 181
Baptist Union 234
Barrowists 234, 239
Bartholomew, massacre of St 248, 253
Beatification 234
Becket, Thomas à 88
Bede, the Venerable 43
Beghards 234
Béguines 234
Belgium 163, 164, 165
Benedict IX, Pope 50, 235
Benedict XII, Pope 78
Benedict XIII, Pope (Avignon) 79,
80, 245
Benedict XIII, Pope (Rome) 145
Benedict XIV, Pope 145, 146
Benedict XVI, Pope 213, 226, 228
Benedictines 18, 35, 238
benefice 234
benefit of clergy 110, 234
Benjamin, anti-Chalcedonian Patriarch 27
Bernard St 237–8, 241
Bianchi 234
Bible: Cologne 98; Complutensian Polyglot
99; English 310–11; Great Bible 111;
Gustavus Vasa 117; modern bible
movement in England 311; modern
versions 311–12; New Testament,
making of 295; Vulgate 269 *see also*
Book of Common Prayer
Bible belt 234
Bill of Rights 1689 149
Bill of Rights 1791 176
Bishop's Book 234
Bishops' Wars 129, 234–5, 241
Bismarck 163; *Kulturkampf* 164, 175, 232,
244, 251
Black Friars *see* Dominicans
Blackwell, George, Archpriest of England
114, 128
Bogomils 61, 72, 235
Bohemian Brethren *see* Unitas Fratrum
Bohemian Protestants 242

Bonaventure 55
Boniface, St 34, 37, 43
Boniface VIII 56, 238, 245
Boniface IX, Pope 79, 80
Book of Common Prayer 111, 112, 129,
130, 131, 191, 215, 234, 235
Booth, William 189–90
Breda, Declaration of 131
British and Foreign Bible Society 152
British Isles, conversion of: Alfred to the
Norman Conquest 44–5; Augustine to
the Vikings 42–4; Celtic Christianity
41–2
Brownists 234, 235, 239
Buffon *Histoire naturelle* 146
Bulgaria, massacre 1876 172
bulls 235; 1478 233; *Ad conditorem
canonum* 78; Americas 124, 125;
Audita tremendi 68; *Clericos laicos*
56, 238; *Cum internonnullos* 78; *Cum
occasione* 250; eighteenth century 144,
145, 146, 147, 250; *Execrabilis* 82, 89;
Exivi de Paradiso 78; French
Revolution 155, 156; Golden Bull of
Eger 54; Golden Bull of Rimini 75;
Inquisition 119; Jesuits 121, 123;
Luther 101; *Regnans in Excelsis* 113;
religious unity 224; *Unigenitus Dei
filius* 145, 250; *Vineam domini* 109;
witchcraft 92
Bunyan, John *Pilgrim's Progress* 131
Byzantine Empire 235; 1054–1453 61–4;
Roman Byzantine Emperors 345–6;
see also Eastern Empire

Calixtines 235
Calixtus II, Pope 51
Calixtus III, Pope 52
Calvinism 235–6, 240; Calvin, John 105–6;
predestination 254, 260
Camissards *see* Enfants de Dieu
Canada 1603–1776 133, 135; 2001 226;
Pentecostalism 220–1
Canonization 234, 236
Canon Law 236
Canterbury: Archbishops 338–40;
Capuchins 59, 60, 236